ETHIOPIA THROUGH RUSSIAN EYES

COUNTRY IN TRANSITION
1896-1898

by
Alexander Bulatovich

Translated and Edited by
RICHARD SELTZER

The Red Sea Press, Inc.
Publishers & Distributors of Third World Books

11-D Princess Road
Lawrenceville, NJ 08648

P. O. Box 48
Asmara, ERITREA

The Red Sea Press, Inc.
Publishers & Distributors of Third World Books

11-D Princess Road   **RSP**   P. O. Box 48
Lawrenceville, NJ 08648   Asmara, ERITREA

Copyright © 2000 Richard Seltzer

First Red Sea Press, Inc. edition 2000

All rights reserved. No part of this publication may be reproduced, stored in a retrieval system or transmitted in any form or by any means electronic, mechanical, photocopying, recording or otherwise without the prior written permission of the publisher.

Cover Design: Jonathan Gullery
Book Design: Wanjiku Ngugi

Library of Congress Cataloging-in-Publication Data

Bulatovich, A.K. (Aleksandr Ksaver'evich), 1870-1919.
   [Ot Entoto do rieki Baro. English]
   Ethiopia through Russian eyes: country in transition, 1896-1898 / by Alexander Bulatovich ; translated [and edited] by Richard Seltzer.
     p. cm.
   Includes bibliographical references.
   Contents: bk. 1. From Enttoto to the river Baro -- bk. 2. With the armies of Menelik II.
   ISBN 1-56902-116-3 -- ISBN 1-56902-117-1 (pbk.)
   1. Ethiopia--Description and travel. 2. Bulatovich, A. K. (Aleksandr Ksaver§'vich), 1870-1919--Journeys--Ethiopia. 3. Ethnology--Ethiopia.
I. Seltzer, Richard. II. Bulatovich, A. K. (Aleksandr Ksaver§'vich), 1870-1919. S voiskami Menelika Vtorogo. English. III. Title.

DT377 .B92813 2000
306'.0963--dc21   99-462347

Contents

Translator's Introduction v

Book One
From Enttoto to the River Baro

Introduction 3
First Excursion 5
Second Excursion 23
Geographic Survey 33
Population of Southwest Ethiopia 51
Ethiopian System of Government 87
Military 101
State Government and Distribution of Land 113
Ethiopian Church and Faith 125
Conclusion 143
Appendix 147
Notes 163

Book Two
With the Armies of Menelik II

Preface 173
Introduction 175
From Addis Ababa to Jimma 183
Jimma 193
Kaffa 209
Andrachi 225
Through Kaffa and Gimiro to the Abyssinian Border 251
From the Borders of Abyssinia to Lake Rudolf 265
From Kolu to Lake Rudolf 315
The Mouth of the River Omo and Return Trip to the
    Kibish River 341
Appendix 383
Notes 389

Bulatovich -- Hussar, Explorer, Monk 407
by I.S. Katsnelson

Translator's Introduction

A young Russian cavalry officer witnessed as Ethiopia vied with Italy, France, and England for control of previously unexplored territory in east-central Africa. His two books included in this volume are an important source of historical and ethnographic information about that little-known but critical and exciting period.

Almost all official Ethiopian documents from the 1890s were destroyed during the war with Italy in 1936. The historical record depends largely on the observations of European explorers and visitors, of whom Alexander Bulatovich was one of the very best. The books included here cover the first two (1896-97 and 1897-98) of his four trips to Ethiopia.

Bulatovich sensed that Ethiopia was in a delicate state of transition, that what he was seeing would not remain or even be remembered in a generation or two. He had the instincts, although not the training, of an anthropologist, trying to preserve some record of fast-disappearing cultures. But he was not a scientist who observed with cool detachment. Rather, he was actively involved in the events he described, particularly on the expedition to Lake Rudolf. He became ambivalent, torn by his military duty (as an officer attached to the army of Ras Wolda Giyorgis) and by his personal values and sense of justice. Time and again, he found himself party to the decimation of the very people whose culture he wanted to preserve.

He approached his subject with enthusiasm, fascination, and, at times, with almost religious respect. He did not presume that European culture and technology were morally superior. Nor did he romantically prefer the "primitive."

Empathizing with many of the peoples he encountered, he witnessed the tragedy of the clash between traditional ways and modern arms. He considered modernization inevitable, but prefered that it be done in the most humane manner. Hence he considered conquest and gradual change under the Amharic rulers of Ethiopia as preferable to the total destruction which would be likely in case of conquest by a European power.

Bulatovich had a strong natural interest in military and religious matters, and that was at the heart of his respect for these people. He saw the Abyssinian military as having recently passed through a golden age of cavalry charges and individual heroism, which called to mind the by-gone days of medieval Europe. He saw the Ethiopian Church as close to the Russian Orthodox Church and the origins of Christianity, and he greatly respected all the details of their belief and practice, and all their unique legends and saints.

He was, however, a product of his time: the time of Kipling and the Berlin Conference. In those days, it was common for Europeans to make judgements about cultures, based on a scale in which their own culture was at the top. He shows great respect for and understanding of Amhara, Galla (Oromo), and several other Ethiopian peoples and cultures, with whom he had prolonged contact and whose languages he learned. But he uses strong negative terms to describe the people and cultures of what is now Southern Ethiopia. In part, this prejudice is due to ignorance—he had little contact with these people and did not understand their languages. In part, too, it was a reflection of the attitudes of his comrade-in-arms—Amhara and Oromo warriors—who also were encountering these people for the first time, and for whom they were just as foreign and incomprehensible as they were to Bulatovich.

His works should appeal to anyone interested in the history or anthropology of Africa and Ethiopia. They also provide a clear picture of the relations between Russia and Ethiopia in the 1890s, which planted the seeds of their present-day relations. And these accounts can help fill in historical details regarding events and individuals during that era, and can serve as a valuable resource to specialists.

Up until now, the main source in English about Russian activities in Ethiopia and their observations of that country has been The Russians in Ethiopia: An Essay in Futility by Czeslaw Jesman. This is an amusing collection of rumors and anecdotes, based primarily on Italian sources. Unfortunately, it is often wrong; but, in the absence of a better source, its errors have often been repeated.

One speech which Bulatovich made to the Russian Geographical Society was translated into Italian and French and is frequently cited. But his two books, up until now, were available only in Russian. Hence his observations and contributions have remained virtually unknown in the West.

Bulatovich's first book, From Entotto to the River Baro, published in 1897, consists of journals of two excursions he went on during his first trip to Ethiopia 1896-97, plus a series of essays based on what he heard and observed during his year-long stay with the Russian Red Cross Mission. The essays deal with various peoples of Ethiopia (Galla/Oromo, Sidamo, Amhara) -- their history, culture, way of life, beliefs and languages; on the governmental system and its historical background, on the army, on commerce, and on the Emperor's family.

With the Armies of Menilek II, published in 1900, is the journal of Bulatovich's second trip to Ethiopia 1897-98, during which he served as an advisor to the army of Ras Wolda Giyorgis as it conquered the previously little-known southwestern territories from Kaffa to Lake Rudolf. Here he builds on his previous knowledge of the country and also recounts an exciting personal story of military adventure, which builds to a climax in the final chapters.

Both books, edited and with an introduction by Isidor Savvich Katsnelson, were reissued by The Institute of Oriental Studies in Moscow in 1971.

I first discovered Bulatovich in the London Times of 1913, while looking for another story, on which I wished to base a novel. The article described how Russian troops had besieged two monasteries at Mount Athos in Greece and exiled some 660 monks to remote parts of the Russian Empire for believing that "The Name of God was a part of God and, therefore, in itself divine." Bulatovich—a former cavalry officer who had "fought in the Italo-Abyssinian campaign, and afterwards in the Far East"—was the leader and defender of the monks. ("Heresy at Mount Athos: a Soldier Monk and the Holy Synod," June 19, 1913).

News was a more leisurely business then than now. The reporter drew an analogy to characters in a novel by Anatole France and drew an interesting sketch of the background and motivations of the main figure. I got the impression of Bulatovich as a restless man, full of energy, chasing from one end of the world to the other in search of the meaning of life. Eventually, he sought tranquility as a monk at Mount Athos, only to find himself in a battle of another kind.

I was hooked by this new character and new story. What would a Russian soldier have been doing in Ethiopia at the turn of the century? What war could he have fought in the Far East? What was it that compelled him to go from one end of the world to the other, and then to become a monk?

After getting out of the Army, I moved to Boston, where my future wife, Barbara lived. There I tracked down all available leads to this story, but could find very little additional information. There was a poem by Mandelshtam about the heresy. The philosopher Berdyayev had nearly been sent to Siberia for expressing support for the heretics. But that was it.

Then in the spring of 1972, the "B" volume of the new edition of the official Soviet Encyclopedia (Bolshaya Sovietskaya Entsiklopediya) appeared. The previous edition had mentioned an "Alexander" Bulatovich who died about 1910. The Bulatovich in the Times article was named "Anthony" and was very much alive in 1913. The new edition made it clear that Alexander and Anthony were the same man. (In the Russian Orthodox Church, when becoming a monk, it is common to adopt a new name with the same first letter.) The new article corrected the date of his death (1919) and referenced books that Bulatovich had written about his experiences in Ethiopia. This encyclopedia item was signed by Professor I.S. Katsnelson, from the Institute of Oriental Studies, in Moscow.

I wrote to Professor Katsnelson, and to my delight, in his reply, he sent me a copy of a recently published reprint of Bulatovich's Ethiopian books, which he had edited, and also gave me the name and address of Bulatovich's sister, Princess Mary Orbeliani, who was then 98, and living in Canada.

From that point on, one lead led to another.

Katsnelson offered to help me gain access to Soviet archives that had some of Bulatovich's unpublished notes and other related materials. But my Army security clearance prevented me from travel behind the Iron Curtain. (I was then in the Army reserves.)

Instead, in the summer of 1972, I traveled to Mount Athos, where I spent a couple of weeks, mostly doing research in the library of St. Pantelaimon, the one remaining Russian monastery there.

Meanwhile, I corresponded with Princess Orbeliani, and visited her for two days the following summer in Penticton, British Columbia. In long tape-recorded conversations and in letters before and after that visit, she provided me with valuable information about her brother's life and insight into his character. At 99, she was very articulate, lucid, and helpful. She was delighted that someone was showing an interest in her brother's work and beliefs. She was a remarkable and inspiring person—unassuming, warm and open. Living in a nursing home, she continued to pursue her artwork, specializing in water colors. Although her fingers were swollen from arthritis and she had difficulty even unwrapping a piece of candy, she could still play Chopin on the piano from memory, smoothly and without hesitation. Her own tale would make an interesting book: flight during the Revolution by way of Baku to Yugoslavia, and hardship there under the Nazis; sending her son to engineering school in Louvain, Belgium; his career in the Belgian Congo; and then eventually joining him in British Columbia. (She passed away in 1977 at the age of 103).

Increasingly, I was getting caught up in the research, carrying it far beyond what one would normally do to write an "historical novel." Each new piece of information raised more questions and pulled me in even deeper.

After Barbara and I were married in 1973, we wanted to travel to Ethiopia. In preparation, we took lessons in the Oromo language with Solomon Kenea, an undergraduate at Harvard who came from the same part of Ethiopia where Bulatovich had traveled. I didn't expect to become proficient in the language, but I felt that learning it was one way to get an appreciation for the people and their culture. And if and when we got to Ethiopia, trying to learn more about the language would be a way to make friends there, as Bulatovich had eighty years before.

Unfortunately, the revolution in Ethiopia then made the trip impossible.

But at Harvard's Widener Library, I was able to follow up references and find related materials. In this manner, I found and photocopied numerous books and articles about Ethiopia, as well as the heresy, and the Manchurian campaign of 1900.

I was fascinated by Bulatovich's character. I wanted to work out the puzzle of his motivations, to figure out what could have led to all the shifts and twists of his life story: from St. Petersburg, to Ethiopia, to Manchuria, then back to St. Petersburg where he became a monk, and on to Mount Athos, becoming the champion of the "heretics" there, then a chaplain at the Eastern Front in World War I, surviving the Revolution and Civil War, and returning to preach on what had been his family's estate in the Ukraine, only to be murdered by bandits.

What drove him to do the things he did? How could I present all these facts I had uncovered in a way that they seemed plausible?

Eventually, I wrote The Name of Hero. Intended as the first part of a trilogy, this novel focuses on Manchuria, with flashbacks to his childhood and to Ethiopia. Professor Katsnelson died in 1981, the year that Hero was published.

Katsnelson (1910-1981) was a professor at the Institute of Oriental Studies of the Academy of Sciences of the U.S.S.R., in Moscow. He was a specialist in ancient Egypt and Nubia, best known for his monograph Napata and Meroe—the Ancient Kingdom of Sudan published in 1971. He had a personal interest in Ethiopia and Bulatovich in particular. In 1975, together with G. Terekhova, he published a popularized biography of Bulatovich entitled Through Unknown Lands of Ethiopia. He also edited and, in 1979, published a book by another Russian explorer of Ethiopia, a contemporary of Bulatovich, L.K. Artamanov, entitled Through Ethiopia to the Banks of the White Nile. Katsnelson also uncovered in the Soviet Archives a series of previously unpublished documents by and about Bulatovich in Ethiopia. These were eventually published in Moscow in 1987 as Third Expedition in Ethiopia by Bulatovich. Selections from his introduction to the first Bulatovich books, with unique biographical details about Bulatovich, are included at the end of this volume.

While I was researching my novel, I translated portions of Bulatovich's Ethiopian books for my own use. The more I read about Ethiopia, the more it became clear to me that experts in the field were unfamiliar with these works and could benefit from them, and also that they contain much that would interest the general reader and lover of history. Finally, with the prompting of Professor Harold Marcus of Michigan State University, I made the time to translate both books in full. I am now writing the next Bulatovich novel.

TRANSLATION NOTES

Up until the Revolution, Russia used the Julian or "old style" calendar, which, in 1897-98 lagged 12 days behind the Gregorian calendar, which was used by the rest of the world. Since Bulatovich used the "old style" and celebrated religious holidays, such as Christmas, in accord with that calendar, his usage has been retained in this translation.

I have not anglicized the names—except Biblic ones in a church or historical context (e.g. the Queen of Sheba), and Bulatovich's middle name Xavieryevich (instead of Ksaveryevich), to indicate the Roman Catholic origins of his father, Xavier.

Ethiopian words in the text pose a particular problem. Bulatovich used non-traditional phonetic methods to render what he heard into Cyrllic characters. Strictly following standard Cyrllic-to-English transliteration practice would lead to unnecessary confusion, making it difficult to recognize when he is writing about well-known historical people, places, and events. For instance, the general he accompanied on the expedition to Lake Rudolph is commonly rendered in English as Wolda Giyorgis, but direct transliteration from Bulatovich's Cyrillic would yield Val'dye Gyeorgyis. And the common title dajazmatch in direct transliteration would have been dadiazmach.

To avoid this problem, where the Amharic original is obvious and the person, place, or thing is well-known, I follow the spelling in The Life and Times of Menelik II by Harold G. Marcus.

In other cases, I deviate from standard transliteration to yield spellings consistent with well-known ones. For instance, the Russian letter "U" at the beginning of a word and before a vowel is rendered "W" in this text (as in Wollo and Wollaga). Also, the Russian character that is normally rendered with the two-letter combination "kh" is transcribed here simply as "h" when it falls at the beginning of a word (as in Haile). And the combination of two Russian letters—"d" and the letter normally rendered as "zh"—is here treated as the single letter "j" (as in Jibuti and Joti). Also, the series of titles ending in -match, such as dajazmatch, are rendered consistently with "tch" rather than just "ch" as in Bulatovich's usage.

For convenience, when Bulatovich uses Russian units of measure for distance (verst), length (vershok, arshin, sagene), temperature (Reamur), weight (pood), I provide a direct translation and immediately follow with the conversion to common American units of measure [in brackets].

The paragraph breaks are the same as in the orginal (for easy comparison of one text with the other).

Ellipses (...) are used here the same as in the original. They do not indicate that material has been omitted.

Thanks to the dozens of people from the Internet newsgroups soc.culture.soviet and k12.lang.russian who took the time to help me decipher obscure and obsolete Russian terms and identify literary quotations. Alexander Chaihorsky deserves special thanks for his insight into the meaning of "sal'nik" based on his experience as an explorer in northern Mongolia. Thanks also to another Internet contact: Zemen Lebne-Dengel, who explained for me the Amharic words t'ef and dagussa.

BOOK ONE

FROM ENTTOTO TO THE RIVER BARO

INTRODUCTION[1]

In the summer of 1896, I had the opportunity to take part in a journey into Abyssinia, and decided to take advantage of it. I set out toward the western regions because Ethiopia was almost completely unexplored in that direction. Only three Europeans had up until then been on that side of the Didessa River:
1) Ilg[2] by order of Emperor Menelik went up the Dabus River, but didn't cross the Gaby River.
2) Schuver[3] went from Gedaref across the Abbay River between the Dabus River and the Tumat River and discovered the basin of that river.
3) And Pino, a French merchant, went on several campaigns with *Ras* Gobana[4,5] and was the only European to have crossed the Gaba River. But he didn't reach the River Baro.

The whole southwestern portion of the Ethiopian highlands was up to this time completely unexplored. This was true not because of lack of people who wanted to, and not so much because of insuperable natural obstacles to such exploration. Rather, up until very recent times, this region was ruled by a series of independent Galla tribes.[6] You could get there only by passing through Shoa; but because of the continual wars between Abyssinians and Galla, that was impossible. Now the Abyssinians rule this country and, only with great reluctance let anyone go there.

In addition, this journey was interesting because, according to informed sources, the western provinces, together with Harar, were the richest in Abyssinia, and were almost the sole source of the state treasury. It would also be interesting to observe how the Abyssinians rule a recently conquered region.

From an ethnographic point of view, it would be interesting to learn the morals, manners, customs, and character of the Galla, who were the native inhabitants of this country and who up to this time were almost completely unknown.

A visit to this region also had interest from a military point of view, because this is where the main forces of Abyssinia are —presenting the opportunity to study the Abyssinian army, which was very difficult to do in Entotto.

I was unprepared for this journey and didn't have the appropriate instruments; so, unfortunately, I couldn't try to solve the scientific questions which I otherwise would have pursued. But it was impossible to obtain the instruments. I received the invitation to make this journey at the end of September. If I had ordered scientific instruments, at best they couldn't arrive before the beginning of January, and there would always be the risk that they would be broken in transit.

Therefore, not setting myself unrealistic scientific goals, I decided to take advantage of this rare opportunity I had been given to visit this interesting country, and I tried to do everything I could to make my journey useful.

This book is an account of my journey and description of the country, its governmental structures, and the beliefs and customs of the tribes who lived there. These are the fruits of my best efforts at observation. I know very well that my conclusions are in many ways inexact and that a more detailed study of the country will reveal that this account is not without errors. I myself, after my trip, frequently had to correct my own errors. But I tried, as much as it was in my powers, to determine the truth. Keeping in mind the proverb, "The one who is mistaken is the one who does nothing," I decided to publish this work.

First Excursion

When Emperor Menelik gave me permission for my journey, the main condition he imposed on me was that I could not cross the borders of his realm. I agreed to that, unwillingly.[7]

On Oct. 28, 1896, the Emperor granted me a farewell audience. Saying good-bye, His Highness wished me a good trip and gave me two letters: one to *Dajazmatch*[8] Demissew (his domain was halfway to Leka), and the other to *Dajazmatch* Tesemma, who lives at the far western frontiers of Abyssinia.

At noon on Oct. 29, cordially seen off by those members of the Russian Red Cross who were staying in Entotto and by several Abyssinian friends, I left by the road to Leka.

My detachment consisted of 17 servants and eight animals (seven mules and one horse). It was very easy to find servants. Knowing of my upcoming trip, they came and voluntarily applied for work, despite the extremely modest conditions (five talers for clothes and pay per servant on our return). I selected just 17 men. This number was a few more than what I needed, but the road ahead was such that we would not be able to pass that way without losses, and it would be impossible to replenish the ranks en route. So I increased by a third the number of people I needed (I estimated 11 for guns and one for tent posts). Our weapons consisted of three 3/8-inch-caliber rifles which were provided by the Red Cross (with 50 cartridges for each gun), one carbine (with 50 cartridges), one double-barreled hunting gun (500 cartridges), six Gra guns (1200 cartridges), and one revolver (18 cartridges). Our side-arms consisted of a sword, three Abyssinian sabers and four metal spears. Our transport consisted of eight pack mules which could carry a total of 45 poods [1620 pounds] of cargo.[9]

On the first day, we only went 15 versts [9.9 miles] because the pack loads were not yet adjusted and required frequent stops and fixing. We spent the night at Mete. On Oct. 31, we crossed the upper reaches of the Awash River and stayed at the home of a Galla. In all, in three days, we went 75 versts [49.5 miles].

Crossing the Awash, we came to the residence of *Dajazmatch* Ubye—the husband of *Woyzaro*[10] Zawditu[11], daughter of Menelik.

At our next stop we met the uncle of the *Dajazmatch*—a gray-haired, hunched old man, 65 years old, of Semitic features and with oblong, suspicious eyes. He was supposed to lead me through the domain of his nephew. The house where we stayed belonged to a rich Galla. Our host was absent, and his two beautiful wives received us. The house was rather large, of a low circular design 15-20 paces in diameter with a gabled roof, propped up with a large number of posts. The house was divided by partitions into three separate apartments. At night the livestock was driven into the apartment nearest to the outside doors, the largest one (Galla houses are not surrounded with fences). The hearth was found in the middle apartment, and the farthest apartment was the sleeping chamber of the host.

On November 1, we stopped in the land of Gura at the house of a *shum*[12] of my friend *Dajazmatch* Haile Maryam, the older brother of *Ras* Makonnen[13]. The domain of Haile Maryam used to be very great; but four years ago, he argued with the Empress Taitu[14] and everything was taken away from him. Now part of the confiscated land has been returned to him—namely Chobo, Gura, and Tikur. The home of the *shum* was located on a beautiful spot on the bank of the River *Guder*. Knowing that I would pass through his land, the *Dajazmatch*, who at that time was in Addis Ababa, sent a courier to the *shum*; and that evening they brought to me a large *durgo*[15]: a plump ram, 200 pieces of *injera*[16], *tej*[17], *tala*[18], honey comb, butter, hens, eggs, and a sauce for the servants. A *gybyr* (feast) was prepared. First Ato Zennakh, Ato Balaynekh and I, and then all the servants and local Abyssinians ceremoniously carried in a ram, which had just been slaughtered and hung it on a post. Ato Zennakh, with the air of an expert of Abyssinian gastronomy, cut it into pieces. A servant with bare shoulders, who had wrapped his shamma[19] around him, lifted the still warm thigh of a ram over a basket with *injera*, around which we sat. (In good homes at eating time, one is supposed to wear the shamma in this manner. In the palace, those close to the emperor in general do not have the right to wear the shamma at all) Each of us chose a piece of meat for ourselves and cut it from the leg. It is hard to imagine anything more delicious than raw fresh-killed meat, but unfortunately, thanks to it, there is scarcely an Abyssinian who does not suffer from tape-worm, and all of them, beginning with the Emperor and ending with the beggar, regularly, every two months, take boiled and crushed berries of the *kusso* tree, and, in low-lying places, of the enkoko bush. At times of severe illness, before receiving the Eucharist, the Abyssinian takes his *kusso*, and he considers it indecent to die without cleansing himself of tape worms.

On November 2 we crossed the rapid Uluk River by a natural stone bridge, which is some sort of wonder of nature. The countryside was of striking beauty. In the narrow and deep ravine, the river rushed past with a roar. The steep banks were overgrown with high *kolkual* cactuses, having found shelter by some miracle on the almost sheer cliffs. This countryside is rich in hot mineral springs, well-known both among the Abyssinians and the Gallas for their medicinal strength. The three main springs are found by the same river, at the bridge. They are named Iesus, Maryam and Giyorgis [Jesus, Mary, and George]. Alongside the river, somewhat higher, there is a lake with a large number of springs, which also bear the names of saints. Nearby there is a market. It was market day and groups of Galla and Abyssinians stretched out on both sides. Along the way, they would plunge into the medicinal water of the lake and water their cattle. My fellow travelers did likewise. All this compact mass of supple and slender black bodies of antique beauty now shone dark bronze under the oblique rays of the evening sun, in the middle of the wild lake, surrounded by ancient forest and rocks.

On this day, passing along the valley of the *Guder* River and having crossed it by a narrow bridge made of liana, we stopped at the foot of the Toke mountain ridge. On November 3, we climbed the mountain ridge; and on November 4, we descended into the valley of the Gibye River[20]. Both the ascent and the descent were extremely difficult because of the steepness and the muddy forest road.

Ato Zennakh asked me to stop over at his house, and I accepted the invitation, because the unsuitability of my pack saddles for mountainous roads was already beginning to tell: one mule was hurt; and the next day, we decided to cauterize its back in the customary Abyssinian fashion. This operation is done in the following way: they bring the mule down on the ground and, having made two sickles red-hot pressed on cow's dung, they seared it in seven places on each side of the backbone, each in the form of a line five vershoks [8.75 inches] long, extending from the backbone down along the ribs. On the following day, in spite of the fact that the whole back of the mule was swollen, they saddled it with a light load, and by evening the swelling had gone away.

In the absence of the *Dajazmatch*, who almost always stays with the Emperor, Ato Zennakh manages all of his vast property. His house is located at the foot of Mount Jibat in a delightful, heavily populated valley of one of the tributaries of the Gibye River. Built on a small terrace with a very steep climb, and surrounded by a high fence, it towers over all the surrounding countryside. There are many legends about Mount Jibat. They say that on the summit there used to be a castle of *Negus* Zara Yakob[21] (fifteenth century A.D.). The ruins of this castle exist to this day, but the mountain has become overgrown with such thick forest that to get to them is very difficult.

Ato Zennakh entertained me as well as he possibly could. An ox and two rams were slaughtered and a feast was prepared, at which was drunk an enormous number of *gombs*[22] of *tej*.

On November 6, the holiday of my regiment, after a sufficiently long march, we stopped at the house of a rich Galla. In solitude, I drank a bottle of red wine in honor of the regiment.

On November 7, our route went along the valley of the Gibye River—wide and low, still swampy from the rain. From the north it is bounded by the Chalez Mountains, and from the south by the Jibat Mountains and Koletcho-Ale. It is said that in these mountains there is a summit to which a cross descended from heaven; and that, to this day, it is guarded by some mysterious old man and old woman. But no one has ever climbed this mountain and seen this cross, since according to popular belief—which scarcely ever is wrong—anyone who dares to climb here will suddenly die.

At noon we crossed the Gibye River, the main tributary of the River Omo. The water still hadn't abated after the rain, and we swam the horses and mules across. Galla carried our goods by hand over a hanging bridge. This bridge was constructed in a very eccentric way. From two enormous trees on both banks of the river were stretched lianas, on which were placed the web of the bridge; several lianas served as hand-rails on the sides. The length of the bridge was 40 paces; its width was one pace. This year, the water was very high and damaged part of the bridge, such that mules couldn't pass along it.

Our animals swam in groups of two or three; and we nearly had an accident. The current took my horse and two mules, and since the banks were steep and the animals were in no condition to scramble out, they were quickly pulled down. But the selflessness of two Galla and of my servants saved the animals. Here, among other things, a humorous episode took place. One of the servants was wearing my old flabby top hat; when the servant was crossing the bridge, the wind caught the hat, and it fell in the water. A Galla, seeing this, jumped straight from the bridge, from a height of at least five arshins [six and a half yards], after the hat into the water, and with celebration brought it to me, apparently thinking it was of great value.

The whole crossing, with and without loads, took an hour and a half.

On November 8 we crossed the property of *Dajazmatch* Ubye into the land of *Dajazmatch* Demissew and stopped at the large market of the village of Bilo. This day we succeeded in killing an enormous chamois-bull (*orobo*). The bullet from the 3/8-inch-caliber rifle, as it turned out that time, hit the cheek and went through, but, in spite of that, the *orobo* continued to run and only fell at a distance of 700-800 paces from the spot where it was wounded. Both the entry and exit holes made by the bullet were scarcely noticeable.

The Gibye River separates the lands of *Dajazmatch* Demissew and *Dajazmatch* Ubye. We parted cordially with Ato Zennakh, and I gave him a watch.

Dajazmatch Demissew sent a large convoy (150-200 men) to meet us and, along with two of his senior commanders—*Abagaz* Bakabil and Ato Wolda Maskal—and, in addition, five flutes, which is considered a great honor. The title *Abagaz* means "father of the estate." Usually this is an old man, who has known the owner from childhood. Sometimes he is a slave, who nursed him. Always he is someone connected to the estate with strong ties of friendship. Such was *Abagaz* Bakabil. Ato Wolda Maskal was the commander of 2,000 soldiers and in the absence of the *Dajazmatch* was his deputy.

The town of Bilo, where we stopped, was one of the most significant commercial centers of western Abyssinia. Although it is located on the land of *Dajazmatch* Demissew, it was not under his command, but rather under the *nagada-ras* (in translation—"head of the merchants"), who is in charge of all the trade of a certain district and of all the merchants found there, in judicial, administrative, and fiscal matters. The significance of Bilo as a commercial point derives from its position at a crossroads. Everything that goes from western Abyssinia to Shoa and Gojjam and from the south to Gojjam passes through Bilo. Through it pass large caravan tracks to Wollaga, Ilu-Babur, Jimma, Kaffa, Leka, and on the north and east to Gojjam, and from there to Massawa, Jibuti and Zeila through Shoa and Harar. Recently, with the increase in export through Zeila and Jibuti at the expense of Massawa, trade from southern Abyssinia and Kaffa goes not through Bilo, but straight to Shoa through Sodo and Jimma. In Bilo itself, there are no more than 300 households, but already with the first steps you feel the difference between this settlement and those which are near it. It is immediately evident that this is a commercial center with lively and exuberant interests. Here one can buy both hay and *injera* and *tala* and *tej* and even cognac and absinthe. At a dinner held in my honor, the *shum* of this city, son of the *nagada-ras*, asked me about the governments of Europe, about Egypt and India, showed interest in politics and in his turn told what he knew about Kaffa and dervishes. As usual, they overloaded us with *durgo*. After the meal, singers sang the victories of Menelik, and also improvised on the friendship of Russians and Abyssinians. Those singers were soon relieved by others who, together with the beggars who had assembled, gave me no peace all night long.

On November 10, we crossed through the Koncho mountain ridge, which unites the mountain groups of Sibu, Chelea and Limu, and descended into the valley of the Wam River, a tributary of the Didessa. On November 11, at noon, we swam across the Wam and climbed on Mount Leka. On November 12, met by all the available soldiers of *Dajazmatch* Demissew, we ceremoniously entered his residence. He himself came out to meet me and accommodated me in his house. Son of an *afa-negus*[23], who had great influence on the emperor, he until recent times was *fitaurari*[24] and ruled a small region of Gera and Guma which bordered on Kaffa. But after the death of the *Fitaurari* Gabayu, Takle, and Damto, killed in the last war, he was given authority over these lands and the rank of *Dajazmatch*. To him was also entrusted the chief supervision over two Galla states which had submitted to Menelik and therefore had maintained their former government: Wollaga—*Dajazmatch* Joti, and Leka—*Dajazmatch* Gebra Egziabeer. Thus the property of *Dajazmatch* Demissew extends from the extreme western and northwestern borders of Ethiopia.

I spent two days as a guest of this amiable host, also becoming acquainted with his wife, who is very nice, but in appearance almost a little girl. She is 14 years old, but, by her own words, Demissew is her third husband. *Woyzaro* Asalefech (literally "forcing to go"), a cousin of the Empress Taitu, got married for the first time at the age of nine and recently, in accordance with the wishes of the *itege*[25], divorced her second husband and married *Dajazmatch* Demissew. The life of women of the upper class in Abyssinia is a sad one. As much as a woman of the lower class is free, the life of a woman of the upper class is secluded. For entire weeks and sometimes months, they do not leave their elfin[26]. They are always surrounded by dozens of maid servants. Here, in addition, several boys are always found, sons of well-known people who are subordinates of the *Dajazmatch*, who teach etiquette and grammar. All this is guarded by several gloomy, wrinkled, beardless eunuchs.

On November 14, bidding good-bye to the *Dajazmatch* and his wife, I left this amiable host. He led me with flutes and with all his army to the banks of the Didessa and at parting gave me a splendid mule with silver gear. In return, at his request, I gave him a Gra gun, 100 cartridges, and part of my traveling medicine chest—some of all the medicines, and likewise several bottles of vodka.

At three in the afternoon we crossed the wide Didessa River. The goods and people were transported by Gallas on small, dug-out canoes, and the horses and mules swam across. During the crossing there was a small accident. One of my servants and a Galla were on one of the canoes. A servant held the reins of my horse and the mule which had just been given to me in order to lead them across to the other side. But the new mule, as soon as it no longer felt the bottom under its feet, suddenly turned back toward the bank. The reins fell under the stern of the canoe and the canoe capsized. My servant, not knowing how to swim, almost drowned, but this was, fortunately, close to the bank, so Galla arriving just in time saved him, at the same time as losing a 3/8-inch-caliber rifle and also some other things. The whole crossing took three hours.

The Didessa here is quite wide (300-400 paces) and very deep. The banks are overgrown with an enormous ancient forest, interwoven with lianas, overhanging down to the water. The river abounds with fish, crocodiles and hippopotamuses. During the crossing the Galla tried to make as much noise as they could in order to scare away crocodiles.

At this place, the forest on the banks of the Didessa stretches out in a narrow strip, behind which lies a wide plain, overgrown with dense five-arshin [four-yard] high grass, completely hiding both rider and horse. The road is intersected by a thick network of interlacing paths, among which it is difficult to distinguish which were made by animals and which by people, and the high grass conceals from you all points of orientation. Because of this, we finally lost our way and were separated from our mules. We had to spend the night in a secluded Galla farmstead, consisting of five houses.

Almost half of the population of this farmstead died this year from fever. At our call, a boy appeared. He was quite emaciated. A sheep skin thrown over his thin shoulders was his only clothing. He was shaking all over from fever, and the moans of several more sick people were heard from the house. At the entrance several piles of stones were heaped up; and bundles of high grass, scraps of material, coffee seeds and some beads and shells were thrown on them. This is how Galla offer sacrifices to the fever in order that it pass by their houses.

The valley of the Didessa is one of the most fever-ridden. The fever here is especially strong and every year takes many victims. But the illness only lasts from May-June to October-November. The other unhealthy characteristic of this place is that every little wound easily turns into an ulcer; almost the whole populace is afflicted by them.

At night I sent everyone to search for the mules and goods, but it took until noon the next day for them to find them and get back together. We spent the night at the home of Ato Balaynekh, a *shum* of *Dajazmatch* Tesemma who had been sent to meet us. He is responsible for the law court—*wambyr*—in the half of the property of *Dajazmatch* Tesemma which lies between the Didessa and Gaba Rivers. But his main duty, aside from managing his own district, is to keep an eye on the collections of taxes by the other *shum*s. Here, as before, I was received extremely cordially.

Ato Balaynekh is an interesting type of Abyssinian of the old stock: lean, lively, sometimes brutal, apparently brave, not as refined as the emperor's courtiers today, rough and proud. He took part in the last expedition to Aussa and, as he asserted, killed 32 Danakils.[26] He doesn't know how to shoot a rifle, but uses a spear exceptionally well.

On this side of the Didessa, the road turns to the southwest; and the countryside changes sharply. Here everything is completely concealed by forest and bushes. The elevated and hilly countryside is broken by narrow, deep valleys, in which many streams, descending from the summits of Kaffa, pour their crystal clear water into the Baro or the Gaba. All these valleys are thickly grown with coffee. The air is very damp, and in the morning the dew is plentiful. Endless spring reigns here, and there is no time of the year when no trees are in flower. Ten to twelve years ago this countryside was completely settled and, of course, there wasn't a piece of good land left uncultivated. But a cattle disease led to famine, and destruction of the population during the subjugation of the region has half depopulated it. Riding through, every minute you come across straight lines of *kolkual* cactus among the overgrowth, indicating former property boundaries or the former fence of a farmstead. Now the territory all around is completely covered with bushes, thickly interwoven with thorny lianas. Rarely, you come upon a Galla settlement, surrounded with banana trees. More often, here and there, clearings are seen, where peas grow among chopped and knocked down trees. By this picture you can judge the fertility of the soil. Uncultivated ground gives just as fine a harvest as that which has been sown. Beehives hang from all the high trees near settlements. The honey from this area is celebrated for its strength. The general impression produced by this region is the most delightful: if it is possible to apply the phrase "flowing in milk and honey" to any country, then truly this is that country.

On November 16, we crossed the Dobona River by bridge and spent the night at the home of a Galla. The family consisted of the host, (the father of whom was killed by Abyssinians during the subjugation), his mother and two wives. One of the wives was exceptionally beautiful. The host himself, apparently, was reconciled with his fate, but his mother looked on Abyssinians with fear and anger and sat by the fire all night long.

On the seventeenth, we took a very difficult road to the Gaba River and, crossing it by bridge, spent the night at the house of *Balambaras*[28,29] Mansur. He was on a raid with the *Dajazmatch*, and his wife took us in.

The banks of the Gaba River are precipitously steep and do not allow crossing by ford. They took advantage of this circumstance and on that side of the bridge built a gate for the collection of duty from all incoming and outgoing merchandise. Aside from the revenue, it also has military significance, since it prevents desertion. An excellent mule of mine died here. The day before, it was still quite healthy; but at eleven o'clock in the morning, descending to the Gaba River, it suddenly took ill. White foam poured from its nostril, and after two minutes it was dead.

On the nineteenth, we crossed the Sor River, also by bridge. The banks of the Sor, like those of the Gaba were entirely overgrown with coffee.

On the twenty-first, we were ceremoniously met by *Fitaurari* Wolda Ayb, a deputy of *Dajazmatch* Tesemma. He had come three versts [two miles] from the town with his available garrison. Together, we went to the town of Gori. This is the last Abyssinian town on the north-west border. The troops who had come to meet me, bowed down to the ground to me, and, surrounding me, led me to the house that had been prepared for us. The clergy came from the church in Gori to meet me with crosses and icons. The priest recited the Lord's Prayer, and then began hymns, accompanied with dancing.

Gori is the residence of *Dajazmatch* Tesemma. At this time, he was on a small expedition against the neighboring Mocha. He had left *Fitaurari* Wolda Ayb as his deputy, an old man, who had also served his father, *Dajazmatch* Hadou. My arrival threw the old man into great confusion. The day before, he had received a letter from the Emperor addressed to the *Dajazmatch*, explaining the purpose of my visit and ordering him to meet me with honor and to receive me well. In Menelik's letter, it was said that I came to look at the country and that he should show it to me. But without a direct order from the *Dajazmatch* the *Fitaurari* was afraid to do that. On the day following my arrival, all this became clear. I demanded that the *Fitaurari* give me a guides to *Dajazmatch* Tesemma in Mocha, but he did not agree to this. Then I explained to him that I didn't come here just to sit around; and, having the permission of the emperor, in two days I would either set out to find *Dajazmatch* Tesemma or go north to *Dajazmatch* Joti. The *Fitaurari* was in despair. He implored me to wait here two weeks, believing that in that time the *Dajazmatch* should definitely return. But I foresaw that two weeks would drag on to two months and did not agree to that. My departure was set for Tuesday. Unfortunately, I could not carry out this intention. The fever which I had suffered in Addis Ababa and which had not left me for the whole time of the trip, now came back in a stronger degree, complicated by a large abscess on my stomach at the place where I had had a hypodermic injection of quinine. On November 25, I finally took to my bed, and only got up again three weeks later.

The twenty-third and twenty-fourth of November, I had a misunderstanding with the servants. They demanded that I give them five talers for clothing, and when I said no, they went on strike. But I forestalled it, firing the chief instigator. I whipped another who continued to stir up trouble, and the commotion quieted down. At first, the one who had been punished was bitterly offended and went to give his gun back to me. I dismissed him and gave him three more talers for the return journey. But in less than half an hour, priests came to ask forgiveness for him, and he himself began to kiss my feet. I was very happy at this outcome, as a moral victory, definitely establishing my authority over him.

My illness, apparently, was not of the lungs, since I suffered badly for three to four days, until I lanced the abscess with a knife washed in sublimate. All the servants sat at the entrance to my tent and wept mournfully.

On December 12, somewhat recovered from the illness, I designated the fifteenth as the day of departure. But this again had to be put off since the chief of my servants, Wolda Tadik, became seriously ill. On December 20 a letter arrived for me from *Dajazmatch* Tesemma, which said that he would be happy to see "the eyes of a Russian friend" and asked me to wait until Christmas, since he hoped to return at that time. The letter was written from Mocha, and it was brought from there by a Galla woman. I answered that I would wait, and I used the free time to hunt, and also to become acquainted with the beliefs, customs and history of the Galla. Through my servants I questioned merchants who came that way, who had relations with Negroes of Bako and Kaffa.

Our internal life was often troubled by my servants fighting among themselves or with the local inhabitants. That kind of business made it necessary for me to dress wounds. On December 23, having quarreled with one another, some took up guns, some took up sabers, and the issue threatened to become a regular battle. Fortunately, I intervened in time and calmed them down. That's the way things were until December 31. Wolda Tadik recovered. There was no news from *Dajazmatch* Tesemma. There was no reason to stay here any longer, but I also didn't want to leave without having seen the lands on the other side of the Baro River. Since there was no legal way I could penetrate beyond the Baro River, I tried to accomplish it by cunning and force. During my stay here, I was treated almost like an honored captive. Fifty soldiers were posted around the house, day and night, in order to "protect me from danger," as the *Fitaurari* asserted. If I went out anywhere, to stroll or to hunt, they all went along with me.

On the morning of December 31, I ordered two horses be saddled (one of which I had bought the day before); and at 8 o'clock in the morning, accompanied by one servant, I quickly set out along the road that leads to the bridge across the Baro. We took several biscuits with us and armed ourselves: I had a sword, revolver and rifle, and my servant had my carbine and saber. Each of us had 40 cartridges. At 12 noon we got as far as Didu Mountain, having covered, along a mountainous road with frequent crossings, 50 versts [33 miles] in four hours. Another 15 versts [12 miles] of difficult, swampy forest road remained up to the Baro. Having given the horses a quarter hour of rest, we moved along farther, but were soon forced to dismount. The road was swampy, and we were sometimes up to our knees in mud. The forest was shady and cool, since the ancient enormous trees blocked the light of the sun. Among the trees everything was completely overgrown with coffee bushes.

Already after eight versts [5 miles], we heard the rumbling of a waterfall. Finally, at three o'clock in the afternoon, we reached the great river. Over the river a bridge had been thrown, for which they used two rocks halfway along the riverbed. In this manner, the bridge was made up of three spans, each 40 paces in length. Beyond the Baro began the theater of military action and Mocha, a state that is kindred to Kaffa, populated by people of the same Sidamo tribe.[29] To the north from Mocha, Negro tribes begin. Not being able to seriously acquaint myself with these regions, I wanted at least to glance superficially at them, and therefore, in spite of the insistence of my servant that we return, I went farther. The sun had already set, but the forest did not end, and there were no traces of habitation. But there in a thicket the sound of voices was heard. We went toward the sound; and in half an hour, we found ourselves in the middle of coffee pickers. The wife of the Abyssinian *shum* on this side of the Baro, had gathered all her husband's remaining soldiers and risked crossing the river to harvest coffee. At the entrance to a hut, hidden by banana leaves, a fire crackled, and fifteen Abyssinian men sat around it, chattering in an undertone. Our arrival absolutely amazed them. In the hut, where they led me, I saw the bold woman leader of this small detachment. Very beautiful, with almost white skin, she reclined on a bed and breast-fed a child. They treated me to flat-cakes made from corn and freshly picked coffee; this was all of their provisions. Chatting cheerfully, we sat around almost to the coming of the new year.

My departure had caused a terrible commotion in the city. *Fitaurari* Wolda Ayb raised everyone to their feet and sent them after me. He wasn't afraid of a trick, but rather that something had happened to me.

On the following day, having taken leave of our hostess, I set out for the border of Mocha. Having gone some distance through a countryside devastated by war, we turned north and reached Alga, the farthest Abyssinian observation point. This was a sort of small fort, surrounded by a deep moat, with little bridges thrown over it. A guard stopped us here in the name of Menelik and wouldn't let us in, until the commandant came and, realizing who I was, admitted me. In Alga, I was overtaken by a unit of men sent by the *Fitaurari*, with *Kanyazmatch*[30] Sentayukh and *Azzaj*[31] Dubal. They asked me to return, saying that I was at risk of being killed and that that would be the ruin of them. On the following day, taking the direction to the north along the slope of the mountains, after a very difficult crossing we reached Sale, the district which borders the lands of Negro tribes. From there, continuing again to the north and descending, we again reached the Baro. At this place it is even more beautiful than where I crossed it the first time. Fifteen versts [10 miles] below the bridge, the Baro divides into two streams which again unite here, forming two beautiful waterfalls, of which the first is several sagenes higher than the second [sagene=2.13 meters]. Pedestrians cross the Baro here by jumping from rock to rock, but horses and mules cannot do that. We tried to have a mule cross by swimming above the waterfall, where the current was not so strong; but the mule and the Abyssinian who was crossing with him almost perished. Halfway across the river, the servant hit a rock under the water, and letting go of the mule, was carried away to the waterfall. Fortunately, we at that moment held out a spear to him, which he grasped and leaped out on the bank. While we saved the Abyssinian, the mule, fighting against the current with difficulty, swam backwards and helplessly floundered and fought in the water, not having the strength to climb up on the steep bank, which had been undermined by water. Passing lianas under his belly and grabbing him—some by the ears and some by the tail—we somehow finally dragged him from the water.

Forced to build a bridge, we made full use of all the cutting weapons we had at hand. We wove the web of the bridge out of lianas. The work moved along at full swing; and after three hours, the bridge was ready. On this side, it began with a climb on a smooth stone surface, along which ran part of the water of the upper channel. My horse slipped and falling, began to slide down the inclined plane to the waterfall. The selflessness of my servants saved it. By some miracle, they held their ground on the slippery inclined plane, caught hold of it as well as possible, and, tying it with lianas, dragged it back up. This day, crossing an uninhabited border zone, that separates the lands of the Gallas and the Negroes of the Bako tribe, we spent the night in the neighborhood of the well-known market of Bure.

Bure is an important point of barter with Negro tribes on this side of the Baro. At Saturday markets, they bring for sale elephant tusks and sometimes their livestock, and in exchange for that they buy ornaments, beads and cloth. Besides this, Bure, located on the road from western Wollaga to Kaffa and from Mocha and western Kaffa to Leka and Gojjam, is important as a market for coffee. From Kaffa, Mocha, and the neighboring districts, coffee goes to Bure, where it is resold by other merchants who convey it to Leka or Bilo and there, in turn, resell it. Together with coffee goes much civet musk. I succeeded in seeing a civet cat[32] at the shop of a Galla merchant, who had a large quantity of them.[33] This animal is found in great numbers in this area; they catch these animals in snares. They put the captured cat in a long round cage, in which it cannot turn around. They always keep it at the hearth in homes. In almost every house, we saw two or three of these cages. They feed these animals meat cooked in butter. Ten civets can eat a ram in a day. Every nine days they gather the musk. This takes three men. One, having opened the cage from behind, takes the civet by the tail; another takes both back legs; and the third, with a horn spoon, carefully scrapes the discharge that has accumulated over this time. In nine days about two teaspoons accumulates.

On the following day, in the morning, before going to Gori, we went to see the market. It was eight o'clock in the morning; and people began to gather at the large square, surrounded with low huts, covered with banana leaves. Old men, women with infants tied behind them at the waist, and youths all stretched out in a long file, and each brought something: this one a hen, that one a piece of salt, that one large banana leaves, that one beads, that one handfuls of coffee... All of them, waiting for the *chekashum*[34], crowded at the entrance and with fear and curiosity looked at the never-before-seen white man. Finally the *shum* arrived and climbed up into his tower. One after the other, they let pass those who arrived. His helpers inspected to see what each had with him, and if it wasn't much, let him go by. From the others they collected a tax. For a ram or goat they took salt (1/20 of a taler); for a shamma they also took a little salt; from a sack of cotton several handfuls of it, from a sack of corn likewise, and so on for all the products. There weren't any large-scale merchants here. The large-scale merchants had houses nearby, and it was an advantage for them to sell at home rather than here. At the market, all the surrounding population gathered, as at a large party. Each had some kind of trifle with him, in order to trade it for something else. For several coffee seeds, they sold a cup of beer; for several bundles of cotton, tobacco in a pipe. There were almost no talers in circulation, and all commerce was exclusively by barter. They brought cows here as well, to mate with a good bull, also for a known price. There were baskets here and palm mats. Most of the Galla wore a shamma thrown over their shoulders, with a small leather apron around the waist; on the head they wore a pointed hat made of the skin of a goat or a monkey. Galla of this district have an exceptionally beautiful physique and are tall. Among the Galla women I saw very many who were beautiful. Around their waist was wrapped a large hide trimmed with beads and shells, which they wore as a [White Russian] kokhlushka skirt; on others even something like a leather sarafan. Most wore their hair shoulder-length, plaited in large numbers of braids. Some had their hair fluffed up and encircled with thin horizontal braids. One Galla woman had the most original hair style: the hair was wound round a large number of sharp sticks which stuck out of her head like needles. The men wear their hair short, and children have their heads shaven all around, with a clump of hair left in the middle.

In addition to the Galla, several Negroes from the Yambo and Bako tribes came to the market. They wore aprons made of leaves. Their upper front teeth were knocked out, and on the cheeks and on the forehead there were three longitudinal lines. They brought cotton with them.

I returned to Gori that day, covering 50-60 versts [33-40 miles] in five and a half hours. Everyone in the town was in complete despair, not having had any news of me. The *Fitaurari* arrested the Arab merchant who sold me the horse, and kept close watch on my servants. Learning of my return, he came with bows and expressions of joy on the occasion of my safe arrival. On my insistence, he freed the imprisoned Arab. I set the day of my departure for January 7.

On the evening from January 5 to 6, we took part in the religious procession to the Jordan. All the neighboring population assembled for the church holiday and the procession became huge. The deacons went first, all the children from eight to twelve years old, after them the priests ceremoniously carried on their heads the holy books and vessels; then came a chorus of scribes—*debtera,* and then an endless crowd of laymen, consisting of a large number of separate choruses, singing songs that were not at all spiritual. The deacons ring little bells, the *debtera* sing hymns and beat on drums, the children and women shout shrilly, several people shoot guns, and the procession ceremoniously proceeds to the Jordan. After the religious procession, the leaders dined at my tent. All night long, the singing and dancing did not stop. This revelry presented astonishing contrasts. Hymns of the *debtera* were interrupted by the loud women's chorus and the song "Gobilye, gobilye", which means "Lover, lover." And in the intervals, when it was quiet, the measured reading of the holy Gospel and the book of Mistir[35] was heard. And among all this, now and then, gun shots resounded.

At two o'clock in the morning, the service at the Jordan began. At five o'clock, the water was blessed. The priest submerged the cross in water three times—in the name of the Father, the Son, and the Holy Spirit—after which he poured it three times on his own head, on the heads of other priests and on me. Then, nearly crushing one another, the people rushed to the Jordan. After dinner on the bank of the river, the return procession began, even more lively than the day before. To the earlier choruses was added another one of Galla, who although pagan were caught up in the general merriment and joined in the holiday and danced their dance. The lead singer, a Galla man of enormous size with a brutal face, stood in the middle of a large circle. The chorus repeated on refrain, in a fury:*"Hoda, Hoda;"* and with the backs of their heads to one another, the Galla made a tight circle and, holding spears straight up and down, jumped up in time to the music. The lead singer was in complete ecstasy, with the song on his lips. He ran up to one and then another and aimed a spear at him. With the sharp end right at your chest, looking at the ferocious, brutal appearance of the Galla, it seemed he wouldn't hold back, and the spear would pierce into your body... Several jumped up, wildly growling and performing unusual body motions during the jump... Finally, the procession reached the church. After a three-time religious procession around the church, a volley of all guns was fired, and the priest went into the church.

On January 8, having written a letter to the *Dajazmatch* with thanks for his hospitality and having given this to the *Fitaurari*, I left, accompanied by a huge convoy with *Azzaj* Dubal and *Kanyazmatch* Work at the head. In the name of the *Dajazmatch*, the *Fitaurari* gave presents to me and all of my servants and also asked me to take a mule with gear, but I declined this on the pretext that not being acquainted with the *Dajazmatch*, I could not take gifts from him. He lead me beyond the city with all his available soldiers, but, in spite of all these honors, I realized that he secretly ordered that no one should lead me to nor show me any other road than the one by which I had arrived. Soldiers were sent far ahead with the order to send away from the path any Galla whom I could ask about the road. I intended to cross the Gaba, to move north by the large road from Leka to Wollaga, but by chance found out that there is another bridge and a better road across the Gaba. Despite all the difficulties and the cunning of the convoy, I turned onto this road, after first reconnoitering it. On January 11 we reached the gates of the bridge across the Gaba. They didn't want to let us pass, but we went by force.

On the far side begins Wollaga, and the countryside changes completely. Here already it is not so humid as in Ilu-Babur and Mocha, and the vegetation is not as rich, but the country is more populated and the soil, although not as black, is nonetheless apparently fertile. The prevailing type of tree is mimosa. The inhabitants are the same type, but apparently they are wealthier here. All of them were dressed in shammas, and many even had trousers. Likewise the houses are better and larger and as was the livestock—true sign of abundance. I came upon many women with chocolate-colored skin: some seemed from a distance white-skinned. Their hair was divided into many thin locks, covered with a layer of light yellow clay.

On January 12, we crossed the border of the property of *Dajazmatch* Tesemma, and entered the estate of *Dajazmatch* Demissew, and going past the large markets of Supe and Sodo, we spent the night in the land of *Abeko*. On January 13, we reached the large commercial settlement of Gunji. Gunji and Sodo, just like Bilo, is under the authority of a *nagada-ras*. Here I received news that completely changed my former plans. I found out that *Dajazmatch* Demissew was actively gathering provisions to go on an expedition against Abdurakhman (who rules over Beni Shangul and the course of the Tumat River), and *Dajazmatch* Joti had been called to *Dajazmatch* Demissew and already was on the way. Since the expedition, evidently, could not be postponed because the rains were coming, I decided to go as soon as possible to *Dajazmatch* Demissew to find out from him the true state of affairs; and if there was going to be an expedition, to try to take part in it. At seven o'clock in the morning, accompanied by one servant and a guide, who led us to the main road, I went to Didessa. After a five-hour fast trek by very difficult mountain road including crossing the Dobana River, we reached the gates on that side of the Didessa. I demanded that the leader of the guard post give us a guide to show us the ford, but he refused. My servant and I had to find it ourselves. The difficulty of finding it was heightened by the fact there were a large number of trails on the other bank and it was hard to distinguish which of them had been made by people and which by hippopotamuses. We used guess-work and crossed successfully. At six o'clock in the evening, having made a 80-90 verst [53 to 60 mile] passage, we reached the outpost of the *Dajazmatch*. He was sick, but finding out about my arrival greeted me with extreme pleasure, like an old friend. From him I learned that the Emperor had indeed commanded him to prepare for an expedition, and, at the first order, to quickly advance to the western borders for action against Abdurakhman. He had everything ready for the expedition, except 1,000 guns which he should receive from Addis Ababa and for which men had already been sent. Knowing of my desire to take part in the expedition, he replied that he would be in the highest degree happy if I would go with him, but it was necessary to get permission for this from His Majesty. On the following morning, I sent letters: one to the Emperor asking for permission to take part in the expedition, and the other to Russia with the same request.

On the third day after my arrival, the rest of my servants and mules arrived. There had been an accident while the crossing the Didessa, and crocodiles had carried off one of my servants.

Waiting for the answer from the Emperor, I went hunting. Having waited in vain for 14 days for the answer to my letter, I began to fear that some difficulty had arisen, and decided to go in person to Addis Ababa. On January 29, at eight o'clock in the morning, accompanied by one servant—he on a mule and I on a horse—we set out on our journey. The road was familiar, and we moved quickly. We had some biscuits and a few pounds of barley, the supply of which we refilled at local stops. The order of movement was as follows: having fed the mules at dawn, we set out at six o'clock in the morning and went at a trot, where the terrain permitted, otherwise at a walk or by foot up until twelve or one o'clock. Then at noon we took a short break and continued our advance until sunset. In this manner, depending on the road, we crossed from 90 to 110 versts [60 to 73 miles] a day. On the fourth day, February 1, having in this time gone 350 to 370 versts [231 to 244 miles], I arrived in the evening at the capital and stayed at the home of Mr. Mondon-Vidailhet.[36]

On the day after my arrival, I was received by the Emperor. He was very interested in my journey and was amazed at the speed of my passage. He told me that the expedition would not take place, since Abdurakhman had said he was ready to submit and agreed to the demand of the *Negus* to come in person or send to Addis Ababa his father as an expression of submission.

After several days disturbing news came from *Ras* Wolda Giyorgis, who was on an expedition against Kaffa, and the emperor ordered Demissew to go with his troops to help him. Finding out about this, I returned to the Emperor with my former request, but the *Negus* declined, justifying this refusal on the grounds that he was afraid I might be killed in his country. All these troops had participated in the Italian war. Many of them had relatives and friends killed there. Knowing that Abyssinians make little distinction between white men, the Emperor was afraid that that there could be some who would use this occasion to avenge the death of their friend or relative and would shoot me

21

from behind on the day of battle. Despite my argument that I would take all the consequences on my own responsibility, he remained inflexible. I had to reconcile myself with the bitter thought of being so close to war and not taking part in it.

On February 11, my mules and servants arrived, and on February 13, I set out, without luggage, on an elephant hunt with *Dajazmatch* Gebra Egziabeer in Leka.

Second Excursion

My equipment consisted of a small tent, two packs with gifts, linen and clothes, and two large skins with peas.37 The armament consisted of six Gra guns, two 3/8-inch-caliber rifles, one carbine, one double-barreled hunting gun, and one Gra system four-gauge elephant gun (with explosive bullets) weighing 24 pounds, which I bought in Addis Ababa for 120 talers.

Including my personal servant and the senior servant, there were 14 servants, one per gun. Two men carried the elephant gun in turns, since in addition to it, they also had another burden and long marches were planned.

From Addis Ababa to Lekamte, the residence of *Dajazmatch* Gebra Egziabeer is an estimated 360-400 versts [238-264 miles]. The elephant hunting season had already begun. I had little time left. I intended to cover this distance as fast as possible, so that after hunting I could catch the steamer leaving Jibuti on April 2. Therefore, having provided myself with a letter from the Emperor to *Dajazmatch* Gebra Egziabeer, I declined a translator and *durgo* along the way.

We set out at 12 noon on February 13. On the 15th, we camped at the vertex of a road crossing in Chalea. On the 16th, having passed the city of Bareilu, and having made a brief daytime stop at the city of Likamakos[38] Abata, we climbed Mount Tibye. The *shum* of the Likamakos killed a ram for us, and here we took part in the Lenten church service. On the 17th, we passed the summit of Mount Tibye and Mount Amara. On the 18th, we crossed the upper reaches of the Gibye River; and on the 19th, at 12 noon, we arrived at Lekamte. Thus we traversed the whole distance in six days, going 60 versts [40 miles] a day along a very difficult mountain road. We set out at six in the morning and walked till noon or one o'clock, made a short stop and then again walked until evening. We were on the move ten to eleven hours a day. Our food for this time consisted almost exclusively of peas fried in a pan; and for the first days, up until Lent, we ate gazelles killed along the way, for the most part raw, so we did not have to drag them along with us.

Notified by me of my arrival, the *Dajazmatch* sent all the soldiers at hand to meet me. I already knew *Dajazmatch* Gebra Egziabeer from before. During my stay at the home of *Dajazmatch* Demissew, Gebra Egziabeer was gravely ill. He had a severe fever which he had caught on an elephant hunt. It was immediately after the rains, when the huge grass was not yet burnt. Having surrounded the elephants, they set fire to the grass, but a stiff wind suddenly arose and spread the fire over the whole field and carried the flames toward the hunters. They saw too late the danger that was threatening them. Already there was no way out. Fortunately, there was a swamp nearby into which they all threw themselves and hid in mud up to their heads. The fire passed them by, taking several victims. Without exception, all the survivors fell sick with a fever, from which several men died. Being of very strong constitution and not having previously been sick, the *Dajazmatch* suffered especially severely from the fever and asked me by letter to help him. One day I went to him and gave him some of my quinine.

Dajazmatch Gebra Egziabeer is a Galla. From time immemorial, his clan has ruled this region. Twenty years ago it was conquered by the Tekla Haymanot, the *Negus* of Gojjam; but he could not hold out here. *Ras* Gobana, the famous general of Emperor Menelik, subdued all the surrounding Galla lands, and Leka, in view of its hopeless situation, voluntarily submitted to Menelik and now pays him a tribute consisting of 100 *ukets*[39] of ivory (150 pounds), 500 *ukets* of gold (about one pound) and a fixed tax for houses and cattle. Moreover, the inhabitants are obliged to maintain the troops of the Emperor who are stationed within the bounds of the region. At the time of the death of his father, Abakumsa (as Gebra Egziabeer used to called) was christened and had one of his three wives christened and repudiated the rest, giving them to his retinue. Emperor Menelik and Empress Taitu were their godparents. At the christening, he took the name Gebra Egziabeer—which literally means "God's slave." Promoted to *Dajazmatch* by Menelik, he inherited all the possessions of his father: very extensive possessions which, on the west, border on the possessions of Abdurakhman. The *Dajazmatch* is a very sympathetic and intelligent man. He is interested in everything, understands what can interest a European, and recounts very wisely and interestingly the history of his people and their former customs.

On February 20, together with 800 men armed with military guns, we began the hunt and set out to the north toward the valley of the Abbay—the Blue Nile. Each soldier, in addition to a gun, also carried little skins of grain or flour, enough for ten days. The kitchen went with us: two servants, carrying on their shoulders in rope nets large broken pumpkins in which hung dough that was being made sour for *injera*. It was a luxury which I would have liked to have foregone, but the *Dajazmatch* insisted on it.

My whole cargo was packed on one mule and consisted of a small tent, one change of linen and two large skins of corn for the servants—enough for ten days.

The leader of the hunt was Baljeron[40] Haile Maryam, also a Galla, but baptized and trying in every way to imitate the Abyssinians.

The hunt was unsuccessful. We wasted ten days, sending out scouts and looking for elephants where they had been before. We found old tracks, but there were no elephants.

We came across other game in great quantities, but it was forbidden to shoot them.

On the last day, I killed a hippopotamus in the Angar River. Since the provisions had run out, the Galla had not eaten for a day. They dragged the dead hippopotamus with lianas to the shore and quickly ate it up, roasting its white flesh on the campfire. On March 2 we returned to Lekamte.

Handek, the area where we hunted, embraces all the southern course of the Angar River and the rivers which flow into it from the left, and likewise the valley of the Didessa River. Beyond Angar begins Lima, the property of the Gojjam *Negus*, which extends to the Abbay River. Both the one region and the other are uninhabited in their low-lying parts because of dreadful fevers that reign there. Enticed by the fertility of the soil, Galla go down there at the good time of the year, sow seeds, and come back later to harvest. Large areas of land are planted with cotton. It's hard to imagine a place more beautiful than this. Bounded on the southeast, the east and the northeast by high mountains, cut by frequent streams and rivulets, the banks of which are overgrown with thick forest, it is all covered with low fruit trees with bright green glittering leaves. These trees bear varieties of fruit which all have a very thick layer of flesh and a stone in the middle. In taste, they are for the most part sour.

On the day after our return, the *Dajazmatch* assembled another party of hunters; and on March 4, we set out again, this time with a detachment of a thousand Galla men, armed only with spears, to places where no one had disturbed the elephants for three years. The leaders of this hunt were *Azzaj* Haile Iesus and *Agafari*[41] Wolda Giyorgis. Of the thousand men, four hundred were on horse and armed with three small spears each, and the other six hundred were on foot, half with small spears and the other half with four-arshin-long [three-yard-long] spears with huge points and yard-long blades. This long spear is called a *jambi*. They throw it from the top of a tall tree when an elephant passes under it. The force of the fall of the spear is so great that it sometimes pierces all the way through an elephant. Usually, one such spear is sufficient to bring an elephant down.

Only my servants and several soldiers of the *Dajazmatch* were armed with guns.

At first we divided into two detachments, one of the *Azzaj*, the other of the agafari, and set out toward the west to the Didessa valley. After fruitless searches in the forests surrounding the Didessa, on the third day we united again and went up north, toward the watershed between the Angar and the Didessa. For five days, our searches were fruitless, despite the fact that setting out at dawn we only began to set up camp at sunset. I was simply amazed at the endurance of the Galla and, in particular, the endurance of the scouts who were sent out ahead. If we did 40 versts [26 miles], then they, probably, did at least 60 [40 miles], through dense bushes overgrown with thorns, in part through high grass which was half-burnt with sharp hard stalk bases. When you look at that terrain, you are amazed at how they, barefoot, not only walk through it, but even run.

We usually made camp in the valley of some rivulet. When night fell and the campfires were lit, all the old Galla would gather in conference with the *Azzaj*, discussing what to undertake and where to go tomorrow. Gray, taciturn, with an invariable pipe between the lips, they seated themselves around the fire and sedately deliberated, sometimes conjectured. When the camp began to quiet down, each day a dialogue took place that on the one side was the orders for the following day and on the other side was a public prayer.

"*Abe, Abe,*" was heard from one end of the camp.

"E,e,e," they answered from the other end.

"Tomorrow we will set out early to this place."

"Good. Good."

"We have a guest with us."

"I know. I know."

"Until he shoots, no one else attack."

"Good. Good."

"May God help us find the elephant."

"Let it be so."

"Let Maryam help us."

"Let Giyorgis, Mikael, Gabriel help us."

"Listen, listen," cries one to the other. "May Satan not get mad at us."

"May he not send a *goro*[42] at us."

"Let him not strike us with sickness."

"May the Angar, the Didessa Rivers help us."

"Let the Jirgo, Tume Sibu, Tibye Mountains help us."

"All pray God that He help us." And amid the night stillness there begins a drawling, plaintive song. Someone asks for mercy upon him. Someone asks for an elephant to be sent to him. Someone asks that his spear be guided. Some enumerate their previous triumphs. And long, long into the night stillness, these plaintive sounds are heard.

Finally, on Sunday, March 9, we came upon a fresh night track. The scouts who had been sent ahead reported this to us; and the whole band, those who were on horseback at a trot and the rest at a run, rushed there. Up until noon, we couldn't catch the elephants. Finally, at 12:30, the scouts reported that the elephants were resting in the shade of trees by a nearby stream. The *Azzaj* gave the order to surround the elephants, and seventy mounted men (including me, since a week before I had bought myself a hunting horse) rushed at a gallop straight to the indicated spot. Having galloped three versts [two miles], we suddenly heard cries, "There they are!" Fifty paces in front of us, we saw a huge herd of elephants fleeing from us. A hundred head of elephant, big and small and all red from the clay of the stream bed, flapping their ears and trembling with their whole bodies, raising high their trunks, ran in panic. I shot several times from my horse. Some of my companions shot, too. But the elephants hid. Meanwhile, the bearers of *jambi* succeeded in climbing into the trees which stood in the middle of the stream. The other spear-bearers on foot likewise came in time. The elephants, having tried to flee to the other side of the stream, turned when they saw the mounted hunters. The grass was set afire, and the frightened elephants scattered, like a broken brood of partridges. There was no escape for them. In the forest, the *jambi* struck them; on the edge of the forest—the spear-bearers on foot and my servants with guns. Just as they broke out farther, we surrounded them, like a swarm of flies, and even behind them along the plain, where high grass grew and thick trees, we struck with whatever we could. Those who had guns shot. The others hurled spears which plunged into the elephants' bodies and which the elephants pulled out of their wounds with their trunks and angrily threw back at us. Anyone whom an elephant charged saved himself by fleeing while others distracted the animal off to the side. If an elephant pursued someone all the way to the hill, it was almost impossible to escape. I saw how one elephant, having rushed at a Galla who had galloped by at twenty paces from me, in the twinkling of an eye snatched him from the saddle with his trunk, let forth a cry and threw the man against the ground, intending to trample him. Fortunately, others succeeded in distracting the elephant, and it left his victim. In another case, an elephant threw a large broken branch at a Galla who had been with us and broke his arm. Five, ten, fifteen minutes of pursuit and an elephant fell. It was then considered the catch of the one who first wounded it, and the fortunate hunter rushed to cut the tail and the end of the trunk and the ears as material evidence of his triumph.

The field of the hunt presented an interesting picture. All around the grass blazed with a crackling sound. In the woods, there was endless shooting and cries of terror or triumph, and all this uproar was drowned out by the bellow and screech of the panic-stricken elephants, throwing themselves now at one person, now at another. The Galla believe that at such moments of despair the elephants are praying to God, throwing sand and grass to heaven. I personally saw elephants doing this.

Only at 7:30 in the evening did this hunt, that was really more like a battle, end. None of us had had any food in our mouths since morning, nor a drop of water. It was impossible to drink from the stream because it was all red with blood. But no one bothered to think of food or drink.

On this day forty-one elephants were killed. Five were my share. (I killed three and my servants two). We lost five men killed: three crushed by elephants and two killed by our shots. One man had a broken bone in his right arm. With triumphant songs, we returned to camp, not feeling tired. On the following day, one group set out to extract the tusks and another set out to pursue the wounded elephants. Meanwhile I examined the wounds inflicted by my elephant gun. It had a remarkable effect. I killed all my elephants with it, and with a single bullet in the head.

On Tuesday, all the elders gathered and sorted out the disputes about who first wounded an elephant. The Gallas do anything to show their right to an elephant. They resort to bribes and to guile. But the *Azzaj* knew the people he was dealing with. He waited until the provisions had been exhausted, so that hunger would separate the true from the false. He didn't miscalculate. I didn't wait for the end of the disputes. Since my elephants were without question, I hurried off with my trophies to Lekamte. On Thursday, March 13, at noon, the *Dajazmatch* ceremoniously met me; and on Friday the 14th, at three in the morning, I set out for Addis Ababa. The send-off was moving, since during the hunt the Galla had grown fond of me. As a gift, many of them on the day of the hunt had brought me their spears, covered with the not yet dry blood of elephants. They did this completely unselfishly. Gebra Egziabeer and I exchanged gifts. I gave him the elephant gun, and he gave me his own saber and a large buffalo goblet. I forgot to mention that on the trip back to Leka, the Galla drove out a buffalo. We pursued it on horseback. The buffalo adroitly evaded and beat off the javelins with its horns, but, nonetheless, loss of blood and the long gallop tired it. Its head sunk all the lower. It raised high its tail and breathed heavily. At that moment, a Galla ran up to it and finished it with his spear.

The city of Lekamte, which I was leaving, is a very important commercial center. All roads from southern and western Abyssinia to Gojjam and from Gojjam to Massawa pass through it. In addition, fords across the Didessa and the Abbay are nearby. Through it also passes the road from Wollaga to Shoa. Finally, apart from other considerations, here is concentrated all the trade in gold, and here is found the main trade in civet musk bought in the southwestern territories. Lekamte is a very lively place and presents a motley mixture of languages, dress, and peoples. You see here Arabs from Beni-Shangul, and Negroes, and people from Gojjam, and Tigreans, and Galla. There is even a Greek and an Englishman here. There are two very interesting characters. The Greek, *Balambaras*[43] Giyorgis, settled here 25 years ago. He fought in the ranks of *Negus* Tekla Haymanot and took part in rebellions against him, was several times imprisoned and again pardoned. At one time, he molded the guns of the *Negus*, now he lives in Lekamte as a merchant. He is the main buyer of gold and civet musk. He described his life in a book, illustrated with drawings. This book is written in the Geez language.[44]

The Englishman, Mekkelby, is a former lackey who deserted his master, the name of whom he no longer remembers—apparently, he was one of the members of the embassy to *Negus* Tewodros. He now serves *Balambaras* Giyorgis and has completely forgotten his native tongue.

Of the sights of Lekamte, one worthy of note is its newly built church. It is large, stone and decorated by local artists. Like the majority of Abyssinian churches, this is a round building with a quadrangular altar and four gates to the four sides of the world. On the royal and west gates are depicted Archangels Gabriel and Raphael, the former on the right side of the door, the latter on the left. Gabriel is dressed in a colorful shirt, red hat and red turned-up shoes, and in his hand is a raised sword; under him is depicted the sea in which Pharaoh and his Egyptians drown; and on the bank, Moses, with a long black beard, dances and claps his hands among a chorus of Levites. Archangel Raphael is dressed the same as Gabriel, and is shown standing over the sea with fish swimming in it. He has pierced one of the fish through the gills with a spear. According to legend, the fish turned into an island, on which saints hid in time of persecution. To the right of the royal gates, under a large icon of the Mother of God, Menelik and Taitu are depicted, pointing to *Dajazmatch* Gebra Egziabeer and his wife with two children. The *Dajazmatch* devoutly looks upward and holds in his hands the Psalter. To the left of the royal gates, under icons of Archangel Michael and George the Victorious, the *Dajazmatch* is also depicted, with his associates—*Azzaj* and *Nagada-ras*—his uncle and his brother.

I once attended mass in this church and saw a large number of newly christened Galla receiving communion. Christianity here makes enormous progress, and each Sunday the newly converted number in the dozens. In spite of the fact that the *Dajazmatch* does not collect taxes for himself personally, the palace of the *Dajazmatch* is notable for its splendor and comparative comfort. One sees the desire to imitate Abyssinian etiquette in everything.

Leaving Lekamte on March 14, at three in the afternoon, we spent the night at a distance of 20 versts [14 miles], at he house of the uncle of the *Dajazmatch*. Early in the morning of the day of my departure, I sent a letter to the Emperor with news of the successful hunt.

Because of the addition to our baggage of ten tusks and two buffalo horns, I had to add another horse to our previous two mules.

The animals had rested during the time of the hunt, staying in the town; but after uninterrupted, tiresome marches in very poor conditions the servants were, apparently, exhausted. Out of the 29 days, counting from the day we left Addis Ababa, they had had only one day of rest and one day of partial rest, when they took the tusks. In the first six days, we went 360 versts [240 miles]; for the rest we journeyed for no less than seven hours a day. Many had broken toenails and cracks in the soles of their feet and limped. But their spirit was cheerful, and on the sixth day, on Wednesday, March 19, we made camp in the evening at a distance of three versts [two miles] from Addis Ababa (one stage of the journey, from Bilo to Jibat, we made without stopping, starting at 5:30 in the morning and finishing at 8 o'clock at night. One mule stopped, and I replaced it with a horse).

On March 20, the Emperor, learning of my arrival, sent a large convoy to meet me. With firing of guns, singing and dancing, as is customary in such cases, they led me to the palace, where Menelik ceremoniously received me. After the reception, he invited me to lunch, and likewise fed all my servants. On the following day, he gave me a private audience and, knowing that I intended to leave on Saturday, asked me to postpone my departure to Tuesday, March 25.

My mules were exhausted, and my servants also. Therefore, for the journey to the coast I had to refill the ranks. (On leaving, I sold the mules remaining from the first trip, since they were almost all done for). I found servants very quickly and hired 12 men, the same as the number of guns. The Emperor gave me six mules for as far as Harar.

The Emperor ceremoniously received me in a farewell audience, and expressed the desire to see me again in Abyssinia. Saying good-bye to my friends and the European colony, I left on Tuesday, March 25, at one o'clock in the afternoon. The Emperor bestowed on me a lion's battle dress and lion's head band.

On April 4, at 7 o'clock in the morning, we arrived in Harar, having gone a distance of about 600 versts [400 miles] in ten and a half days along the mountainous Chercher road, despite the fact that during this time I went 40 versts out of the way to meet the caravan of Ato Iosif, for my goods. On April 8, at 10 o'clock, I set out with eight servants and the same mules to Geldessa, where I arrived that same day. On the following day, at 12 o'clock, having put together a caravan of five camels and having sent the mules back, I moved on to Jibuti, where I arrived on April 16 at 8 o'clock in the morning, having left the caravan 50 versts [33 miles] behind. (It arrived on the following day at 12 o'clock). On April 21, the French steamship "Amazon" arrived, and I left the shores of Africa, which had been so hospitable to me. I took with me the best and warmest memories of this country where I had been and of the people whom fate had destined that I come to know.

GEOGRAPHIC SURVEY

The western regions of southern Ethiopia belong to the following basins: 1) Awash, 2) *Guder* (tributary of the Blue Nile), 3) Gibye (tributary of the Sobat), 4) Didessa (tributary of the Blue Nile), and 5) Baro (tributary of the Sobat).

1) The Awash rises in the mountains of Mecha, among the peaks of Dolota and Elfek. At first it flows to the south and then going out of the mountains into the plain, it receives several insignificant streams from the left and from the right. Reaching the mountains of Sodo and having taken into itself from the left the Akaki River, which descends from the mountains of Entotto, the Awash turns east, and then going 200 versts [132 miles] in this direction, to the north, where from the left it takes the Kassam River, which descends from the mountains of Shoa. Not reaching the sea, the Awash disappears in the sands.

At the spot where I crossed the Awash, its river-bed differed from other rivulets, which discharge into it and flow in the same plain, by its seemingly polished stone bottom. The banks of Awash are very beautiful. To the right and the left in a strip a hundred sagenes [213 meters] in width, they are overgrown with beds of young trees, like islands, isolated amid the high grass. In each such clump, the trees grow close to one another and belong to various species, of which many only grow in much lower zones and are not normally found in places near the Awash. It must be that their seeds were brought here by the wind. I think that such an eccentric grouping of trees must be attributed to the yearly flooding of the Awash and the speed of its current.

2) The *Guder* arises on the Tikur plateau from a small swampy lake. It flows at first to the north, and from the mountains of Mecha turns northwest and empties into the Abbay. Its current is very swift and rough, with frequent waterfalls. Its banks are rocky. Of its more significant tributaries one can mention the Uluk River, which descends from the mountains of Chobo. It empties into the *Guder* from the right. The Haratit River flows from the mountains of Toke and empties into the *Guder* from the

left. Both of those flow in rocky banks. On the Uluk River, in the vicinity of Ambo, there are hot springs.

3) The Gibye arises in the mountains of *Guder* and flows in deep canyons among the mountains of Tibye and Sibu to the south, where, passing these mountains, it enters a wide plain. Here it takes on from the left the Alanga River, which gathers into itself all the waters of the southern slopes of Chalea and the western slope of Toke, and continues to go to the south along a wide valley. Having taken into itself from the right another river also named "Gibye," which flows from the mountains of Limu, and joining with the Omo River, which falls down from the mountains of Kaffa, it is a river with many names, which turns to the west, skirts Kaffa from the south, then turns north and empties into the low-lying marshy plain of Bako, where it joins with the Baro and rivers of the western slopes of the Kaffa heights and flows out to the west under the name of the Sobat[45] River.

I believe that after the loss of the expedition of Captain Bottego[46] there can no longer be any doubting the fact that the the upper reaches of the Gibye River are the same as the upper reaches of the Sobat River, and not some other river, which empties into Lake Rudolf, as had been supposed before. D'Abbadie had even earlier proposed that the Gibye is the upper reaches of the Nile.[47]

The goal of the expedition of Captain Bottego was to discover the course of this river. The expedition was annihilated at the end of February 1897 approximately 800 versts [528 miles] to the west of Entotto and 200 versts [132 miles] to the north of the city of Gori in the property of *Dajazmatch* Joti in the province of Wollaga. The fact that it was destroyed at this place serves as evidence of what was said above, since, following the course of the river, the expedition left Kaffa behind and arrived at this place, which is the low-lying plain in which the tributaries of the Sobat join together. From time to time, news of this expedition was received from Abyssinian sources, which made it possible to draw conclusion about its whereabouts. So, in the summer of 1896, the expedition was at the upper reaches of the Webi, since several of its soldiers fled from there. In the fall, rumor had it that there were Europeans with guns to the south of Mocha.

The campaigns of Abyssinians to the south likewise confirm that the Gibye is the upper reaches of the Sobat. In his last campaign from Ilu-Babur to Mocha and Gimiro, *Dajazmatch* Tesemma went with his armies to a large river which was impassable. They named it Nichsar, which means "white gra*s*s," and are convinced that it is the Nile.

The Gibye at the place where I crossed it, flows in low-lying banks. Its width is about 75 paces. The current is not very fast. The banks are overgrown with a narrow band of forest, behind which stretches steppe, covered with grass five arshins [four yards] high.

4) The Didessa River flows from the mountains of Gomo to the north and empties into the Abbay. From the right, it takes into itself the Rivers Enareya and Aet which flow from the mountains of Lima, and then the large Wam River, which arises in the north in the mountains of Sibu, 100 versts [66 miles] to the north from Abbay. The Wam flows at first to the south, and skirting the mountains of Leka, turns to the north and empties into the Didessa. Not far from where it empties into the Abbay, the Didessa takes on from the right the large Angar River, which flows from the mountains of *Guder*. From the left side, the Dobana River, which rises in the mountains of Guma, empties into the Didessa.

The Didessa and its tributaries in its upper reaches is very rough and swift, and flows in rocky banks, but passing into the plain it flows quietly and is only occasionally interrupted by rapids. The banks are low and overgrown with a thick band of forest. In the place where I crossed it, the speed of the current was one to one and a half sagenes [2 to 3 meters] per second. Its width was about 100 sagenes [213 meters]. At the time of our crossing in November, it was so deep that I couldn't reach the bottom with a long spear. In January, we were able to wade across. After its junction with the Angar there are no longer any rapids and, according to reliable individuals who know the area, both it and the Abbay can be navigable.

5) The Baro River descends from the mountains of Kaffa and flows at first to the south. Going down into the low-lying valley of Bako, it joins with the Gibye or the Omo.[48] The Baro takes into itself from the right side the Gaba River, and from the left the Gunji River. The Baro and all these rivers flow in deep canyons, overgrown with coffee forests. Their current is very swift, with frequent waterfalls. The bottom is stone. The width of the Baro at the place where I crossed it is 120 paces. The depth in the middle is more than two sagenes [4 meters]. On the stone banks there are characteristic craters. The Gaba River flows down from the mountains of Goma and flows between rocky cliffs, with only two crossing points, where there are bridges. The Gaba takes from the left the Sor River, which flows down from the mountains of Soyo, and from the right the Birbir River. The Birbir is a significant river. After joining with the Didessa, the Abbay does not have any significant tributaries until the Dabus, since along its left bank stretches a mountain ridge, which consists of a continuation of the mountain ridge of Darima.

Therefore, all the water of the southern slopes of this mountain ridge, despite its closeness to the Abbay, cannot join with it, and, going into the Birbir River, empties into the Gaba.

Thus we see that with the exception of the Awash, which flows in the direction of the Red Sea and is lost in the sand, all the other waters belong to the two main tributaries of the Nile, to the basins of the Sobat and the Abbay.

The water of these rivers is exceptionally clear and clean. In time of rain, it becomes red from mixing with clay from the mountains. This clay is composed of the same fertile components as the silt of the Nile.

The mountains of the south-west regions of Ethiopia are the heart of a mountain range, extending from three mountain masses.

1) The Mountains of Metalla and Mecha are a continuation of the plateau of Shoa. Mecha is a plateau with separate summits of Tulu, Elfek and Dolota. To the south they end in rocky cliffs.

2) The Gurage plateau, turning into the Tikur plateau, is continued by the mountain ridges of Toke, Chalea, Tibye, Guder and Lima to the northwest, where it breaks off in the valley of the Abbay.

The appearance of this mountain range is extraordinary along all its extent. Chobo and Dandi look like a plateau strewn with round hills. The Tikur plateau looks like a plain with the summits of Bolo and Roge towering in the middle. Toke is a group of cone-shaped mountains covered with forest. Following it, the mountains of Chalea have a peculiar form of oblong heights with the appearance of an ellipse with two cones on both ends, of which the southern is larger than the northern. The tributaries of the Guder flow in the rocky cliffs of the mountains of Chalea.

The Chalea-Wobo rises and intersects the mountains of Tibye, which look like a row of raised mountain ridges with separate cone-shaped sharp rocky summits. Such are the summits of Tibye, Tulu, Amara, Shumbera, Araresa-Ganou and Tulu-Gomdo.

North of Tibye, the mountains get lower and, rising again on that side of the Gibye River, form the high Sibu mountain group with the summit of Tuka (3,120 meters). Tuka Mountain has the appearance of a pyramid with very wide base compared with its height, such that from a distance it does not give the impression that it is as high as it is. A series of peaks, joining with the mountains of Nonno stretches out from it very characteristically to the southeast. They look like stone posts or rock caps.

To the north, the mountains of Sibu intersect with the mountains of Guder, which intersect the mountains of Lima. One of the spurs of Sibu descends, getting lower to the south. Going to the banks of the Didessa, it again rises and forms the mountain ridge of Leka.

The average height of these mountains is 2,500 meters, and individual peaks attain 3,000 meters. The summit of Tuka, the highest, is 3,120 meters.

3) To the west of the just described mountain ridge, the mountains are in essence mountain ridges, extending from the Kaffa heights. One of these goes to the east and consists of the mountains of Lima or Enareya. The latter get lower to the north and intersect with the mountains of Nonno with the mountain peak Koncho. Nonno is a group of mountains in the shape of cones, surrounded by cap-shaped rocky hills.

Another mountain ridge goes to the north along the left bank of the Didessa and is divided into two spurs. One of these spurs, which at first is called Buna and then Dolati, goes along the left bank of the Didessa, separating it from the Dobana River. The other, named Darima, at first follows along the left bank of the Dobana River and separates the basin of the Dobana from the basin of the Gaba River. Then it separates into two spurs: one goes to the west, separating the basins of the Gaba and the Birbir, and the other continues to go along the left bank of the Didessa, then turns to the west and follows along the left bank of the Abbay until it empties into the Dabus.

The following summits are found on these spurs: in the land of Guma at the point where the main mountain range separates into two spurs is the summit of Tulu Jiren, which from a distance looks like an extinct volcano; in Buna is the summit Anna, covered with forest, which gives the impression of a large hill; on the mountain ridge of Dolota are the mountains of Tulu Amara and Tuto, which also look like large hills, but not covered with forest; on the Darima mountain ridge is the extinct volcano Mako, and farther is a mountain group with the extinct volcano Tulu Jirgo. The height of all these summits is no greater than 3,000 meters, and the general average height of the mountain ridge is 2,200 meters.

The third mountain ridge goes from the Kaffa heights to the west, forming the mountain group of Sayo, with a summit of the same name which is shaped like a hill and covered with forest, then, in turn, separates into several mountain ridges which, spreading out like radii, separate the tributaries of the Baro River and the Gaba River. The western spur is the highest and ends in the Dida mountain group. On one of the middle spurs there are several rocky summits, and its northern extremity is crowned with Guratcha Mountain. The average height of these mountain ridges is about 2,000 meters above sea level. The summit of Sayo is about 2,500 meters high, as is Dida.

All the mountain ridges and the separate heights of these mountains are covered with thick forest.

The fourth mountain ridge goes from the Kaffa heights along the left bank of the Baro, forms the mountain ridges of Alga and Sale and comes to an abrupt end in the Bako plain. It also is covered with forest.

By its outward appearance and geological structure, part of the mountains of the west Ethiopian heights are undoubtedly of volcanic origin. All the mountains to the east of the Gaba River are of volcanic origin. To the west of the Gaba and to the north of the Birbir, they do not have that nature. The difference is apparent in the shape of these mountains. The soil is also different. Red and black volcanic clay on the east changes to black earth in areas of rich vegetation and sands in the lowlands. The difference is noticeable also in the fact that the eastern mountains abound in iron, and gold is extracted from the northwest mountains. Hot sulfuric springs are found very often in the eastern mountains.

This region should be extremely interesting from the geological point of view, but to my deepest regret, I am not well enough acquainted with that field of human knowledge to make useful observations and draw correct conclusions.

Depending on the elevation of the area above sea level, Abyssinians distinguish three climatic zones: *dega*, *wayna-dega*, and *kola*. Those areas which are higher than 2,500 meters above sea level are called *dega*. Areas from 1,800 to 2,500 meters are called *wayna-dega*. And those lower than 1,800 meters are called *kola*. In translation *dega* means "elevation" or "cold". *Wayna-dega* means "grape elevation," or "place where you can grow grapes." *Kola* means "hot place." Almost all the territory of this part of the western Ethiopian heights belongs to the *wayna-dega* zone. The only exceptions are individual summits, which cross into the *dega* zone, and low-lying valleys of rivers and likewise the whole Handek area which are kola.

But aside from this division by elevation above sea level, southwestern Ethiopia is also categorized into three separate climatic zones by its humidity, and the time of year and quantity of rainfall:

1) The area to the west of the Didessa and the Sibu mountain ridge and Leka, and likewise the elevated area on the right side of the Gaba River—Wollaga and *Abe*ko;
2) the low-lying area along the course of the Didessa and Abbay; and
3) the area south of the Gaba River.

In the first area there is one rainy season, which begins in June and continues to September. This period is called keremt. The period of time that follows that—*baga*—has no rain, and in November the level of the rivers goes down. The hottest season is January and February. Then the sky is cloudless and there is no wind. In March rain falls rarely and there are southern winds. In May strong eastern winds blow and keremt comes, at the end of which strong western winds blow.

In the second area, the winds are the same as above, but the rainy season begins later and ends earlier, and rain falls less frequently. There is one rainy season in July and August. The air is also much drier than in the first area.

In the third area, there are two rainy seasons. The first and strongest lasts from July to September. The second begins at the end of January and lasts to the end of March. The air is extremely humid. During the first rainy season eastern winds blow, during the second southern winds, and in between there is calm.

Such a difference of climate between the first two areas and the third can, I believe, be explained by the location of the mountains. The mountains of Kaffa and Gurage prevent free access of southern winds in the first two areas, while they cannot prevent access to the third area, because this area is on the western slopes of the Kaffa heights, which in this case rather prevents free access of eastern winds. The climate here must be similar to the climate of the great lakes. The most healthy of these climates is that in the first area. Dry air is healthy. The climate of the second area is also very favorable, but the air is too humid, and diseases there are more frequent. The most unhealthy climate is the third area. For six months of the year, from April to November, strange fevers reign there. Furthermore, every little wound opened in that area almost always turns into a malignant sore. This territory is entirely uninhabited. Galla from lands that border this region go down there in the better time of the year, do their sowing, and go away, returning again at harvest time.

The temperature of the first and third areas is very moderate. It does not go higher than 40° Reaumur [122° F] in the sun during the day, and at night does not fall to lower than 12° Reaumur [59° F]. On the summits of mountains the temperature at night drops to 8° Reaumur [50° F]. In low-lying areas the temperature during the day goes up to 45° Reaumur [133° F] in the sun, and at night does not go lower than 15° Reaumur [66° F].

The transparency of the air changes depending on the time of year. It is clearest for some time after the end of the rainy season, when the air is not yet filled with mist. In January they begin to burn the dry grass and the air is filled with particles of smoke and dust and becomes very opaque. Because of the dryness, the air is clearer in the eastern regions than in the west.

Thunderstorms happen most often in March and April and at the onset of the rainy season. There are no thunderstorms during the rainy season. Sometimes these storms are very violent and local inhabitants fear them. You repeatedly hear about fatal lightning accidents.

The length of the day is the same as in the rest of the tropics in general: between the longest and the shortest day there is a several minute difference which depends on latitude. Night falls extremely swiftly. About half an hour after sunset, it is already completely dark.

Vegetation differs in the *dega, wayna-dega,* and kola zones. The western and eastern regions also differ from one another.

The characteristic tree for the *dega* area is the *kusso*[49]—a very beautiful leafy tree, which attains great size. Its fruit has the appearance of large red clusters. The Abyssinians use them to purge themselves of parasitic worms. They take *kusso* regularly every two months. The characteristic grain of the *dega* is barley, which is not sown in lower areas.

The majority of trees are common to both the *dega* and *wayna-dega*. The forests mainly abound in ted and tis—two kinds of juniper. These trees attain great height and size. Old trees are covered with white moss, picturesquely mixed with the branches, which the Abyssinians call zaf shebat—"the gray hair of the tree." A dense network of thin lianas covers the trees. Large fig-trees and sycamores—vanza[50] and worka[51] are found near settlements. You could arrange an entire battalion in their shade. There is also a very beautiful leafy tree—the *birbirsa*. In forests the gesho[52] bush grows in abundance. Its leaves are useful for cooking honey: they take the place of hops. The *kolkual* are remarkably enormous cactus trees, which Galla plant around their farmsteads. From the trunks of the cactus they also hollow out beehives, because the wood is very soft and light. On the plains of Wollaga, Leka and Shoa *gerara* trees grow separately. These acacias are characteristic of the landscape of these plains. In Abyssinia there are several varieties of *gerara*; the variety changes depending on the altitude of the place and the quantity of moisture. In addition, the jibara[53] is a characteristic plant, with its sharp thorny leaves, with a lilac-colored flower on top of its long stem. Of the cultivated trees, we mention the kogo or banana ensete—musa ensete. The root of this tree is used as food. Around their homes, Galla also plant trees which bear nuts from which they press out oil.

The grain plants which belong in the *wayna-dega* zone are very diverse: wheat, *mashella* (sorghum), tef[54], dagussa[55] from which beer is made, and bakhr *mashella* (corn); but bakhr *mashella* is mainly grown in the kola zone. They grow a lot of red pepper, ater (peas), *shumbera* (another variety of peas, which does not twist and the seeds of which are not round, but rather faceted), and bakela (beans), a plant which gives pods with very small seeds. The bakela is very poisonous and strikes the nervous system; but, nevertheless, Abyssinians cultivate it. After cooking, when the water is poured out, it loses its poisonous properties. In their gardens, they plant a cabbage, which does not have heads and attains enormous height. They sow onions (shunkurt), garlic (nachshunkurt), and lentils (mysyr). In several areas, they sow *talby*, a kind of flax. Its stalk isn't used, but they eat the seeds which, they say, restore one's strength. They cultivate the following rootcrops: potatoes, which are less oblong and harder than ours; and *guder*, a twisting plant with fruit like small red spotted pumpkins. The *guder* has a root that is very tasty and resembles the taste of potatoes.[56] The Gallas also sow pumpkins. One species of pumpkins, almost hollow inside, serves in the manufacture of containers for water. From these they also make canteens for travel. The huge burdock[57] is characteristic of the uncultivated plants. Its stem is similar to the trunk of a tree, and its flowers are the size of a man's head.

The steppe is covered with grass that reaches a height of one to one and a half arshins [about 28 to 42 inches]. No sooner does it dry than it burns.

The vegetation of the western regions, thanks to the moisture of the climate, is much richer. Huge forests have grown up, dense with trees of every possible species, and a non-botanist has difficulty distinguishing among them. Enormous trees with triquitrous [triangular] stems are characteristic of these forests. For instance, coffee trees grow in abundance along the banks of rivers. These coffee trees attain a height of two sagenes [4.26 meters] and in November are entirely strewn with seeds, which are harvested at the end of December, when they are already falling from the trees. Since the seeds turn black by lying on the damp ground, this coffee loses part of its value. Among these trees there are many which possess medicinal properties, for instance the enkoko tree. Its fruit, which looks like a cluster, is used as a laxative and to purge parasitic worms. There are poisonous trees, such as the acacia, which bears fruit which looks like beans. These beans poison fish, which, having eaten them, die instantly. A very wide-spread soapy tree is the *entod*. Its fruit is dried, turned into flour and serves as an excellent soap. Bamboo and palm trees are found in the forests. All the trees are thickly interwoven with liana of several varieties, one of which has terribly sharp thorns. Its leaves and fruits do not at all differ from our Raspberries. In general, the forests abound in thorny trees. There is even one tree which has thorns on its trunk.

The cultivated plants in the west are the same as those found in the east, with the exception of a few which are not found in the east or which are very rare there. For instance, in the west, they sow sugar-cane, which closely resembles *mashella* among plantings of *mashella*. They eat it raw: they clean the skin from the stalk, then chew the stalk, and having sucked out the sap, spit it out what remains.

The forest abounds in flowers. Twisting plants with round fruit two and a half inches in diameter are among those which are characteristic of these forests. The fruit is covered with a rind which is green with spots and has a white core with black seeds—in a word, it is similar to a watermelon. The forests of the western regions are strewn with them: Abyssinians call them yasaytan duba, that is "the devil's own pumpkin."

The vegetation of the kola, and for the most part of Handek, differs from the vegetation of the areas just described. All along the steppe are scattered separate trees, which are small with bright-green shiny leaves without thorns. By their appearance they resemble peach and apple trees. The Galla distinguish 12 varieties of this tree, depending on the fruit which they bear. Unfortunately, at the time when I was there, there was no fruit, because it only ripens in August and September. I tasted only one species—red berries with a very thin layer of flesh and a huge seed, with a sour taste. The banks of streams are overgrown with huge forests.

At the good time of the year, when there is no fever, Galla descend to the kola regions and sow corn and cotton. Many of the herbs are medicinal and spicy. There is ginger, a spicy plant called *korkoruma*, and a kind of red pepper mit-mita, which is terribly hot. Grass in the kola attains enormous height, hiding both horse and rider. In river valleys, the stalks of grass are five arshins [four yards] high.

In these areas, it would be possible to successfully grow chinona, cinnamon, cork, and tea trees, and likewise many other trees which yield valuable products.

The insect kingdom is very rich. Huge red and black ants are characteristic of the western regions. They are the scourge of the population, destroying edible supplies and flooding the house every evening. Another species of ant, the white, mist, destroys buildings. Every three years the inhabitants have to build their houses over again. Furthermore, bees abound in this area. They give three kinds of honey.

Especially black honey, from which very strong *tej* is made, is found in the western forest regions. Especially white and particularly fragrant honey is found in the lower regions in Handek. And a honey which is the average between these two appearances is found in the other regions. There is a kind of wasp, named *tasm*, which gives honey. It is found in the ground. This honey is very tasty, somewhat sour, particularly nutritious and restores one's strength. The inhabitants recommend it for its medicinal properties.

In the west, in January I came upon a swarm of locusts, accompanied by flocks of white birds, which were feeding on them. Thanks to the fact that the farmsteads were widely dispersed, the inhabitants succeeded in not allowing them to get to the crops, chasing them into the forest.

In the west, the flies are larger but, in general there are not very many of them. Of reptiles, there are lizards, turtles, and snakes, including many poisonous ones. There are huge snakes the teeth of which are considered a talisman and remedy for diseases. These teeth are very difficult to obtain and therefore are very costly—up to 15 talers per tooth. Crocodiles are found in the rivers.

The fauna, which depends on the elevation of the area, is divided into two groups. In the first group belong animals which inhabit the heights of the *dega* and *wayna-dega*. In the second belong animals of the kola. The most wide-spread animals in the *wayna-dega* are antelopes and chamois-bulls of several varieties. The chamois-bulls (*orobo*) live in the lowest plains, but are seen also in the kola. They have sleek, brown hair. In their size and in the shape of their face, they are like an ox. They have huge horns (one to one and a half arshins [28 to 42 inches] long), which stand straight up. The surface of the horn is not smooth, but spiral shaped. They are very easy to shoot because they are not watchful and not easily frightened. An *orobo*, having heard a shot, will at first look for where the shooting came from and who his enemy is. If he doesn't see a human and isn't wounded, he does not run away. This means that you can shoot and stay put several times in the ox's vicinity. Another type of chamois-bull is the dukula. It is the size of a calf and has a face like an ox, but its horns are lighter and straight, from 4 to 6 vershoks [7 to 10-1/2 inches] in length. Its hair is sleek and brown. They are very watchful and it is difficult to hunt them. They are found in the *wayna-dega* zone and rarely descent to the kola. Antelopes belong in two categories: bokhor and *myeda-feyel*. The bokhor is the size of a goat, with sleek brown hair, and horns bent a bit backwards. The *myeda-feyel* is smaller, with gray hair and straight horns. The word *myeda-feyel* in translation means "billy-goat of the plain." They live in plains and in mountains of the *wayna-dega*, rarely going down from there. These animals are very sensitive and watchful and it is difficult to hunt them. You have to shoot from a very great distance.

The forest of the *wayna-dega* abounds in four species: zinjero —large baboons—live in the higher places, on rocky mountains. They attain the size of a large dog. They have an oblong, dog-like face, a long tail that stands up when they travel by land, and bristling, long, rigid, dark brown hair. They are very watchful and it is quite difficult to shoot them.

The *gureza* is ape-like. They live in less elevated places. There are lots of them in the forests of the western regions. Their hair is very beautiful—black, long and silky. On the middle of the spine, on the stomach and on the tail they have long white hairs. Their face is very ugly and flattened out. They bear some resemblance to human beings. Their teeth are almost black. The Gallas and Abyssinians hold them in high esteem. They don't disturb them and can't bring themselves to touch a dead *gureza* because of fear of bad luck. They consider that these animals have human characteristics. Abyssinians confirm that *gureza*s fast on Wednesdays and Fridays and that they never disturb the crops, exclusively feeding on the leaves of trees. *Gureza*s rarely come down on the ground, almost always staying in the trees.

Small monkeys known as tota live in the forests of *wayna-dega*. They have light-gray hair and on the face white whiskers. They always settle near farmsteads and are the scourge of farmers, since they destroy crops. They seem to have great love for one another. Relatives almost always carry away a wounded or killed tota, as the Abyssinians assert. I never saw this happen, but, having wounded a little tota, I at the same place killed a large female and male, who openly came out to save it, in spite of the fact of our presence. They are said to be revengeful and malicious. Abyssinians affirm that captured and domesticated totas will set fire to houses in revenge for some offense.

A very rare species, which I succeeded in seeing, the so-called small monkey chana only appears in Ilu-Babur. It is about the same size as the tota, but its hair is very beautiful: an ashen color with some gray.

All species of predatory animals known in Central Africa live in the *wayna-dega*: lion, panther, leopard, the spotted hyena, the jackal, and the wild cat. There is a special species of predatory animal which no European has yet seen, but which Abyssinians and Gallas affirm exists. They say these animals, which they call vobo or asambo, are the most terrible. The animal known as tryn, which gives a musk called zebad, also belongs to the species of predatory animals. This animal is similar to a cat: its hair is multi-colored, its tail is comparatively short, and it is the size of a small dog. They catch them in traps, then lock them in cages and keep them at the hearth in their homes, feeding them meat. They are found in the lower moist regions of the *wayna-dega*. Of the remaining animals in the *wayna-dega* there are wild boars and hares. Predatory animals abound on the plateaux of Tikur and in the mountains of Chalea and Chobo. In the west, in general, there are fewer, with the exception of panthers, which are only found in the west.[58]

The kola, which is uninhabited by humans, abounds in animals even more than the *wayna-dega* region. Predatory animals, such as the lion, go down there for hunting. The characteristic inhabitant of the kola is the elephant. Unfortunately, from year to year, they decline in numbers because of systematic destruction. The Abyssinian elephant is smaller than the Indian and more malicious than it. It possesses large tusks, which sometimes attain six poods [216 lbs.] each. Elephants usually travel as whole herds, but those which have the largest tusks go separately and are very cunning, quick-witted and malicious. A hunt for such solitary elephants always costs many casualties. Handek above all abounds in elephants, since this area gives elephants every comfort: forest, plenty of shade, many fruit trees whose leaves they eat, an abundance of beautiful water, and an entire uninhabited country measuring several hundred square versts [verst = 2/3 mile]. Aside from elephants, in the kola are found rhinoceroses, hippopotamuses, buffalo, and a species of antelope called sala with straight and very long horns. This antelope is about the size of a calf, with light brown hair.

There are many birds both in the kola and in the *dega* regions. You come across the most diverse species, from the smallest to the largest. There are very beautiful little birds with yellow and black feathers. There is a little bird with a very long tail which sometimes does not fly straight, but rather describes a parabola in the air. In the forests of *wayna-dega* there are many song birds. Of large birds, in the *wayna-dega* you come across the workum—a non-predatory bird which attains the size of a large turkey. It has a long, very strong beak, with a horny crest at the base and red crop under the beak. There are several different varieties of dove. There are particularly many of them in the kola. Their trilling is characteristic of these steppes. Many partridges and guinea fowls are found here, and on the plateaux you come across bustards. The lakes and rivers abound in various species of duck and geese. In the swamps, there are many snipe and woodcock, and you chance upon ibises and herons. There are especially many predatory birds. There are enormous eagles. There are species of crows—black and of the same size as ours, but with long beaks bent downward. There are white predatory birds which destroy locusts. In the kola there is also a particularly small bird which is a friend of the hippopotamus and never leaves it.

In the large rivers there are many fish.

All the land from Addis Ababa westward up to the Baro River and from Abbay on the south up to the Kaffa mountains is settled by Galla (Oromo). Beyond the Baro River to the west live Negroes. The Kaffa highlands are populated by Sidamo, and the region to the north of the Abbay is settled by Abyssinians (Amhara).[59]

Although the whole area under consideration, as we saw above, is very favorable for settlement, with the exception of the lower kola, the distribution of population in these regions is unequal and depends on political principles (the better the leader of a province, the larger the population) and on whether more or fewer people were destroyed during the recent conquest of the territory.

I tried to determine the size of the population, based on the number of aba-koro (chiefs of tribes) and the number of aba-langas (assistants) found under their leadership. I also used for this determination official data regarding fortifications. These observations made it possible for me to determine the number of Galla in the territory 200 versts [132 miles] wide and 400 versts [264 miles] long, stretching from Addis Ababa to the west—over an area of 80,000 square versts [35,556 square miles]—to be 1,200,000 to 1,500,000 people. The distribution of population in this zone is as follows: the densest population center is between the rivers Didessa and Gibye —approximately 8,000 [3,556 square miles] with 160,000 inhabitants; the least populated are the extreme south-western provinces, west of the Didessa and south of the Gaba, which have no more than 10 people per square verst—in total 115,000 inhabitants in an area of 11,500 square versts [5,111 square miles]. The density of population of the remaining areas is approximately 15 people per square verst, which for 60,000 square versts amounts to 900,000 to 1,000,000 inhabitants.

This calculation is, of course, very rough, but it is justified by many facts, which I observed: 1) the density of Galla settlements, 2) the quantity of cultivated land, 3) the number of chiefs (aba-koro) in each region and the number of their assistants (aba-langa), 4) information regarding fortifications, staffed with soldiers and leaders, and which have their very own separate leaders, 5) the number of troops stationed in the given area (in all, there are from 30,000 to 40,000 men stationed in this zone, which is also in keeping with the proposed number for the population).

The just enumerated population of this zone belongs to two Galla tribes: east of the Awash River is the Tuluma tribe, and west of it is the Mocha tribe. The Mocha is divided into five main clans. The Liban clan inhabits the regions south of the Awash— Sodo, Chobo, Dandi, and also Mecha. The Afrenjo clan inhabits the valley between Mecha and Chobo and likewise the mountains of Toke and Nonno. The Javi—the most numerous clan —lives in Lima, Jimma, Chalea, Tibye, Siba, Wollaga, and Ilu-Babur. The Homo clan inhabits Leka, and the Tuma the left bank of the Didessa.

But besides this division of the whole tribe into five main clans, each of these main clans is also divided into a number of small clans, which occupy some region, separated from others by natural boundaries and forming an independent state. The Galla gave their land names which came from either the name of a clan leader or from some important geographical name of their country, such as a high mountain or a river in their territory. This name is sometimes characteristic of the place. For instance Guratcha is "black," which means wooded. These names serve as almost the only names to guide a traveler, since there are no villages, and towns are extremely rare. In each region there is a marketplace, but it does not have a special name and is not found near settlements, but simply among the more heavily populated areas at the intersection of roads.

The main regions are the following: Meta, Bocho and Ejirsalafu, all three of which are the personal property of the Emperor. They are governed by *Azzaj* Gyzau. There are no towns nor significant marketplaces there. The countryside is level, steppe-like, and without trees.

Mecha is a plateau, populated by the Liban clan. It is ruled by *Dajazmatch* Ubye. Chobo, Dandi, and Tikur are plateaux populated by the Liban clan. They are governed by *Dajazmatch* Haile Maryam. His residence is in the town of Chobo. Toke, Dano, Bake and Nonno are inhabited by the Afrenjo tribe. This area is mountainous with forests. *Dajazmatch* Ubye rules it. These regions supply the capital with bamboo for building and with gesho leaves for the production of honey.

Chalea, Chalea-Wobo, Gobu, Tibye, and Sibu are populated by the Javi tribe. The area is mountainous, and covered with forest in places. They are governed by Likamakos Abata. The town of Bareilu—a large, permanent military camp—has about 2,000 residents. It also has some commercial significance, lying on a major caravan route from Wollaga to Shoa.

The mountains of Budera-Lima are inhabited by the Javi tribe, and are ruled by the Gojjam *Negus* Tekla Haymanot.

On the little river Bilo, a tributary of the Gibye River, the Bilo commercial center with 3,000 inhabitants is found. It is settled exclusively by merchants and is ruled by *Nagada-ras* Ingeda Gobaz.

Bilo is located at the intersection of several major roads: from Shoa to Wollaga, from Shoa to Ilu-Babur, from Jimma to Gojjam and from Ilu-Babur to Gojjam.

At the center of the town is a large square and marketplace. On Mondays and Fridays large markets are held. There are no streets in the town. The buildings are of brushwood, covered with thatch. Homestead are surrounded with high fences and follow one another without interruption.

Botor, Enareya-Lima, Jimma-Aba-Jefar are mountainous regions, populated by Galla of the Javi clan. Jimma—an independent Galla kingdom—is under the chief supervision of *Ras* Wolda Giyorgis. Botor and Lima are governed directly by him. Judging by the accounts of eye-witnesses, Jimma is very densely populated and very industrial. The best iron items and cloth are fashioned there. Merchants from Jimma conduct trade with the southern regions and with Kaffa. Their caravans pass from Berber through Kofir. All the residents of Jimma, as well as King Aba Jefar, are Mohammedan.

Leka, *Degay*, Gurangur, Bayo, Bunaya, Dabo, Guma, Goma, and Gera are inhabited by the Homo or Gomo tribe. Leka is very densely populated. Part of it represents an independent state under the rule of *Dajazmatch* Gebra Egziabeer, a christened Galla, It is also under the main supervision of *Dajazmatch* Demissew, who rules all the chasvanymi regions. In Leka the main town is Lekamte with 8,000 inhabitants. It is located at the intersection of important trade routes from Shoa to Wollaga and from Kaffa and Ilu-Babur to Gojjam. Here is found the residence of Gebra Egziabeer. For the most part, the inhabitants are merchants. Every Saturday a large market is held. Leka is the main marketplace for buying gold, musk, and ivory. Twenty versts [14 miles] from it is another town—Gatama, which like Bilo is populated exclusively with merchants and is independently governed by a *nagada-ras*. There are about 2,000 inhabitants there. Each Monday a large market is held. The residence of *Dajazmatch* Demissew is in Leka in the town of Deseta, which was recently built. It used to be in the nearby town of Roga. Both the one and the other are located on the heights of the mountain ridge that stretches along the right bank of the Didessa. This mountain ridge is partly covered with forest. In Deseta, there are about 4,000 inhabitants, mainly soldiers of the *Dajazmatch*, with their wives and children. Roga has about 1,500 inhabitants. Dabo, Guma, Goma and Gera are likewise densely populated.

Dabo, Guma, and Goma are mountainous, and partly covered with forest. But Gera, which is lower, is located on the lower course of rivers which flow from Kaffa to the Omo.

Guma and Gera produce lots of wild coffee. In Gera, in addition, many elephants are killed, a little fewer than in Handek of *Dajazmatch* Gebra Egziabeer. In both regions they get up to 150 pairs of tusks a year. Through Guma and Goma a large road runs to Kaffa.

The towns of Deseta and Gori each consist of a group of homes of military leaders dispersed here and there, around which huddle little shacks or, rather, huts of their soldiers. All the buildings are of wood, covered with thatch.

*Abe*ko, Wollaga and Darima are also governed by *Dajazmatch* Demissew. Wollaga and *Abe*ko are populated by the Javi clan. This mountainous region is, in places, overgrown with forest. A large part of Wollaga is an independent state, governed by *Dajazmatch* Joti, who pays tribute to the emperor and is under the supervision of *Dajazmatch* Demissew. His region is very rich and quite densely populated. Gold and ivory are obtained there. Through Wollaga a trade route passes to Khartoum, to the dervishes, and Joti has dealings with them. He is married to a daughter of one Arab ruler of a bordering province.

Darima is a very mountainous area, populated by the Tuma clan. Darima is rich in forest and produces lots of honey. Near it is found the large independent commercial town of Gunji and large markets, surrounded by the homesteads of the merchants of Sodo and Supe. Gunji is ruled by a *nagada-ras* on the same basis as Bilo and Gatama. In it are found up to 2,000 inhabitants, mainly merchant families. On Tuesdays a large market is held. From the outside, this town does not differ from Bilo. Sodo and Supe are just marketplaces with the homesteads of merchants spread out nearby. All these points are located on the large trade route from Ilu-Babur and Mocha, which abound in coffee, to Wollaga and Gojjam, where coffee is resold.

Buna and Chiro are populated by the Tuma tribe and are a wooded mountainous area. These regions are relatively sparsely populated. In the lower areas, a lot of cotton is produced. A lot of honey is also obtained. These regions are ruled by *Dajazmatch* Demissew. Gosho, Embo, Ayo and Orumu are populated by the Tuma tribe. Ilu-Babur, Make, Abiyu-Bure, Alga and Dida are populated by the Javi tribe. The population is very sparse. *Dajazmatch* Tesemma rules these regions. The country is wooded, mountainous and abounds in coffee. In the region of Abiyu-Bure lies the significant trading center of Bure. This is a marketplace with the homesteads of merchants spread around it. Bure is on outskirts of Galla settlements and on the border with the Negro tribes Gambi and Bako, which bring there ivory, cloth, ornaments and iron items to exchange. To Bure also come the sellers of coffee from Wollaga and Leka. The town of Gori in Ale is the residence of *Dajazmatch* Tesemma. This town is a large permanent military camp, with up to 4,000 inhabitants. In the domain of *Dajazmatch* Tesemma there are several gates built at fords across rivers that are not passable at other places. There are two of them on the Gaba River. In addition, there is one gate on the banks of the Didessa and one at a ford across the Baro. At these gates they collect taxes from merchants—a known percent of the goods transported. In addition, the garrisons at these gates are responsible for arresting deserters. Each such gate consists of a high watch post surrounded by a fence, and has about ten soldiers with guns.

On the far side of the Baro, in the border region of Sale, there is a small fort that looks like an observation post. It is surrounded by a deep ditch, across which is built a small bridge with a permanent guard. The garrison consists of 500 men, armed with guns. They live in the fort on a permanent basis.

Beyond Sale to the west begin the Negro settlements of the Gambi, Bako, and Masanko tribes, and to the south the Sidamo tribes: Mocha and Kaffa; and beyond those again the Negro tribes of Gimiro, Shiro and others.

According to wealth, industry and abundance of means of development, the population is distributed in the following manner:

The richest and most industrial settlements are Leka, Jimma and Wollaga. The inhabitants of these regions are involved in agriculture, commerce, and crafts. They extract gold and grow cotton. They have many live-stock, particularly cattle. There are only a small number of horses, mules, and donkeys, which among them are very expensive. As a consequence of this, the means for development of these regions is insignificant.

The inhabitants of the steppes of the Tikur, Chobo, Chalea, Tibye and Mecha plateaux are less rich. They are primarily involved in raising live-stock and produce excellent horses, mules and donkeys in large quantities. The means for development of this region are enormous.

Even poorer are the inhabitants of the wooded and unusually fertile regions found to the west of the Didessa. They harvest coffee and also do farming. But all the cultivation is done by hand since the live-stock died partly from the conquest of the area and partly from the plague which followed it. There are almost no horses, mules or donkeys, and the means for development of the country are nonexistent.

The Population of the Southwestern Regions of Ethiopia

The population of southwestern Ethiopia consists of the following main groups: Galla, Sidamo, and Amhara[60]; and on the western and southern borders—Negroes.

The Galla dwell to the west of Entotto up to the River Baro. There are two tribes of them: Tuluma and Mocha. The latter extends from the Awash River to the Baro River in the west and from Abbay to Kaffa in the south. They belong to the Galla—Oromo.

The inhabitants of Kaffa, Mocha, Gurage, Kulo, Kusho, Sidamo, and Amaro are called "Sidamo." Some authors suggest that these were the first inhabitants of the Ethiopian plateau.

Amhara, or, as we have become accustomed to called them, "Abyssinians," constitute the latest, military, and official population of these regions and are scattered among them rather uniformly.

The origin of these people has still not been accurately established; and, with regard to this question, there are only hypotheses, often contradictory.

Some authors call all three groups "Cushitic." Others, considering the first two Cushitic, count the Abyssinians as of Semitic race. But to call Galla and Sidamo descendants of Cush, the son of Ham, doesn't mean anything at all. Why between the ones and the others is there such a huge difference with regard to culture and customs and language? Where did the ones and the others come from? I am too little acquainted with this question to take upon myself its resolution. But bringing my personal observations together with works I have read about this question, I believe the most probable explanation of the existing ethnographic grouping is as follows. Galla, Somali, Adali (the latter two are steppe nomadic tribes who occupy the coast of the Red Sea from the Ethiopian plateau) are all Cushites and occupied these places, it must be, in the time when the descendants of Mesraim occupied Egypt. They arrived here, probably, by a dry route with their herds, and to the present have remained semi-savage.

In the reverse movement of Cushites from Africa to the Arabian peninsula, (which was mentioned by Lepsius), they encountered Semites, who, so to say, cut them in half. The Finikiyane were driven toward the Mediterranean Sea, and the other part toward the Arabian Sea. This forced the migration of the latter to Africa across the Bab-el-Mandeb Gulf. These immigrants occupied the Ethiopian plateau. They must have been culturally higher than the Galla and drove the Galla to the south. Aren't these the ancestors of those peoples we call Sidamo, Agau, Bylen, the original inhabitants of the country? And don't the inhabitants of Harar likewise belong to them? Much data inclines me to accept this hypothesis. Firstly, the type of the Harar and the Sidamo; secondly, the similarity of sounds in the languages of these groups; and thirdly, the level of culture.

From the fifteenth century B.C., a vast movement of Semites into Africa began. Between Ethiopia and the Arabian peninsula there were very active trade dealings. They spread out on the plateau, but unevenly. In all probability, their port of entry, so to speak, the point for settlement of the plateau was Massawa. Therefore, we see the greatest concentration of Semites in Northern Ethiopia: Felasha, Abyssinian Jews in the mountains of Semien, and Tigreans in Tigre. Southern Ethiopia was under the least influence of Semitism. From the Arabian peninsula, they brought with them the language that belongs to the Hamitic root —this is the present-day Geez language (literary). The Semites, having mixed with the inhabitants of the country, changed their language and pronunciation and hence came about the present-day Amhara, or Abyssinian, or Amharic language. "Amhara" is the name that the Abyssinians give themselves. The name "Abyssinian," accepted now in Europe, came about thus: Arabs call them "Habesh," which means "mixture" (confirmation of what we surmised that the Abyssinians are a mixed race). The Portuguese changed the word "Habesh" to "Habeks," and German scholars from "Habeks" made "*Abe*ssinen."

Although the Amharic language differs in grammar from the Geez (literary), many of its roots are borrowed from the Geez; so that the Amhara language is really Geez changed by mixing with other languages. The pronunciation of it likewise differs from the Geez. The Amharic language has no gutturals, which are characteristic sounds for Semitic languages, whereas Geez does have them.[61]

Let's now consider these nationalities in more detail.

GALLA—OROMO

The first mention of the Galla in The Abyssinian History of the Kings ("Tarika Negest") is attributed to 1480 A.D. During the reign of Iskander, the Galla made their first invasion into Abyssinian land and destroyed the monastery of Atones Maryam. In 1539 appears Gran.[62] He is a native of the Harar region, which at that time already belonged to Galla who had adopted Mohammedanism. On the one hand, using the Galla's desire to occupy Abyssinian lands and on the other hand raising the banner of the prophet among the Moslem population of the coastal zone and declaring holy war, Gran invaded Abyssinia, burning and destroying monasteries and churches.

At first, the Galla attacked Shoa and the provinces of Menjar and Ankober. But then, while the Arussi Galla independently waged war against the tribes of South Ethiopia, gradually ejecting them and occupying their places, Gran, inspired by the idea of Islam, made his way to North and Central Abyssinia, to the cultural and religious center of the empire, and destroyed Aksum. In 1545, Gran was killed in Damby, at Lake Tana. With his death, the Galla invasion lost its significance as a religious war. The Galla-Mohammedans who came with him occupied the best land in the province of Wollo. In the south, too, and in the west, Arussi Galla continued to gradually oust the indigenous inhabitants of these lands—Amhara and Sidamo: the first to the north beyond Abbay, the second to the south to the mountains of Kaffa.

This gradual conquest continued until very recent times. The Galla of Leka, for instance, consider that they occupied this country only 180 years ago. Thus, in Abyssinia we meet Gallas of two kinds. Some, Mohammedans, came from the east, from Chercher—they are Wollo Galla. Others, pagans, came from the southeast, from Arussi—these are the Tuluma and Mocha tribes. The first occupy the territory between the Kassam and Awash Rivers; the second are found to the south of the Abbay River and to the west of the upper Awash. Each of these tribes is divided into small clans. Tuluma is divided into seven clans, and Mocha into five (Liban, Afrenjo, Homo, Tume, Javi). Each of these small clans occupies a separate region, separated from the others by accurately established boundaries. But they all recognize that they belong to the Galla nation. They all call themselves "Oromo." Almost all of them have the same customs, language, type, and character, despite the difference of faith which exists between Galla pagans and Galla Mohammedans.

The Galla physical type is very beautiful. The men are usually very tall, with statuesque physique, lean, with oblong face and a somewhat flattened skull. The features of the face are regular and beautiful. The nose though sometimes fleshy is not a snub-nose. The mouth is moderate. The lips are not thick. They have excellent even teeth; large and in some cases oblong eyes; and curly hair. Their arm bones are of moderate length, shorter than the bones of Europeans, but longer than among the Amhara tribes. The feet are moderate and not turned in. The women are shorter than the men, and very beautifully built. In general, they are stouter than the men, and not as lean as they. Among them one sometimes encounters very beautiful women. And their beauty does not fade as quickly as among the Abyssinians. The skin color of both men and women ranges from dark to light brown. I did not see any completely black Galla.

The separate clans of the Mocha tribe differ somewhat. The far western clans are more thick-set and taller than the eastern and northern. Among them there is a more uniform and consistent type. This, I think, must be explained by the greater purity of their clan, since, being farther from the Abyssinians, they could not mix with them.

Galla Clothing

The various tribes also do not dress all the same way, depending on the location of the settlement. Tribes which are closest to the Abyssinians wear the shamma[63], but they do not drape it as beautifully as the Abyssinians, tossing most of both ends on one shoulder and leaving the right arm and half the chest bare. In the southwestern regions, where cotton is scarce, instead of a shamma they wear lamb or goat skin. You only see trousers on rich Galla or those who live in border areas. They usually tie some kind of leather apron around their hips. Often you can see on their heads a pointed cap made of goat skin. (A piece of skin from a recently slaughtered goat is stretched on a sharp metal casting. When it dries, the ends are cut off and the hat is ready.) Women's clothing also changes depending on how close they are to the Abyssinians. In the border regions, they wear the long women's shirts of the Abyssinians. In places more distant from the border, they tie around their body a piece of material or treated oxhide, sewn with shells and beads, such that it looks something like a White Russian plakhta. Some women make themselves a kind of sarafan out of leather.

The men wear their hair shaved close to the skin or standing in a shock. The Galla who border on the Abyssinians adopted from them their manner of braiding hair in small plaits, lying close to the head and connected together at the back of the head. This is a sign of bravery. The right to wear such a hairstyle belongs to: he who has killed a man—for one year; a lion—for two years; and an elephant—40 years. Women usually wear their hair separated into small matted locks, each braided into a small plait and dangling in this manner on all sides. Some spread an abundance of butter on their hair; others, who in particular are encountered in Wollaga, spread on their hair a yellow clay taken from water and renew this layer of clay each two to three weeks. Then, from a distance, they appear to be blond, and the color of their face takes on a special shade which can be compared with the color of cinnamon. In Leka, after treating hair this way, they gather it in a bun in the middle of the head. The ends of the braids stick out then above the head in all directions in the form of a hat. In general, such a hair style resembles sheaf of grain, planted down the head. Sometimes they arrange even more original hair styles, inserting long wooden needles in the hair.

Galla love all kinds of decoration: bracelets and rings are in wide use among them. These are made out of copper, lead, ivory and iron. They even wear rings on their toes. They put bracelets in bunches on their arms, on the arm above the elbow and on their feet. You sometimes come across such large and heavy bracelets that your are amazed at how they can work with them.

Children up to the age of ten to eleven do not wear any clothes. Usually their head is shaved and only in the middle do they leave a shock of hair. Mothers carry infants usually either from the side at the waist, or from behind. The mother ties the baby to her skirt and works with the baby on her.

Galla Family Life

The family life of the Gallas is just as simple as all the rest of their life. They do not build villages. Each family settles separately. Among them, polygamy is widespread. Each wife lies in a separate house since a separate household is established for each wife. The construction of their houses differs from that of the Abyssinians in that the roof rests not on a single post but on many. Inside, houses are divided into three parts by partitions. The first section from the entrance is intended as an enclosure for cattle at night, since houses are not protected by fences. In the middle part, the hearth burns and food is cooked. The part farthest from the entrance is covered with mats and serves as the bedroom. Strangers are not allowed there. The food of the Galla consists of cooked cabbage, or cooked roots of ensete and *guder*, cooked seeds of *mashella*, peas or *shumbur*, and lentils. They make of this something similar to our porridge [kasha], which they call gunfo and which they eat with spoons made of horn. They almost never use butter in their food, but rather use it exclusively for garnishing of hair. Instead of bread they make unleavened flat cakes—kita. They also make a kind of bread. The leavened dough is spread out on an earthenware pan and from the top in the middle of a round loaf another smaller pan is squeezed. Fire is lighted under the large pan and on top of the small one. A somewhat heavy, but tasty bread results. They prefer to eat meat raw. They eat their food without flavoring, not adding either salt or pepper. They love milk and meat. As for beverages, the most widespread is a beer, which they make from barley with the addition of finely minced leaves of the gesho plant, which substitutes for hops. Galla beer is thicker than Abyssinian. They don't know how to make mead, but they drink honey, diluted with water. They do not wash their hands before dinner, as the Abyssinians do. The wife first feeds her husband, and then eats with the children.

They buy themselves wives, paying the parents of the girl an amount that depends on the beauty of the bride and the wealth of the groom, up to 50 cows. In addition, they give the bride jewelry in the form of bracelets, rings or shells. On the day of the wedding, a feast is held at the house of the parents of the bride. After the feast, they take the bride to the house of the groom, where the feast continues, but without the parents of the bride. After the wedding, the husband cannot show himself to his father-in-law or mother-in-law until a child is born. In case of an accidental meeting, he must hide in the bushes. The number of wives is not limited and depends on one's prosperity. Each wife usually lives separately. The husband roams from one cabin to another. They sleep separately; to sleep together is considered indecent. Marriage takes place late: for men not earlier than 18 years, and for women not earlier than 16. When parents consider that their daughter has reached maturity, they perform an operation on her (removing the clitoris) and then give her in marriage. (I ascertained that this operation is performed by Galla of Wollaga, Leka, and Ilu-Babur). Once married, the wife becomes the slave of her husband, and there is no divorce under any circumstances. Conjugal infidelity is very rare. It is not considered infidelity if the younger brother of the husband has relations with the wife. In case of discovery of adultery, the husband can kill his wife on the spot; but for the most part, he exacts a fine from the culprit.

The birth of a child is not at all celebrated in the family, and no operation is performed on the new born. The mother gives him a name; but in the plateaux, the head of a family is always known by the name of his horse, for instance Aba Morke, Aba Jefar (the name of the king of Jimma).

Death is mourned by the whole family and all the neighbors of the deceased. They bury the dead in a deep grave, men to the right of the entrance to the house, and women to the left. First they lay brushwood on the body, and then pour earth. In eastern regions, they pile on a high stack of stones, and on top they lay reed stalks, coffee seeds, barley, and *mashella*. By the quantity and type of what is spread on it, one can determine the fortune of the person who is buried. In the city of Gunji, for instance, I saw an enormous grave with cruets spread out on stakes driven into the ground. In western regions they do not make such large graves, but in contrast to the eastern ones, they surround their graves with fences. They bury the deceased beside the house where he lived; and for twenty years after and sometimes for her whole life, the wife guards the grave of her husband. After twenty days, the wife can pass on to the brother of the deceased. During the twenty days after the death, several times relatives and neighbors of the deceased gather and, sitting in a circle, weep and remember his brave deeds. In addition, they have one very original custom. While living, a Galla rarely boasts of his deeds, and it is considered improper if he himself begins to talk about how many enemies he killed (completely the opposite of Abyssinian behavior). After death, his brother or friend has the responsibility to recount where, when and in what circumstances the deceased distinguished himself. On the death of the father, all the property passes to the eldest son, to whom also passes the leadership of the tribe, if the father was its chief.

In the family, the authority of its head is recognized, but only to a certain degree. The Galla family is not comparable to our Northern Russian family, but rather is closer to the White Russian. The son, as soon as he marries, separates himself from his parents; and although he respects his father and older brother, he is, in actuality, quite independent.

Galla Culture

For the most part, the Galla are a settled (rather than nomadic) people. But here one can distinguish three shades of their culture. There are settled Gallas who are almost exclusively satisfied with the products of their raising of livestock, who almost never work the land, and for vegetable food make use of the roots of banana ensete [or kogo]. But at the present time, losses of cattle and recent wars have almost deprived them of livestock. Others occupy themselves almost exclusively with tilling the soil and bee-keeping. A third category occupies itself now with the one and now with the other equally and also with domestic crafts. The entire center and the Javi and Gomo tribes belong to this last category. The inhabitants of the extreme western provinces are exclusively tillers of the soil. The inhabitants of the plateaux and the eastern provinces are primarily breeders of livestock. These three shades correspond to the three transitional stages from a nomadic to a completely settled state. Related to this is the development of the idea of the right of land property separately from the right of ownership. In the first case, all the land and water is the general property of the tribe. In the second case, the individual has a right to land which he actively possesses. In the third case, we see an exact differentiation of lots of land, purchase, sale and obligation.

Where I was, I did not see nomadic Gallas, but they are still found in Arussi. In Ilu-Babur, in Sale and in Alga up until the conquest of those last provinces by the Abyssinians, inhabitants there were in a semi-nomadic state. Now, having lost their cattle, they have been forced to turn to tilling of the soil. Since there is a lot of free land in these regions and it is all equally fertile and abundant in water, the inhabitants rarely stay long at the same place, but each three to four years select for themselves another; all the more so because they often build new huts, which termites usually destroy very fast.

Although those Gallas who till the soil dig in the ground less than Egyptian fellahs, they love their land and cultivate it comparatively well enough. A Galla farmstead makes a remarkably fine impression. Usually there is a small round hut for those who do not have livestock and a large one, surrounded by high banana trees (musa ensete) for those who do have cattle. The huge leaves of these trees completely hide the low pointed straw roof of the house. Several trees, from the nuts of which oil is squeezed, are planted at the entrance to the house and among them are woven root-crop plants which they call *guder*. Around the house there is a silky crop of tef (a kind of very small millet), a huge *mashella* (a Turkish millet), corn, a high cabbage which attains two arshins [56 inches] in height and does not have cabbage-heads, peas, and another plant like peas but not twisting, that is called *shumbur*, crops of tobacco, beans, lentils and pumpkins. On the plateaux there is wheat and barley. From what has been enumerated, it is clear that there is quite a wealth of various kinds of crops that, with small changes, depending on the elevation of the place, you find almost everywhere.

The techniques for cultivation are the same in the various regions. There are two kinds: by oxen and by hand. They were forced to resort to cultivating by hand after the loss of livestock in Bune, Ale, and Ilu-Babur. The tool used for this is a small shovel or axe, sitting perpendicularly on a handle about 3/4 arshin [21 inches] long. They do not dig the earth with it, but rather chop. In those places where they cultivate with oxen, they use a tool which is like a wooden plough. A pole with an iron tip serves as a ploughshare. Into the ground that is ploughed or dug this way, they toss seed, and that's the end of all the effort of sowing. The fertile soil takes care of any defect in the cultivation. In Ilu-Babur I saw an even simpler technique. There the countryside is wooded, the climate is humid, the soil is soft, black earth, and the entire effort of cultivation is limited to just cutting out a clearing in the forest, and sowing right on top of the wood that was felled, not even taking away the felled trees. I saw a field which was sowed in this way with peas, and which produced an excellent harvest. They reap with sickles with a toothed blade, and they bind in very small sheafs. In those places where livestock remain, they thresh the grain by driving oxen in a circle over ground which is covered with it. In the other places, they thresh with a long flexible stick. The soil throughout the whole extent is fertile to a high degree and, depending on irrigation, produces from two to four harvests a year.

The raising of livestock, which formerly was originally the main form of farming, has now fallen greatly and in some regions it is rare that you see a cow. But in the eastern plateaux cattle are still kept and without them no family at all would be thinkable there, since the countryside is completely deforested and the absence of firewood is made up for with pressed cow dung. The Gallas love their livestock and look after them, and at night they drive them into their homes. They have a curious breed of horses. In all probability these horses are descended from the Arabian breed, but their type is very different from them. The head of the horses is larger. The cheek is short, narrow and low placed. The chest is narrow and the ribs are insufficiently long. Very often, the legs are wet. Key factors of the hind quarters leave much to be desired. The sacrum sags. (I enumerate their bad qualities in comparison with Arabian horses.) In spite of all these deficiencies, this is a fast horse, with great endurance and a large heart. For their small stature (rarely larger than two arshins [56 inches]), they carry a comparatively heavy weight. Mares, mated with donkeys, produce excellent mules. These mules are not as tall as European ones but in endurance, strength, and speed of step they are indispensable on journeys. The donkeys are very small and not as hardy as the Egyptian ones. The hooves of horses, mules, and donkeys are of striking strength and grow very quickly. Neither the clearing nor the shoeing of hooves is known there, but nevertheless they carry out journeys of a thousand versts [700 miles] and even longer, along mountainous roads.

Cattle, bulls and cows are of the same kind as in Egypt, with humps. The cows produce very little milk: this is a more meat kind of cattle. The sheep are without tails. They have goats. Of domestic birds, you only see chickens.

Bee-keeping is an important branch of farming but it is not spread equally everywhere. Above all to the west of Didessa, where, as you go past houses, you see all the large mimosa trees surrounding them hung with beehives. In December and January, the bees swarm, and at this time the Gallas spread out their beehives. These hives are made either rolling up bark with wood and wrapping it in straw, or hollowing out a crude casting from the trunk of *kolkual* cactus trees. When the time comes to take out the honey, this is done in two ways—either smoking out the bees with smoke of pressed cow dung, or cutting the rope which holds up the beehive. The hive then falls from a height to the ground, and the frightened bees fly away. Depending on the vegetation there are three kinds of honey: very black and bitter in the southwest in Ilu-Babur; quite white, aromatic and very sweet in Handek; and an average between these two in the other places.

Artisans such as blacksmiths and weavers are found among the Galla. Blacksmiths forge knives and spears from iron, which is mined in the country. The manufacture of steel is unknown to them. Weavers weave rough shammas from local cotton. The loom is set up very simply. The weaver sits in a hole and, pressing his feet on the treadle, in turn raises and lowers the the appropriate row of basic threads. With dextrous movement of his arms, he passes the shuttle through, after which another horizontal bar, hanging above the cloth, adds the thread that has just passed through to those already woven. In addition to this, there is also the production of earthenware from unbaked clay. They make large gombas, somewhat like large pitchers without handles, with a volume from half a vedro [ten and a half pints] to four vedros [84 pints], earthenware pans for baking bread and pots for cooking food. There are joiners who make saddle-trees and wooden supports for the head, which serve in place of pillows. You find the above mentioned handicrafts among all the Galla, but in addition at the courts of the rulers there are also goldsmiths, and in Leka and Jimma there are leather craftsmen, who make excellent Morocco; harness makers who make the most intricate riding gear; artisans who make shields; weavers of straw hats (all Galla know how to weave parasols and baskets); armorers who make steel sabers; weavers who weave delicate shammas, etc. Commerce among the Gallas is in a transitional state from barter to monetary.

The monetary units, the Abyssinian taler and salt are accepted by the Gallas, but talers are found in the country in relatively small quantities and are concentrated in the hands of merchants. Three-pound bars of Abyssinian salt, which go for five to seven for the taler, are cut into four pieces by the Galla. These pieces go for from 16 to 20 for the taler. Galla have great love for commerce and exchange. In each little area there is at least one marketplace, where they gather once a week, and there is hardly an area which is relatively larger and populated which does not have marketplaces strewn throughout. Usually the marketplace is a clearing near a big road in the center of Galla settlements. In the middle is an elevated place for the collector of taxes from those who have brought things for sale, on which sits the head of the market, an Abyssinian. Rarely does any Galla man or woman skip market day. They come, even with empty arms or with a handful of barley or peas, with a few coffee beans or little bundles of cotton, in order to chat, to hear news, to visit with neighbors and to smoke a pipe in their company. But besides this petty bargaining, the main commerce of the country is in the hands of the Galla, and they retain it despite the rivalry of the Abyssinians. Almost all the merchants are Mohammedan. They export coffee, gold, musk, ivory, and leather; and they import salt, paper materials, and small manufactured articles. They are very enterprising and have commercial relations with the Sudan, Kaffa, and the Negro tribes. But they rarely take their wares to the sea, and prefer to sell them in Gojjam, Shoa or Aba Jefar's Jimma.

The customs, manners, religion and language of the Galla correspond to their state of culture. Industrial Jimma, the merchants and Galla who have distinguished themselves by their position have accepted Mohammedanism, but the remaining masses are still pagan. Their beliefs are not fixed, and are not put together in any system. There is some indeterminate expression of instinctive feeling of belief in a higher being, but they have no definite concept of God. Believing that God—Wak—is in heaven, that he is great and omnipotent, they do not try to explain him further to themselves and to represent him more definitely. In this way, they have avoided idolatry, to which inquisitive intellect inevitably led other nations. "Wak is there in heaven," says the Galla, pointing upward and lowering his eyes (in the Galla language the word "wak" also means heaven).

Galla Religious Beliefs

The religious beliefs of the Galla are not reduced to a logical system. All that is out of the ordinary strikes the Galla. He loves nature, feels her, lives with her, and, to him, it seems that she likewise is endowed with a soul. River, mountain, large tree—all these are living beings, particularly interested in this or that side of human life. First comes Borenticha—the bearer of evil and of all misfortune. Men worship him under the name of "Borenticha," and women under the name "Borentiti."

Secondly, Adbar—the bringer of the harvest and rain. Third, Oglye—the spirit whom women worship in order to have children. Fourth, Atelye-hora, masculine, and Atetye-dula, feminine—also influences child-bearing, fertility, and reproduction of cattle.

The Galla pray to all these beings and offer sacrifices which vary with the importance of the occasion and the supposed power of the deity—from a bull to a little bunch of grass or handful of pebbles. Usually each year on one of the Tuesdays or one of the Saturdays of May, each family offers a sacrifice to Borenticha. A ram is killed, beer is brewed, honey is gathered, flat cakes are cooked, and to this feast come all the relatives and neighbors. During the feast, some of everything is thrown on the ground. For instance, some beer is poured out saying "Here's for you, Borenticha. Here's to you, Borentiti. Pass us by. Don't touch us."

Trying to explain to themselves why they offer sacrifice once a year, namely in May, you hear two motives which, apparently affect this. First, the time coincides with the approach of the rains, and the well-being of the Gallas depends on the quantity of rains. Borenticha, as the great evil being, can hurt this. Secondly, this time coincides with great feasts in honor of the Mother of God in Abyssinia and with "Bayram" among the Mohammedans. Seeing the ones and the others celebrate at this time, they made a holiday for themselves, and at the same time they sacrifice to Borenticha.

Aside from this annual sacrifice to Borenticha, they pray when undertaking anything like a hunt or war and also in case of illness. Prayer consists of song in which the one who prays expresses by his words the essence of what is asked. In time of illness, relatives of the sick man sing in a toneless voice, and growl and leap, trying to chase away the sickness.

They offer two sacrifices to Abedara, spirit of the Earth: before sowing and after harvesting. Usually, women cook some flat cakes made of tef, go into a thicket, throw the cakes under a big tree and sing and dance there in honor of Abedara.

Women often pray to and offer sacrifices to Atetye, throwing bunches of grass under big trees.

"Oglye" in different places signifies something different. In Leka, for instance, this god is identified with an elephant. In other regions he is considered of feminine gender, giving fertility. In any case, each time when a ram or a bull is killed in the home, women smear their neck and chest down to the stomach with fat and hang a piece of "white fat"[64] in the form of a necklace around their neck. Men, too, having gathered blood in a shield and having mixed it with ashes of grass, cover their forehead and cheeks with this blood and hang "white fat" around the neck, and on the arms wear bracelets of fat. The latter give them good luck in war. The entire night after this, wild singing and dancing continues.

Thus, we see gods entangled among themselves. But this original polytheism is even more entangled when it gets mixed with worship of Christian saints: the Mother of God, Saint George the Victor, and Archangel Michael. This should not be taken as an indication that they were formerly Christians. Rather, simply being neighbors with Abyssinia and seeing how the Abyssinians worship these saints, the Gallas came to the conclusion that these are probably likewise great beings whom they didn't know about before; and they began to worship them too. They always call one of the olive trees near the house "Maryam," and during the big Abyssinian feasts of the Mother of God in January, they offer sacrifices: they pour a handful of barley or wheat and pour some beer under the olive tree and sing songs.

They also offer sacrifices to mountains and large rivers. As already mentioned above, these sacrifices are very diverse, beginning with a bull or a ram and ending with only a bunch of grass. But there is still another unique kind of charm at times of sacrifice that I came upon accidentally. In Wollaga, in the middle of the road, I saw a clay figurine that represented a four-legged animal with a horse's head, lying on a pile of stones, sprinkled on the top with little bunches of cotton. I ordered my servants to pick it up for me, but they wouldn't, saying that you shouldn't do this, that this is an enchanted object which would bring misfortune to anyone who picks it up. Then I myself picked it up. To my questions about what this meant, they explained to me that probably this figurine, which represented the devil, was thrown along the road by a Galla out of malice to his enemy.

By the way, when in a great hurry, instead of a ram, for instance, Gallas offer a clay image of it as a sacrifice.

There is one more interesting rite. At the exit of the path which leads from the house to the big road, you almost always come upon a little bed of stones, and on it lies dry grass. This is made so that Borenticha, having seen the sacrifice, won't stop at the house, but will pass by.

The Gallas don't have their own weekly or annual feasts, and they also don't have fasts. But living as neighbors with Abyssinia, the Gallas adopted from the Abyssinians some annual feasts: Holy Cross Day, which coincides with the end of the rains and the onset of spring, called in Abyssinian Maska and in Galla Maskalya; and Christmas, called Guma by both Abyssinians and Galla.

The Galla have no public worship, no priests, no altars, no idols. But in their midst there are soothsayers, whom they call kalicha. Conditions necessary to become a kalicha are not fixed: anyone who has a calling can make himself one. But the degree of respect for a kalicha depends on the degree to which his predictions and advice are good. Sometimes the name kalicha is hereditary and passes from generation to generation to the eldest in the generation. A kalicha who advises well and speaks the truth is very respected by the people. They come to him from afar to get advice and offer gifts.

When the country was subjugated, the first thing the Abyssinians did was to capture and execute the kalichas. Now there are almost none of them in the country, or they hide secretly in thickets. In appearance, they differ from others in the fact that they grow very long hair.

The Galla have many superstitions, for instance belief in werewolves which they call buda. One glance of a buda is enough to kill a man, especially at meal time.

From what has been said above, it can be seen that the faith of the Gallas is not in any way fixed. But at the same time, because it includes an understanding of God-Spirit, and of the origin of evil—Borenticha—as well as a precarious understanding of life beyond the grave, it cannot present a serious hindrance to their conversion to Christianity.

Right now, in Shoa, and particularly in Leka, Galla are baptized in large numbers. But unfortunately, this is superficial, since the Abyssinian clergy have no missionaries who would try to explain the essence of the Christian faith to the Galla.

Galla Language

The language of the Galla people is melodious and simple, and the words are easily pronounced because of the abundance of vowels. It has none of the guttural sounds of Semitic languages, and I didn't notice any differences between abrupt and drawling consonants, as, for instance, in the Amharic letters "k" and "t". The form of sentences is simpler and less flowery than that of the Abyssinians. Clauses are short and abrupt. And in conversation, the listener after each sentence of the speaker answers "yes" with a drawling "e" sound, after which the speaker continues.

In conversation with a person of higher station, the Galla begins his speech with the word duguma, which means "this is true." This must be because, in general, they often lie.

For conjugation, they use pronouns and auxiliary verbs for the future, present, pluperfect tenses. The perfect past, as in Amharic, is a basic verbal form.

They use participles and gerundives, but to less a degree than the Abyssinians.

Unfortunately, I am not well enough acquainted with this language to resolve its detailed and exact nature.

I tried to find out if the Galla have any epic folk tales, but only managed to collect a few proverbs and stories. I didn't find any epic folk tales.

By the way, here's a little story that an old Galla man told me as an amiable introduction to a gift: "A mouse came to an elephant to ask for the hand of his daughter. The elephant said, 'What! You, who are so little, want my daughter?' 'Never mind,' says the mouse. 'Give me your daughter.' The elephant did so. Some time later, elephant hunters came to this place. The mouse having found out about this went by night to the hunters' camp and gnawed through all the saddle girths and horse gear and in this way saved the elephants."

Galla National Character

The main character trait of the Galla is love of complete independence and freedom. Having settled on any piece of land, having built himself a hut, the Galla does not want to acknowledge the authority of anyone, except his personal will. Their former governmental system was the embodiment of this basic trait of their character—a great number of small independent states with figurehead kings or with a republican form of government.[65]

Side by side with such independence, the Galla has preserved a great respect for the head of the family, for the elders of the tribe, and for customs, but only insofar as it does not restrain him too much.

The Galla is a poet. He worships nature, loves his mountains and rivers, considering them animated beings. He is a passionate hunter.

The Galla are a warlike people. They are very brave, and killing among them, as among other peoples, is elevated to a cult. Very recently there were some Galla tribes where a youth did not have the right to get married until he killed an elephant, a lion, or a man. Having killed one of them, a Galla greased his head with butter, wore bracelets, rings, and an earring.

But comparing their bravery with the bravery of other peoples, I should say that this is not the nervous enthusiasm of the Abyssinian, not the selflessness of the Russian, but a quicker bent for blood. This bent makes the Galla dreadful to such a point that he doesn't notice danger.

The armaments of the Gallas consist of a metal spear (which has a different shape among the various clans), a knife in his belt, and a large shield. Whether or not a Galla is a cavalryman depends on his place of residence. On the plateaux of Chalea, Wobo, Tikur, Shoa, and Leka, which are abundant in horses, all the Galla are cavalrymen. In the mountains and forests of the west and southwest regions adjacent to Kaffa, almost none are.

The ambush, the night attack, the single combat—those are the favorite tactics of the Galla.

Both on horse and on foot, the Galla fights for his personal goal—to kill and to get trophies. There is no general concept of "patriotism." To run away is not considered a disgrace. The Galla likewise have no concept of all being related to one another by blood and kinship. In the recent subjugations of the Galla by the Abyssinians, the most violent fighters in the ranks of the Abyssinians were themselves Galla.

Galla make excellent cavalrymen. Their horses are plain and small, but hardy and fast. In battle, they very rarely get close to the enemy. Instead, having galloped at the enemy in full career and having thrown a spear, they abruptly turn around and gallop away. In general, the Galla are marvelous military material, and particularly now, after that school of obedience and discipline that they pass through under the power of the Abyssinians.

The ambition and sense of honor of the Galla do not go very far. The Galla passionately wants to kill somebody or something in war or in a hunt to have the right to grease his head with butter and to return home with songs. But you can defeat a Galla without risk. In case of injustice, the beaten man feels indignation, but never outrage.

The Galla is a beggar, sooner generous than stingy, sooner good than bad. You can only believe him with caution. Formerly, there was almost no thievery among the Galla, but this was not due to principled honesty, but rather to the absence of want—all the more so because the distribution of property was very equal. But now, theft has become very common.

As regards the difference between separate clans of the Mocha, those who inhabit the plateau are more warlike and blood-thirsty than those who live in the lowland. As regards culture, the inhabitants of Wollaga, Leka, and Jimma differ sharply from the others. These are mainly trading and manufacturing regions.

The Original Form of Galla Government

The original form of government of the Galla and the beginnings of their legal procedure and of criminal law were entirely changed with the conquest of the area by the Abyssinians. Originally, they were separated into a mass of separate clans, and each clan was a completely independent unit. A large part of them, namely all the western clans, had a monarchic form of government. But some southern clans had a republican form of government.

The republics of Goma and Gera chose several rulers, whom they drove away quickly whenever they had the slightest cause for dissatisfaction. In all the other clans, the eldest in the clan, descended by the eldest line from the founder of the clan, was the head of state. But his rights were completely fictitious. He did not have the use of any revenues from his subjects, because he did not have the right to collect taxes. His revenues consisted of rare voluntary gifts, portions of military plunder and revenues from his own properties, cattle, and land. This was because, in the primogeniture system of inheritance he, descended by the eldest line from the founder of the clan, was the richest landowner in his tribe. In case of war, he was at the head of his clan, but he could neither begin nor end war, nor undertake anything at all independently without having consulted with the elders. He presided in the lube, but all the business was decided there without his knowledge.

The lube is a very unique institution. Each head of a family in the state has the right each 40 years to become a member of the lube for five years. If the head of a family turns out to be a young boy, this does not prevent him from taking part. This assembly of the leaders of the families of the state perform all the functions of court and of state government.

The court, whether civil or criminal court, is conducted in the following manner. The plaintiff and the respondent, or the accuser and the accused, each entrust their business to one of the members of the lube. Those entrusted explain the essence of the matter to the council, wrangle with one another; then when the matter has been made sufficiently clear, the lube decides on the verdict. For the duration of the trial, neither the respondent nor the plaintiff have the right to interfere. They are not asked about anything. There are two criminal punishments—fine and exile. And, in some western regions there is still sale into slavery.

There is no capital punishment for ordinary criminal acts. Premeditated murder is punished the most severely. The property of the killer is confiscated for the use of the family of the victim, and he himself is expelled from the borders of the country. But if after some time he arrives at an agreement with the family of the victim on the extent of compensation, then he can return again. Theft is punished by large fines and, in some border regions, by sale into slavery. Adultery is punished by fines, if the deceived husband did not already deal with the insulter in some way.

Since the right of property in land in the majority of regions up to now has been identified with actual possession, law suits on this question could only arise in the thickly populated regions of Leka, Wollaga, and Jimma, where already there exist not only property in land but also servitude.

Aside from the administration of justice, it was likewise the duty of the lube to reconcile quarreling clans.[66]

Such was the form of government of Galla states up until their conquest by the Abyssinians. But from that time the peaceful, free way of life, which could have become the ideal for philosophers and writers of the eighteenth century, if they had known of it, was completely changed. Their peaceful way of life is broken; freedom is lost; and the independent, freedom-loving Gallas find themselves under the severe authority of the Abyssinian conquerors.

The Abyssinians pursue two goals in the governing of the region: fiscal and political—security of the region and prevention of an uprising. All families are assessed a tax. This is very small, not more than a unit of salt a year per family. In addition, families are attached to the land. Part of the population is obliged to cultivate land for the main ruler of the country, and part is divided among the soldiers and military leaders. The whole region is divided among separate military leaders who live off their district and feed their soldiers.

The dreadful annihilation of more than half the population during the conquest took away from the Galla all possibility of thinking about any sort of uprising. And the freedom-loving Galla who didn't recognize any authority other than the speed of his horse, the strength of his hand, and the accuracy of his spear, now goes through the hard school of obedience.

The lube no longer exists. The Abyssinians govern through clan leaders aba-koro and aba-langa (the aba-koro's assistant). The aba-koro is the head of the clan, who gathers the Gallas for work, gathers coffee for the leader of the region, levies taxes for them, and, when it is necessary, collects *durgo*. The Abyssinian leaders only supervise the correctness of the actions of the aba-koro. The court of the first instance is the aba-koro, but important matters go straight to the leader of the region who punishes in accord with Abyssinian laws, and, in the case of political crimes, robbery, attempted murder or murder of an Abyssinian, uses capital punishment.

That's the way things are done in the conquered regions. But aside from these there are three states—Jimma, Leka, Wollaga —which voluntarily submitted to Abyssinia and pay it tribute. In those places, the former order has been preserved, although the lube no longer exists. The Abyssinians obtain taxes from them and do not interfere in their self-government. Aside from payment of taxes, they also feed the troops stationed there.

After all that has been said above, the question automatically arises—what are the relations of the conquered to the conquerors? Without a doubt, the Galla, with their at least five million population, occupying the best land, all speaking one language, could represent a tremendous force if they united. But the separatist character of the people did not permit such a union. Now subjugated by the Abyssinians, who possess a higher culture, they little by little adopt this culture from the Abyssinians, and accept their faith. Since there is no national idea, in all probability, they will with time blend with the Abyssinians, all the more because the Abyssinians skillfully and tactfully manage them, not violating their customers and religious beliefs and treating them lawfully and justly.

Only those states that pay tribute and preserve their independence represent a danger. Among these, hate for the Abyssinians is apparent in the ruling class, although they have adopted all the customs and even the household etiquette of the Abyssinians. In case of internal disorders, these states will certainly try to use such opportunity to their advantage. But Emperor Menelik doesn't disturb these states for the time being, in view of the fact that they are the most profitable regions of his empire.

Sidamo

Pressed from the north by Abyssinians, from the south and east by Galla, Sidamo tribes ceded to the newcomers almost all the territory they formerly occupied, partly merging with them, and keeping some territories, such as Kaffa, Mocha, Kulo, Sidamo, Amaro and Gurage. Kaffa and Mocha to this day retain their independence. The others have been subdued by the Abyssinians. Up until the invasion of the Galla in the sixteenth century, these regions, judging by the Abyssinian Tarika Negest, belonged to them. For example, the names Kaffa and Mocha were given to them, according to legend, by Atye Zar Yakob, who in the fifteenth century conquered them. The word "Kaffa" derives from the word kefu meaning "wicked," and Mocha from the word mot meaning "death," because the conquest in all probability did not come easily to the Abyssinians, thanks to the war-likeness of the inhabitants and the difficult mountainous and forested terrain.

At the time of the invasion of Gran (sixteenth century), one of the sons of Atye Zar Yakob reigned. The Gallas, having occupied all the intervening country, waged uninterrupted war against the remnants of the former population, but the difficulty of the terrain and the bravery of the inhabitants of the above-named regions, preserved them like islands up until today. It is worthy of note that the Galla call all Abyssinians

"Sidamo," not seeing the differences between the two nations. This serves, besides, as an indication that the Galla came from Arussi, since Sidamo is the name of the province which borders Arussi and Ethiopians inhabit it. Having first become acquainted with the Ethiopians of Arussi, they called all the other Ethiopians by the same name.

The Sidamo type is very beautiful, particularly the women. The color of the skin is lighter than that of the Galla and the Abyssinians. The women are quite light. The features of the face are very regular: thin straight noses, thin lips, oblong eyes, small hands and feet. The skull is not flattened out and is more round than among the Galla. The hair is curly. Their stature is smaller than that of the Galla. The women are thinner and more graceful.

I passed through the regions of Mocha and Alga, which are inhabited by them, during time of war and did not have a chance to become acquainted in detail with their way of life and character. But, judging by questions, their character differs little from that of the Abyssinians. They dress similarly in shammas, have the same food, and have a similar governmental organization. For example, Kaffa has a *Negus* (a descendant of Zar Yakob) and is divided into 12 provinces governed by *Ras*es (six Christian and six Mohammedan).[67] Mocha is also ruled by a king, who they call tetchuchanochi, and the four regions into which it is divided are ruled by aga-rases.

Kaffa is half-Christian. There are churches and priests. But the question arises—who assigns the priests, since they do not have relations with the Abyssinian clergy and do not have their own bishops. Mocha also preserves a memory of Christianity. They call God Erotchi, believe in Jesus Christ, the Mother of God, and several saints. They fast on Wednesdays and Fridays, and celebrate on Saturdays.

All the Sidamo tribes speak dialects which are different, but very close to one another. They are very brave and warlike. Their weapons consist of spears, shields, sometimes bows and arrows. They say that there are guns in Kaffa. Their spears are not the same simple shape as the Galla's, but are very intricate and almost always poisoned. The Abyssinians consider war with them much more difficult than with the Galla. It is said that they poison the water and resort to all possible measures of war against the enemy, in which the terrain which is rugged, mountainous and forested helps them greatly.

I decided not to recount here everything that I heard about them since, not being in a position to verify what I heard, I could easily fall into error.

The relationship of the Abyssinians to these tribes is different from their relationship with the Galla. They consider the Sidamo as related with them by blood, and many highly placed persons among them have Sidamo wives (for instance, the *afa-negus*, the chief judge).

The Abyssinians rule the subdued Sidamo tribes the same way as they do the Galla.

NEGROES

The western borders of Abyssinia and part of the southern are inhabited by Negroes. The borders between Galla and Negroes in the west are the Baro and Dabus Rivers. To the south from Mocha on the slopes of the Kaffa Mountains there also live Negroes of the Gobo, Suro or Shiro, and Gimiro tribes; and on the western borders on the far side of the Baro are the Gambi, Bako, Masanko and Madibis[68] tribes.

I did not succeed in going to Negro settlements, but I saw several Gambi and Bako inhabitants, and likewise saw captured slaves of the Madibis and Gimiro tribes.

The type of the Bako tribe is of very tall build, dry, long-legged, with very large feet, which are turned inward, and large arm bones, an oblong shaped skull, a turned-up meaty nose, thick lips, curly hair, and skin that is completely black. They extract their two upper front teeth and pierce the lower ends of their ears. In addition, they tattoo their cheeks, making three lines on each side. They dwell in a very unhealthy, low-lying, swampy valley, in which all the tributaries of the Sobat join together. It is extremely difficult to make your way there. Hence very little is known about them, and they are rarely seen at markets in the town of Bure. They don't wear clothes, but instead they make aprons out of leaves. The Gambi tribe has just as much tattooing as the Bako, but differs from it in smaller stature and not such long legs. The language of the Gambi and the Bako is the same. The Gambi build wooden houses, similar to those of the Galla. Their food consists mainly of roots of ensete bananas (fruitless bananas). They have cattle.

The Madibis tribe is found to the north of the Bako. Judging by answers to questions, it is under the authority of Arabs. There reigns someone named Amati, who according the words of the Negroes is white. He has only one wife who also is white. He has double-barreled guns. (This is according to the words of a Negro boy, whose sister was a slave at the court of Amati. He was sold to Galla lands several years ago.) The type of the Madibis is very well built with a round skull, turned-up meaty nose, thick lips, small eyes, and curly hair. Their arms and legs are large and their feet are turned inward. They make three marks on each cheek and extract the front upper teeth. They build stone houses, have monogamy, and married people, under threat of being sold into slavery, do not have the right to sleep together. They have many livestock, but they eat only those that have died. On those rare occasions when they hold a feast, they do not just butcher a cow, but rather murder it, removing its head. Their usual food consists of soup, and they are not squeamish about putting mice in it. The same slave who told me all this showed me how they dance. The women run in place and cry piercingly, "A-a-a!." The men at first do not run like the women, and then going into an ecstasy begin to jump back and forth, spreading their legs wide and crying "Bum-bum!" All these Negro tribes are related to one another, in all probability. It must be that they belong to the Shilluk[69] [Nilot].

Bordering Mocha from the south, the Gimiro tribe represents a different type than the rest. They are very ugly, with a very turn-up nose and a huge mouth. They have a different kind of tattooing: two vertical marks on the bridge of the nose and two such marks at the ends of the mouth. They build straw houses, like huts. They are involved in agriculture. By the testimony of the Abyssinians, all these tribes are very brave and warlike and adults never surrender themselves into captivity—only women and children fall into the hands of the conqueror. They very quickly accustom themselves with their new position and completely forget their former life and language. I managed to transcribe several words of the Gimiro and Madibis languages,[70] from which it can be concluded that these two peoples have completely different languages.

Relations between these tribes and the Abyssinians have up until now been such that the Negro tribes have served the Abyssinians as the target of wars and raids. Abyssinians have tried to take as much livestock and as many prisoners as possible, and then would go back home. Now this predatory way of conducting war is being replaced by another, based on the annexation to the empire of new territories and the general expansion of the empire. Evidently, the Negroes will not be strong enough to defend themselves against this, and in all probability, the time will soon come when all the surrounding Negro tribes, who inhabit places that are not extremely unhealthy, will be annexed by Ethiopia.

AMHARA OR ABYSSINIANS

The Abyssinians, rulers of the country, call themselves "Amhara" in contrast to the inhabitants of Tigre. Through all the extent of my journey to the west, I did not come across any areas that they had completely settled, but, on the other hand, in those most recently conquered, all the rulers and troops are Abyssinian.

As said above, being a mixture of all the peoples who gradually occupied the country, they are not of one uniform type. The shape of the skull, the shade of the skin, the height, the features of the face are all diverse. Side by side with a clearly Semitic type, you see the regular facial features of the ancient Egyptians and a turned-up nose. But, in spite of this apparent diversity, the national character is very determined and homogeneous, with small deviations that could lead to two types —Gojjam and Shoan.[71]

It is hard to imagine so many contrasts united in one person, as are united in the Abyssinian character. Their character is like the nature around them—where precipices, cliffs, mountains and plains alternate among one another, and cold is mixed with tropical heat. If I allow myself a rather free comparison, this is how I would characterize the Abyssinian. He is talented and receptive, like a Frenchman. With his practicality, with the way he deals with those he has conquered and his governmental abilities, he is like an Englishman. His pride is like that of a Spaniard. By his love for his faith, his mildness of character and tolerance, he is like a Russian. By his commercial abilities, he is like a Jew. But in addition to all these characteristics, he is very brave, cunning, and suspicious.

At the present time, Abyssinia—with its ancient culture, Christianity, and historically shaped governmental order— appears like an island among other peoples who are almost in a childlike condition. Abyssinians have professed the Christian faith since 343 A.D., and before then, from the time of Solomon, they professed the Jewish faith, which even today is reflected in their ceremonies.[72] To this day they separate animals into pure and impure; they give great significance to the ability to butcher cattle; and they circumcise their children. There are many other similarities, but I will tell of them in greater detail later.

Abyssinian Language

Their language is of Semitic origin and of Hamitic root, since their ecclesiastical and literary language, Geez, derives from the Hamitic. The Geez language was brought to Ethiopia at the time of the Semitic migration. The Semites, becoming the ruling nation, made Geez their language. Mixing with Ethiopian tribes, Cushites who lived on the Ethiopian plateaux, they modified their language, adopting much from the surrounding tribes. Since the distribution of Semites was not uniform, with more to the north than to the south, to the north the language retained a greater purity, and at the present time we see in Abyssinia three dialects: Geez, ancient Hamitic, is the ecclesiastical and literary language; the Tigrean dialect which differs little from Geez; and the Amharic language, which has many Geez roots, but which has a grammar and pronunciation which is completely different from Geez. The Amharic language is very sonorous. In it there are not of the characteristic guttural "ha-ga" sounds of Semitic languages, including Geez and Tigrean. Conjugation and declination are also completely different between these two languages. The alphabet of both consists of 202 letters. Each syllable is represented by a different letter. The written form of the letters is similar to ancient Chaldean. They write from left to right. (It is significant to note that the all eastern people write from right to left.) Regarding the pronunciation of several consonants there are several complications. For instance, there are three different ways to pronounce the letters "h" and "t"; there is a difference between "ts" and "t-s"; and there are two ways to pronounce the letter "s." All books are printed in the Geez language, and only in recent times have several appeared in Abyssinian: Feta Negest and Tarika Negest. The first of these is a modified Code of Justinian; and the second is the history of the reigns of kings. The people have preserved some legends relating sometimes to former kings, but mostly to saints. Of the kings, Atye Zar Yakob (1434-1468) still lives in the memory of the people. He ruled all of present-day Ethiopia, including Kaffa and Mocha. I was unable to find any epics. There are some stories and proverbs.[73] There are very few songs about the country, almost none, because their singers prefer to touch upon lively interests of the day with their songs or to sing unceremoniously about the person who invited them, in hope of getting a good tip. If the tip isn't good enough, the praise slowly turns to insulting abuse. Songs with indecent contents are also very wide-spread. In Abyssinia there are two kinds of itinerant singers: azmari and lalibala, which are always at odds with one another. The azmari sing, accompanying themselves on a single-stringed instrument like a violin, which is called a masanko.[74] The lalibala sing heroic couplets with great enthusiasm, and with them there is a chorus of boys or girls who sing the refrain. These singers represent a completely different class of people, and are not subject to the general laws of the land. No one has the right to bother them, under threat of severe punishment, and the singers can ridicule and blame whomever they please, even the emperor himself to his face. They all are afraid of this mockery and generously reward singers, using them also as a way to increase their popularity. Azmari sing with great affectation, somewhat nasally, and during the song and roll over with their whole body in time to the music. For the most part, what they sing is improvised. Some of their tunes are very nice. Lalibala do not sing, but rather yell or growl some kind of heroic recitative; then the chorus sings some monotonous tune.

Abyssinian Family Life[75]

The family life of the Abyssinian is very simple and almost the same in all classes. Houses in Shoa are wooden; those in the north are stone. Their structure is very simple. They drive sticks or stakes that are two and a half to three arshins long [70 to 84 inches] into the ground around a circle with a radius that is also three arshins [84 inches]. In the middle is a large post which serves as the base for the roof. The roof and the walls consist of the same kind of stakes and are connected together with ropes or pieces of bast. The house is not divided by partitions, but from one of the sides they make a back shed for horses or sheep. In the middle of the house is the hearth, on which they cook food in clay pots. By one of the walls is the alga—a bed, consisting of a wooden frame on supports and a belt binding. All the rest of the space is covered with large clay pots. There are no kitchen-gardens. Large houses of leaders are built by the same system and attain 16 arshins [12 yards] in diameter. Sometimes they build them without a central post. Around the circumference, they stick large slivers of wood or stakes five arshins [4 yards] high, and in the middle around the circumference of a little circle drawn inside are several large posts. On these posts is placed a circle of flexible bamboo poles, tied together with ropes, and on this circle is held the whole roof, which consists also of flexible thin spokes or slivers, joined together above in a conic shape and fastened to a whole series of intermediate horizontal circles made of bent bamboo. They wrap these circles with multi-colored skins, and obtain a very beautiful appearance.

Abyssinian Clothing

The clothing of the Abyssinians consists of white trousers. The well-to-do have white thin cotton shirts. The highest personages wear silk ones. The waist is wrapped in a long wide piece of cotton material, over which they wear a bandoleer, if they have one, and a saber. On the shoulders they throw a shamma, a large square piece of white cotton material made locally. It is worn like a Roman toga, and there are many nuances in the way it is worn. At home, where each Abyssinian considers himself as an independent lord with full rights, like the emperor in the empire, the Abyssinian dons the shamma throwing the ends behind both shoulders and wrapping it around his whole body. The extreme expression of pride is a sitting or quietly moving Abyssinian, wrapped up to his nose in a shamma, looking with disdain on all that surrounds him. In the presence of or in the home of a higher person, no one other than this person can wear his shamma in this way. Others wear theirs in two ways. Half the shamma is wrapped around the waist, forming a kind of skirt; and the other, free half is picturesquely thrown over the shoulders. This is how all wear it when they speak with the *Negus.* for instance, or a slave before his master. In addition, during a conversation the rule is observed that the younger when speaking to the elder, covers his mouth with the free end of the shamma. Furthermore, a courtier, when leaving the emperor or his leader, covers both of his shoulders with the free half of the shamma. Also, in law court, the plaintiff and the defendant wrap half the shamma around the waist and, hold the other hand in their hands. They like to cover their head with white muslin. This is in imitation of Menelik. Previously each brave man who had killed an elephant, lion or man braided his hair in plaits. Menelik always wears a headband. In recent times, felt hats with wide brims have come into use. They usually don't wear footwear and only when going to hot places do they wear something resembling sandals. The highest persons put on over the shamma what they call a kabba. This is a satin cloak with a hood, bordered with fringe. For covering from rain and cold, they have something like our felt cloak. This consists of thick felt, but sewn so that it doesn't come undone. The hood is on the back of it. The clothing of the women differs from that of the men in that, instead of trousers and a thin shirt, they wear a long, thick shirt that extends to the heels. The wealthy have them embroidered with silk. Around their waist they wrap the same kind of sash as the men, and on top they throw a shamma, and some a cloak.

Abyssinian Food

The usual food of the Abyssinian consists of *injera* (a kind of pancake bread, which is round, about 3/4 arshin [21 inches] in diameter), which they eat dipped in sauce made of pea meal with pepper. The wealthy add to that butter and meat. Their national and favorite dish, which they succeed in eating quite rarely is brindo, raw fresh-killed meat. A huge fillet or thigh is held by a servant over a basket around which those who are eating sit. Each chooses a piece for himself and cuts it out. They can eat an enormous quantity of raw meat, but all Abyssinians without exception have the inevitable consequence of that—tapeworm. Therefore, it is the established practice among them to eat once every two months the cooked berries of the *kusso* tree to expel the parasitic worms. They very strictly observe fasts. On Wednesdays and Fridays they do not eat until noon; and during fasts, even fish is forbidden.

Abyssinian Way of Life and Etiquette

In his own home the Abyssinian is the complete master and zealously protects his right of the inviolability of his dwelling, like an Englishman. In the home of each wealthy Abyssinian the same strict etiquette is observed as at the court of the emperor, although, of course, to a lesser degree. There is a whole series of various domestic posts. For instance, the agafari, is the one who admits those who wish to see his master. There are agafari of the husband, the wife, who manage large receptions. They are usually very important and full of their own dignity. They always have in their hand a thin stick or little whip. The *Azzaj* manages the house and all the property. There are chiefs of the various departments of the household economy. The kitchen chiefs are the cookers of honey, the *injera*-byet, wot-byet, and *tej*-byet. The chief of the stables is the balderas. The asalyfi is the one who cuts the food in pieces and serves the food and drink. The elfin ashkers are the servants of the bedroom. They are usually notably good-looking youths with gentle, graceful movements, with refined Abyssinian manners, always remarkably draped in their shammas.

The day of an Abyssinian noble usually begins and ends very early. He gets up at sunrise and with his secretary—tsafi—and get down to work. The secretary reads to him the correspondence that has been received and answers to these letters are composed. Having finished that the noble goes to the courtroom to dispense justice. All available soldiers and chiefs have already assembled in the yard to accompany him. He sits on a richly attired mule. Over him they unfurl a parasol, and the huge procession moves to the courtroom. At eleven o'clock on ordinary days and at two to three o'clock on fast days they have dinner. The wife is not at this meal. She sits in the elfin—the bedroom. Nobles dine with their closest leaders. After the dinner of the master, the servants who are in attendance on him eat what remains, and if the master wants to especially distinguish one of them, he gives him his partly eaten piece of meat or partially drunk decanter of mead. After dinner, mead—*tej*—and beer—tella[76]—is brought in decanters. And conversation begins, the thread of which is always maintained by the master. In this regard they have striking talent, and the popularity of a leader to a large extent depends on his skill in conducting conversation.

At every minute people come to disturb the master about this or that matter. Only in the evening do all the retainers go away, business ends and he can spend a few hours with his family. At about seven o'clock he has supper with his wife, and at about nine o'clock he has already gone to bed.

Abyssinian Family

Families, as we know them, do not exist among the Abyssinians. Therefore, mutual love among members of a family, with very rare exceptions, does not exist. The absence of family is due to the position of women in Abyssinia and the instability of marriage. With very few exceptions, all marriages are civil. As a result, it is sufficient if the groom and bride in the presence of two witnesses—kuas—declare in the name of the *Negus* that the marriage is made, and then the witnesses look after the property brought by the wife and also are responsible for the obligations which the groom takes on himself in relationship to the family of the bride. From the moment of swearing by the name of the *Negus*, the marriage is completed, but to divorce is just as easy as to marry. In front of two witnesses, the husband sets the wife free, and then if the divorce was not a consequence of discovering unfaithfulness of the wife, then in going she has the right to half of all the property which they then divide. Only after many years of peaceful life together do the husband and wife decide to have a church wedding, which is inviolable. Priests are all married in church weddings.

Because divorce is so easy and families change so frequentl, one mother might have children from several fathers; and the position of the children is extremely uncertain. For instance, having divorced the first husband, the mother takes an infant with her and leaves another with the husband. Then she marries a second time, also has children from the second husband and a second time divorces, and this time leaves all the children both from the first and from the second marriage with the second husband. I saw little love of parents for their children. Above all, brothers and sisters are friendly to one another. At a strikingly early age children cease being children. They are very serious, rarely play pranks and you can entrust them with important things to do, which they will take care of and not make a mess of it. Their independent life begins very early.

The Abyssinian woman is terribly coquettish and beautiful; but for the most part, she is short, poorly built and rarely has many children. Having few children must be due to the very early marriages. I knew a case where a girl seven years old was given in marriage. They marry quite frequently at nine years old, regardless of whether they are physically completely developed. The position of women is very free in the lower class and completely closed in the higher class. Eunuchs watch over them. They cannot go anywhere without a huge escort. In other words, on those rare occasions she is accompanied by her whole staff of chamber maids and eunuchs, and they sit her on the mule and take her off the mule, closely screening her by shammas from the view of strangers. In the higher class, almost all women are literate and even well-read. Very often, important correspondence is carried on between husband and wife. Since relations between the sexes are very easy, there are almost no instances of love affairs and jealousy. Catching the wife in infidelity at the scene of the crime, the husband has the right, with impunity, to kill both of them, and usually does so. But until such time as the infidelity has not been clearly discovered, the husband does not express either jealousy or suspicion. The closed conditions of women of the upper class are stipulated by etiquette.

The birth of a child is not a prominent, happy event in the family. For the Abyssinian woman a child is almost always a burden. At birth, a male child is circumcised on the seventh day and christened on the twentieth. A female child is circumcised on the fourteenth and christened on the fortieth. At the christening, the child is given the name of some saint. They never call themselves just by this name but always with prefixes, for instance Wolda Mikael—"birth of Michael," Gebra Maryam—"slave of Mary," Haile Iesus—"strength of Jesus." For the most part they do not call themselves by the name given at christening but with a nickname. There are some very original nicknames, for instance, Setayukh—"How much I see" or Enatenakh—"You are to mother," Sefraishu—"Find the place", and for women, for instance, Terunesh—"You a clean person," Worknesh—"You are gold," Deseta—"Happiness."

Death among them is a very sorrowful event, mourned by all the relatives and acquaintances. And on this occasion there appears a contradiction of their character. Indifferent in his family feelings, the Abyssinian comes from afar to mourn at the grave of a relative. The Abyssinian dies quietly, in spite of the fact that during a grave illness for several days before death, in his house a mass of people crowds together, before time, to mourn him. (By the way, this happened to me when I was seriously ill in December of 1896, and my servants believed that my end was coming.) When it is apparent that death is unavoidable, the person who is sick takes *kusso* (a purgative) to drive out parasitic worms before death. (It is considered indecent to die with these in one's stomach). Then he takes confession and is given communion. They wash the corpse, roll it up in linen and, with loud weeping, carry it to the church where, after mass, they bury it with the head to the east. They have mourners, but they do not collect the tears in a vessel. Relatives wear mourning clothes, consisting of dirty, torn and old clothing. For several days the closest relatives do not leave the house, and during this time everyone who knew the deceased pays his relatives a visit of sympathy; and, over a small bottle of *tej* (mead), they weep together with them. In such cases the effusiveness of the Abyssinian character is expressed. Whether he rejoices or grieves, he tries as much as possible to express this and let it be known. Their mimicry and manner of conducting themselves always corresponds remarkably to the occasion. For instance, mourning the death of someone who is a complete stranger, the Abyssinian seems at this time to be completely crushed by grief, and finally having convinced himself of this, he weeps almost sincerely.

The property of the deceased is divided among the children and among them they do not have the right of inheritance by the eldest. Always the land, and very often all the property of the deceased is inherited by whoever of the children was closest to him.

Abyssinian Division into Classes

Some writers compare present-day Abyssinia with Europe in feudal times and identify its system with the feudal system. But is this really so? The first condition of a feudal system is the division into classes and hereditary ownership and class advantages, which Abyssinia does not have. In Abyssinia there is an aristocracy of position—people who at the present moment are in power. There are merchants, priests, monks, soldiers, artisans, and peasants. But all of these are differences in positions or occupations, and not separate closed classes.

In Abyssinia there is no hereditary nobility, and it would even be unthinkable given the country's family structure. There are some families which lead their kin from afar. There are some who consider themselves descendants of kings and at this time are in the lowest position. In the Abyssinian language, there isn't even a word to express "nobility." Sometimes in an argument they say, that "I am bale abat," which means "one who has a father." But this is not to determine his noble parentage, but rather in contrast to someone whose father was a slave or who himself was a slave. The concept of hereditary nobility is incompatible with the practical mind of the Abyssinian. They admire wealth, position, and personal servants, as long as these elements of strength are evident. But if they should go away—if the wealthy man is impoverished, if the leader had his territory taken away from him, if someone who was powerful at court falls into disgrace, or if children of a powerful and great man do not represent anything remarkable by their wealth or position—then these people become equal with all others and the lowest soldier will talk down to them ["tutoyer" in French]. But nevertheless, when distinguishing among gentlemen, they always give preference to individuals whose fathers were in the same position.

Selection for the highest government posts is based on the principle of personal merit. And in addition to that, in order to be recognized as emperor, besides the actual power, one must have the ability to show that one is descended from Solomon.

*Ras*es and *Dajazmatch*es are very often relations by marriage or by blood with the reigning emperor and his wife. The emperor and empress try to tie them closer to the throne by having them marry their relatives. But some of them came from the very lowest positions.

Thus we see that nobility as a class does not exist, but there is a class of those in high positions; or you could call it a service aristocracy, the membership of which is half by chance. The concept of "mesalliance" does not exist in the upper class. They select their wife by desire, and sometimes from among the servants. Children of the upper class usually start out at a young age at the court of the emperor or of one of his principal leaders. There they carry out the responsibilities of a house servant and receive the highest Abyssinian education: they learn to play the lyre (*bagana*),[77] to play chess, reading, writing, theology and military exercises. Becoming personally known by the emperor or another individual at whose court they serve, and finally, winning the favor and confidence of him, they obtain some appointment. But at court are found not only the children of those in the highest posts, but also many who are there by chance. Posts are neither for life nor progressive. Each person who holds a post considers himself the direct servant of the person who gave him that assignment. The only similarity between present-day Abyssinia and Europe in feudal times is the apparently considerable independence of those who govern the territories, but as we will see later, this autonomy is very relative and the proprietorship is not hereditary.

The life of the upper class is very simple and uniform. In this regard it differs from the life of others. This crowded court and etiquette represents in miniature the court of the emperor. Their manner of conducting themselves with subordinates is notable for remarkable restraint and dignity. In general, the upper serving class have great qualities. They are very devoted to the leaders who assigned them to their job and zealously guard the interests of their patrons.

The Abyssinian clergy consists of "white"—priests and deacons, "black" and *debtera*—scribes, who are secular individuals who live in churches. The similarity to feudal times lies in the existence of ecclesiastical lands, very large and independent properties controlled by them. Each church has its land, half worked by peasants. Each monastery also has lands, and, in addition, their bishops and *ychygye* (the leader of the monastic order of Saint Abun Tekla Haymanot) own extensive lands. Each man who feels the vocation can go into the clerical ranks. But only those who have been prepared for it and who marry in a church ceremony are consecrated as priests. All deacons are children. Those who have prepared themselves for the clerical calling, but have not been consecrated as priests, not feeling this vocation, continue to live in churches and are called *debtera*—scholars or scribes. They have great influence on the affairs of the church. In each church, the leader of all the clergy who live there (the clergy of a parish can reach as high as 300 men in a single church and never is less than 25) and of the church lands is appointed from among the *debtera*. The clergy —especially the *debtera* and itinerant monks—have great influence on the people. Each person of the upper class has a confessor, who plays a large role in his family life. In the Abyssinian clergy, many characteristics of Judaism have been preserved. *Debtera*, for example, take the place of the former scribes and Levites. They sing during the church service, devote themselves to theology and copying holy books. The Abyssinians have preserved some ceremonies borrowed from the Jews. They read the Psalms of David more often than the Gospels. But, in spite of all that, Abyssinians, and especially their clergy, are ardent and sincere believers, and among their monks there are many ascetic heroes. (For more details on that see the chapter "Church and Faith.")

Military service is the favorite profession of Abyssinians, but having the full freedom of a person in the limits of the responsibilities he has taken on for himself, each enters into service by his own desire and choice. The army is very well paid and in peace time does not entail any work. (The army will be described in detail later.)

Merchants constitute a somewhat separate class and are subordinate to *nagada-rases* ("chief of traders"—of which there are three). Some towns are populated exclusively by merchants and regardless of the fact that they are located among other estates, they are governed separately from the others. The merchants are distinguished by great resourcefulness and commercial abilities, which they inherit, in all probability, from their Semite ancestors. They usually buy goods from Galla merchants and take them to the sea. Some even take them to Aden. Membership in the merchant class is as random as is membership in the other classes, and is not based either on heredity or on other positions.

Those who work the land (peasantry as a class does not exist) become such by their own desire. There are two kinds of them: those who pay rent to whoever has title to their land, whether this is the emperor or someone else, and those who in some provinces possess their own land. Abyssinian farms have less of a many-field system than Galla ones. They do not grow roots, as the Galla do. But they work the land well enough using the same tools as the Galla. The livestock among them is the same as among the Gallas: bulls, cows, sheep, goats, horses, mules, donkeys, and in the north there is a special breed of rams with very long wool.

The artisans—for the most part descendants of the Felasha—are concentrated at the courts of rulers. Weavers and smiths often live separately. Among the artisans are smiths, joiners, tanners, saddle makers, weavers, goldsmiths, and gunsmiths.

Abyssinian Slavery

Continuous wars which yield many prisoners, and the necessity for a large number of workers to support the way of life of the upper class gave rise to slavery. But this slavery is only similar in name to what we are accustomed to understanding by this term. By a law issued by the Emperor Menelik, slavery has been abolished in the country; and at risk of having one's hands cut off, it is forbidden to sell or buy slaves. Nevertheless, those who were captured earlier, and recently captured Gallas and Negroes stay at the homes of their masters and continue to work for them, receiving food and clothing in return. This is a very indefinite condition, which could not be called either slavery or freedom. For instance, a runaway when captured is returned to his former master and is punished for escaping, but the children of slaves are not slaves, and willingly, faithfully, by force of habit stay at home and serve their masters. To buy or sell slaves is forbidden, but you can give them. Today you can also say with certainty that the last remnants of slavery will soon be abolished and Abyssinians will change to paid labor since the way they conduct wars has already begun to change its character, turning from the former raids to conquest of new lands and annexation of them. Since all the conquered inhabitants are attached to the land, war will not yield slaves. But the slavery there is today is a very mild variety of it. They treat their slaves very well, do not force them in their work and consider them as members of the family.

Abyssinian Distribution of Property

The distribution of property in the country, despite the existence of a large number of beggars, is rather even. Few are those who stand out conspicuously above the general level. The right to own land only exists in a few provinces, namely Tigre and Shoa and others at a distance from the imperial power. All land belongs to the emperor. The distribution of land in central Abyssinia took place historically. Part is owned directly by the emperor, part is granted to the church, part is given to the proprietorship of private individuals half and half or by other arrangements, and part is distributed to military leaders in the form of pay. Galla lands together with their population belong to the emperor by right of conquest. All Galla are considered obliged to pay rent, and at the present time the same process is beginning which took place in Russia at the time of Boris Godunov —the process of turning people into serfs. Considering himself free, a Galla who is dissatisfied with the governor of the territory or with the burden of taxes abandons his home and goes to another Galla, who willingly accepts him. This phenomenon serves, in the first place, as a curb against too greedy administrators, but then, on the other hand, it gives rise to a large number of complaints against neighbors—a constant correspondence with demands for returning those who have left, which, of course, rarely succeed. In former times, the majority of Galla fled to the autonomous Galla lands—Leka, Wollaga and Jimma. But now the emperor has forbidden the rulers of these lands from accepting new immigrants. This should be the first step toward finally turning the whole Galla population into serfs.

The export and import trade of Abyssinia is in the hands of Abyssinians and a few Europeans: French, Armenians, and Greeks. For the most part, imports consist of guns (through Jibuti), cheap paper linen from India, glass vessels (small decanters), silk and velvet cloth, and small items. Exports consist of coffee, ivory, gold, musk, and skins. Both imports and exports are directed to four points—Massawa, Jibuti, Zeila, and Berber. Massawa has now, with the shift of the political center of Abyssinia to the south, lost its former significance. Jibuti is gaining more and more importance as the sole point for import of guns, but the main part of the native trade goes by way of Zeila to Aden. Berbera serves as the port for Somali lands and the southern regions of Jimma and Kaffa. Merchants sell their wares at marketplaces which are found at each little populated point. Exchange is conducted in money. The monetary unit is the Maria Theresa taler and pieces of salt (amulye) which are six vershoks [nine inches] long, and one vershok [one and three-quarters inches] thick. They give seven pieces of salt for one taler. Now the emperor is trying popularize coins of his own mint of various values, but up until now he has been unsuccessful.[78]

Abyssinian Games

It is said that how they pass their free time and games indicate the character of a people. In this regard, the Abyssinians have a wide range of games according to the time of the year and their appropriateness for big holidays. The Abyssinian sometimes does not play an unseasonable game, even though all the circumstances favor it.

In the month of September on the holidays of Maskal, Holy Cross Day, everyone who owns a horse plays guks. They prepare horses for this big game, and on the day of the holiday they all go out on the plain. This game is an imitation of actual individual cavalry combat. Dividing themselves in two groups, several dare-devils engage in battle. They fly at full career at someone on the opposite team and, not having galloped a hundred steps, sharply turn and gallop away. Those who are summoned and others with them pursue those who summoned them and throw at them a javelin without a point, which the others parry with their shield, and some who are dextrous parry with a javelin. Once started the battle becomes general: clouds of flying javelins, sometimes the dry sound of one striking a shield and a mass of riders racing forward and backward at full career. Among the horses, servants of the gentlemen dart in and out and bring them javelins. It is rare that such a game takes place without unfortunate accidents, sometimes ending in death, since besides the force of falling of the javelin, even without a point, is so great that it pierces the shield. And I know of an incident when one Abyssinian broke his arm because a javelin pierced through his shield. (By the way, the Gallas, having adopted this game from the Abyssinians, are enthusiastic about it even more than the Abyssinians are.)

In November begin the games that lead up to the great games of guna on Christmas. The people call the holiday of Christmas also guna. The reason for this, I believe, is the same as that among us in Russia, where a holiday of a pagan cult is timed to take place with a Christian one. For example, kolyada, Shrovetide, is the celebration of John the Baptist.

The game of guna consists of two teams, armed with wide sticks that are an arshin (28 inches) in length, try to drive a small piece of wood to the enemy's side. All, old and young, play at Christmas this game that, like guks, rarely can take place without unfortunate accidents.

From the beginning of Lent begins the time for the playing of was—a ball made of rags. One person, sitting on the shoulders of another, throws in a heap the playing balls. Whoever gets the ball sits on the shoulders of the one who threw it, and the game goes on forever.

At Easter again they play guks and the so-called giji. A thin pole is set us and they throw javelins at it from 50 paces. When someone hits the target three times, all the others lie on the ground and the winner goes past them.

In August after the rains, they play jiraf—long whip. All, having armed themselves with a long strap, are divided into two teams and try to drive one another away. In the end, the weaker team runs away. This also doesn't happen without mutilation.

These games have great educational significance. The whole nation takes great interest in them and these games demand from the player great endurance, dexterity, and quickness of understanding and accustom them to danger.

Their household games are senterei (chess) and gebeta, a kind of backgammon. The chess moves are the same as the way we play the game, but the circumstances are different. For example, the game is not considered lost if the king is taken. Gebeta is similar to backgammon, but dice are not thrown. Rather the game is based on calculation, so it requires very quick wits. On a board or simply on the ground, there are 12 or 18 little holes. At the beginning of the game half the holes belong to one player and half to the other. In each little hole there are three pebbles. Shifting these pebbles in accord with known rules, they win over from their opponent his holes and pebbles. The person whose last pebble arrives at a hole where there are three pebbles takes possession of that hole.

THE ETHIOPIAN SYSTEM OF GOVERNMENT

The empire of the now-reigning Menelik II, king of kings of Ethiopia, consists of the following domains. Listing them from north to south, they are:

Ras Mengesha Yohannes—Tigre. *Ras* Mengesha is a natural son of Emperor Yohannes IV.

Yohannes' legitimate son and heir to the throne was *Ras* Area, who married the daughter of Menelik—*Woyzaro* Shoareg. *Ras* Area died. The boundaries of Tigre once extended to the shores of the sea; but first Turks and Egyptians and, especially in recent times, Italians drove back the Abyssinians to the other side of the Mareb River. Although the Italians were defeated in the last war, in the peace treaty it is assumed that the boundaries stay at Belesa-to-Mareb.[79]

Ras Wali—the mountain province to the south of Tigre: Lasta Samyen, Eju.

He is a brother of the Empress Taitu and son of the Tigrean *Ras* Wolda Giyorgis.

The dynasty of the Wag*shum*s—the provinces of Wag and Derru. There are two brothers: Wag*shum* Wangul and Wag*shum* Kabeda. They are a strong Jewish type, but in all probability their ancestors were Felasha kings, since the mountains of Samena and Wag are populated by them. (Felasha are Abyssinian Jews).

Ras Mikael—Wollo. *Ras* Mikael, baptized by the Emperor Yohannes, is a Galla, formerly king of Wollo.

Negus Tekla Haymanot is king of Gojjam, Damot, Amhara, Gindeberat, Jimma, Lima, Guder and Horro.

Negus Tekla Haymanot, formerly *Ras* Adal, is the son of *Ras*

Gosho. He was crowned *Negus* by Atye Yohannes in 1881 for the conquest of Kaffa.

Ras Mengesha Bituaded[80]—Gondar and Begamedyr. The title bituaded means "favorite." It is usually given to one of the *Ras*es who is closest to the reigning emperor. He is entrusted with the government of the provinces of Gondar and Begamedyr. The city of Gondar was formerly the official capital of Abyssinia. (Today, besides *Ras* Mengesha Bituaded there is a Bituaded Atnafi, an old man, ruler of a small area, and a favorite of the *Negus*.)

Azzajs—those who rule lands of Emperor Menelik, are generals of his own army. They rule parts of the kingdom of Shoa, the hereditary domain of Emperor Menelik. Shoa consists of the provinces of Tegulet, Ifat, Menjar, Bulga and Ankober.

Ras Makonnen—Harar, Chercher, Itu, Erer, Ogaden. *Ras* Makonnen is a nephew of the emperor on his mother's side.

Dajazmatch Wolda Gabriel—Bali and part of Arussi.

Ras Dargi—Arussi, the homeland of the Galla people. *Ras* Dargi is the son of Atye Sahle Selassie, the grandfather of Menelik. Besides this recently conquered province, he also rules a small region near Gondar. He is very dear to the emperor and has great influence.

Dajazmatch Balachio—Sidamo. Formerly Lyj, Balachio is a son of *Dajazmatch* Beshakha. Balachio was in Petersburg with the embassy of Damto. This year on the occasion of the death of his father, killed at Adowa, the emperor gave him the government of his father's former lands. The other half of Sidamo is ruled by *Dajazmatch* Mul Saged.

Fitaurari Abto Giyorgis—Gurage and Sodo.

Dajazmatch Haile Maryam—Chobo, Bocho and Tikur.

Dajazmatch Haile Maryam is a nephew of the emperor, the oldest brother of *Ras* Makonnen.

Dajazmatch Ubye—Mecha, Ejir-Salafu, and Nonno. Ubye is married to *Woyzaro* Zawditu, the second daughter of Emperor Menelik.

Dajazmatch Demissew—Gera, Guma, Gomo, Buna, Leka and Wollaga. He is the son of *Afa-negus* Nasibu, the chief judge. He has the main supervision of the autonomous Galla provinces of Leka, under *Dajazmatch* Gebra Egziabeer and Wollaga, under *Dajazmatch* Joti.

Likamakos Abata—Chalea, Tibye, Wobo, and Sibu. Likamakos is a court rank equivalent to Adjutant General.

Dajazmatch Tesemma—Ilu-Babur, Buna, Burye, Alye, and all the southwestern areas of Abyssinia. Tessema, the son of *Dajazmatch* Nadou, is married to the god-daughter of Empress Taitu, the daughter of the Galla king
of Guma.

Ras Wolda Giyorgis—Botor-Limu, Kulo, Kosho, Konta-Shiro. He also has main supervision over the kingdom of Jimma of Aba-Jefar. (*Negus* Aba-Jefar is a Mohammedan.)

The recently conquered province of Walamo is directly under the command of Menelik. These days, Abdurakhman, the king of Beni-Shangul has submitted to the Emperor.

All these domains are not hereditary, but rather are bestowed by the Emperor (with the exception of the domains of *Negus* Tekla Haymanot, Tigre, the kingdom of Jimma, Leka, and Wollaga). The size of each domain depends purely on personal factors—on the relationship of the Emperor to the proprietor and on his personal merit, and consists of one or several provinces. The connection between these provinces is not permanent and can always be broken either by one of them being taken away or by the addition of a new area. All these "polymarchs," as these rulers of regions can be called, are completely independent in internal affairs, justice, the distribution of lands and jobs. But in all else they are absolutely under the command of the Emperor. They recognize his power and pay him tribute in the form of taxes or presents.

In general, Ethiopia represents a single state, divided for government among the main military leaders, under the absolute imperial power of the king of kings, all the strength of whom rests in the army and in the love of the people.

A necessary condition to becoming Emperor is belonging to the house of Solomon and Menelik I. (The exception to this was the dynasty of Zagye and the Emperors Tewodros and Yohannes.)

From this we see that the Ethiopian Empire is a purely military state. It became this historically, having earlier experienced many other phases.

It is not within the limits of my work to describe the history of Ethiopia, but I consider it necessary to indicate some of its prominent moments.

History of Ethiopia

The name "Ethiopia," which the Abyssinians give to their country, is a Greek word and in translation means "black face." Homer called all of Central Africa "Ethiopia," stretching from the Red Sea and the Indian Ocean to the Atlantic. Diodor the Sicilian distinguished three Ethiopias: Western—the Congo Basin, High—the present-day highlands of Ethiopia, and Eastern—which included the lower, east coast of Africa and South-Western Arabia.

In the history of Ethiopia, the following moments can be distinguished:

1. The period which preceded the Queen of Sheba. This period is almost completely unknown with regard to what is now Ethiopia, and apparently doesn't have any connection with it.

2. The Queen of Sheba and the Solomonic[81] dynasty which followed her were displaced by King Del Noad of the Zagye dynasty in the year 901 A.D. According to the Abyssinian Tarika Negest, the Queen of Sheba, having heard about the greatness of Solomon, went to him and had by him a son named Menelik or Ybnakhakim. There is much disagreement regarding the etymology of this word. Several believe that it derives from the Amharic words men which means "what" and alykh which means "you say." In other words, "what you say or tell." Others translate Menelik as "second I." But the name Ybnakhakim, which is equivalent to Menelik, comes from the Arabic, and the most probable translation for that is "descended from a wise man." Hakim—"wise"—was the Arabic name for Solomon.

The Queen of Sheba, Azyeb or the Southerner, also had many other names: Makeda and Nikola. The Abyssinians affirm that Aksum was her capital, but others say it was Yemen. There is also dissension among scholars on this question. Some, such as, for example, Patriarch Mendes and Bruce,[82] accept the legend about her journey to Solomon and consider her to be actually a queen of Aksum. Others (such as Pined) consider her to be an Arabian queen. Most probably, she ruled both present-day Ethiopia and the Arabian peninsula, at least part of the one and the other, since between Arabia and Ethiopia there was a close connection at that time, based on the continual migration of Semites to Africa.

The legend says further that Menelik, having come of age, was sent to Jerusalem. He was supposed to give Solomon gifts from his mother. Abyssinians have preserved the legend that at the time of his reception for the first time by Solomon, Solomon, wanting to test his son, stood in the ranks of his retinue, and on the throne placed one of his retainers. Menelik, although he had never seen his father, having first bowed to the man on the throne, did not give him the gifts, but rather began to search with his eyes among the retinue and, having finally seen Solomon, bowed to him.

He was very similar to his father and enjoyed great popularity. As a result of this, it is said that Solomon, having generously given him presents and many Levites, priests and children of many noble families, let him return to his homeland. On leaving, Menelik, it is said, stole the Ark of the Covenant and one of the tablets of Moses.

He reigned under the name of David. He converted his whole people to Judaism and abolished idolatry in the country.

In the ninth year of the reign of Bazen, a king of this dynasty, Christ was born.

At the time of the fortieth king of this dynasty, Abrekh-Atsebakh, the light of Christian learning penetrated Abyssinia in the person of Saint Frumentius, called by the Abyssinians Aba Salama (343 A.D.)

From this dynasty in 521 A.D. there reigned King Kaleb who had undertaken a campaign against the Jewish King Zu-Nuvas,[83] well-known for his oppression of Christians of Nauad. Kaleb defeated Zu-Nuvas, and the Ethiopian kingdom was founded by the son of Kaleb, Abrekh, who then died at the siege of Mecca. His two sons were routed by the Persians and the kingdom was destroyed.

3. In 901 A.D. the Zagye dynasty was established and reigned until 1255 when on the imperial throne again appeared a king from the dynasty of Solomon thanks to the insistence of Saint Tekla Haymanot. The man who re-established the dynasty was Ikuna Amlak. The most outstanding member of the dynasty of Zagye was King Lalibala, ranked by the Abyssinians as one of the saints. He is known as a builder of churches. Legend also attributes to him an attempt to divert the water of the Nile to the Red Sea.[84]

4. Beginning with Ikuna Amlak in the Tarika Negest more detailed descriptions make there appearance. This period, which continued until the invasion of Gran in 1534 A.D., is very similar to the Middle Ages in Europe. Apparently, in this era, the feudal system flourished. The king was only the first feudal lord of his kingdom. There existed individual land property of the gentry with hereditary rights and privileges.

From 1434 to 1468 Atye Zara Yakob reigned, and in his reign Ethiopia attained its highest brilliance of power and majesty. He was an ardent Christian and was interested in church dogma.

In his reign, a church council was convened, and the dogma was established about the Holy Trinity—one in nature and three in persons. The first relations with Europe were started by him. At the time of the Florentine Council he wrote through Aba Nikodim, the father superior of the Abyssinian church in Jerusalem, a letter to Pope Eugene IV. He conquered Kaffa, Mocha, and Enareya and converted them to Christianity. According to tradition, he gave those lands their names. "Kaffa" comes from the word kefu which means "evil." Mocha comes from mot, which means "death." And Enareya in translation means "slaves," since those who were conquered were turned to slaves.

After the death of Atye Zara Yakob, relations were opened with Portugal.

In Europe, the legend of "Prester John" circulated. He reigned somewhere in the East—in India or in Africa. The Portuguese King John sent John Covilha and Alfonso de Paiva to find him. The second died on the way, but the first reached Ethiopia, visited at the court of Atye Eskender and reported to his government that he had found "Prester John."

When Eskender died, there ascended the throne the under-age Lebna Dengel, known by the name of David. His grandmother, Eleni, threatened from the east and the south by Mohammedans, sent Covilha with an Armenian named Matthew to the Portuguese King Dom Manuel with a request for help. In reply was sent a mission, consisting of Duarte Galvano, Rodrigo de Lima, Alvares and Bermudes. All of them, with the exception of Galvano, who died in the Kamaran Islands, reached David II in 1520.

The wars of Gran and the mission of Portuguese and Jesuits that took place then are sharply distinguished from the rest of the history of Ethiopia, almost constituting a separate epoch. The Abyssinian Tarika Negest says almost nothing about these events. But Portuguese sources, and in particular Jeronimo Lobo ("Voyage historique d'Abyssinie")[85], elucidates for us this epoch, which lasted from 1534 to 1635, when the Jesuits were expelled by Emperor Fatsilidas.[86]

The embassy of Rodrigo de Lima and Alvares returned in 1526 and brought with them an Abyssinian monk—Saga za Ab or Christovl Likonat. Rodrigo carried with him a letter to the Portuguese king and Alvares carried one to the Pope. But in 1534 Gran appeared, and the frightened David sent Bermudes to the Portuguese king with a request for help and promise to adopt the Roman faith and give a third of his lands to the Portuguese. King John III appointed Estevano da Gama, son of the famous Vasco da Gama, as viceroy of India. ("India" at that time was the name for all the eastern coast of Africa and present-day Abyssinia.) He ordered him to destroy the Turkish and Arabian fleets in the Red Sea. He didn't succeed in finding the Turkish fleet, and he put ashore 400 Portuguese under the command of Christovao da Gama (his brother) at Massawa. This landing of troops was very opportune since the Ethiopian empire was at that time in a critical position. Gran had for several years managed to put all of Abyssinia to fire and sword, beginning with Menjar and up to Aksum, which he torched and destroyed. But what kind of man was Gran and what were these hordes that came with him?

Lobo calls him a Moor from the cape of Guardafui and his horde also Moors (however, Portuguese called almost all Mohammedans "Moors.") Bruce also calls his army "Moors." In Portuguese sources he is called King of Adal and Emir of Zeila, and they conjecture that he was Somali. But how is this? In Lobo's book, the entire east cost of the Gulf of Tajura is called Zeila, and nothing is mentioned of Harar, which at that time was a considerable city and an independent region. Evidently, he did not know about Harar. The province of Harar was originally populated by a people related by blood to Agau, Guragye and Kaffa —in other words, pre-Semitic inhabitants of the plateau. Before their invasion into Ethiopia, the Galla occupied all the lands of Harar, and its surviving inhabitants gathered in one place and built the city of Harar and preserved their national independence up until that time. Both Galla and the people of Harar, who were close to the coast and consequently in the sphere of influence of Islam, were among the first to adopt Mohammedanism. According the unanimous traditions of the Abyssinians, Galla and people of Harar, Ahmad Gran was born close to Harar and was a Galla. The indication in history that he was king of Adal (the inhabitants of Aussa on the coast of the Gulf of Tajura, located to the north from the Somalis, are called Adalis) doesn't prove anything, because, in all probability, he was the chief of the whole Mohammedan population, including Adalis and Somalis, and they, for a certainty, helped him in his campaigns. But the main part of his armies consisted of Galla. This is demonstrated by the fact that all the conquered Abyssinian lands were settled by none other than the Galla— Galla of Wollo, Borena, and Tuluma. In the ranks of his armies were janissaries, Turkish riflemen and artillery, who were sent to him at his request after the defeat inflicted on him by the Portuguese. I give very little credence to the indication that the Adalis were armed with guns, since if in the last expedition of the Adalis to Aussa, instead of using Rozdan or Italian guns, they preferred to hang them on trees, then, I think all the more that, at that time, they were not capable of operating fire-arms.

The Portuguese who had landed were ceremoniously met by Eleni, who saw them as her saviors. The Emperor Galawdewos was at that time in Gondar. Da Gama went to him. At Belut the first battle with Gran took place, where 400 Portuguese, thanks to their fire-arms, completely crushed a many-times stronger enemy. Nevertheless, in view of their small numbers, they were forced to spend the winter in Membret, surrounded by once again assembled hordes of Gran, to whom were now joined Turkish riflemen and artillery. In the battle that took place there, Christovao da Gama was killed, and the remaining Portuguese joined forces with Emperor Klavdiy in Damby. Gran went there and attacked Galawdewos, but the Portuguese Peter Lev killed him, and this decided the outcome of the battle and the Galla invasion. This happened in 1547.

Gran was an outstanding personality and to this day still lives in the memory of the people, who ascribe to him supernatural qualities. For example, they say that on the Chercher road a spring summoned forth from a stone by a stroke of Gran's spear; and as evidence of that, they point to traces of his sword in the rock, etc. He was able to unite and direct toward a single general goal tribes that are extremely freedom-loving and independent, and of which, besides, some are completely different from others by their lineage and their language. The epoch of Gran threatened Abyssinia with terrible danger. But with his death, this danger went away, because neither before Gran nor after him was there a personality who could unite all these tribes together. Part of his forces went back, and part stayed on the conquered lands and engaged in raids against Abyssinians and civil war. In the south there continued a war of separate families for land, and the Galla, not stopping, a little at a time, gave way more and more to the west.

The despotism, exactingness, and lack of tact of the Portuguese meant that they could not excite sympathy toward themselves, and we see that discord began between Emperor Klavdiy and them, and that he expelled Patriarch Bermudes. But with this expulsion the pretensions of the Vatican on Ethiopia did not end. We see a whole series of Catholic patriarchs of Ethiopia, a whole series of Jesuit missions, which busied themselves more with politics than faith, and relied more on the strength and prestige of Portugal than on their strength of persuasion. The results were the same as in the states of Europe—hatred of the people, civil war, plots, discord and finally the expulsion of the Jesuits. This was a significant period in the history of Abyssinia. Having started relations with Europe, freed by Europeans from ruin, Abyssinia was very close to complete unity with Europe, if only the Europeans had been a little more tactful and not so demanding. But instead of this, what happened was completely opposite. They had to save themselves from their saviors. And having learned such a lesson, the Abyssinians have been prejudiced against whites up until this time, and will be so even longer.

6. The epoch that followed this one, from 1635 to 1769, the year of the death of Atye Ayto Ioas,[87] can be called the time of development of imperial power on the ground of the feudal system which had been destroyed by the Galla invasion. In this epoch was laid the foundation, which, completed by King Tewodros, would constitute the basis of today's empire. This basis was the military organization of the empire and the fact that the well-being of everyone depended on the kindness of the emperor.

The native lands of the Abyssinians which had been conquered by the Galla were once again taken back by the emperors and, as if by right of conquest of new lands, were declared the property of the king. This produced a revolution in the life of the people. Up until that time in Abyssinia there existed class division: there were nobles, who owned land, and there were peasants, who worked half and half for large landholders. In this way a blow was dealt to the nobility, but the peasants continued to live in their former conditions, with this difference—that they became obligated for the land to the emperor himself. This revolution took place imperceptibly. At first only the legal situation was proclaimed—that all land belongs to the emperor. But by the smallest steps, little by little, lands were taken away and given to others. In addition, separate districts were formed which were responsible for some special service, for instance a district of spear carriers etc. Each possesses a district on condition of known obligations to the empire. The small districts carried out the above named auxiliary service. Those that were more sizable were obliged to supply a known number of soldiers in time of mobilization. The number of soldiers depended on the size of the district.

In this manner, the old feudal system was completely destroyed, and a new foundation was established which gave the empire great strength. The population was divided into two parts. One went to the land on known conditions. The other grouped itself around the throne, the source of charity and prosperity, and placed all their hope in service to the emperor. Around the emperors there formed a significant army, which they used more for the expansion of the boundaries of the empire than for internal wars, whereas before it had been the reverse. The army itself was almost obliged to conduct war, since without it there would be no means to satisfy its needs. Thus we see that the former citizens who took up arms only for self-defense, were turned into soldiers for whom war is a profession, and the hereditary feudal lords turned into non-hereditary polymarchs.

7. In this epoch the same cause which gave rise to the previous epoch now brought it down almost completely. This era, beginning with the death of Atye Ayto Ioas in 1769, continued to the accession to the throne of Emperor Tewodros II in 1855.

Due to the greatly increasing power of separate military leaders, civil wars occurred in the country. The strongest of the military leaders captured Begamedyr and crowned his pretender to the throne from the house of Solomon, having forced him to proclaim himself "*Ras* Bituaded." And Begamedyr ruled the empire under this title. Among these Bituadeds was the remarkable dynasty of *Ras* Guksa. Guksa was the grandson of Ali the Great, a Galla Mohammedan, chief of the Iju tribe.[88] The descendants of Guksa for a long time disposed of the throne of Ethiopia by their arbitrary rule.

The reign of Tewodros II[89] marked the beginning of the revival of imperial power, which has now attained its apogee.

I am not going to enlarge upon the reigns of Tewodros II and Yohannes IV[90]. In general outline, these reigns are well known to all, and in detail each of them could be the subject of a separate work. I will stop only at the history of the accession to the throne of Emperor Menelik and several years of his reign. Menelik was the son of the Shoan *Negus* Haile Malakot, grandson of Sahle Selassie,[91] (patron of Europeans) who is well known from the works of d'Hericourt.[92] He traces his family from Solomon. The kingdom of Shoa, separated from the rest of Ethiopia by Gallas of Wollo, kept its independence and ancient traditions and peacefully prospered while the rest of Ethiopia was torn apart with civil wars. Originally, the ruler of Shoa, one of the sons of Zara Yakob, had the title of meridazmatch.[93] With the fall of imperial power, the meridazmatches of Shoa took the title of *Negus* and declared themselves independent. Emperor Tewodros, having set his sights on uniting and restoring the empire, launched a campaign against Haile Malakot, the king of Shoa. In 1856, the Shoans were beaten, Haile Malakot was killed and the government of Shoa was given to the brother of Haile Malakot, Ato Ayale,[94] with the title of meridazmatch. Eleven-year-old Menelik (who was born in 1845)[95] was taken prisoner together with all the remaining relatives of Haile Malakot.

As soon as Tewodros went away, a brother of Ato Ayale who had fled, Ato Seyfu united with Ato Bezaby[96] and went against Ayale. They defeated him and divided Shoa among themselves. But four years later, Tewodros returned to punish the rebels. Ato Bezaby was able to obtain pardon and gain the confidence of Tewodros, but Ato Seyfu fled and was killed. The government of the whole kingdom of Shoa was given to Ato Bezaby, who ruled until 1866, the time of the return of Menelik. That year, 20-year-old Menelik fled with only one slave Wolda Tadik (now *Azzaj* Wolda Tadik, ruler of Ankober) to the ruler of Wollo. The son of that ruler was at that time in captivity at Tewodros,' and he, intending to do Tewodros a service and mitigate the lot of his son, put Menelik, who had come to him, in chains and decided to give him to the emperor. At this time news arrived that his son had been executed. In revenge for this, he freed Menelik and with honors and an escort sent him to Ankober. Menelik ceremoniously entered there and was accepted by the populace as the legal king. The cruelty and injustice of Ato Bezaby for the time when he governed the region succeeded in setting the whole population against him. Around Menelik quickly gathered the former soldiers of his father and grandfather, and he declared himself *Negus*. Having learned of all this, Ato Bezaby, who was at that time at the borders of Shoa, hastened to Ankober with his whole army, but the day before the battle all the soldiers went over to the side of Menelik. Bezaby was taken prisoner and the *Negus*, having forced him to pay a fine of 2000 talers for "disrespect to the legal king," pardoned him. Regarding this episode, I heard the following story, that on the day of battle not accompanied by anyone, Menelik set out for the enemy side; and that with a speech, in which he declared himself the legal king and gave himself into their hands, he drew them all to his side. Later Bezaby again rebelled and paid for it by dying. In 1868 Magdala fell and King Tewodros killed himself.

After a short interregnum the Tigrean *Dajazmatch* Kassa ascended the throne and was crowned in 1872 under the name of Yohannes IV. *Negus* Menelik at first did not recognize him and in the year of his accession to the throne wrote a letter to the English resident in Aden, explaining his legal right to the imperial throne. In 1881 Emperor Yohannes, pursuing, as had Tewodros, the idea of uniting and restoring the empire, went against Menelik. The matter did not reach a battle, since Menelik, having secured beforehand the consent of Yohannes, went to him at his camp with an expression of submissiveness—a stone around his neck. Yohannes pardoned him and confirmed him in kingly dignity.

The personality of Emperor Yohannes was in the highest degree remarkable. He was a Christian fanatic and made up his mind not to have any Moslems among his subjects. He forcibly converted them to Christianity. Just as Tewodros, he dreamed of the restoration of the greatness of the Ethiopian empire. He intended for the empire to consist of four kingdoms: Tigre, Gojjam, Wollo, and Shoa. In each kingdom he intended to have a separate bishop and to this end he sent for four abunas from Alexandria, paying 10,000 talers for each. In 1881 he, with this aim, crowned as the Gojjam *Negus Ras* Adalya, who took the name of *Negus* Tekla Haymanot. But the great plans of Emperor Yohannes were not destined to come true. In 1889 he was accidentally killed at the siege of Metamma.

At that time Menelik, supported by Italy, had put together a conspiracy with *Negus* Tekla Haymanot against Yohannes.

Relations of Menelik with Europe began from the very first year of his rise to the throne of Shoa. When Italy took Assaba there started up the most lively relations between him and it. Having aroused his ambitious intentions, Italy thought to raise Menelik against Yohannes and having divided them to conquer them separately, following the principle of "divide et impera" [divide and conquer.]

The Red Sea coast belonged to Ethiopia up until the seventeenth century. But with the loss of a large part of its lands at the time of the Galla invasion it also lost the coastal region. In 1557 Massawa was taken by the Turks which gave it to the Egyptians in 1866. In 1869 the Italian steamship company Rubatino bought from the Adal Sultan of Rakheyta, Beregan, the port of Assaba with adjacent territory up to Rakheyta, and in 1879 gave all this to the Italian government.

From this time there were engendered in Italy interests in Eastern Africa, and Italy used every chance to expand its possessions. In 1881 a convention was concluded with Beregan, the Sultan of Rakheyta, concerning the mission of the Italian protectorate (perhaps this convention was just as hollow as the Treaty of Wichale). On March 15, 1883, a treaty was concluded with the Aussa Sultan about free transport of goods through his possessions. On May 22 1883 a commercial treaty was concluded with Menelik, *Negus* of Shoa. In 1885, the Egyptians abandoned Massawa and their possessions on the eastern shore, and Massawa was slowly taken by Italy. The new possessions received the name of the Eritrean Colony, and with this was laid the beginning of the struggle between Italy and Abyssinia which so tragically ended for Italy last year.

Italy was extremely interested in these new acquisitions. Diplomatic ties were begun with Ethiopia. A whole series of travelers set out to study the country, and many of them paid for it with their life (Jullietti was killed in 1881, Bianchi was killed in 1884, Count Porro, Chiarini).[97] Ambitious plans were engendered in Italy.

In 1887 the first catastrophe happened. Considering the seizure of the territory adjacent to Massawa an encroachment on his rights, Emperor Yohannes sent his best military leader, *Ras* Alulu, who at Dogali destroyed an entire Italian detachment of 500 men. This led to the equipping that same year of an entire expedition which without opposition took Saati in 1888.

An Italian diplomat, Count Antonelli, energetically worked at this time to sow discord and civil war in the country. They incited Menelik against Yohannes, promised him support and supplied him with arms. They also tried to incite the Gojjam *Negus* to revolt. In 1888 the Sultan of Aussa accepted the protectorate of Italy.

Negus Menelik, who for a long time had felt his dependence on the emperor as a burden, conspired against the Emperor Yohannes, having agreed to act together with the Gojjam *Negus* Tekla Haymanot. Emperor Yohannes, having found out about this, wrote insulting letters to both of them with the threat of punishing them. But his position was difficult. Enemies surrounded him from all sides. Having left the Italians, Yohannes went against the Gojjam King and forced him to submit again. Having finished with him, Yohannes wanted to deal the same with his second opponent, Menelik, but at this time in the west dervishes swept into Galabat, and Yohannes, putting off the punishment of Menelik for another time, proceeded against them, where he was killed at the siege of Metamma on March 11, 1889.

When he received news of the death of Yohannes, Menelik immediately went to Gondar where he was crowned emperor. Between him and *Negus* Tekla Haymanot, who also had a claim on the imperial throne, civil war broke out, which ended in the complete victory of Menelik, who took from his opponent almost all the land to the south of the Abbay River and left him only his native possessions.

Ras Zaudi was appointed *Ras* Bituaded in Begamedyr, but he soon conspired against Menelik. At first, it seemed that everything favored Zaudi, but at the decisive minute the troops went over to the side of their legal king. Zaudi was captured, put in chains and to this time still lives on one of the mountains in Ankober.

The government of Menelik was distinguished for its justice, restraint, lawfulness and concern for the people and the army. The war cry of his soldiers: Aba Danya—"father judge" (the name of his horse)—serves as his best character reference. For the soldiers he did not grudge them money nor food and tirelessly tried to obtain as many more guns as he could. His popularity was very high, and the number of his troops grew. He divided them into regiments of 1000 men each, and gave them to rulers in the outlying districts, to ensure against rebellion by those rulers. His reign was marked by continuous wars against the Gallas and constant expansion of territory. He had some outstanding military leaders: *Ras* Gobana, *Fitaurari* Gabayu and several others. *Ras* Gobana is now a legendary personality in Abyssinia. He was a Galla, a remarkable cavalryman, an outstanding athlete and courageous man. He conquered for Menelik all the Galla lands to the west from Entotto to Beni-Shangul and to the southwest to the River Baro, to the east and south together with the Emperor he conquered Harar, Arussi and Guragye. He died in 1890 as a result of an accidental fall from a horse during a game of guks. Arussi was conquered in 1886. In 1887 in a battle at Chialanko, Emir Abdulakhi was defeated; and a result of his defeat was the annexation of Harar. In 1892 Walamo was subdued. In 1896 Menelik covered himself with glory at Adowa and showed Europe that such was the present-day Ethiopia and such is her power.

But we will turn to a continuation of the history of the relations of Menelik with Italy. Making use of the troubled times, of the change of regimes, the Italians tried to seize as much land as they could, and succeeded in doing so. In the year that Menelik ascended the imperial throne, they concluded with him the Treaty of Wichale. That is so well known that I won't say anything further about it.[98]

The friendship of Italy, which at first was advantageous for Menelik, now became a burden for him, thanks to the claims and seizures of the Italians. Relations quickly changed for the worse and ended in an open break and war. At this time another power, interested in the failure and weakening of Italy—France —appeared to help Menelik. France also owned the coast of the Red Sea which was closest to Shoa and Harar. In 1862, Frenchmen bought Oboka. In 1884 it established a protectorate over the Somali coast of the Gulf of Tajura from *Ras*-Dumeyra (to the south of Rakheyta) to the the well of Hadu (to the south from Jibuti). In 1888 the spheres of influence were demarcated between France and England. In 1886 was established the governorship of Oboka and the Somali coast, and from this time France had active official relations with Abyssinia, vigilantly and jealously following its politics.

The help of France to Menelik at the time of his struggle with Italy consisted of admission and delivery of firearms. We know how this struggle ended. We are familiar with its details. And the war that followed is fresh in our memory.

From this short outline we see that the history of Ethiopia is one of continual war with both internal and external enemies. The basis of imperial power can only be actual military strength, and on the army as on a foundation, has been built all the rest of the edifice of the Ethiopian Empire. What kind of an army is this?

The Military[99]

Almost all those who have traveled in Abyssinia and written something about it always have given information about the military. They described the hierarchy, the numbers, the tactics and other details. Many have admired its bravery. But isn't it strange that none of them has touched upon the most important feature of this army? Why is it that one person has a large army and another a small one? Perhaps because one has greater means and land? No, that is only partly true. Most important here is the soldiers and how to pay them and how to rouse them.

The Abyssinian army is the Abyssinian people with its distinctive characteristics—independence and a critical attitude to everything. It is more developed than the rest of the population, extremely sensitive and rather spontaneous. The soldier goes to serve whoever suits him best, whoever is popular for his generosity, good fortune and personality. For example, Menelik now has 60,000 of his own soldiers and Tekla Haymanot has 5,000 in all; and formerly these numbers were the reverse.

The Abyssinian army—this spontaneous army, seems to us, Europeans, disorganized. But in the apparent disorganization are contained historically developed traditions, internal discipline and a manner of conducting war. Its relation to the European manner of conducting war can be compared to the relation of a trained horse to one which has not yet been broken. Anyone who is somewhat acquainted with the rules of riding can ride a trained horse. But only a good horseman can ride one which has not been broken. The Abyssinian army requires outstanding military leaders and, in actuality, has an excellent cadre of officers. But let's look into it in more detail.

Numbers and Organization of the Military

The Abyssinian army consists of the following types of troops:
1) The personal regular troops of the emperor.
2) Private regular troops of individual military leaders.

3) Territorial troops assembled only in case of mobilization.
4) Irregulars.

The personal regular troops of the emperor or, as they are called, gondari constitute the main body of the army and support of the throne. There are about 60,000 of them, part divided in regiments of 1,000 men under the leadership of bashi, and each regiment divided into companies (units of a hundred) and half companies. Companies are under the leadership of a yamato alaka. Half companies are under a yaamsa alaka. The leader of a half company appoints a sergeant major to help him. In addition, a half company is divided into squads of five to ten men.

The field army is divided into two parts. One half is found near the emperor, and the other half at the borders and with separate rulers with the aim, first, of increasing their military strength against internal and external enemies, and second, in order to hold them well in hand.

Private regular troops of individual military leaders consist of soldiers personally recruited by them, armed and paid by them, and serving them personally. These troops are not broken into regiments like the personal troops of the emperor.

They are distributed among officers of this or that military leader, each of whom has the right to recruit their own soldiers as well, in addition to soldiers given to them by their senior leader. The number of troops of individual leaders is not determined by law for each separately, but rather depends on the wealth, the popularity of the leader, and the size of the region that provides the means for maintaining the troops. At the present time, the largest of these is that of *Ras* Darga, with up to 30,000 men. In total, there are about 90,000 of this kind of troops.

Territorial and auxiliary troops consist of owners of plots of land, which are connected with the obligation of service in time of war. There are plots which supply porters and others which supply warriors. The number of men supplied by each plot of land depends on its size. These auxiliary troops are not organized in separate detachments; but rather are distributed in units that already exist. Their total number is between 80,000 and 100,000 men.

Irregular troops consist of inhabitants who voluntarily join the army. Most of them are Galla. Their number is very indeterminate and depends on the circumstances and the expedition which is being undertaken.

MILITARY HIERARCHY

As we already saw, only part of the regular troops of the emperor are distributed in thousand-man regiments. The rest of them are unequally distributed among military leaders.

The Military

The military hierarchy is extremely involved and cannot in any way be reduced to a table of ranks. In concept, the gradation of ranks seems to be in the following steps:

Negus negasti—the emperor, commander-in-chief of all armies.
Negus—king, commander of the army of his own kingdom.
Ras—field marshal, independent commander of the army of his region or of one of the armies of the emperor or of a *Negus*.
Dajazmatch—full general or lieutenant general, commander either of his own army or of a detachment of the emperor, of a *Negus* or of a *Ras*.
Fitaurari—major general, leader of either a separate army or one of the detachments of the emperor, a *Negus*, a *Ras*, or a *Dajazmatch*. Etymologically, *fitaurari* means "to plunder forward," in other words, leader of the advance guard.
Kanyazmatch—colonel, leader of a detachment. This word can be translated as "leader of the right wing," but this is completely untrue. They are just as often on the left wing as on the right. Zmatch means "nobleman" and kan means "right."
  In other words, "nobleman of the right." Formerly, in ceremonial processions, they stood to the right of the throne, just as the *likaunts* and *Azzaj*s were of the right and left sides. *Dajazmatch* means "noble of the doors." They stood in front of the throne and even farther in front of them stood the *fitaurari*.
Gerazmatch—lieutenant colonel, noble of the left, leader of a detachment of the emperor, a *Ras*, a *Dajazmatch*, or a *fitaurari*.
Balambaras—commandant. Literally translated "leader where there is a fort"; corresponds to captain.
YamAto alaka—leader of a company, captain, junior captain.
Yaamsa alaka—leader of a half company, lieutenant.
  In the thousand-man regiments of the emperor, their commanders —bashi—correspond to *kanyazmatch*es or colonels. These are military ranks, but in addition, each civilian and court occupation is connected with command over its own soldiers, the number of which sometimes exceeds 1,000 men.
Afa *Negus*—"mouth of the *Negus*," the chief justice, general procurAtor.
Azzaj—court marshals or those who govern estates.
Bajeronds—also court posts of paymasters or heads of workshops. Of all of these we must note the likamakos—the post of adjutant general. They constantly must be near the emperor and have great influence. Formerly, they had the responsibility of dressing in the clothes of the emperor in time of war. They have their own soldiers and are comparable in importance to a *Dajazmatch*—commander of a detachment.

This hierarchical sequence exists only in concept. In reality, there is no such sequence. There are *fitaurari* who are much more important than *Dajazmatch*es. And the correlation of *fitaurari*, *kanyazmatch*es, gerazmatches, and *Balambaras*es is impossible to establish, even in comparison with civilian ranks. For example, an *Azzaj* of the emperor is more important than any *Dajazmatch*, and a *Balambaras* of the emperor is more important than a *Kanyazmatch* of anyone else, and near the emperor there are gerazmatches who are more important than *fitauraris*.

As I already said before, the national character does not permit any abstract limits and regulations. They always consider the actual situation, and if a gerazmatch is stronger and more influential than a *Ras* then he makes use of his great importance.

Promotion in the ranks is not based on gradual succession but rather depends solely on the will of the person doing the promoting. A private can, on the spot, be made a *Ras*.

Once someone has a certain rank, he cannot be demoted. He might be removed from a post and suffer any criminal punishment, but the title stays with him forever.

Independent commanders of regions—*Negus*es, *Ras*es, some *Dajazmatch*es, and *fitaurari*—have the right to promote in the ranks. In this regard, each of these has the right of promoting to all ranks up to the one that comes just before his own. In other words, a *Dajazmatch* can promote up to *fitaurari*, and a *fitaurari* up to *Kanyazmatch*.

These leaders have nagarits—kettledrums—as signs of independence and power. These nagarits can be bestowed only by the emperor, a *Negus*, or a *Ras*. The number of nagarits that the various rulers have differs greatly and depends largely on the size of the region. The emperor has more than 40 of them. The prerogatives of power connected with the possession of nagarits include: the right of commanding one's own army, independent government of a region in all its relations, the right of criminal punishments up to and including cutting off of hands, and the right of promoting in the ranks, as noted above.

Distribution of Troops

The troops are distributed in the area of the Ethiopian empire in the following way:

On the northern borders in Tigre, the *Ras*es Mengesha, Wali and Wag*shum* Wangul—in total about 10,000.

In Central Abyssinia, *Ras* Mengesha Bituaded—15,000.

In the northwest and west, in Gojjam, *Negus* Tekla Haymanot—5,000.

In the northwest and west, *Ras* Mikael in Wollo—4,000.

In the present-day political center of Abyssinia, in Shoa—30,000.

In the west and southwest in Harar and Ogaden—18,000.

In the south in Arussi and the far southern borders, *Ras* Dargi, *Ras* Wolda Giyorgis—40,000.

In the near western Galla lands—*Dajazmatch* Demissew, *Dajazmatch* Balachio, *Fitaurari* Abto Giyorgis—17,000.

On the far southwestern border—*Dajazmatch* Tesemma—8,000.

On the far western border, the autonomous Galla states—Wollaga of *Dajazmatch* Joti and Leka of *Dajazmatch* Gebra Egziabeer—4,000.

Thus we see that the main body is grouped around the capital of the emperor. A large mass is in the former political center of the empire for protection from internal disorders. The northern, northwestern and northeastern borders are occupied comparatively weakly, and the southern, southwestern and southeastern borders are strongest of all since in these directions the empire is expanding its conquests, from year to year getting all the larger.

RECRUITING FOR THE ARMY

In peacetime, not all the soldiers of the regular army are under arms, but only the necessary part of them. The rest take leave and live on their plots of land.

The recruiting of regular troops is based on the principle of free individual will and personal choice. Troops are recruited voluntarily and they join the service for an undetermined period of time. A soldier serves only as long as he wants. The age of the recruit at the time of joining has no significance. They take men who have attained some degree of manhood, but also who are not yet decrepit. The induction itself takes place in the following manner: the person who has joined receives a gun (this is not obligatory) and presents a guarantor—tayaja—who is responsible for him in case of flight or loss of the gun. The newly recruited solider is assigned to one of the commanders and from that moment his real service begins.

The territorial troops are recruited from those who wish to work plots of land which are connected with obligations. Ownership of such plots of land for the most part passes from father to son.

Irregular troops are formed from volunteers at the moment of declaration of war.

KINDS OF ARMS, WEAPONS, EQUIPMENT AND CLOTHING

The Abyssinian field troops consist of one kind of arms—infantry. The cavalry is almost all irregular and does not consist of separate tactical units. The emperor himself has artillery and several of his military leaders have some cannon, but that's the exception.

Infantry (neftenya) is armed mainly with guns of all sorts of systems. There are Veterli, Gra, Winchester, and Remington; and the newest systems are also seen. Each soldier has a cartridge belt with 35-40 cartridges. The total number of guns in the empire together with those taken in the last war amounts to 125,000. This quantity suffices for the majority of regular troops of the emperor and private commanders. Those who do not have guns are armed with spears.

The sidearms of the infantryman are a saber in the form of a curved, double-edged yataghan or a large straight sword. In recent times, a saber of European manufacture is in greater use. The defensive weaponry of the Abyssinian is a shield made of the hide of buffalo, hippopotamus or ox. From the development of battle with firearms, shields fell into disuse in the infantry.

The clothing of soldiers does not in any way differ from that of other citizens. Only when he goes into battle, he winds his shamma around his waist or leaves it in camp and puts on his shoulders a lemd—the hide of a ram, of some wild animal, or velvety clothing made to look like hide. The purpose of this clothing is to protect the body from thorns. Commanders dress especially splendidly—their horses in rich silver gear, sabers trimmed with gold; they wear lion or velvety lemds trimmed with gold decorations, and on their heads they distinguish themselves with lion manes.

The troops do not wear footgear. Only when they go down into low-lying, sandy plains do they wear a kind of sandal.

Each soldier receives either a plot of land or a ration in the form of meal, mead, and meat. In Galla lands, together with a plot of land, they are given some gabars—serfs. The monetary allowance is several talers a year for clothing and gifts in the form of a mule, a horse or a donkey. In general, besides rations, each soldier costs not less than 5-7 talers a year. I personally as a witness as was distributed 50,000 talers sent by Menelik to be given out to men of Gondar who were under the command of *Dajazmatch* Demissew. They received the gifts variously and not all got them. Some received 12 talers for a mule, some 8 for a horse, and some 4 for a donkey.

It appears that the commander is responsible for entertaining his soldiers. The emperor gives banquets twice a week (Thursdays and Sundays) for his personal guard and all commanders who are in the capital. On important holidays he feeds all available soldiers, and the other commanders do likewise at their own homes.

Having given a soldier a gun and cartridges and having satisfied him with a ration or land and salary, the commander lets the soldier himself take care of his own equipment. This equipment is extremely diverse and depends on the prosperity of each individual soldier.

Territorial and auxiliary troops are armed with spears, sabers, and shields. Their clothing is the same for all. They don't receive any allowance.

Mounted troops consist of cavalrymen who voluntarily follow the army. They are irregular and are not divided into tactical units. In addition, all commanders fight on horseback and those of the soldiers of the field armies who have horses. The cavalryman—*farasenya*—is armed with several light spears, a saber and a shield. The horses are of the local breed (see above). The saddles are small, light, with front and back arches, stirrups in the form of small rings, letting through only one large toe. The bit is a mouthpiece with a ring instead of a chain, extremely severe. Riding is all based on balance. All the managing of the horse is by the outward reins and by the legs. The clothing of cavalrymen does not differ from that of others. They do not receive any allowance.

The artillery of the emperor consists of 101 guns—32 former ones and 69 taken in the last war. In the number of recently taken ones are 8 machine guns; the rest are mountain guns. Of the former guns, three are bronze, three machine guns, and the rest are Hotchkiss 37 millimeters. Artillerymen—*medfanya*—are selected from the more well-developed men, primarily from those who are on the coast. The main command over the emperor's artillery is entrusted to Likamakos Abata, a favorite of the *Negus*. He is assisted by Bajerond Balcha and Gerazmatch Iosif. There are six men for each gun. They receive comparatively greater pay than others. Their dress in normal times is the same as that of the others, but in battle they dress in red shirts, green wide trousers and green with red turbans. In addition to that of the emperor, the following individuals have artillery: *Ras* Makonnen has four Krupp guns that were taken from Sultan Abdulakhi, *Ras* Dargi has three guns, and *Ras* Mengesha Bituaded has six former guns and two newly taken ones, *Dajazmatch* Wangul has one gun; *Azzaj* Wolda Tadik and *Dajazmatch* Demissew each have one, and *Negus* Tekla Haymanot has three.

MOBILIZATION

The mobilization of the Abyssinian army takes place very quickly, which considering the bad roads and the fact that in peacetime most of the army is dispersed at their homes, is especially remarkable. Mobilization, either general or private, of separate military leaders, is announced with beating of kettle drums—nagarits—in squares and marketplaces and at the courts of commanders of provinces. The mustering point is designated and how much provisions each should bring with him—and with this all anxiety about mobilization ends. The army assembles itself at the designated place with striking speed. I was present at one such mobilization in the lands of *Dajazmatch* Demissew. No sooner did they beat the nagarits than on all roads there stretched out an endless line of separate caravans of soldiers. Each soldier went by himself to the mustering point.

The whole Abyssinian army can be mobilized and concentrated in one and a half to two months.

Movement by Marching

Abyssinian soldiers, setting out on a march must take care of their own clothing. For the most part, they take their wives, sometimes children, slaves or servants if they have such since each soldier goes with his own transport, which greatly impedes and slows the movement of the army.

On the march each goes there where he finds it more convenient for himself, but in bivouac that are in groups, surrounding the tents of their commanders. Near the enemy, the transport is left behind under escort of the rear guard—wobo, and the troops go in battle order, either making use of several roads or the commander-in-chief goes by a path and the rest go in a compact mass forward, right and left, conforming with the movement of the commander, about which they judge by the parasol held over him. The supply of provisions during a march inside the state consists of *durgo*—products brought by local residents on order of the authorities as a gift. In enemy country they supply themselves by pillage and only in extremity do they resort to their own provisions.

Conduct of War

Judging by the recent campaign against the Italians and wars against Gallas, the Abyssinians, depending on the enemy, conduct war by two different methods. In the first case, against Europeans, the Emperor tried to keep his army assembled, and conducted guerrilla warfare with local residents and with Italian troops of *Ras* Sebat who had changed sides. Going to the bounds of a hostile tribe, all troops dividing into small groups, lay waste the country, burning houses, taking prisoners and livestock, and at night usually assemble in camp. The main aim of war was to take the king or the leader of the tribe, since by this the war would end and the tribe would be subdued. For this they set in motion both stratagems and bribery. In case the enemy troops are concentrated, they also concentrate their troops and if the matter turns into a battle, then it takes on the character of a series of isolated battles.

Tactics

The tactics of the Abyssinians are the tactics of outflanking and turning movements. Reserves do not exist. All troops are brought into battle at once. Since each man tries to get to the enemy as quickly as possible, outflanking seems to be a natural consequence of this. Troops in the rear, seeing before them the whole front occupied, catch up from the flanks.

The formation is difficult to categorize under a concept of loose or close order. It is not close since the separate parts do not know close order, and not loose since it does not have the form of a chain. In general, it is more or less a thick crowd of people, adapting itself to the ground.

Management of troops up until battle is in the hands of the main commander. At the time of attack the parasol of the commander-in-chief serves as the direction of it and the leading subject. Each soldier goes after his direct leader, who already independently, if he has not received special orders, is adapting to the surrounding circumstances. The attack is usually accompanied by beating of kettledrums and playing of horns—malakot—and flutes—embilta. Troops introduced into battle go out of the hands of their commanders.

The Activity of Separate Kinds of Arms

The infantry strives as quickly as possible to meet the enemy at the distance of a near rifle shot. Then they seek cover, adapt to the ground, and open fire. As soon as the opponent begins to waver, they throw themselves into the attack with sidearms and tirelessly pursue the enemy who has turned in flight. In case the attack does not succeed or having learned of the death of their leader, his soldiers leave the battle and, mourning the leader, carry away his body or run. In the latter case, running is not considered a disgrace. Infantry prefers closed and rugged terrain for battle.

A cavalry battle is a battle of isolated riders who, having picked for themselves a place that is convenient for racing, in full career ride up to their opponent and throw spears at him. In case of confusion in the infantry or of flight, the cavalry merges with them. A battle of cavalry against cavalry consists of a whole series of isolated mounted encounters that occur in one place. The cavalrymen ride up to the enemy and throw spears at them, then sharply turn back and ride away. Several cavalrymen rush in pursuit of those who had attacked, but already new cavalrymen from the other side fly to the rescue. In this way, the battle continues until some, having felt the moral and numerical superiority of the opponent, are forced to run, and then others follow them.

Artillery in the Battle of Adowa was formed all together as a battery. The emperor was well satisfied with its activity. It fired frequent shots. By our understanding, it leaves much to be desired. In the recent battle, it had rather a moral significance.

Action with sidearms and firearms differs greatly from ours. When firing from canons, they badly adapt to the gunsight and aiming of shrapnel. From rifles, they always shoot with a constant sight, changing the gunsight only depending on distance. With saber, they always cut from the right down to the left, and saber wounds are less serious than they would be with skillful chopping. Their ability to wield a spear is striking, especially the ability of cavalrymen. Cavalrymen can throw a spear at full gallop for 150-300 paces.

Military Spirit

The spirit of the Abyssinian army is extremely high, and to each individual soldier his purpose is clear—to kill his opponent. They do not make for themselves any illusions on this account and do not consider it necessary to adorn this fact in any way. He knows that war is murder, and he goes to it with joy. In addition, war for an Abyssinian is a pleasant pastime, a source of income, a means to gratify ambition, to show one's valor and to receive well-known honors.[100]

Murder is raised to a cult. Each man keeps track of the number of men he has killed in war and for each one killed has the right to braid his hair and grease it for a year. On the return of a hero, he is met with songs and dances, and accompanied by his friends he goes to his leader where with enthusiasm he tells about the victory.

The main psychological difference between their army and European ones consists in the fact that war as they understand it seems more active. The Abyssinian soldier goes to kill. In the soul of the majority of Europeans, there is rather a feeling of preparedness for self-sacrifice than a desire to personally kill an opponent.

The whole spirit of the army is formed in agreement with this. For the weaker to run is not considered a disgrace but rather good sense. At first, an attack is extremely energetic; but, once repelled, they rarely return. Incidents of heroic self-sacrifice by entire units, to the best of my knowledge, simply don't appear in the annals of their military history. They adore battle and go to it with joy. They are brave and, although hot-tempered, are quick-witted in battle and know how to use the terrain and circumstances. Their youngest leaders and the majority of the soldiers understand the situation. In addition, this army has extremely great endurance. They content themselves with a very small quantity of food, and endure cold, heat, and long marches extremely well. But this army requires good leaders. The leader who does not enjoy the faith and respect of his subordinates cannot lead them into battle. In the opposite case, soldiers are in the highest degree devoted to him, even to the detriment of the general concept. In battle each soldier fights not for the general concept, but for himself and his direct commander and repeats only the war cry of that commander.[101] There is no patriotic pan-Ethiopian concept, but there is the concept of "ashker"—servant of someone or other.

DISCIPLINE AND SUBORDINATION

As regards discipline and subordination, they have the one and the other, but in a unique way that is not similar to ours. They have a constant, conscientious and critical relationship to everyone, and they do not obey their commander if he orders them to do something that in their opinion is not appropriate. Beginning with the most junior and up to the highest, the commander is the spokesperson of the general will of individual persons and rarely is in a position to oppose that will, except perhaps only if he has such real exceptional moral strength as Menelik II.

But as much as the opinion is erroneous that the Abyssinian army is ideally organized and disciplined, so too it would be untrue to consider it an undisciplined horde. Although it is organized on the basis of personal will and therefore only he who wants to serves and serves whom he wants, this does not have an effect on the total number of the army, since militarism is the characteristic of their national spirit, and only the particular grouping of separate commanders changes. Although in their army one can note the rudiments of "praetorianism," in the form in which they are, they do not represent a danger for the empire. Although in form their army seems undisciplined, this is more than made up for by their quick wits and understanding of the situation, and one can dare to say that their military order is that ideal of personal initiative and ability to adapt to the circumstances for which European armies strive. The lack of training is made up for by their upbringing and by historical traditions. Training in the European manner would be for them at the present time extremely out of place, since as they say "to teach the learned man only corrupts him."

STATE GOVERNMENT AND THE DISTRIBUTION OF LAND

The whole internal government of the state is closely connected with the military organization. With regard to government, the whole country is divided among the main military commanders, with the exception of lands that belong to the church (about a tenth of all land) and to the emperor.

Having received the authority to govern some region, a commander chooses a piece of it for himself, distributes a piece among his officers and soldiers, and leaves a piece in the possession of peasants obliged to some auxiliary service in the army.

A distinction is made between gabar and gindebelt peasants. Gabar—etymologically "tributary," means "serf." For the use of land of the owner or of his officers or of his soldiers, the serf is obligated to work for him or pay taxes to him. For this tax, he sows a known quantity of land on the estate and separates a part of the mead and meat for the owner. Galla are all considered gabars. In Central Abyssinia only those who voluntarily agree to it are serfs. Gindebelts are owners of separate plots of land, and this ownership has known obligations connected with it, such as supplying porters for a march. The leaders who manage gabars are called melkanya, and those who manage gindebelts are called meslanye. The general management of both kinds is in the hands of *Azzajs* of the emperor or of separate rulers. Each minor leader manages his province in all these relations: collects taxes, looks into complaints, maintains appropriate administrative order, declares mobilization, and performs judicial functions. But he is obliged to give a detailed account to a senior commander regarding everything that he does. Senior commanders govern lands distributed to officers on the same basis as the main commander of the whole region. They are not obliged to pay a tax to him, but it is accepted practice periodically to give one's commander products of one's farm or some article obtained in war. Soldiers hire out their land to gabars in exchange for half the produce.

The lands of the emperor are also distributed among his officers, soldiers, gabars and gindebelts. The gabars and gindebelts are under the supervision of *Azzaj*s.

Such is the general administrative structure and distribution of land. In each region there are some exceptions, but I will not enlarge about that, not having been able to become more deeply acquainted with it.

The owner in his own home is the absolute boss within the limits of his competency—that is the distinctive trait of the national character. Such is their government. Each little leader is in the highest degree independent in all particular questions of government. The home of each such leader is in miniature the home of a *Ras* or the emperor. Etiquette is strictly observed. But, although they are so independent in particular questions, they cannot undertake anything that can infringe in the slightest on the interests of a commander. Each of them is responsible for anything that could lead to damage for a senior commander. This makes them extremely suspicious and cautious.

POLICE

There is no organized police in the country, but each Abyssinian, seeing some illegal act, considers it his duty to stand up against it in the name of Menelik or of the main ruler of the country. In this case, their great sense of lawfulness.[102] is striking.

JUDICIAL SYSTEM AND PROCEDURE

The exercise of judicial functions rests partly in the emperor and commanders of regions and districts, and partly in the people itself.
1) Each leader has the right to judge and punish his subordinates, and each individual person has the same right over his servants.
2) Minor civil and criminal cases that end in fines are judged by whomever is chosen by the litigants.
3) Important civil cases and land disputes which end in punishment not higher than cutting off of hands are judged by the main commander of the territory.
4) In the second instance, important cases are judged by the *afa-negus* ("mouth of the *Negus*," the chief judge and general procurator.

5) Cases of murder and repeated robbery and civil cases in the highest instance and also especially important cases are judged by the emperor himself.

In all these cases, the trial is public and open.

If the litigants turn to a third party for resolution of their dispute, this third party judges them "ba Menelik alga" which means "by the throne of Menelik." This takes place in the following fashion. The judge and all those present sit on the ground. The litigants, having wrapped half their shamma around their waist, and holding the other half in their hands, explain the case at issue. This is always accompanied with gestures, mimicry, picturesque poses, exclamations, and swearing.[103] When the case is sufficiently clear and witnesses have been interrogated, the judge, having asked the advice of those present, decides the verdict.

The law court of commanders differs from this only in that it takes place at the court of this commander and, also, the commander sits on a bed covered with carpets during the judicial session. The emperor himself goes out to hold law-court two or three times a week—most often on Wednesdays and Fridays from 6 to 10 or 11 o'clock in the morning. At this law court all the highest secular and church officials—likaunts—gather. The emperor sits on his throne in a special building that is called Saganeyt, near doors which open on the square. Behind the emperor sits his whole suite. Below on a platform is the *afa-negus*—the chief judge; wambers—judges; and higher clergy—likaunts. Commanders of the guard and gentlemen in waiting (agafari) stand in front, keeping order. The case of the litigants is set forth by one of the judges. They stand in front of the emperor, surrounded and separated from one another by gentlemen in waiting; for this occasion, their shoulders must be bare. During the exposition of the case, judges ask them several questions. In reaching a decision, in important cases, the emperor consults with the clergy and his retinue. The *afa-negus* announces the verdict. Some criminal punishments are carried out there and then, such as flogging (punishment with a whip or jiraf). For the cutting off of hands, the executioners are kettledrummers.

Law and Custom

Written law—Fetanegest—and custom—serat—serve as a guide for criminal and civil cases. Fetanegest was translated from the Arabic in 1685 during the reign of Emperor Iyasu I, at the insistence of Empress Sabla Wangel. This book consists of a collection of articles of the Justinian Codex, several decrees of the Nicaean Council and other supplementary items. It is divided in two parts:

1) 22 chapters about ecclesiastical law; and
2) 51 chapters about state, civil and criminal law.

In the forty-fourth chapter, it talks about imperial power. The time of appearance of this book coincides with the apogee of imperial power.

CRIMES AND PUNISHMENTS

The first guide in determining criminal punishments is the principle: an eye for an eye and a tooth for a tooth.
Crimes and punishments are as follows:

1) State crime—capital punishment (in very rare cases); cutting off the right hand and left leg; most often, putting in chains and life imprisonment.
2) Insulting majesty—cutting out the tongue.
3) Murder—the murderer is given to the family of the person killed, who kill him in the same manner that he killed.
4) Robbery—capital punishment (in this way, Emperor Menelik eliminated robbery, which formerly was very widespread).
5) Petty theft—first conviction: monetary fine and flogging (with jiraf), up to eight lashes; second: monetary fine and flogging up to 50 lashes; third: monetary fine and cutting off of hands; fourth: capital punishment.
6) Insulting a personality by action or word[104]—monetary fine.
7) Rape—monetary fine; obligation to marry.
8) Fraud—monetary fine.
9) Accidental manslaughter—monetary fine from 50 to 1,000 talers.
10) Non-performance of instruction of the government—monetary fine and flogging.
11) Criminal breach of trust—removal from job, putting into chains, monetary fine, confiscation of property.

The imposition of punishments by separate individuals goes in the following steps:
1) Each private individual in relationship to servants and minor commanders have the right to throw someone into chains for an indeterminate time and to impose 25 lashes by birch rods (kurbach).
2) The commander of a marketplace can impose monetary fines and flogging with whip (jiraf) up to 8 lashes.
3) The commander of an area—cutting off hands, up to 50 lashes (jiraf), and monetary fine.

4) *Afa-negus*—cutting off hands, up to 75 lashes (jiraf), and monetary fine.
5) The emperor—capital punishment, up to 100 lashes (jiraf), monetary fine, and life imprisonment.

Capital punishment is carried out by hanging, or, in case of murder, it is carried out by relatives in the same manner in which the murderer killed. When the murderer is sentenced, he is given over to the relatives, who take him outside town and kill him. Very often, this task is entrusted to a child.

The cutting off of hands is carried out by kettledrummers. One of them holds the arm of the criminal at the elbow. Another, having taken the hand, quickly cuts through the veins and skin that surround the bone and, with an abrupt movement, removes the hand.

Flogging is also carried out by kettledrummers.

Putting someone in chains is the lightest punishment and corresponds to our disciplinary punishment—arrest. It is done very often—sometimes only for a few hours. It consists of the right and left arms being put into irons or simply being tied with rope.

Prisons are very rare in Abyssinia and only state criminals are imprisoned there. An important criminal is chained with his right arm to the left arm of another free man who takes care of him until the end of the trial.

Economic Condition of the State: The Treasury

The economic condition of the state, in view of its purely military character, of course, cannot be brilliant. Constant wars do not give the rulers time to indulge in cultural improvements and development of commerce in their region. They all, not worrying about tomorrow, sooner exhaust their region than enrich it. A large part of the land serves for supplying the army, for satisfying the needs of the court, part for support of the clergy, and very little directly brings revenue to the state treasury.

In general, the annual income of the state treasury is about 800,000 to 900,000 rubles, which for a population of 15 to 17 million amounts to 5 or 6 kopecks per person. These 900,000 rubles are spent as follows: about 300,000 a year goes to pay the army; about 20,000 as gifts to churches; about 100,000 for weapons; about 80,000 to buy cloth and similar things, for making silver articles for gifts; part is set aside each year; and part, paid in kind, is spent on the court.

The sources of income of the state treasury (in rubles per year) are as follows:

I. Tribute of Wollaga, Leka, Jimma (Aba Jefar): Leka (gold, ivory, and money) 60,000
Wollaga 60,000
Jimma 50,000
II. Customs duties—10% of all goods in Harar and from other regions about 100,000
   Income from the personal lands of the emperor 100,000
III. Income from Galla land 200,000
IV. Income from the right of trade and from marketplaces, collected by *nagada-ras*es (chiefs of merchants) 100,000
V. Gifts paid in kind and income from remaining regions 200,000

Obviously, both expenses and income are expressed here in extremely rough numbers and by eye, since the Abyssinians themselves do not know what they collect.

At the conclusion of this chapter, I consider it necessary to describe the family and court of the emperor.

FAMILY OF THE EMPEROR

The family of the Emperor consists of his wife—Empress Taitu; two daughters—Shoareg and Zawditu from his first wife Bafana; his grandson from *Woyzaro* Shoareg—*Balambaras* Ayale; his uncle *Ras* Dargi; cousins, sons of *Ras* Dargi—*Dajazmatch* Tesemma, Mul Saged, and Lyja Tasfa; cousins—*Ras* Makonnen and *Dajazmatch* Haile Maryam.

The Emperor was married in a church ceremony to Empress Taitu in 1881. She comes from a very good family in Tigre. Her grandfather was the well-known *Ras* Wolda Giyorgis. Before Menelik, she was married three times. Her first husband, *Dajazmatch* Wandi, is still alive and has a little land, but he does not appear at court. Her second husband, *Dajazmatch* Wolda Gabriel, was killed by Tewodros who took Taitu for himself. But she refused to favor him, saying it was because of illness, for which she was put in chains. On the death of Tewodros, she married a third time, to *Kanyazmatch* Zakargacho; and then married Menelik, with whom she had a church wedding in 1881, at the age of 30 (she was born in 1851).[105] She has had no children with Menelik; but from a previous marriage, she has a daughter who is married to *Ras* Mengesha. She is very beautiful, with very light skin. She is short and dresses the same as other Abyssinian women. She is notable for her intelligence and her great influence on the Emperor in matters of faith and internal government.

The Emperor's daughter Shoareg was first married to *Ras* Area, son of Atye Yohannes. After the death of her first husband, she married *Ras* Mikael, the ruler of Wollo. During her latest marriage she had a son by *Dajazmatch* Waju, son of *Ras* Gobana. Her son, *Balambaras* Ayale, is now ten years old. He is a very lively, intelligent child, the very image of Menelik.

Woyzaro Zawditu, married to *Dajazmatch* Ubye, is childless. She is short, very light—a rather good-looking woman.

Ras Dargi is the third brother of Menelik's father, Haile Malakot, the son of Sahle Selassie. He was imprisoned together with Menelik at the court of Tewodros. On Tewodros' death, he returned to his nephew who met him with great honor, and to this time he continues to play an important role at court. The Emperor consults with him about everything, and in conversation *Ras* Dargi always addresses Menelik with the familiar form of "you," rather than the formal "you." (This is exactly how Menelik treated *Ras* Gobana, his celebrated military commander.) *Ras* Dargi has three sons—*Dajazmatch* Tesemma, Mul Saged, and Tasfa. They sent Tasfa in 1894 to Switzerland to be educated on the guarantee of Count Ilg, who put him in boarding school. But the translator who was with him, having been bribed by Italians, convinced the boy to go over to the side of Italy, and he did so. All who know Tasfa are sorry about this because it is said he was a boy with exceptional abilities.

Dajazmatch Tesemma, the oldest son of *Ras* Dargi, is the grandson of Atye Sahle Selassie. They say that he is ambitious. They keep him at a distance from the court, and *Dajazmatch* Wolda Gabriel constantly keeps an eye on him.

Ras Makonnen is a cousin of the emperor, a grandson of a sister of Menelik's father. At the present moment he is the most popular of all the Abyssinian military commanders—the richest and the strongest. He is very well liked by the emperor. All foreign affairs are conducted through him and on his advice. This is a man remarkable for his abilities and intelligence. He is a widower with two sons.

Dajazmatch Haile Maryam, brother of *Ras* Makonnen, is the former type of a feudal lord. Alternately with *Dajazmatch* Ubye, he stands guard over the emperor and the capital,

Thus, from this list we see that there are three possible pretenders to the throne: first *Dajazmatch* Tesemma, second *Balambaras* Ayale, and third *Ras* Makonnen.

We will be careful not to predetermine what the future will show, except only what you can almost guarantee—namely that there is no way to avoid civil war if Menelik does not name his successor before his death and prepare the ground for him. The succession to the throne is the sorest subject in the present-day Ethiopian empire.

The personality of Emperor Menelik is probably so well known that I can scarcely add to his character, and there remains to me only to repeat what others have said—that this is in the highest degree a bright, genial, cheerful person. He is one of those historical figures who appear at intervals of many centuries and who make their own era in history.

Abyssinians are filled with deep respect and love for their Emperor. They relate to him prophecies that came to King Zadyngylyu from Angel Raguil and to Sahle Selassie from Auriel.

They have besides a whole book of prophecies that they keep in secret. There are prophecies that they relate to Russia. In one of the prophecies of Raguil to Atye Zadyngylyu (he received revelations in his sleep and then wrote them down), it is said that a king from the north will be with a king of Ethiopia one in spirit and one in heart. In another prophecy of Angel Auriel to Sahle Selassie, it is said that a king of the north and of Jerusalem will meet with a king of Ethiopia in Mysyr (Egypt) and will conquer Egypt. After this, they will divide among them all the land.

The government of Menelik is distinguished for its gentleness, in contrast to the previous reign, and for its justice and tact. Menelik's motto is justice and his main rule is: never stretch the strings too hard so as not to break them. All these qualities have strengthened the throne for him, and his wisdom, military abilities and military good fortune have expanded the boundaries of the empire to an extent that his predecessors never dreamt of.

The court of the emperor and court etiquette are determined by a special book Kybyra Negest "The Honor of Kings."106 There is found the ceremonial of coronation. At the present time not all the rules of the Kybyra Negest are carried out.

In the eighteenth century, judging by the accounts of d'Abaddie and other travelers, at the court of the emperor there was a council of four likaunts (clergy chosen from several ancient families) and four *Azzaj*s. This council shared with the emperor the functions of justice and government and could, in some cases, exercise a veto. I did not find such an institution today. At this time, they do call the highest clergy likaunts, and they are present during trials; but there are not four of them—rather there is an undetermined number—and they are not specially chosen. There are five *Azzaj*s at the emperor's court, but they are exclusively for economic necessities, and do not wear turbans, like clergy.

Let's add the following list of court ranks:

Likamakos—adjutant general, a title which is held by two people: Abata (commander of the artillery) and Adenau. Abata is a young, talented man, who distinguished himself at Adowa, a favorite of the Emperor and Empress, but not liked by the rest of the court. Adenau did not manifest valor at Adowa and therefore is in disfavor.

Bajeronds are chiefs of separate divisions of the economic management. There are three of them: Bajerond Balcha is a favorite of the Emperor, a hero of the recent war, wounded at Adowa. He guards the whole treasury and jewels and is an assistant of Likamakos Abata in the management of the artillery. Bajerond Katama is the commander of the imperial guard. He is also responsible for distribution of all letters and decrees of the Emperor in the whole empire. Bajerond Wolda Giyorgis manages the gold and silver smiths of the Emperor.

*Azzaj*s manage the personal lands of the Emperor and parts of the court household.

Azzaj Wolda Tadik escaped from Tewodros. He is a favorite of the Emperor and managers Ankober.

Azzaj Bezaby manages Menjar and part of the court household.

Azzaj Gyzau manages Meta and all the food supply parts of the court of the Emperor (to him also is entrusted the care of distinguished foreigners).

Ato Vadaju is the assistant of *Azzaj* Gyzau.

Azzaj Aba Tekhsas manages the court of the Empress. (He is noted for great personal bravery. At Adowa he carried the imperial parasol.)

There are several agafari, "those who bring in" or gentlemen in waiting.

Ya elfin askalakay Ishaka Ibsa is "he who forbids entrance to the inner chambers." He commands all the court guards and stays near the Emperor all day. He manages admittance to the emperor. Ishaka Ibsa is still a young man, raised from childhood by the Emperor.

Agafari Wolda Gabriel manages the official audiences of the Emperor.

In addition to these main ones, there are still some more agafaris, and one separate agafari for the court of the Empress.

Walderas is the chief of the stables.

Asalafi is the gentleman carver and high cup bearer. During dinner he cuts the Emperor's food in pieces and gives it to him.

Elfin ashkers are servants of the inner chambers, in the sense of gentlemen-in-waiting. There are many of them. Most of them are children of former chief officers of the army. There are several relatives of former emperors. From childhood they are raised at court as pages, and then become *elfin ashkers*. their responsibility is to escort the emperor here. Those among them who distinguish themselves and demonstrate their abilities are chosen for higher posts.

In addition to these people, there are managers of separate parts of the court household: managers of cooks, of bakers, of makers of beer and mead, and of smiths.

At court there are two translators: *Gerazmatch* Iosif, a favorite of the emperor, accompanied *Ras* Makonnen during his journey to Italy. This very intelligent person has influence in foreign affairs.

Ato Gabriel translates clippings from French and Egyptian newspapers and manages foreign mail.

The Emperor's priest is *Ychygye* Gebra Selassie.

The chief secretary of the Emperor, who manages all the emperor's correspondence on all matters is Alaka Gebra Selassie. The abilities and memory of this man are truly enormous. He works like no one else. His office consists of several copyists. He conducts all the internal correspondence, and he must remember everything. There are no incoming or outgoing journals. Correspondence with all the provinces is enormous, and he must really be notable for outstanding capabilities in order to be in condition to look into all these matters and not confuse them.

Protection in the capital is entrusted, in turn, to the troops of *Dajazmatch* Haile Maryam and those of *Dajazmatch* Ubye.

There are several Europeans at court: Count Ilg serves as Minister of Public Works and Chief Advisor on Foreign Affairs. His position has now become official since he received in March, together with Mr. Mondon, the rank of state councilor—mangyst mekerenya. (Mondon is the official representative of the French government. Another person from the French government, Mr. Clochette,[107] a former captain of the French naval artillery, is their secret military agent.)

Mr. Dyuba manages the suburban forest of Mangasha. He is a French deserter, a former lieutenant of a cuirassier regiment. He deserted in 1870.

Tigran, an Armenian goldsmith, is very well liked by the Emperor and Empress. An Armenian is gardener. A Greek is baker.

The Emperor's day begins at dawn. At 6 o'clock in the morning he already takes the daily report of his secretary *Alaka* Gebra Selassie. In good weather, this takes place on the terrace in front of the court, and no stranger can be present during it. Having finished with the report, the Emperor goes to look at construction that is under way and work in the court or rides to the quarry, to the forest, etc. He always takes advantage of such occasions to utilize the soldiers who accompany him. For example, if he rides past a quarry, then he gets down off his mule and takes a stone, and all those traveling with him must do likewise.

On such excursions, he usually rides on a luxuriously adorned mule, dressed just like all the others except that there is a large felt hat with gold lace on its head. They carry a red parasol over the Emperor. In front they lead two of his horses in case His Majesty wants to play *guks*, which happens very frequently. (The Emperor is an excellent cavalryman). Supper is served at eleven o'clock on meat days and at two or three o'clock on fast days. With the exception of Thursdays, Sundays and high holidays, the Emperor dines in the *elfin* (inner chambers) with the Empress. Only the very closest associates are allowed there, as, for example, *Ras* Dargi, *Ras* Makonnen, and some other *balamuals*. (People who have permission to enter the inner chambers without previous announcement are called *balamuals*). Dinner continues long and consists of dishes that are generally accepted in Abyssinia. After dinner, the Emperor rests for an hour or two and then again he either receives or takes care of business or visits workshops. At six o'clock in the evening, the suite dissolves to their own houses. At seven o'clock, supper is served in the inner chambers. Only some of the very closest *elfin ashkers* and Ishaka Ibsa are present there. At nine o'clock, the Emperor goes to bed. On Wednesdays and Fridays, the Emperor goes out personally to hold court. On Thursdays, Sundays and on high holidays, there is a *gybyr*—a meal for all officers, soldiers of the guard, and, on high holidays, for the whole populace. One is notified about dinner by the beating of kettledrums. Dinner is held either in large tents or in a separate building called *Aderash*. First, the Emperor himself eats, separated from others by a red silk curtain. Inside, behind the curtain, only *balamuals* are allowed. Our mission also had this honor. After the Emperor has finished his meal, the curtain is opened and others are admitted. Trumpeters and flutists go in front. After them, a dense crowd goes. Not bowing to the Emperor, but only wrapping themselves in their *shammas* in accord with etiquette, they take seats close around baskets with *injera*. Over each basket, a servant holds a large piece of raw fresh-killed meat. Other servants pass out large horn goblets of *tej* to those who are dining. Having sated themselves, the dinner guests, without saying anything and not bowing to anyone, leave just as they had come. During dinner, the trumpeters play malakots and the flutists play embiltas. During breaks, they drink and *azmari* [itinerant musicians] play violins. Dinner lasts several hours; and on high holidays it lasts from nine o'clock in the morning until four o'clock in the afternoon.

Twelve times a year, during the monthly Mother of God holidays, there are dinners of the Society of Mary (*Makhaber Zamariem*). This Society consists of the Emperor and eleven of his closes balamuals. On these days, the Emperor eats on the floor from one basket with the rest of the members of the Society. When a member is absent, in his place they seat another person chosen by the Emperor. Each member in order treats the others to dinner. (The main members of this Society are *Ras*

Dargi, *Ras* Makonnen, *Afa-negus* Nasibu, *Ras* Wolda Giyorgis, *Ras* Mengesha Bituaded, *Dajazmatch* Ubye, *Dajazmatch* Tesemma, *Dajazmatch* Haile Maryam, *Likamakos* Abata, and *Alaka* Gebra Selassie.)

Ceremonial receptions take place in a separate building called *Adebabay*. This is a pavilion made of carved wood. The platform ends in railings to which is attached, from inside, an *alga* (bed) which signifies the throne of the Emperor. From the platform downwards goes a wide staircase, and under the throne a second platform, where stands the person who is being received in audience. During the reception, everything is covered with carpets. The Emperor is surrounded by his whole suite. The Emperor received the Red Cross Mission in *Aderash*, which was specially outfitted for this occasion. Appointments to posts and ceremonial receptions of those who have killed elephants and lions take place in Saganeyt, the same place as the law court. On the appointment of someone to a post and the granting to him of a region, they announce this by beating on kettledrums, and an auaj or herald proclaims the new appointment. The newly appointed person bows down to the ground before the Emperor; and then, accompanied by all his friends and servants, goes home with songs, dances, and firing of guns, and gives at home a feast for all who come, which lasts several days. Such ovations and feasts also take place in case of someone having killed an elephant or a lion.

The Emperor very zealously fulfills his duties as a Christian. He strictly observes fasts and during the great fast on Wednesdays and Fridays does not eat until sunset and sometimes spends the night in church on the floor. Each holiday he attends mass. He also makes large donations to churches.

$\mathcal{E}$THIOPIAN CHURCH AND FAITH

The Ethiopian church is under the authority of the Alexandrian patriarch. Abyssinians consider themselves attached to the Alexandrian church by decree of the Nicaean Council, at which it was also decided that they should receive bishops from Alexandria. Thanks to this dependence on the Alexandrian church, the Ethiopian church did not send representatives to the ecumenical councils and separated itself simultaneously from the Alexandrian church and from the rest of the church after the censure of the monophysite doctrine of the Alexandrian patriarch *Aba* Dioskuros by Pope Leo at the Chalcedonian Council.

Like the Alexandrian church, the Abyssinians consider the Apostle Mark as their enlightener. They acknowledge only five councils, receive bishops from Alexandria, but in spite of this outward unity, they differ from the Copts in many dogmas and in the divine service; and their relationship with the Alexandrian church and the *abunas* (bishops) they receive from them is rather one of antipathy. The Debra-Libanos religious belief that now predominates in Abyssinia is closer to Orthodox diophysitism than to Coptic monophysitism.

According to Latin sources, the Abyssinians were converted to Christianity by Saint Frumentius. Saint Frumentius was going to India together with Edeziy and Merope, but they were lost in a wreck in the Red Sea. Saint Frumentius found himself at the court of the Ethiopian king. From there he returned to Jerusalem, then was ordained by the Alexandrian patriarch as bishop of Ethiopia, and, returning there, baptized King Abrekh-Atsebakh and the whole nation. The Abyssinians named him *Aba* Salama.

There are several versions of this story in Abyssinian sources.

In an authentic copy that I have of the Abyssinian *Tarika Negest*, it is said, "At the time of the reign of Abrekh-Atsebakh, the baptism took place when they were in Aksum. At this time, there were no Turks. The father of *Aba* Salama was a merchant. *Aba* Salama came with his father. At this time, the

Ethiopian people in part bowed to the Law of the Prophets and in part to wild animals (*baauri*). After this, *Aba* Salama taught them about the descent of Jesus Christ—the birth, suffering, crucifixion, death, and resurrection. He performed many miracles before them. At that time, they believed in Christian baptism and were baptized. The conversion took place in 343 A.D. and they built Aksum." (R. Basset, *Etudes sur l'histoire d'Ethiopie*, "Chronique ethiopienne," Paris, 1882, issue No. 30, page 220). In the book Synkysar (a collection of sacred books, arranged according to the day of the year), Frumentius(Frementos) and Edeziy (Adzios) are called relatives of Merope.

One Abyssinian scholar, *Alaka* Sou Aganyekh, father superior of the church in the city of Gori, recounted to me a completely new version of the *Aba* Salama story, that has a legendary character. (I cite it since it is very curious.) In Tigre, there was a good man who got sick and died. They washed him and wanted to bury him, but by some indications, they noticed that he wasn't completely dead. They waited three days, but the situation didn't change. Then, on the advice of a wise man, they decided that this was some very important sign and that one should not oppose the clearly expressed will of God. For a large sum of money, they got a blind beggar woman and took her to the dead man. After this the dead man quieted down, and after nine months and five days the blind woman gave birth to a son whom they called "Fre Mentotos," which means "creation of an unknown guest." In three years his mother died; and in his seventh year, merchants brought him into slavery and took him to Egypt. He spent twelve years there. After this, the man who had taken him to Egypt died himself and, in dying, set the slave free. In four years, after having visited Jerusalem, he returned to Abyssinia. There, at this time, reigned Abrekh-Atsebakh, who, having found out about his arrival, summoned him to him and began to ask what he had done in Alexandria and Jerusalem. He told about the birth of Christ, the suffering, death, and resurrection from the dead. The king having given him much money, sent him to Jerusalem in order that, after studying theology there, he could give Abyssinia a new faith. He stayed in Jerusalem for seven years, and in the eighth year was consecrated as a bishop by the Alexandrian patriarch and returned to Ethiopia where he baptized the king and all the people. *Aba* Salama brought with him 45 books of the Old Testament—*Billugat*—and 36 books of the New Testament—*Hadisat*—translated by him to the Ethiopian language.

After the death of *Aba* Salama, in 383, Abyssinia continued to receive its bishops from Alexandria and was under its influence. Together with the Alexandrian church it separated itself from other churches, but this separation took place imperceptibly for

Abyssinians and they were not responsible for it. The spiritual influence of the Alexandrian church was strong in Abyssinia. The works of Alexandrian theologians played a large role in this case. The works of *Aba* Dioskuros were were translated into the Ethiopian language and his fate was explained as an unjust persecution by Pope Leo. In their eyes, Dioskuros was a martyr since they only knew one side of the dispute.

After the moderate monophysite teaching of Dioskuros, there appeared in Abyssinia the more extreme teaching of Eustaphy. It got most of its followers in western Ethiopia—Gojjam

Both new teachings penetrated Ethiopia from the west and north and spread more in these parts. The south preserved its original apostolic faith, the apologist and the interpreter of which was the most revered saint in Abyssinia *Abuna* Tekla Haymanot. I consider it my duty to dwell on him at greater length.

The time of Tekla Haymanot coincides with the return of the imperial throne from the dynasty of Zagye to the dynasty of Solomon. According to Abyssinian sources, he was born in 1350 and died in 1443. Here is how the life of Saint Tekla Haymanot is described in *Synkysar*. The Abyssinian scholar *Dabtara* Sou Aganyekh translated *Synkysar* to the Amharic language and wrote it down for me.

Abuna Tekla Haymanot came from the tribe of Levi, from Azariya, a Jewish high priest, sent by Solomon to Abyssinia together with Menelik. The father of Tekla Haymanot, Tsara-Zaab, was a priest in the vicinity of Tisa in the province of Bulga, which belongs to Shoa. His mother was Egzioharaya. Both of them were married for a long time and had no children. At this time, King Matolome (in all probability not pagan, but Jewish) arrived from Damot and abducted the wife of Tsara-Zaab. He liked her and decided to marry her. On the way, he sent word to his people about his decision and ordered them to prepare a marriage feast with 10,000 oxen, 20,000 sheep, lots of *injera*, beer, and mead. Egzioharaya cried day and night, and prayed to God and on the day of the wedding when she had already put on her wedding dress, she saw Archangel Michael with sword in hand. He took her to the church where at this time her husband was serving dinner. From church they returned home, and on this day she conceived a son, who was born after nine months and five days on the 24th of *Tekhsas* (December 19). They called him Tekla Haymanot. At the moment of his birth, light filled the whole house. On the third day, when they anointed the mother with oil, the whole house was filled with fragrance. In the third year, they sent Tekla Haymanot to church to study and in four years he was consecrated as a deacon. After this, he was consecrated as a monk—"put on monastic belt and hood" as the Abyssinians say. His spiritual lineage is as follows. Saint Anthony put on the hood and belt by order of Archangel Michael. Anthony ordained *Aba* Markariy, who ordained *Aba* Pakhomiy, who ordained Aba Aragaui, also known as Zamikael. *Aba* Aragaui ordained *Aba* Krystos Bezana. Krystos Bezana ordained *Aba* Maskal Moa. *Aba* Maskal Moa ordained *Aba* Iokhani, who ordained Iisus Moa, who ordained *Abuna* Tekla Haymanot. At first, he was in Haik, then in Debra Damo, and then he founded the monastery of Debra Libanos, where he stayed to the end. His life story is filled with descriptions of miracles performed by him. Abyssinians claim that on his spine there were six wings, thanks to which he flew four times to Jerusalem. In four days, on his return for the third time from Jerusalem, he resurrected someone who had died twelve years before. In Damot, he in one day resurrected a thousand men. In Haik, he fasted for seven years, standing in one place without food and drink. In the sixth year, one of his legs broke and one wing was burnt by a wax candle, but he put a piece of wood under the leg and continued to stand. In the seventh year, he saw the Lord in the clouds. And the Lord told him to ask for whatever he wanted. Tekla Haymanot asked for three things: first—for Ethiopia and all pious people who were there—that God forgive them, for his sake; second—for the monastery of Debra Libanos—that God illuminate the whole place where it stands; third—for the kings of Ethiopia from the family of Solomon—that God bless them and keep the throne in their hands. In four days at the end of his fast, he flew again to Jerusalem and, having returned from there to Debra Libanos, he extracted water from a stone with a cross, and to this day this spring has healing powers and masses of ill people, both Abyssinians and Gallas, gather there.

From this story it is evident how much the personality of Abuna Tekla Haymanot is legendary. It is known for certain that he was in holy orders *ychygye*—head of all monasteries, that he founded the monastery of Debra Libanos, and that he served as an apologist of the faith in the spirit of Orthodoxy. His relics to this day are preserved in undecayed form and are greatly revered.

Thus we see in the Ethiopian church three successive influences: remnants of the original apostolic faith (the teaching of Tekla Haymanot), the extreme monophysitism of Eustaphy, and the moderate monophysitism of Dioskuros. In the sixteenth century, there appeared in addition the Catholic influence of Portuguese Jesuits. From this time, disputes of faith began in the Ethiopian church, which led to bloody wars.

Political questions became associated with questions of faith, and this or that dogma became the catchword of this or that party. At one time, Catholicism triumphed, but not for long. It was superseded by the extreme monophysitism of the Gojjam Eustaphiants, who believed the human nature in Christ is special and not material like other men. Eustaphiants were superseded by followers of the Debra Libanos doctrine, and they in their turn were replaced by Tigreans who were followers of Dioskuros, the so-called faith of the knife—Kara Haymanot. These last believe that the humanity in Jesus Christ is absorbed by his divinity.

The disputes in the Ethiopian church have been remarkably well described, the action of Catholic and Protestant missionaries has been well characterized, and the conditions of missionary work in Abyssinia have been recounted in a book by our well-known professor of the Ecclesiastical Academy, V. Bolotov—Some Pages from the Church History of Ethiopia, published in 1888. The only point for which I did not find confirmation is the belief in three births of Jesus Christ, which he attributes to the Debra Libanos doctrine, and his assertion this doctrine differs in this regard from the party of Kara Haymanot, which recognizes two births.

I have in my hands a Debra Libanos book of catechism, Emada Mistir, given to me by their *ychygye*. I spoke with many Debra Libanos scholars, and they all quite definitely told me that they recognize just two births. I suspect that they may have formerly believed in three births, and I think that the conclusion drawn by Mr. Bolotov from foreign sources, was, it must be, a mistake of the authors of those other works. The struggle of the three doctrines ended with the triumph of the Tigrean doctrine—Kara Haymanot or moderate monophysitism. Emperors Tewodros II and Yohannes IV professed this faith. Coptic bishops also were followers of that faith. Emperor Yohannes definitively gave this faith the upper hand. The doctrine of Eustaphy was judged heretical and ceased to exist any longer. (There are only secret adherents in Gojjam). The followers of the Debra Libanos doctrine—all Shoa—kept their former faith, so that now this question is in the following position. Under Yohannes, Menelik attended the council called by Yohannes to discuss the dogmas and formally joined the moderate Kara Haymanot monophysitism of the Tigreans. But in his soul, he remained an believer in the Debra Libanos doctrine. The Empress Taitu, who is very interested in questions of faith, since she is of Tigrean origin professes Tigrean monophysitism. Abunas, Coptic bishops, are monophysites. All monks of the order of Abuna Tekla Haymanot (and now this is the only monastic order in Abyssinia), all Shoa, and the *ychygye* —all of them are followers of the Debra Libanos doctrine, professing if not complete diophysitism, then, in any case, very moderate monophysitism, which in its dogmas differs very little from Orthodoxy. Menelik doesn't raise questions of faith, leaving them open. Since a numerous majority adhere to Debra Libanos and their clergy grow in strength, I think that the Debra

Libanos doctrine is prevailing. The six demands which the church makes on a Christian are:

1) to go to mass on Sundays and holidays;
2) to fast on Wednesdays and Fridays for the duration of four fasts;
3) to confess once a year;
4) once a year, come what may, to receive the Eucharist;
5) to give alms; and
6) to not arrange feasts and not get married at unauthorized times.

The seven sacraments of the church are the following: baptism—*maternek*,
anointing—*miron*,
receiving the Eucharist—*kurban*,
confession—*manazaz*,
extreme unction—*kyba kedus*,
entering priesthood—*ekakhat shum*at, and
marriage—*bakhyg magbat*.

The Holy Scripture includes 45 books of the Old Testament (Biluyat) and 36 books of the New Testament (Hadisat). These 36 books are the following: 4 gospels, 8 synodic books (decrees of apostolic councils), 14 letters of Apostle Paul, 3 letters of John, 2 letters of Peter, 1 letter of James, 1 letter of Jude, the Acts of the Apostles, and decrees of two ecumenical councils.

In addition, books inspired by God include the essence of the works of John of Damascus [Golden Mouth], of Vassily [Basil] the Great, of Marisakhak, of Efrem, of Aragaui, of Manfasaui, and several others.

The collection of all the holy books of the Ethiopian Church is Synkysar. It looks like a huge calendar with saints and works of some of the fathers of the church corresponding to each day.

Each Abyssinian year has the name of one of the evangelists in order. The first year after leap year is Matthew, the second Mark, the Third Luke, and the fourth (leap year) is John. Their counting of years is eight years behind ours. Right now for them it is 1889 Matthew. They have 365 days in a year, except 366 in leap year. The year is divided into 12 months of 30 days each and, in addition, there is a remainder of 5 or 6 days. The year begins on September 1. There are monthly and annual holidays.

I'll briefly describe their calendar:

September—*Maskarem*, 30 days
1st—Saints John Raguil, Iov, Bartholemew
5th—*Abuna* Gebra Hyyauat

6th—Aba Pataleon
7th—holiday of the Holy Trinity
10th—birth of George
11th—Hanna
12th—holiday of Archangel Michael
14th—Stephen
16th—Kidana Mykhrat
17th—*Maska*l (Holy Cross Day)
18th—*Aba* Eustatios
19th—Archangel Gabriel
21st—holiday of the Mother of God
23rd—holiday of George the Victorious
24th—holiday of *Abuna* Tekla Haymanot
25th—Mercury
27th—*Madhani Alem* (holiday of the salvation of the world)
29th—*Baala Egziabeer* (the Lord's holiday)
30th—John

Tykymt, 30 days
4th—Abrekh-Atsebakh, king of Aksum (who had Ethiopia baptized)
5th—Abo (a highly revered saint)
6th—Pataleon
7th—holiday of the Holy Trinity
11th—Anna, Fasilyadas, Klavdiya [Claudia]
12th—holiday of Archangel Michael, Matthew the Evangelist
14th—*Abuna* Aragaui
17th—Stephen
21st—holiday of the Mother of God
22nd—Luke the Evangelist
23rd—holiday of George the Victorious
25th—Abuna Abib
27th—*Madhani Alem* (holiday of the salvation of the world), Aba Tekla Maryam
29th—*Baalye Wald* (holiday of the Son)
30th—John

Hedar, 30 days
1st—Raguil
6th—Kissakuan
7th—holiday of the Holy Trinity
8th—holiday of cherubim and seraphim
11th—Anna
12th—Michael
13th—legion of angels
15th—Minas
17th—Saint Waletta Petros
18th—Apostle Philip

21st—holiday of the Mother of God
23rd—holiday of George the Victorious
24th—heavenly host
25th—Mercury
26th—Samaatata Nagyran
27th—holiday of the salvation of the world
29th—holiday of the Son

Tekhsas, 30 days
1st—The prophet Ilya [Elijah]
4th—Apostle Andrew, *Abuna* Tekla Alfa
12th—Archangel Michael, *Aba* Samuil [Samuel]
15th—Aba Eustaphy
19th—Archangel Gabriel
21st—holiday of the Mother of God
22nd—Daksios
23rd—holiday of George the Victorious, David
24th—holiday of *Abuna* Tekla Haymanot
27th—holiday of the salvation of the world
28th—Gehenna
29th—birth of Christ [Christmas]

Tyr, 30 days
3rd—Libanos
4th—John the Thunderer
6th—Galilee
15th—Kirkos the Younger
18th—George the Victorious
21st—holiday of the Mother of God
29th—the Lord's holiday

Ekatit, 30 days
8th—birth of Simeon
10th—Jacob [or James] Alfeev
16th—Kidana Mykhrat
21st—holiday of the Mother of God
29th—the Lord's holiday

Magabit, 30 days
5th—*Abuna* Gebra Manfas Kedus
8th—Matthias, Haria
10th—the Lord's cross
12th—Archangel Michael
21st—holiday of the Mother of God
23rd—death of George the Victorious
24th—holiday of *Abuna* Tekla Haymanot

29th—the Lord's holiday
30th—Mark

Miazia, 30 days
7th—holiday of the Holy Trinity
12th—Archangel Michael
17th—Apostle James
19th—Archangel Gabriel
21st—holiday of the Mother of God
23rd—death of George the Victorious
24th—holiday of *Abuna* Tekla Haymanot
29th—the Lord's holiday
30th—Mark

Gynbot, 30 days
1st—birth of the Mother of God; Yared, teacher of Ethiopia
5th—Abo
12th—Archangel Michael, John of Damascus [Golden Mouth], death of *Abuna* Tekla Haymanot
21st—holiday of the Mother of God
23rd, 24th, 25th—days of the holiday of the Mother of God
26th—Apostle Foma [Thomas?]
28th—Emmanuel
29th—holiday of the Son

Saniye, 30 days
8th—holiday of the Mother of God
12th—Archangel Michael, King Lalibala
20th—Hyntsata Biyeta
21st—holiday of the Mother of God
23rd—George the Victorious, Solomon
27th—salvation of the world
29th—the Lord's holiday
30th—John

Hamlye, 30 days
2nd—Faddey [Thaddeus]
5th—Peter and Paul
7th—holiday of the Trinity
8th—*Abuna* Kiros, Abo
10th—Nathaniel
12th—Michael
17th—*Aba* Garema
18th—Jacob [or James]
19th—Archangel Gabriel
21st—holiday of the Mother of God
29th—the Lord's holiday

Nakhasye, 30 days
1st—holiday of the Holy Virgin
3rd—Queen Sophia
10th—Council of 318 fathers of the church
11th—Anna
12th—Michael
13th—the Lord's Transfiguration
16th—Felseta (Assumption of the Mother of God)
17th—death of George
18th, 19th, 20th, 21st—holiday of the Mother of God
23rd—George
24th—*Abuna* Tekla Haymanot
27th—salvation of the world
28th—Abraham, Isaac and Jacob
29th—the Lord's holiday
30th—John

Pagume, 5 or 6 days
3rd—Archangel Raphael

Nine annual holidays of the Lord are the following: baptism [Epiphany], resurrection from the dead [Easter], Ascension, the descent of the Holy Spirit on the Apostles [Pentecost], Palm Sunday, birth of Christ [Christmas], Transfiguration, Feast of the Purification, and Holy Cross Day.

There are 33 holidays of the Mother of God.

Over the year, there are four major fasts which are comparable to ours in time and duration, except for Lent, which lasts for eight weeks. They also fast on Christmas Eve, Epiphany, and the day of the beheading of John the Baptist. Two weeks before Lent there is a minor fast, which lasts three days—Wednesday, Thursday, and Friday. In addition, they fast every Wednesday and Friday.

A fast consists of not eating meat, eggs, or milk. On usual Fridays and Wednesdays, those who are fasting do not eat anything until afternoon, and for Lent on Wednesdays and Fridays they do not eat anything until sunset. Ardently pious people do not eat anything at all on Fridays and Saturdays.

The Abyssinian church is very rich in holy traditions. For example, they have preserved the names of the two thieves crucified on the right and left sides of Christ. They are named Titos and Koridos. The name of the soldier who pierced Christ with a spear is Longinos. Anna, the mother of Mary, was the second wife of Ioakim, who inherited her from his brother. They consider, as far as I can understand, that James and John are relatives of Jesus Christ, children of the first wife of Joseph.

By tradition, the gall which they gave Christ to eat on the cross was the gall of an elephant.

The Abyssinian Creed is literally the same as ours. They do not make the sign of the cross during prayer. In those rare times when I saw them make the sign of the cross, they did so in the most diverse ways—courtiers with one finger raised high, squeezing the rest of the fingers in a fist, crossed from left to right; clergy who had been in Jerusalem crossed themselves in the Orthodox manner.

The worship service of the Abyssinians differs from ours. Services are as follows: performing of the seven sacraments, midnight and morning vigils, and prayers. I did not see all the sacraments performed, and it was very hard for me to find reliable witnesses about the method of their performance. Consecration to ecclesiastical rank is performed at the end of mass. The abuna (bishop) goes to the altar. (During this same mass he stands facing the king's gates, beside the *ychygye*, to the right of the emperor). There he, apparently, lays hands on those to be consecrated. I'm afraid I am mistaken, but it seems that the whole ceremony of performing the sacrament consists only of this.

The sacrament of marriage consists of those who are betrothed receiving the Eucharist together. (I also do not guarantee that this ceremony is limited just to this).

The sacrament of confession consists of confessing one's sins to a priest.

The sacrament of baptism consists of the parents of the infant, together with his god-parents, bringing him—if he is a boy, on the fortieth day, and if a girl on the eightieth day—to the church where he at first is baptized and anointed and then, after mass, receives the Eucharist. Judging by what one Abyssinian priest told me, the sacrament of baptism, is performed in the following manner: when the infant is brought into the church by his parents and by his godfather and godmother, the priest, serving together with a deacon, consecrates the water. Before the consecration, they read the Creed; letters of Apostle Paul; the Gospels; the 50th, 68th and 123rd Psalms; and then the prayer of the Mother of God. The water is scented with incense spread with a censer and is blessed with a cross. Having taken the infant, the priest says, "I believe in one God the Father. I believe in one God the Son. I believe in one God the Holy Spirit." Then the deacon, having taken the infant, bows with him down to earth three times in the primary directions of the world, saying: "I bow to the Father. I bow to the Son. I bow to the Holy Spirit." Then they pour water on the infant three times, in the name of the Father and the Son and the Holy Spirit. After the baptism, they anoint him with myrrh, just as among us, and then after mass they give the Eucharist.

Some writers assert that the Abyssinians consider it necessary to be baptized each year, and that this takes place on the Holiday of Baptism. This is totally wrong, since in their catechism and Creed it is definitely stated that baptism can be performed only once. This error was made because the pouring of holy Jordan water must have made the Jesuits think of baptism. I personally witnessed the blessing of water on the Holiday of Baptism, and a priest three times poured water on my head. But no one thought to consider this a ceremony of baptism.

The sacrament of Eucharist takes place during mass. Mass is called kedasye, and Eucharist is called kurban. They have 14 masses. These include masses of Jesus Christ, the Mother of God, and the twelve apostles; in addition to which, there are the liturgies of John of Damascus [Golden Mouth], Vassily [Basil] the Great, and Gregory the Theologian. The liturgy consists of only one part—the liturgy of the faithful. There are no liturgies of catechumen and offertory. The gifts are prepared at the end of the all-night [vespers and matins] mass. Communion bread is baked of leavened wheat dough in the form of large round flat cakes, the surface of which is notched into small squares with lengthwise and transverse cuts. They do not use wine. In its place, they moisten dried grapes and squeeze the juice from it. Grapes are obtained from Gondar. The wheat flour is ground at the church itself by some innocent boy. The liturgy must be served by no less than five clergymen—two priests and three deacons. There can be seven, nine, or 12 clergymen, but never less than five. The whole mass is sung by priests and deacons, without the participation of the choir. Only once, after the consecration of the holy gifts, when the prayer for the whole world is spoken, the choir sings Ekzio maren (Lord have mercy).

The giving of the Eucharist is performed in both forms. At first one of the priests offers the body, having separated a square with his fingers. Then he offers the blood. The gifts are carried in by all the clergymen through the western doors. On this occasion, a deacon rings a little bell and all fall on their knees. The gifts are also carried back out through the western doors.

The liturgy of John of Damascus [Golden Mouth] differs, as far as I could tell, from our liturgy of John of Damascus. First there is no liturgical prayer. In all probability the liturgical prayer is a later addition made by the Byzantine church. There is likewise no liturgy of the catechumen. As for the rest, apparently, there is much similarity to ours. At the consecration of the holy gifts, the clergymen mourn for the suffering and death of Jesus Christ. For the most part, the clergymen are completely carried away in spirit to the events they are mourning.

Matins together with the midnight service precede mass. The service begins at two to three o'clock in the morning and continues until sunrise, when mass begins. *Kidan* consists of the reading of books of the Old and New Testaments and singing by a choir of *debtera*.

At times, a priest and deacon go out from the altar with a censer and crosses. The Gospel is read by one of the priests.

After mass, there is some kind of public prayer. All the priests and deacons who are serving go out from the altar with crosses and censer and stand silently in front of the king's gates facing the people. A choir of *debtera* sings an improvisation in honor of the emperor, then in honor of the holiday, and in honor of the Holy Mother of God. For the most part, the alaka (father superior of the church) improvises; the choir repeats his words or sings the refrain haile (glory) or haleluya (hallelujah). If the improvisation is successful, then all those gathered round approve it, saying "Malkam, malkam" ("Good, good"). The singers get more and more enthusiastic. They sing while swinging in beat with their whole body, ringing copper rattles and beating in time with staffs on the ground. The movement becomes more and more energetic. The beating on drums becomes more frequent and louder. The singers leave their rattles and clap their hands. Some squat and act like ducks [pochards], describing a cross with the movement of their heads. The priests, standing in front of the people, also sing. Some of the *debtera* go to the middle of the circle, making smooth and graceful steps and swinging a staff in time to the music. The oppressive heat becomes dreadful. Sweat pours in torrents from the singers. But all are terribly electrified. The religious enthusiasm is enormous. And there are not at this moment any other than purely religious sensations. But now the singing stops abruptly. One of the *debtera* goes around to all who are present and, dividing them into groups, designates to each a saint to whom to pray. He goes around thus several times until he has enumerated all the saints. After this, a priest says some prayers which end with the prayer "Our father" (Abuna zasamayat) and lets the people go. Leaving, each considers it his duty, just as when arriving, to kiss either an icon or the door of the church.

Many are inclined to condemn the Abyssinians for their "holy dance." But in the form in which it takes place among them, there is nothing immoral about this dance. It is only an expression of the highest degree of religious enthusiasm. Somewhere I read that the Spanish also have holy dances. Among the Abyssinians, the dances appear to be a legacy of paganism.

The worship service on major holidays differs from the usual one only in the greater length of the songs after mass. For christening, the church is carried in a tent to the Jordan and all the local inhabitants arrange themselves in a camp around it. On Holy Cross Day, a religious procession is performed around six high, upright stacks of firewood, stuck into the ground, which are then set on fire at night.

The structure of the church itself is different among them from among us. The altar is in the middle of the church and looks like a separate square room or house. In some churches, the walls of the altar are painted with icons, on which the Abyssinians never give their saints black skin, but rather the color of the faces on the icons is always yellow. In the altar, there are four gates from the primary directions. Some altars only have three gates—northern, western, and southern. Sometimes the gates are made double in each of the four primary directions. The credence [altar] is partitioned off with curtains. The gifts are always brought in and taken out through the west gates. Worshipers arrange themselves in the church in the following manner. In the capital, opposite the king's gates to the left stands the emperor, to the right the abuna (bishop) and the *ychygye* (head of all monasteries). Behind them stands a choir of *debtera*. During mass, the father superior of the church stands right at the king's gates; at the end of mass, he goes to the choir. The men arrange themselves on the northern and western sides; the women on the southern, separated from the men by a curtain. And on the eastern side stand the priests and monks and those clergy who are not taking part in the choir. There are always many men and women behind a fence. These are people who did not keep known rules and, considering themselves unclean, do not have the right to enter the church.

Holy vessels and church utensils used in the divine service are a Communion cup—for the most part, a glass cup. I did not see a paten. The lamb is carried out on a large dish (what kind I was never able to find out). They carry it out covered with large silk shawls, just the same as they carried it out the day before a baptism, when the church moves into a tent. Then the Abyssinians call it *tabot*. Isn't this the *tabot* mentioned by many who have written about Abyssinia, some of whom assert that it has the form of a box and others of a board? It seems to me most probable that the *tabot* among them plays the role of communion cloth and substitutes for the paten.

The church spoon is for the most part silver. There is no duplicate. They separate pieces of the lamb by finger. The gifts are covered by large silk shawls.

The church utensils consist of parasols, censers, crosses, staffs, little bells, rattles, and drums. Parasols play a very important role. They are unfurled above the holy gifts. Little bells are rung when the holy gifts are carried in. The censer is very large, made of fretted copper with attached bells. During the exits, a deacon leaves with the cross, and a priest with a censer. They stand in front of the king's doors, face to face and turn around one another three times, bowing. During this time, the priest swings the censer. The staff consists of a long cane stick with an iron or other kind of cane-head. It serves for resting the shoulders on it during the service. It is about two arshins [56 inches] long. The rattles are similar to a very long tuning fork; among its prongs on the transverse pivot are hung copper ringlets. Their drums are very long. They beat them with the palms of their hands, while sitting on the floor. On the roofs of churches, they make crosses out of ostrich eggs embedded on reeds. In recent times, in some churches there have appeared bells, but the Abyssinians still do not know how to ring them.

The clothing of priests consists of a long silk shirt; and over it, a silk chasuble, which extends to the knees, is worn on the shoulders. For the most part, there are hoods with tassels behind these chasubles. The dress of deacons is similar to that of priests, with the difference that priests' heads are covered with muslin and the deacons' heads are clean shaven. In ceremonial worship services, priests and deacons put silver, gilded headgear in the form of crowns on their heads. This headgear is in different shapes for deacons and for priests. Those who perform the divine service are obliged to change all their clothes, and they do not have the right wear these clothes outside the church. They serve barefoot.

The ecclesiastical ranks of the Ethiopian church are as follows: deacon, kes (priest), *komos, kiros, episkopos, papas,* and *likapapas.*

The *likapapas* is the Alexandrian patriarch. The *papas* is the metropolitan, *Abuna* Mateos, one of the three abunas in Abyssinia. Two *abunas* have the rank of *episkopos—Abuna* Petros and Abuna Lukas. (At the time of Emperor Yohannes, *Abuna* Petros was the metropolitan). *Ychygye* Gebra Selassie has the rank of *kiros.* All father superiors of monasteries and other high church figures have the rank of *komos.*

There are now three abunas in Abyssinia, of whom Mateos fulfills the duties of metropolitan and the others—Petros and Lukas—the duties of bishops. They arrived in Ethiopia at the time of Emperor Yohannes, together with a fourth *abuna*, Markos, who died. Emperor Yohannes intended to divide the whole empire into four kingdoms and to establish a diocese in each. The bishop of Tigre carried out the duties of a metropolitan, but with the ascension of Emperor Menelik, that duty shifted to the

Shoa bishop. For each of these bishops, Yohannes paid the Alexandrian church 10,000 talers.

The duties of the bishops consist almost solely of ordaining for church posts. Sometimes during agitation over important church questions, the bishops send circular messages throughout the diocese. But this happens very rarely. In normal times, they live on their lands, rarely going to the capital. And when they do go to the capital, they are never at court, except for one occasion—the holiday of Maskal (Holy Cross Day). In case of need, the emperor himself goes to them.

The relationships of the bishops among themselves are strained. They openly do not agree with one another on many questions. For instance, Abuna Petros strongly condemns Abuna Mateos for taking money from those who are being ordained. Relationships of the Abyssinian clergy to the abunas are very hostile. They call the abunas mercenaries. The current metropolitan by far does not stand on that moral height which is demanded by his high position. Nonetheless, he has great importance.

The highest church figure after the abunas is *Ychygye* Gebra Selassie. With the rank of *kiros*, he is the father superior of the monastery of Debra Libanos and is the head of all monasteries and the head of all monks of the order of Tekla Haymanot. This old man is a very sympathetic and is loved by all. He also serves as confessor of the emperor. From the very beginnings of Christianity in Abyssinia, an *ychygye* has existed together with *abunas*. Saint *Abuna* Tekla Haymanot was also *ychygye*. The *ychygye* owns large lands. They do not have the right to ordain those who perform the divine service. In Aksum, the father superior of the cathedral church there carries the title of *nabr hyda*. This title derives from High Priest Azariy, who was sent by Solomon together with Menelik. He has the rank of komos. His duty is to preserve the Ark of the Convenant, which was brought by Menelik from Jerusalem, as if it still existed to this day. The father superior of all the churches in Gondar carries the title of *akibe saat*. He also has the rank of komos. The head priests in large monasteries are called *kes hatse*, They, just like *mamhyry*, who are the father superiors of these monasteries, have the rank of *komos*. *Kes* (priests) are ordained when they have reached maturity and are already married. Before ordination they undergo something like an examination. Priests must be married in the church ceremony; and in view of this, they all take as wife the very youngest girls. Deacons are boys from eight to twelve years old. Those who have been prepared for a clerical vocation, but then for various reasons are not ordained as priests nor as deacons and who do not become monks, stay in churches, constituting a special class reminiscent of ancient scribes. They are called *debtera* (scholars). Their duties in the church consist of singing. One of them is selected as the head of the church and of church property. He likewise designates who of the priests and deacons serves. (In this regard, they are extremely punctilious. Only those priests serve who are notable for their irreproachable behavior.)

Monasticism in Abyssinia is very widespread. Formerly, there were two orders: the order of Saint Tekla Haymanot and the order of Eustaphy. The latter was in Gojjam. But now this order apparently does not exist. There are monks who are itinerant, and others who live in the world, and others who live on the summits of cliffs in monasteries. There are also nuns. Abyssinian monks are notable for their asceticism. In general, the clergy have many good qualities. They have a very strong influence on the people. They always take on the role of supporters of the weak and as peacemakers. Each church has the right of sanctuary. In civil relations, each church represents itself as an independent entity. Each church owns land, which is worked by its peasa

Conclusion

Finally, I consider it necessary to summarize my impressions of Abyssinia and, on the basis of these impression and observations, to draw some conclusions about this country in the form of answers to questions which commonly interest us Russians:

1) *Are the Abyssinians savages?*
I think that having become acquainted, just in my short overview, with their faith, morals, customs and governmental structure, no one should have the slightest doubt that the Abyssinians are an old cultured race, although considerably backward today, compared to Europe, as a result of historical causes. They are surrounded by savages.

2) *What kind of government does Abyssinia have? Is its power based exclusively on the extraordinary personality of Menelik or does it rest on firm foundations? Does this government have vitality or does it contain within itself many corrupting elements?*
From the historical overview we see that Abyssinia has passed through a period of civil war. On the debris of the power of separate military leaders and independent rulers, which was broken by Emperors Tewodros and Yohannes, there grew a single strong imperial power, supported by the whole people in the form of a volunteer army. The state is bound to this new phase not exclusively by the personality of Emperor Menelik, but rather it was prepared for it by the preceding destruction of the old foundations. The reliability of the foundations of the state comes from the deep feeling of lawfulness and the consciousness of the people, and likewise from the fact that there are no strong opponents of the imperial power. There may be disturbances when there is a change of ruler, but they could not be serious. Internal opposition to the imperial power has been done away with. There are no external enemies who are close and sufficiently strong. Consequently, the state has all the prerequisites for a long existence.

3) *Are the Abyssinians Christian or is their faith a mixture of pagan, Christian and Jewish beliefs?*
From my perspective, they are very close to Orthodoxy. They are deeply believing Christians, who have preserved many peculiarities of the ancient apostolic church. They have some vestiges of Judaism, but these do not appear to have influenced their basic Christian faith.

4) *Is Abyssinia a poor country, or, on the contrary, is it rich?*
While the people are poor, the country, especially the Galla lands, is very rich.

5) *What kind of relations does it have with Europeans?*
After all that they learned from their recent bitter lessons, it is hard to expect great love. Those who are at the helm of power fear the Europeans. Some envy them, and the majority hold them in contempt. But in this case, it depends on the tact of each individual person to make himself respected or even loved, or the reverse. In any case, Abyssinians show much greater sympathy for Russians, especially those Abyssinians who have had the opportunity to get to know us. "Moscow is Christian" is the general belief of the people, while they aren't convinced that other Europeans really are Christian.

Let's move on then to the question that is most interesting to us: *What kind of relations can we have with Abyssinia?* We'll break that into two questions: *What can the Abyssinians expect from us? And what benefit can we get from Abyssinia?*

The Abyssinians can want from us: first, moral support in their relations with foreign powers; second, material support in the form of delivery of weapons and shells to them, in the form of teaching young Abyssinians handicrafts and technical sciences, in the form of sending to Abyssinia our doctors, technicians, artisans, and artillery instructors.

For us, Abyssinia can present the following interest. Having cast a glance at the map of Central Africa and on the borders of the Ethiopian Empire, you can easily see that being located in the vicinity of the Middle Nile, halfway between Egypt and the great lakes, which belong to England, Abyssinia, which is expanding each year more and more and taking large tracts of land which had been free—rich and densely populated territory—must become the natural and main enemy of England in Central Africa. England is also our main enemy. To help the enemy of our enemy, to make him as much stronger as possible—that is our main goal in Abyssinia.

But apart from this main goal, we have other important interests. As is evident from what has been said before, trade with Abyssinia can be very advantageous for Russia.

In the not too distant future, a union of the Ethiopian church with Orthodoxy could take place.

Considering how easy it is to recruit soldiers in Abyssinia, we could use this source to put together several detachments of Abyssinians for action on our south-eastern and eastern borders. In case of European war, they could be of great use to us thanks to the great moral effect which they could have on our enemies. Their endurance and fighting qualities are well known. The cost of maintaining them would exceed by little the cost to maintain our field troops.

But to bring all this about, it is necessary first of all to transfer the accidental and sometimes odd relations between Russia and Abyssinia to serious ground. It is my deep conviction that Abyssinia can stand us in good stead, and that Russia can benefit from paying attention to it.

Appendix

Equipment

My equipment consisted of:
- One round tent of the Abyssinian style, six arshins (14 feet) in diameter.
- One small tent of the Abyssinian style for each servant.
- One caldron (25 pounds) for the servants.
- Two field mess-tins.
- One Abyssinian frying pan (one and a half pounds) for cooking flat cakes.
- One copper coffeepot.
- One enameled teapot.
- One large enameled mug.
- 500 Abyssinian biscuits, weighing about six poods [216 pounds], (a gift from Emperor Menelik).
- One sack of rye flour, two poods and 5 pounds [77 pounds] of millet grain.
- One 30-pound wineskin of ground pepper and *tef* meal.
- Five pounds of oatmeal.
- Two jars of concentrated milk.
- One jar of cocoa.
- Five pounds of tea and two pounds of sugar.
- Five bottles of vodka.
- Ten bottles of cranberry essence.
- Twenty-five pieces of salt (money and food), one pood and 10 pounds [46 pounds).
- 400 Maria Theresa talers.
- 12 pounds of candles, at eight to the pound (96 candles).
- 300 packets of matches.
- One Red Cross lantern.
- One Red Cross field bed.
- One tarpaulin.

Field First-Aid Kit

Two packets of wadding and 12 gauze bandages in a holster. One two-pound packet of quinine and 35 powders. Forty laxative powders. Seventy powders for rheumatism. Twenty mustard plasters. Two bottles of castor oil. One bottle of opium. One battle of sublimate in tablets (50 tablets). One bottle of iodoform. One bottle of Dzhevinskiy eye drops, unknown in medicine. One bottle of strychnine. Sticking and mercurial plaster. One spool of American antiseptic plasters.

Tools

Two axes. Six sickles. A screwdriver, tongs, and cleaning rods for cleaning guns. Two awls. Two stakes for horse lines, a brush, and a horse comb. One pair of scissors. Needles and thread. Forty arshins [about 31 yards] of towing rope.

Clothing

Felt cloak, overcoat, greatcoat, raincoat, full hussar uniform, Swedish jacket, Austrian jacket, and four pair of blue trousers. Two white canvas suits. Five changes of flannel underwear. Twelve pairs of woolen socks. Twelve handkerchiefs. Six towels. Five pairs of boots (one hussar, one personal, one hunting, and two half-boots.).

Gifts

Six Abyssinian shammas. Forty arshins [about 31 yards] of silk cloth. Forty arshins of red calico. Ten arshins [about eight yards] of muslin. Four nickel-plated watches with chains. Five Swedish knives. Sixty silver crosses and little icons. Six silk shawls. Six bottles of perfume. Books, writing materials, and washing set.

All of these amounted to a weight of 45 poods [1620 pounds], including 20 poods [720 pounds] of powder, three poods [108 pounds] of shot, and 800 cartridges. It was carried by eight mules, which amounted to about six poods [216 pounds] per mule.

Packing

The packing was done as follows:
The large tent with appurtenances was wrapped in the large tarpaulin. The field bed was packed in the trunk that goes with it. Writing and washing materials, blanket, felt cloak, two changes of underwear, Swedish jacket, quarter pound of tea, one

candle, two boxes of matches, sack of coffee, sack of salt, spoon, knife, fork, and one bottle of vodka were all packed in a hold-all. Clothes, gifts, and money were packed tight in two field pack-loads, ordered by me in Petersburg. Wine was carefully packed and taken in a sack. A tin box with alcohol and a tin box with water were each taken in a skin. Axes and sickles were in a separate sack. Powder, shot, and hunting gear were in two boxes. Biscuits were in a pack trunk of the Zvyagin system. (On the third march, I had to throw this trunk away and repack the biscuit in a wineskin). Rye flour was in a sack. Victuals of the servants were in a wineskin. Five pounds of millet, five pounds of oatmeal, dried vegetables, two jars of milk, one jar of cocoa, candles, matches, and tea were all in two wineskins. Salt was tied up in ropes and taken in a skin. The caldron, mess-tins, teapot, coffeepot, frying pan, and tin box for water were strapped to packs. The first-aid kit was packed in a holster and carried by one of the servants; likewise the photographic apparatus.

Distribution in packs

All this was divided among seven mules as follows:
Mule Number 1: The large tent in a tarpaulin with the tools.
Mule Number 2: Sack of meal on one side; hold-all with everyday necessities and bed on the other.
Mule Number 3: A pack with dried crust, strapped teapot, coffeepot, and tin for water; and on top a box with 400 Gra cartridges.
Mule Number 4: A small tent and on it two boxes with powder and shot; on top a caldron, strapped mess-tins and frying pan.
Mule Number 5: Two pack trunks with clothing, gifts, and money; on top, wine.
Mule Number 6: Two wine skins with supplies; on top, a tin with alcohol and salt.
Mule Number 7: One wineskin with victuals, little wineskins and individual knapsacks; on top, a tin with water and a box with 400 Gra cartridges.

For packing, the tent was put together in such a way as to make a bale two and a half arshins [about two yards] long and one arshin [28 inches] wide. It was put on the back of the mule in the middle.

A sack of meal on one side and the bed with the hold-all on the other, each package strongly tied with ropes, thoroughly tightened and placed on the saddle so that the pressure fell on the base of the ribs.

The biscuits were first put in the trunk of the Zvyagin system. Each of the biscuits were 14 vershoks [24-1/2 inches] long, 10 vershoks [17-1/2 inches] thick, and 6 vershoks [10-1/2 inches] wide. The first day we tried to pack them ingeniously but this turned out to be too uncomfortable. The middle bank connecting both trunks was too long and the trunks hung on the sides, weighing heavy on the spine and squeezing the sides. In addition, this position was very unsteady and required constant adjusting. Thanks to that position of the trunks, the straps for packing touched the mule at only two points: the middle of the back and under the belly. On the following day, the servants packed it in their own way, and in this new way the mule was more comfortable. But nevertheless on the third day it succeeded in throwing and shifting off two wineskins of biscuits.

Two boxes with powder and shot were tightly connected to one another, making two sides of a pack. For softness, a small tent was placed under them. Four hundred Gra cartridges were placed in the gun box and packed lengthwise on top of a mule.

Two pack trunks were tightly connected with rope. Two wineskins with supplies were tightly connected as the previous packs, and on top was packed a large tin with vodka.

Thus, for the anticipated six-month journey my goods were distributed by sections in the following way:

Articles of comfort: tent, bed—five poods [180 pounds].
Clothing and footwear—one pood [36 pounds].
Gifts—3 poods [108 pounds].
Food stuffs—meal victuals, biscuits—seven poods [252 pounds].
Alcohol, vodka, and wine—two poods [72 pounds].
Salt and money—two poods.
Lighting—12 pounds.
Powder, shot, and cartridges—eight poods [288 pounds].
First-aid kit—7 pounds.

The most meager section was food stuffs. But, according to the information I had, a large part of the journey passed through thickly settled places, and the food stuffs were taken as an inviolable reserve to make sure. With my 17 servants, we could be satisfied for 15 days with the biscuits and meal we had taken. I threw away the meal on the sixth march since one of my mules opened the old packing, and meal was always easy to obtain on the way.

Loading on Mules

The main principle of loading is that one must arrange the pack in such a way that it lies on the base of the ribs evenly, not touching the spine. Tightly connected, both sides of the pack are lifted by two servants who going behind the mule place the pack on its back. A third servant holds the mule by the reins. The pack is attached with long straps—one inch wide and 10 to 12 arshins [about 8 yards] long. In the middle a noose is tied, and the strap is placed in such a way that it lies in the middle of the load along the back of the mule, with the noose behind. Then the strap from both sides is placed under the front part of the pack, and the ends are pushed through the noose and thrown over to the opposite side, forming in this way in its turn a one and a half to two arshin [42 to 56 inch] noose. [The original showed this in a drawing.] These nooses are stretched to the opposite side under the stomach and are drawn by the ends of the straps. This method of packing is very simple and in case of unhurried travel is completely satisfactory. But for quick marches is it insufficient since it requires constant pulling of the straps, and especially if the mules will trot. The limit of speed of movement with light and balanced packs is eight versts [a little over five miles] an hour.

APPENDIX NUMBER 2

Composition of the detachment

14 servants, two pack mules, and one saddled mule.

Equipment

One small tent. Two pack-loads including: two changes of underclothing, two pairs of boots (the usual hussar kind), gifts, two watches, 20 arshins [about 16 yards] of silk cloth, and three bottles of perfume.

Mule Number 1

Rolled up thick felt for bedding at night and in it a blanket. Abyssinian shamma. Twelve candles. Twelve boxes of matches. Wadding and bandages for dressings. One bottle of cognac. One pound of coffee. And 300 talers.

Mule Number 2

Two wineskins with peas, field mess-tin, frying pan, teapot, five pieces of salt, bag with tools, two axes and three sickles, and 400 spare cartridges.

A field first-aid kid and photographic apparatus were carried separately.

Appendix Number 3

The description of several wounds, inflicted on several animals by a 3/8-inch-caliber rifle 1891 model. (Excerpt from my hunting journal).

On November 8, 1896, a chamois—*orobo* was killed. It was wounded by a first shot at a distance of 200 paces and, having been wounded, it ran. We followed it for 1,000 paces from the place where the first shot struck him. The bullet punched a two-vershok [three and a half inch] hole in its neck in front of the shoulders. The cervical vertebrae were not touched. The wound was barely noticeable.

On November 7, an antelope (bokhor) was wounded. It ran after the first shot. On the second shot from a Gra rifle my servant laid it low, hitting it in the head. The first bullet from a distance of 100 paces punched a hole in him through both lungs, not touching the ribs. The wound was scarcely noticeable. There was internal hemorrhaging.

On March 6, a hippopotamus was killed. A bullet from a distance of 200 paces struck it at the base of the neck, punched through the shoulder bone, making a crack in it and passing out through the lower part of the stomach. The wound was more than two arshins [56 inches] long. The entry opening was scarcely noticeable. The exit had two openings. The bullet went along the skin and in the lower part of the stomach—two lacerated wounds in the shape of longitudinal sections, the first about one vershok [one and three-quarters inches] long, and the second somewhat larger.

On March 9, an elephant was killed with a shot to the head from a distance of 50 paces. The bullet punched through the base of the right tusk and went into the skull. In the meat there is a scarcely noticeable little hole. The bone was splintered.

Appendix Number 4

Words of the Gimiro and Madibis Languages

Gimiro	Russian	Madibis	[English]
	bog	Babata, Iuda	God
	dyavol	botya	devil
	chelovyek	agara	man
ay	voda	fere	water
	zemlya	tiaka	land
damu	ogon	fala	fire
	otets	baba	father
	mat	aa	mother
	devushka	bempel	girl
	brat	abolonka	brother
	ruzhe	alemendi	gun
ebo	kopye	beri	spear
	loshad	nokhti	horse
gali	golova	okholo	head
	zhilishche pokhlebkas	katenna, shuli	dwelling
	myshami	kukum	soup with mice
donka	durra	terbakero	sorghum, a Turkish millet
	reka	wolo	river
	kamen	balye	stone
inchu	les	chicho	forest
bo	zhivot		stomach

Appendix Number 5

Commerce in Abyssinia

Constant wars, poor means of communication, the poverty of the populace and the absence in it of capital mean that the trade and industry of Abyssinia are insignificant in comparison with what they could be under other circumstances. As a matter of fact, Abyssinia itself is a poor country. Not for nothing, the English, having taken Magdala in 1867 and, evidently, having had, in that troubled time, the possibility of securing a firm footing here, did not take advantage of this and completely repudiated any pretension to it. Evidently, the game was not worth the candle. But at that time, Abyssinia did not yet own the marvelous lands of the Galla—the homeland of coffee, gold deposits, and lowlands teeming with elephants. The present-day capital, Entotto, was still inaccessible for Abyssinians and in the hands of Galla. Since then, the times have changed and the commercial revenue of Abyssinia grows from year to year. But, of course, there still remains much to desire. The poverty of the inhabitants makes for very limited demand. Guns, cheap cotton and silk cloth, some cheap household articles such as, for instance, tin cups and glass decanters—such are the main imported articles. Exports consist of gold, ivory, musk and primarily coffee. The export of exclusively expensive and difficult to obtain articles is caused by the poor means of transportation. Were that not the case, the country could quickly develop agriculture, cotton-growing, tobacco-growing, and others. Constant wars also, evidently have a great influence on commerce.

The absence of a convenient monetary unit and the constantly changing rate of exchange also have bad effects. The existing monetary unit is the Maria Theresa taler, and recently the talers of Emperor Menelik, minted in France. The value of both is the same, but inside Abyssinia they accept the taler of Emperor Menelik at a lower price than the old one. The rate of exchange in Aden fluctuates from 2 francs 50 to 3 francs 10. Each taler weighs 27 grams, and consequently, you need to have a separate mule for loading 3,000 talers. In Central and Southern Abyssinia, bars of salt six vershoks [10-1/2 inches] long and one vershok [1-3/4 inches] thick and weighing from 3 to 4 pounds serves as small change.

Articles for export usually pass several times from hand to hand before reaching the sea. For instance, coffee is bought in the west and southwest from local landowners. It is carried by Galla merchants to some central point, as for instance, Bilo, Supe, or Lekamte, where it is resold to other merchants who take it to Shoa or even to Harar. There it falls either into the hands of Europeans (mainly the trading house "Tian and Company") or of Arabs and Indians. They take it to Aden. Such resale within the country is made necessary by the fact that usually after a 300-400 verst [210-280 mile] trip, the mules, which carry very important cargo, which weighs up to eight poods [288 pounds], by bad roads and eating exclusively scanty pasturage, find themselves completely emaciated and beaten and demand rest. Gold comes from Wollaga and from the basin of the Tumat River, which belongs to Abdurakhman, until this time an independent ruler. The Galla gather the gold beyond a waterfall in a hole at the bottom of the river. They thoroughly wash the gold sand in the most primitive way and then they melt the gold they obtain into ringlets. It differs greatly in purity: from 1000 to 810 parts of pure gold. It is of a light yellow color, very soft and easily squeezed. Twenty-seven grams (the weight of a taler is called an uket) is worth 28-30 talers locally, and in Aden is worth 34 talers. Apparently, trade is not very profitable, but taking into account the rate of exchange of talers and the fact that for gold they are paid in merchandise and make a profit on that, all this turns out to be not as unprofitable as it seems at first glance. Considering the taler at 2 francs 60, a pound of 19-carat gold costs 444 rubles locally. But 30 talers for an uket is a price which French traders consider little profitable for themselves. In Aden a kilogram sells for 3025 francs, that is one pound—467 to 468 rubles, which amounts to 24 rubles per pound of gross profit, i.e., 5%. But in essence, as I mentioned above, in view of the fact that for this traders are paid in merchandise, gold brings much greater profit, all the more in view of the fact that its small volume means transport costs very little. As far as I know, among us at the present time one pound of gold costs about 400 rubles, but this is the cost of 14-carat gold; pure gold costs about 500 rubles.

Consequently, trade in gold with Abyssinia could be profitable.

Civet musk is obtained in the humid forested western regions from an animal which the Abyssinians call tryn. The method of obtaining the musk is described by me. The cost in Aden of one kilogram is 1,600 francs, which amounts to one pound or 246 rubles, i.e. almost 17 times more valuable than the same weight of silver. In Entotto, musk sells for eight times more than the same weight of silver, that is one uket for 8 talers, or one pound for 118 rubles. Consequently, for 246 rubles you can obtain 128 rubles of gross profit, i.e. 52%. But trade in this article is very difficult and unreliable, since pure musk is hard to get usually pass several times from hand to hand. Here they dilute it with the feces of this animal and also cow butter, and these admixtures are very difficult to detect; so in Aden they are very suspicious of musk and knocking down the price for it even for good musk. Frequently, local French merchants do not send musk to Aden, since they conduct direct dealings with Paris.

Ivory is sold for the most part from the court of the emperor. Sometimes the emperor pays his debts to suppliers with tusks. The ivory is of very good quality. In Aden, one pound of ivory costs more than 4 rubles for tusks weighing not less than a pood [36 pounds] and less for other tusks. Locally, one uket of ivory, i.e. the weight of 840 talers or 1 pood 28-1/10 pounds [64-1/10 pounds], costs 77 talers, i.e. one pound costs a little more than a ruble. This is the price of large tusks. Thus, the gross profit amounts to 300 to 400%. But this trade, more than all others, varies in price. The fluctuation makes trade in it very difficult. Scarcely does someone announce a large quantity of ivory for sale, and the price immediately drops terribly, and many Frenchmen who are in Abyssinia suffer great losses. The largest trading house that buys ivory is "Tian and Company," which, however, holds in secret the quantity of goods it has for sale, and sometimes tusks lie in its storeroom for many years before they are sold. In Petersburg at the present time, one pound of ivory from large tusks costs six rubles, and this article could find a direct market in Russia.

Coffee is divided into two main kinds: wild coffee of Kaffa, Mocha, and western regions, and cultivated coffee of Harar and Chercher. Both of them are of excellent quality, comparable to the very best kind of Mocha coffee. Harar coffee costs more since it is harvested at the right time. Kaffa coffee is harvested after it falls from the tree; which means that from lying on the ground it blackens and loses part of its aroma and hence its value.

Buyers of coffee in Abyssinia itself are almost exclusively Abyssinians and Galla. Europeans in this trade do very little business inside the country since transport of coffee demands a great quantity of mules. The representatives of the large companies from Aden which buy coffee are found in Harar. In Aden, the price for one kilogram of the best coffee is 3 francs 50 centimes. In Harar, it costs half that; and inside Abyssinia the price is a quarter or a fifth what it is in Aden. In Harar a frazla (measure of weight) is equal to 37-1/2 pounds and sells for 6 to 8 talers, i.e. one kilogram for 1 franc 38 centimes, a Russian pound for 21 to 22 kopecks. In Petersburg, one pound of the best coffee costs 65 kopecks. Coffee could likewise become an article for import into Russia from Abyssinia; and, undoubtedly, quite a lot of coffee could be sold here since it is accepted practice mainly to call "Abyssinian" the Mocha coffee that reaches us far from the first hands.

Of the remaining articles exported from Abyssinia, we must mention wax, which is of very good quality but is exported in small quantities; and skins which are exported in very large quantities. A lot of incense is exported from the port of Zeila. It is obtained in the coastal Somali steppes. Gum arabic is also from there. From Abyssinia, many mules were exported in the past, but in recent times that export has been stopped since in the recent war many mules were killed.

Agricultural produce is not exported from Abyssinia despite the great fertility of the region. Likewise they do not export cotton, which they get there in excellent quality, but all of which is consumed inside the country. This results from the low price of these articles compared with their volume and the difficulty of transporting them.

The main imported article is guns. Most of all they import guns of the Gra system, which the Emperor buys for 18 talers each. On the side, they are sold for 20 to 25 talers.

The revolvers they import are mostly second-hand and old and sell for 12 to 20 talers each.

Saber blades are very expensive, especially thin, long ones. They sell for 12 talers each.

Silver is imported annually in large quantities in the form of money—Maria Theresa talers. Because the value of exports exceeds the value of imports, this money stays in the country. These talers are made in Austria, and the silver is of very low purity. Other imported metals include: iron in the form of wires and small manufactured articles, copper and lead in ingots, steel and mercury for gilding. All of these are imported in very small quantities.

Cotton fabric is imported into Abyssinia in small quantities. Above all they import inexpensive, thin, white cotton fabric of Indian manufacture, which is used in Abyssinia in the sewing of trousers and tents. In Addis Ababa a piece of abujedi—which is what the Abyssinians call this fabric—sells for 4 talers. One such piece measures 18 meters or 26 arshins, or 48 "elbows" (the local measure of length from the elbow to the end of the fingers). Aside from abujedi, they also import a better kind of cotton fabric, but in very small quantities. Usually all the caravans which carry coffee sell their coffee in Harar and buy abujedi there, and take them to Entotto where they buy salt and take it to the far western regions where they exchange it for coffee.

Salt is obtained from Lake Assal and Lake Massovy. The salt is set in the form of bars six vershoks [10-1/2 inches] long and 1 vershok [1-3/4 inches] thick, weighing from three to four pounds. Now in Addis Ababa for one taler you can get six new salt bars or seven old ones, which comes to about four kopecks a pound. They import silk fabric (in the form of part silk material for shirts), velvet, and velveteen. They import a lot of these fabrics because they go in shirts and in the battle dress of officers of the army.

Silk fabric is required in bright colors with narrow lines of mixed-colors (two colors) alternating among themselves. They prefer thick fabric, including cotton underwear. One kend of this fabric, i.e. an "elbow" ten vershoks [17-1/2 inches] long, sells in Abyssinia for one taler, i.e. an arshin [28 inches] for one rubles 60 kopecks.

Velvet in solid bright colors sells in Addis Ababa for the same price.

Silk thread of various colors, especially dark blue, almost black (the latter manufactured in Smyrna), which all Christians wear around their neck, is sold in Addis Ababa by weight. A bundle of silk that weighs as much as 12 talers sells for 6 talers, i.e. a pound goes for 7 rubles 40 kopecks.

Cognac and vodka of very poor quality are imported in large quantities.

The very cheapest cognac, of Greek manufacture, sells in Addis Ababa for one and a half talers per bottle. Vodka sells for one taler. They import red Greek wine and cheap champagne, but in very small quantities.

Sugar is imported in small quantities, in the form of small lumps or in grains. It is of French manufacture and very poor quality—soft, with a small percentage of pure sugar. It is sold in Addis Ababa for 40 kopecks a pound.

Small glass decanters of Venetian manufacture are a necessary possession for each Abyssinian house that is in the slightest degree prosperous. In Addis Ababa two decanters cost one taler, or a decanter for 50 kopecks.

Enameled tin cups for drinking mead in Addis Ababa sell for two for a taler.

Cheap printed rugs likewise are imported.

They import many such objects as: cheap watches; perfume of the very worst quality, brightly painted cotton shawls, beads, felt hats with wide brims, pa*Ras*ols, and soap.

Aden is the main marketplace of Abyssinia and the place where its exports are concentrated and through which imports go.

Trade in the direction from the sea to the middle of the country goes by four routes: 1) Massawa to Gojjam, 2) Jibuti to Harar to Shoa, 3) Zeila to Harar to Shoa, and 4) Berber to Kofir to Jimma to Kaffa.

The first route lost its significance with the shift of the political and economic center of Abyssinia to the south, and likewise after the capture of the Sudan by the dervishes.

The second route is the most convenient since it has almost weekly steamship communication with Europe.

The third route is the richest in means of conveyance through desert. It is the favorite of local merchants.

The fourth route is unknown to Europeans, and about its existence one can rather conjecture.

Consequently, the two main points are through Jibuti and Zeila to Harar and Shoa.

The conditions of transport and the cost of transporting one pood of cargo by both routes is the same. They differ only in the internal order of each port and its transport connections with Europe. Jibuti belongs to France and was built recently. Thanks to the regular and frequent transport of the General-Madagascar "messagerie maritime," which has two lines—Indochinese and Madagascar—the steamships of which visit

Jibuti almost weekly, this port has very quickly gained great significance. One of the two steamships that come to Jibuti goes through Aden. The significance of Jibuti to Abyssinia is bound up with the fact that up until now this was the only port through which guns were allowed to pass into Abyssinia. Aside from the steamships, Arab sail-powered barges also carry on frequent commercial transport with Aden and other coastal ports.
These conveniences of Jibuti are paralyzed by:

1) The establishment of import and export duties. For example, import duties: for one gun—2 francs 65 centimes; for a revolver the same; for 500 cartridges 2 francs 50 centimes; for one kilogram of powder 3 francs; for cognac and strong drinks 20 centimes per liter; for alcohol 80 centimes per liter. Export duties: for each animal—horse, mule, cow, ox —4 talers 11 francs.

2) The punctilliousness of the French administration. The administration has established many rules, putting useless restraints on the inhabitants. For instance, it requires that camel-drivers remove from the streets the manure left by their camels (in case of refusal they are put into prison). I heard about this requirement in Leka, in the commercial town of Bilo, where merchants were indignant about this, saying that it would be necessary to tie a sack to the tail of the camel. And finally,

3) The comparative difficulty of transport connections with Aden. Zeila is 40 versts [28 miles] east of Jibuti. It belongs to the English. The port does not present conveniences like Jibuti, and large ships cannot put in there, having to drop anchor very far from shore. Transport with Aden is carried out by small steamboat, which completes a trip once every two weeks, and by Arab sail-powered barges. Nevertheless almost all the trade in coffee and a large part of the imports go through Zeila. For comparison, I will present the data on exports of coffee through Jibuti and Zeila for 1891. From Jibuti coffee valued at 250,000 franc was exported; from Zeila 1,380,310 francs—i.e. almost six times as much. The remaining articles of export are distributed more evenly between these two ports. French merchants in Abyssinia send their goods to Jibuti (Messieurs Savure, Monat, Trule, Stevena, Pineau and some others). And all the Armenians and Greeks together with Arabs and Abyssinians send their good to Zeila (the main Armenian merchant is Tigran).

I do not have exact data on annual exports through Zeila and Jibuti. But there is data on exports and imports through Jibuti for three months (January, February, and March) from which I derive several characteristic numbers:

There was imported:
guns—394 boxes (4728 guns)
cartridges—592 boxes
cotton fabric—3450 items (valued at 604,000 francs)
silk fabric—14 items
strong drink—53 boxes (valued at 1,590 francs).

There was exported:
ox-hide and sheepskin—11,549 items (valued at 86,544 francs)
coffee—4,180 frazla—62,700 kilograms (valued at 53,440 francs)
musk 1,000 *ukets*—27 kilograms (valued at 43,200 francs)
gold worth 20,000 francs
ivory worth 18,000 francs
raw wax worth 2,000 francs.

The cost to transport a pound of cargo to Addis Ababa includes: 1) what you pay to hire camels from Jibuti or Zeila to Erer or to Harar, what you pay to hire camels from Erer to Balcha and then from Balcha to hire mules to Addis Ababa, or by the high road in Harar to buy mules and carry cargo to Addis Ababa; 2) the pay and cost of up-keep for servants and 3) customs duties at a rate of 1/10 the value of all products which they pay either in Harar or in Addis Ababa.

1) Transport by the road through Harar amounts to: the price of hiring a camel which can carry a load weighing 500 pounds or 12-1/2 poods, or for two camels each carrying half a load equals 14 talers or rubles.

From Geldessa (an Abyssinian border point and customs house) to Harar other camels are hired at a cost of 1-1/2 talers for a full load of 12-1/2 poods.

The composition and movement of caravans is very simple. From Jibuti or Zeila you announce the news to these people that you need so many camels, and they supply them to you quickly enough if camels are available at that time and not too weakened at the end of the hot season. If they are not available, you must wait or send the cargo in parts. The leader of a caravan, called the aban, selects the members of the caravan. He is the person responsible for all the belongings entrusted to him, and he carries out his responsibilities honestly enough, since from Jibuti or Zeila to Harar special care and protection are not required. You promise and give the aban several talers as a reward. You pay part of the money for the transport at the outset and part at the delivery of the cargo. For best protection of belongings, it is good if some of your own servants with guns go along with the caravan—servants whom they usually pay 5 talers at Harar and give upkeep. The caravan workers and the abans are Somali, but for servants you must hire Abyssinians.

You buy mules in Harar. The average price of a pack mule is 32 to 34 talers. For slow going, for every five mules you must have three servants. The pay to them from Harar to Entotto is 5 talers plus upkeep. The upkeep for three servants costs about two talers for the whole trip. Consequently the transport of cargo by five mules, i.e. 30-35 poods [1,080 to 1,260 pounds], amounts to, including the purchase price of the mules, 187 talers; and not including the purchase price of the mules—17 talers. Consequently, transport of a pood [36 pounds] of cargo from Jibuti or Zeila through Harar to Addis Ababa costs, taking into account the cost of buying mules:
to Harar—one pood for one ruble and 20 to 25 kopecks
from Harar to Addis Ababa—one pood for 5 rubles 34 kopecks
total for one pood = 6 rubles and 54 to 60 kopecks.

The distance by this road is 850 to 900 versts [570 to 600 miles]; the total per verst per pound is .73 kopecks. If you do not take into account the cost of the mules, then the transport from Jibuti and Zeila to Addis Ababa costs for one pood one ruble 75 kopecks, i.e. .2 kopecks per verst.

By the second route the cost is as follows.

2) From Jibuti or Zeila to Erer with a fully loaded camel costs 16 talers and a reward to the aban. In Erer they change Somali camels for Danikil ones, with the help of their leader from the Tumbakho tribe. He designates one of them as the responsible aban, but this serves as a very bad guarantee of the safety of the belongings, which they deal with very carelessly. The price of a camel for a full load from Erer to Balcha is 18 talers. For the safety of the cargo, it is necessary to send several armed servants with the caravan, and you pay these servants about 10 to 12 talers for the trek from Jibuti to Addis Ababa. In Balcha you hire mules, donkeys, and horses to Addis Ababa at four talers for the cargo of one mule. Thus, by this road the transport of a pood [36 pounds] of cargo costs about three rubles, which for a distance of 900 versts [600 miles] amounts to .33 kopecks per verst.

Delivery through Harar is faster, but does not allow for transport of bulky items and requires the availability of one's own mules. Therefore, Europeans prefer the second route for their caravans. All the local merchants use the first route as safer for passenger trips and because it passes through territory in which the climate is not as hot.

From this overview, it is evident that trade with Abyssinia does not involve insurmountable difficulties. It is completely possible and would be far from unprofitable for us Russians.

All the articles of export from Abyssinia which find a ready market in Russia, we obtain second hand and overpay considerably, (for instance, coffee or gold, which at the first-hand price would be profitable for our state treasury to obtain).

Some items of import to Abyssinia, as, for instance, silk, cotton, iron, steel, and glass manufactured articles, guns, sugar, alcohol and strong drinks, and kerosene, for which they need a seacoast, we make in Russia; and ours cost no more than the foreign ones.

The distance from Odessa to the Red Sea coast is equal to the distance from Marseilles. Consequently, the transport couldn't cost us more. There remains only to establish direct communication with some port of this coast. And one can not only express the hope, but truly say that profits of trade will become so evident that owners and capital will be found to put our commercial relations with Abyssinia on firm foundations.

Notes

B: = Bulatovich, author
K: = Katsnelson, editor of the Russian reprint
S: = Seltzer, translator

1K: With insignificant abridgments, this is published in accord with the text of the book From Entotto to the River Baro. An Account of a Trip to the Southwestern Regions of the Ethiopian Empire 1896-97, 204 pages. Entotto, the first residence of Menelik, is located on the heights that have the same name, is quite close to the present-day Addis Ababa, which became the capital of the country in 1889.

2K: Alfred Ilg (1854-1916) was a Swiss engineer. He spent 30 years in Ethiopia (1878-1907), and from 1897 to 1907 was a minister. He was engaged in the building of railroads, helping very much the penetration of foreign capital into Ethiopia. His influence at the court of Menelik was very significant, especially in questions of external politics. In 1880 Alfred Ilg went as far as the River Baro (C. Keller, Alfred Ilg. Sein Leben und Wirken als schweizerischer Kulterbote in Abessinien. Frauenfeld—Leipzig, 1918).

3K: Dutchman Jan Maria Schuver made a trip to this region in 1881-1882 (see: J. M. Schuver, Reisen in oberen Nilgebiet. Erlebnisse und Beobactunguen auf der Wasserscheide zwischen Blauen und Weissen Nil and der agyptisch-*Abe*ssinischen Grenzlandern, 1881 und 1882, Gotha, 1883).

4B: A distinguished military leader of Menelik.

5K: *Ras* Gobana (1817-1889) subdued the Galla tribes for Menelik. He went as far as Bure on the River Baro in 1886.

6K: The Galla tribes (who call themselves "Oromo"), arrived from the south in the sixteenth century and settled in the central, western and, partially, in the north-western regions of Ethiopia. At the present time, they number about five million. The Galla language is related to the Cushitic group. They partially mixed with the Amharas and adopted Christianity. In the eastern regions, where their basic occupation is cattle-breeding, Gallas profess Islam. However, they still preserve many vestiges of more primitive religious beliefs. See: G.M. Huntingford. The Galla of Ethiopia. The Kingdom of Kaffa and Janjero, London, 1955 (Ethnographical Survey of Africa. North-Eastern Africa, part II).

7B: Before this I petitioned the commander of the Russian Red Cross Detachment, General Shvedov, for permission to undertake a journey to Kaffa.

But the Emperor categorically refused, saying that to let me go there would be to doom me to certain death, and he didn't want me to die through any fault of his.

8K: *Dajazmatch*, see section on Military Hierarchy: "full general or lieutenant general, commander either of his own army or of a detachment of the emperor, of a *Negus* or of a *Ras*."

9B: For details about equipment, packing, and loading, see Appendix 1.

10B: Lady.

11K: Zawditu was a daughter of Menelik II. From 1916-1930 she was empress of Ethiopia.

12B: Head of an administrative district.

13K: *Ras*, see section on Military Hierarchy: "field marshal, independent commander of the army of his region or of one of the amries of the emperor or of a *Negus*."

14K: Taitu, the wife of Menelik II, had significant political influence (see the section on the Emperor's Family).

15B: A duty paid in kind, consisting of what the inhabitants furnish as provisions and forage to all who travel with the permission or under the orders of the Emperor.

16B: Flat round pancakes, which serve as a substitute for bread.

17B: An intoxicating drink made from honey.

18B: A drink like the Russian "kvas," made from sugar.

19K: See the section on Abyssinian Clothing.

20K: Here he means the valley of the River Omo (its upper reaches). Also see note 46.

21K: Zara Yakob (Constantin I) ruled from 1434-1468. Under him, Medieval Ethiopia attained the apogee of power, since Zara Yakob was able to, although with cruel means, achieve the unification of the country.

22B: A large earthenware pitcher.

23B: "Mouth of the *Negus*"—chief judge.

24K: *Fitaurari*, see section on Military Hierarchy: "major general, leader of either a separate army or one of the detachments of the emperor, a *Negus*, a *Ras*, or a *Dajazmatch*."

25B: Empress.

26B: Home of a woman; in translation "bedroom."

27K: Danakils are nomad cattle-breeders who inhabit the Danakil Desert and the sea coast of Eritrea (the northern part of the region of Harar, the eastern regions of Wollo and Tigre). Their language, Afar, belongs to the Cushitic group. Their general population is about three hundred twenty thousand. Their religion is Islam.

28B: Military rank. [K: *Balambaras*, see section on Military Hierarchy: "commandant. Literally translated 'leader where there is no fort'; corresponds to captain."]

29K: Sidamo is the collective name of a series of peoples of Ethiopia.

30K: *Kanyazmatch*, see section on Military Hierarchy: "colonel, leader of a detachment."

31K: *Azzaj*, see section on Military Hierarchy: "court marshalls or those who govern estates."

32B: Civetta viverra.
33B: The traveller Bianchi [K: G. Bianchi, Alla terra dei Galla. Narrazione della spedizione Bianchi in Africa nell' 1879-1880, Milano, 1884 (second edition 1886)] in his works claims that civets are kept in special yards with furances built in them and from superstition they do not show them to Europeans. I never came across such yards, and I doubt the truth of this story.
34B: The chief of the market; literally "chief of mud."
35B: Abyssinian catechism.
36K: C. Mondon-Vidailhet, the author of several scientific works (and likewise of many newspaper articles) about the languages of Ethiopia, arrived there in 1892. He soon became "state councillor of the emperor of Ethiopia" (see the section on the Emperor's Family).
37B: Likamakos is a court rank. The main function of a likamakos is to stand under a red umbrella in the attire of the *Negus* during a battle, while the *Negus* in simple attire, having mixed with the soldiers, takes part in the battle.
38B: An uket is a unit of weight the quantity of which varies with the kind of goods. An uket of gold is lighter than a uket of musk, which is lighter than an uket of ivory.
39B: Military rank.
40B: Court rank.
41B: Court rank.
42B: Evil elephant.
43B: Military rank.
44K: The Geez language, now a dead language, is related to the Southern Semitic branch of the Semitic group of the Semitic-Hamitic family of languages. From the thirteenth to the twentieth centuries it was the literary and cultural language of Ethiopia.
45K: At the time of his first journey, A.K. Bulatovich mistakenly supposed that the Gibye River (a tributary of the River Omo) forms the upper reaches of the Sobat River, unites with the Baro River and then flows west. In reality, the Omo and the Baro do not unite. The Omo flows into Lake Rudolf, and the Baro and the Pibor River, flowing together, form the Sobat River.
46K: V. Bottego succeeded in going to Lake Rudolph from the east and in proving that the River Omo flows into it. Then he went as far as the valley of the Sobat River. In 1897 he was killed by local residents. For information on his second expedition see: L. Vannutelli and C. Citerni, Seconda spedizione Bottego. L'Omo, Milano, 1899; I.I. Bok, "Successes of Europeans in the Eastern Half of Africa," News of the Russian Geographical Society [Izvestiya Russkogo geografpicheskogo obshchestva], vol. 35, 1899, issue 5, pages 473-474. About Bottego, see: A. Lavagetto, La vita eroica del capitano Bottego, Milano, 1935.
47K: The brothers Antoine (1810-1897) and Arnaud Michel (1815-1893) D'Abbadie. Over the course of a 12-year (1837-1848) stay in Ethiopia, they gathered much valuable information about the geography and ethnography of this country and published it in accounts of their journeys. For the areas visited by Bulatovich, especially important is Antoine d'Abbadie, Geographie d'Ethiopie. Ce que j'ai entendu faisant suite a ce que j'ai vue,

volume 1, Paris, 1890; Arnaud d'Abbadie, Douze ans de sejour dans la Haute Ethiopie (Abyssinie), volume 1, Paris, 1868.
48K: See note 45.
49B: Brayera anthelmintica.
50B: Ficus daro.
51B: Cordia abyssinica.
52 B: Rhamnus prinoides.
53B: Phynehopetalum montanum.
54S: Tef is a type of very small diameter grain (smaller than sorghum). It is the basis for *injera*, the staple food of Ethiopia. Native to Ethiopia, it is now also being grown in the American Mid-West and is used to make a flour which is sold in many health stores. (Thanks to Zemen Lebne-Dengel).
55S: Dagussa is slightly larger than tef in diameter. It is used to make the drink tella.
56B: Enchot—also a rootcrop, with the leaves of the waterlily, very sweet and tasty.
57B: Echinops giganteus.
58B: They are captured with traps (large pits, covered with leaves). Some surpass the size of lions. Their hair is dark brown, almost black, with clear , small completely black spots.
59B: For more details see the chapter "Population of the South-West Regions of Ethiopia."
60K: Bulatovich uses a transcription system which is now dated. Thus he writes "amara" instead of "amkhara", "amarinskiy" language instead of "amarskiy," "khushity" instead of "kushity."
61K: Problems of the settlement of Ethiopia and the classification of languages are very complex and up until now cannot be considered to be definitively resolved. At the present-day level of knowledge, the majority of scholars agree that in the Medieval period the country was settled by tribes which spoke Sudanese languages. Then with the arrival of conquerors—Hamitic, mainly Cushitic tribes which held the commanding position—began the process of mixing of languages. As a result of this, Hamitic languages dominated. Still later there appeared in Ethiopia immigrants from South-West Arabia, bringing with them the Sabean dialect of the Southern Arabic language, i.e. a Semitic langugae. They subdued the country, as a result of which the semitization of the local dialects began and the cushitization of the language of the newcomers. Thus, the Amharic language, now the most wide-spread language in Ethiopia, ought to be defined as "a Semitic language on a Hamitic base," i.e. an organically integral Semito-Hamitic language.

As regards Cushitic languagess, they differ from other Hamitic languages, for example the Galla, Somali and others. The languages of the Sidamo tribes (Gonga, Gunza, Gimirra, Kaffa and others) belong to them. Formerly they were considered one group, in which was included the languages of Yamma, Sidamo, Ometo, Gimiro, Kaffa, Mao, and Shinasha. However, now the classification of M.M. Moreno is recognized ass correct. It distinguishes groups: Sidamo (Sidamo, Kombatta, Hadiya, Alaba, Darasa), Gimirra (Gimirra, Maji), Ometo (Wolamo, Basketo and others), Kaffa. See: E. Cerulli, "Peoples of South-West Ethiopia and its Borderland," London, 1956 (*Ethnographic Survey of Africa. North-Eastern Africa,* part 3), p. 87. One must emphasize one should not, in any case, identify linguistic classification with anthropological. They do not at all coincide. The present-day population of Ethiopia arose as a result of the mixing of various ethnic elements:Ethiopian, Berber and Negro.

62K: Gran "the Left-Handed," is the nick-name of Ahmed ibn Ibrahim, who in 1527 invaded Ethiopia at the head of Galla tribes. Only with great difficulty did NegusLebna Dangel succeed in repelling the invasion of the enemy and defending the independence of the country.

63B: A large rectangular piece of white cotton material, which is thrown on the shoulders.

64S: There is no simple English equivalent of the Russian word "sal'nik." Found in the abdomen of a sheep, "white fat" is a paraffin-like substance which is basically like fat, but with a higher melting point. It looks like rounded aggregates of white spheres. (Thanks to Alexander Chaihorsky for this information. He became familiar with "sal'nik" as an explorer in Northern Mongolia.)

65K: By "republican system" the author means communal-tribal system.

66K: About the luba system (more precisely, gada) which up until now has still been insufficiently studied, see for more detail: D.A. Olderogge, "Population and social system," in the collection Abyssinia, Moscow and Leningrad, 1936, pages 116-123.

67K: For more detail regarding Kaffa, see With the Armies of Menelik and also the introduction [Katsnelson's] to this book.

68K: Under the heading of "Negroes," A.K. Bulatovich unites quite different tribes and peoples. For instnace, the Gobo, more precisely Jimma-Gobo, is one of the Galla tribes; likewise to the Cushites also belongs Gimirra, which is in the group of Sidamo peoples. As regards Bako and Gamba, in spite of the significant language differences, they are counted as belonging to the Western Sidamo group of Ometo peoples, with which their common culture unites them. In general, these tribes are little known (E. Cerulli, "Peoples of South-West Ethiopia and its Borderland," page 96). Only comparatively recently did there appear a detailed description of the Ometo people in the first volume of the series Peoples of Southern Ethiopia: "Volker Sud-Athiopiens. Ergebnisse der Frobenius Expedition 1950-52 und 1954-56," volume 1. "Altvolker Sud-Athiopiens," hrsg. von Ad. E. Jensen, Stuttgart, 1959. Suro or Shuro and likewise Masanko belong to the number of tribes which speak languages of the solitary Suri-Surma-Mekan group, which sometimes are brought together with languages of the Murle tribes, in so far as these tribes have some general cultural features in common (A.N. Tucker and M.A. Bryan, Non-Bantu Languages of North-Eastern Africa, London, 1956).

69K: The assumption of A.K. BulAtovich regarding the fact that these tribes belong to the Shillukam, i.e. Nilotic, is mistaken. See note 65.

70 B: See Appendix No. 4.

71 B: The inhabitant of Gojjam differs from the Shoan with a more industrious character. He also is more proud and vain. The Shoan is more warlike that the Gojjam and less hot tempered.

72K: This is not true. In ancient times, up until the conversion to Christianity, polytheism predominated in the kingdom of Aksum. As regards Judaism, it began to spread later, basically at the time of the christianization of the country (M. Rodinson, "Sur la Question des 'influences juives' en Ethiopie," Ethiopian Studies, Manchester, 1963, pages 11-19.).

73K: In reality, the literature of Ethoipia, in particular the folklore of its different peoples and tirbes, is quite rich and varied. See: E. Cerulli, Storia della letteratura etiopica, Milano, 1956; Golden Land. Stories, legends, proverbs and tales of Ethiopia, [Zolotaya zemlya. Skazki, legendy, poslovitsy i pogovorki Efiopii], edited by E.B. Gankina, Moscow, 1960.

74B: The masanka is a single-stringed instrument. They play it with a bow made of hair, holding the masanka in the left hand, with the long part below, against the chest.

75K: About the way of life of the peoples of Ethiopia, in particular the Amhara, for more detail see: M.V. Rayt, Peoples of Ethiopia, [Narody Efiopii], Moscow, 1965.

76B: Drinks of the Abyssinians. *Tej* is made from honey, dissolved in cold water. To it they add leaves from the gesho tree, which serves as a substitute for hops. This is a very strong drink. Tella is made from barley, also with gesho leaves.

77B: The bagana is a wooden multi-stringed lyre. They play it while sitting, holding it between the knees and both arms. Abyssinians assert that it is the lyre of David.

78B: By the way, it is interesting to note the means that the emperor resorted to in order to put this little coin into circulation. In the palace he built a shop where one can buy bread, *injera*, candles, vodka, mead, wine, and meat, where one can drink coffee and eat. In order to force his retinue to use the shop, he often went there himself, gave them some money and forced them to buy something edible that was eaten or drunk here. Now the shop is in full swing.

There are several coinages of the Maria Theresa taler, and the Abyssinians are extremely discrimating about them. Although one year appears on all of them, even on those which are minted at the present time, the Abyssinians distinguish between talers with straight and hooked noses, not accepting those with a face obliterated and insufficient relief in the bow on the shoulder. In some places they prefer old talers and in others they prefer new ones. It weights 27 grams and is minted in Vienna.

79B: Now these borders are disputed by Menelik.

80K: *Ras* Bituaded (more precisely Bituadded) the highest court title, evidently was already established in the fourteenth century. Originally there were two bituadeds, who occupied the places to the right and left of the king. Their position was so significant that the son of the king gave himself this title. Subsequently, the number of bituadeds, trusted high officials, increased.

81K: Here and farther on, A.K. Bulatovich tells legends which do not have anything in common with historical reality and which evidently arose in the surroundings of the Ethiopian clergy, who wanted to sanctify the origin of the Ethiopian state and of the ruling dynasty with the help of Biblic tradition.

82K: J. Bruce (1730-1794), a well-known traveller in Africa, was Scottish in origin. He explored the coast of the Red Sea and Ethiopia, and spent time in the Sudan and other countries. In 1770 he discovered Lake Tana and the source of the Blue Nile. His description of his travels has been published many times (J. Bruce, Travels to Discover the Source of the Nile in the Years 1768-1773, volumes 1-8, third edition, Edinburgh, 1813).

83K: A.K. Bulatovich uses an unusual transcription system for proper names. He is talking about the Hamitic king Zu-Nuvas, who adopted Judaism under the name of Joseph.

84K: The project of Lalibala is explained by the desire to deprive Egypt of water, to doom it to starvation.

85K: Jeronimo Lobo, Historia de Etiopia, Coimbre, 1669.

86K: Fatsilidas ruled from 1632 to 1667.

87K: Ioas I (Adyam Sagad III) ruled from 1755 to 1769.

88K: The Iju tride, more precisely the Ittu, belongs to the eastern Galla.

89K: Tewodros II reigned frmo 1855-1868. The politics of Tewodros II, which were directed toward the centralization of the country, aroused the discontent of the feudal lords and acted against the colonization intentions of England. Having seized on the murder of Consul cameron and of several Europeans, the English in 1867 disembarked in the Port of Zeila and besieged Fort Mardalu, where Tewodros II was seeking refuge. Seeing no escape from the situation that had arisen, he shot himself.

90K: Yohannes IV (1868-1889) was a protege of England. Incited by England, he went to war with the Mahdists and was killed in battle.

91K: Sahle Selassie, the ruler of Shoa (1813-1847), was the grandfather of Menelik II.

92K: C.E.X. Rochet d'Hericourt, a French traveller, twice visited Ethiopia and gave special attention to the region of Shoa. (See his works: Voyage sur la cote orientale de la Mer Rouge dans la pays d'Adal et le royaume de Choa, Paris, 1841; Second voyage sur les deux rives de la Mer Rouge dans le pays des Adels et le royaume de Choa, Paris 1846).

93K: Meridazmatch, more precisely meredazmatch (from meredi "he who compels to tremble" and azmatch "warrior") is a title which was conferred on the commander of the reserve corps.

94 K: Ato Ayale (Haile Mikael) was the son of Sahle Selassie and uncle of Menelik II.

95K: Menelik II was born on June 18, 1844.

96K: A*baga*ch Bezabe was a pretender to the throne of Shoa. Abagach, "father of the army on campaign," is a title which was given to the commander of the army or the ruler of a border region (in this case it corresponded excellently with "margrave.") Bezabe was appointed by Emperor Tewodros. Regarding these events, see: Guebre Sellassie, Chronique du regne de Menelik II, roi des rois d'Ethiopie, volume 1, Paris, 1930, pages 86-106.

97K: D. Porro and his fellow travellers were killed in the spring of 1886 on order of the ruler of Harar. Chiarini died in 1979.

98K: For the official diplomatic documents see: C. Rossetti, Storia diplomatica dell'Etiopia durante il regno di Menelik II, Torino, 1910.

99K: Regarding the organization of the army in Ethiopia at the turn of the century, see: K. Arnoldi, Military sketches of Ethiopia [Voennye ocherki

Abissinii], St. Petersburg, 1908 (the author often cites the books of A.K. BulAtovich).

100B: Rewards for military distinction include advancement in the ranks and outward signs of distinction: gold trim on the saber, gold miters on the head, lemds made of the hide of a lion and velvety with gold decorations; horses and mules with rich trappings.

101B: In battle the Abyssinians yell entire recitatives, in a hoarse, shrill voice, passionately. For instance: "Koretcha Farda! Aba Sanchayo! Enye Zaraf! Enye Geday! Enye Yaba Danya Lydzh! Anchi man nesh? Enye Yaaba Danya Ashker! Enye Gabro Mariam!" In translation this would be: "Horse of the hero! Killer! I am a robber! I am a killer! I am the child of Aba Danyi—'Father of Justice' (the name of Menelik's horse). Who are you? I am the servant of Aba Danya! I am Gebra Maryam (the name of the person talking)."

102B: For example, one need only by chance come upon hay-mowing of Menelik, and from all sides they begin to cry: "Ba Menelik! Ba Menelik Amlak!" which means, "In the name of Menelik! By the God of Menelik! You must not go there!"

103B: The litigants always begin their speech with the following formula: "Egziabeer asayo, Krystos Iamalaketo." Which means "May God bear witness to you and may Jesus Christ testify."

104B: It is remarkable that insulting someone with words is punished very severely, and that among the Abyssinians there are almost no swear words. "Who is his father" is considered a very strong expression and "Afer Bela" which means "Eat sand" is the height of swearing.

105K: Taitu married Menelik in April 1883.

106K: Kebra Nagest which means "Glory of the Kings" is a collection of historical and church legends and traditions, of the apocrypha, etc. Here appears the well-known story about King Solomon and the Queen of Sheba, from which supposedly the dynasty of Ethiopian kings arose. Mentions of this collection date back to the fifteenth century. (See, Kebra Nagast czyli Chwala Krolow Abysinii. Fragmenty, Warsaw, 1956, page 8).

107K: Captain Clochette died in 1897 in Gore.

Book Two

With the Armies of Menelik II

Preface[1]

This book is the journal of my second expedition to the interior of Africa in 1897-98.

I made my first trip to Ethiopia with the Medical Detachment of the Russian Red Cross, ordered to the theater of the Italo-Abyssinian military actions in 1896. At the end of 1896, the Detachment returned to Russia, but I undertook an independent expedition to the western regions of Ethiopia. That time, I reached the western boundaries of Abyssinia and crossed the River Baro, hitherto unexplored by any European. On the return trip, I visited the lower reaches of the Didessa River, the valley of the Blue Nile, and, in the first days of May 1887, returned to Russia.[2]

In September 1897, the Sovereign Emperor was pleased to enter into direct relations with Abyssinia; and, by command of His Highness, an Extraordinary Diplomatic Mission, headed by Acting State Councilor Pyotr Mikhailovich Vlasov, was sent to the court of Emperor Menelik II. The Envoy Extraordinary was accompanied by his wife and the following members of the Mission: Secretary of the Mission—Titular Councilor Orlov.

Those attached to the command of the Envoy Extraordinary:
-Lieutenant of His Majesty's Life-Guard Hussar Regiment Bulatovich;
-Lieutenants of the Imperial Family's Infantry Guard Battalion Kokhovskiy and Davydov;
-Lieutenant of Her Majesty the Sovereign Empress Mariya Feodorovna's Cavalry Regiment Chertkov.
-The escort of the Envoy Extraordinary:
-Commander of the escort, Sotnik of His Imperial Highness the Sovereign Heir Tsarevich's Ataman Guard Regiment Krasnov;[3]
- and 21 soldiers of lower rank (18 Cossacks of the Cossack Guard Brigade, two Cossacks of His Majesty's Don Guard Battery, and one private of His
   -Majesty's Hussar Guard Regiment).

On business from the War Ministry:
-Colonel of the General Staff Artamonov[4] and

-Lieutenant of the Izmailovskiy Guard Regiment Arnoldi.
The medical staff of the mission:
-Doctor State Councilor Lebedinskiy,
-Doctor State Councilor Brovtsyn,
-Pharmacist Lukyanov,
-Functionary First-Class Sasson, and
-Doctor's Assistant Kuznetsov.

The Extraordinary Mission left St. Petersburg at the end of September 1897 and arrived in the capital of Abyssinia, Addis Ababa, in February 1898. Acting State Councilor Vlasov, his wife, the Secretary of the Mission Titular Councilor Orlov, the entire medical staff of the Mission and some of the lower ranking soldiers of the escort are in Abyssinia to this day [1899]. The rest have returned to Russia.

A courier had to be sent ahead to inform Emperor Menelik that His Highness the Sovereign Emperor was pleased to send an Extraordinary Mission to him. In view of my knowledge of the Abyssinian language and my familiarity with travel conditions in that country, the choice of courier fell on me.

On September 9, 1897, I left St. Petersburg accompanied by Private of His Majesty's Hussar Guard Regiment Zelepukin; and on October 5, I arrived in Addis Ababa at the court of the Emperor.

At the end of November, an important expedition of Abyssinian troops was outfitted with the aim of annexing to the Ethiopian Empire as yet unexplored southern territories, lying between Abyssinia and Lake Rudolf. I took advantage of the opportunity that was offered me to travel with this expedition across unknown lands. On June 5, 1898, I returned to Addis Ababa; on June 14, I left for Russia; and on July 19, I arrived in St. Petersburg. Almost immediately after my return, I fell ill. As soon as I recovered, I started processing the materials I had gathered. Scarcely had I finished this work, when again I was ordered to Abyssinia.

Bringing this preface to a close, I consider it my duty to thank the Chief of the Military Printing Office Lieutenant-General Otto von Stubendorf, the Chief of the Geodesic Office Major-General Iliodor Ivanovich Pomerantsev, the Chief of the Cartographic Department Major-General Andrey Alexandrovich Bolshov, and Colonel of His Majesty's Life-Guard Hussar Regiment Sergei Dmitrievich Molchanov. Owing to their enlightened cooperation and valuable advice, I was able to bring the present work to a satisfactory conclusion. I want to express my deep and respectful gratitude for their help.

March 20 [old style],5 April 2 [new style], 1899, the Black Sea, aboard the Steamship "Tambov"

INTRODUCTION

At the end of 1897 and the beginning of 1898, events were in the making in Africa which were destined to be of the greatest importance for its future. The time had come to answer the long urgent question: Which of the two great powers competing for predominance in Africa—England or France—would get the upper hand in this unequal, but decisive struggle? Would England succeed in realizing her cherished dream—to cut through all of Africa from north to south, from Cairo to the Cape of Good Hope, to take in her hand the inexhaustible wealth of Africa's central lands, and thus to create here a second India for herself—or would France prevent her?

The position of England was much stronger.

The twenty-thousand-strong, excellently equipped corps of Anglo-Egyptian troops under Kitchener was already on the way to Khartoum, the fall of which seemed inevitable. The detachment of Major MacDonald was supposed to advance from the south, from Uganda, toward a rendezvous with him, to take the whole upper course of the Nile, the course of the River Juba and the mouth of the River Omo emptying into Lake Rudolf.

To thwart the plans of her opponent, France, in turn, equipped several expeditions which were supposed to cut off the path of the English, hoisting the French flag on the banks of the Nile.

With this aim, from the west, from French Congo, the insignificant Marchand expedition advanced toward the Nile, and from the east across Abyssinia, the expedition of Clochette and Bonchamps set out to meet it.[5]

But aside from France and England, there was also a third power interested in the question of the possession of the middle course of the Nile—Ethiopia. And her emperor in the spring of 1897 openly announced to the British Envoy Extraordinary Reynold Rhodes that he considers his boundaries "2° and 14° north latitude, the shore of the ocean on the east, and the right bank of the Nile on the west," and that he will support these claims of his with all his might.

What position should Ethiopia have taken?

Africa has long attracted Europeans who seized and divided among themselves all of its coast lands. But the interior long remained a huge park where they hunted for men and obtained slaves to work for the colonists. The abolition of slavery, however, put an end to this state of affairs.

With the development of trade and navigation, the colonies of the Europeans began to spread out. Daring explorers penetrated and crossed Africa from all directions. After the explorers came missionaries and traders. The Europeans developed commercial and political interests which the mother countries encouraged in the newly opened lands. Little by little, the Europeans conquered more and more territory.

At the Conference of Berlin, all of Africa was partitioned by the interested powers into "spheres of influence," that is, regions where they could carry out their aims of conquest and colonization. The rights and interests of peoples living in these "spheres of influence" were completely disregarded; and Abyssinia, in this manner, fell under the protectorate of Italy.

If such treatment of the populace of Africa was justified to some degree by their low level of culture, it was completely unjust and arbitrary in regard to the Abyssinian people, who professed Christianity much earlier than any European nation (in the fourth century A.D.)—a people with a rich historical past. And although this country had recently lagged behind Europe in its development, it had all the makings for a brilliant future.

In the history of the black continent, Abyssinia has played a very important role. Coming into contact with ancient Egypt and because of Semitic immigration, Abyssinia early became the only enlightener and propagator of culture in the Ethiopian mountains and the regions adjoining them. In the Middle Ages, Ethiopia was a powerful state. All the tribes who inhabited the Ethiopian mountains were united under the rule of the Abyssinian emperor. By the beginning of the 16th century, Ethiopia had attained the zenith of its greatness; and, according to well-preserved legends, the Abyssinian Empire was at that time so great and powerful that one of its emperors, King of Kings Lyb-on-Dyngyl (or David II)[6] prayed to God to grant him enemies, regretting that he had none.[7]

The enemy was not slow to appear in the person of Gran,[8] who at the head of fanatic Moslem hordes—of Galla and Adaltsevs— struck heavy blows at Abyssinia. At that time, the southern regions of Abyssinia were subjected to invasion by wild nomadic Galla tribes, who, crowded in their own lands, invaded Abyssinia in an irrepressible stream and took the best lands along the rivers Gibye, Didessa, the Blue Nile and Awash. The Ethiopian

Introduction

Empire was cut in two, and the southern part, Kaffa, remained isolated from the northern part for several centuries.

As a result of these invasions, internal dissensions arose and civil wars, which weakened the imperial power and reduced Abyssinia to decay.

In the middle of the 19th century, Ethiopia was restored to life. The Emperors Tewodros, Yohannes, and, finally, Menelik II reunited Abyssinia. Emperor Menelik entered into a desperate struggle with Italy for the existence, freedom and independence of his state, and won a series of brilliant victories over his enemy. In so doing, he demonstrated irrefutably that there is in Africa a black nation capable of standing up for itself and having all the makings for independent existence.

Of course, at the beginning of 1898 Emperor Menelik could not remain an indifferent spectator to all that was happening in Africa. Possessing in his army a tremendous strength, having put the internal and external affairs of the state in good order, he did not stay indifferent at this decisive moment, but rather moved armies to the western and southern regions to which he had laid claim.

In striving to extend the bounds of his possessions, Menelik is only carrying out the traditional mission of Ethiopia as the propagator of culture and the unifier of all the inhabitants of the Ethiopian Mountains and of the related tribes in their neighborhood, and only makes a new step toward consolidating and developing the power of the black empire.

These are the motives which led Menelik to aggressive acts; and we Russians cannot help sympathizing with his intentions, not only because of political considerations, but also for purely human reasons. It is well known to what consequences conquests of wild tribes by Europeans lead. Too great a difference in the degree of culture between the conquered people and their conquerors has always led to the enslavement, corruption, and degeneration of the weaker race. The natives of America degenerated and have almost ceased to exist. The natives of India were corrupted and deprived of individuality. The black tribes of Africa became the slaves of the whites.

Clashes between nations more or less close to one another in culture bring completely different results.

For the Abyssinians, the Egyptian, Arab, and, finally, European civilization which they have gradually adopted has not been pernicious:borrowing the fruits of these civilizations, and in turn conquering and annexing neighboring tribes and passing on to them her culture, Abyssinia did not obliterate from the face of the earth, did not destroy the uniqueness of any one of the conquered tribes, but rather gave them all the possibility of preserving their individual characteristics.

Thus Christian Abyssinia plays an important role in world progress as a transmission point of European civilization to wild central African peoples.

The high civilizing mission of Abyssinia, its centuries-old, almost uninterrupted struggle for faith and freedom against the surrounding Moslems, the nearness of her people to the Russian people in creed, won for her the favor of the Russian people. Not just educated Russians know of her and sympathize with her, but also the common folk who saw black Christians, devout and often living in poverty, in Jerusalem.[9]

We see much in common in the cultural problems of Abyssinia with our affairs in the East; and we cannot help but wish that our co-religionist nation would assimilate the best achievements of European civilization, while preserving for itself freedom, independence, and that scrap of land which its ancestors owned and which our greedy white brothers want to take.

In the autumn of 1897, I was in the capital of Abyssinia at the time when the decision and preparations were made for expeditions of Abyssinian troops to be sent to the valley of the Nile and to Lake Rudolf. At the beginning of November, Menelik's military commanders arrived in Addis Ababa one after another, and councils of war were held in the palace, with the Emperor himself presiding. On October 20, a partial mobilization of Menelik's own regular troops was declared; and by the beginning of December the plan was finally worked out.

Three main expeditions were proposed:

1) *Ras* Makonnen[10], the governor-general of Harar and Somaliland, was supposed to move west with a thirty-thousand-man detachment and conquer the gold-region of Beni Shangul, and reach, if possible, the banks of the Nile.[11]

2) *Dajazmatch* Tessema, governor-general of the extreme south-western regions of Abyssinia, with an eight-thousand-man detachment, had orders to take possession of the lower course of the Sobat River and the upper course of the Nile.[12]

3) *Ras* Wolda Giyorgis, governor-general of Kaffa and of the southern region of Abyssinia, was supposed to advance from Kaffa to the south-southwest, to annex all free lands found in that direction, and to establish a foothold at Lake Rudolf.[13] The extreme limit for his conquests was set at 2° north meridian and the source of the Nile from Lake Albert.[14]

I was offered the chance to participate in one of these expeditions. In light of the enormous ethnographic, scientific, and military interest which the journey at hand could offer, I decided to take advantage of the opportunity and to join the expedition which was going through as yet completely unexplored regions. From this perspective, the expedition of *Ras* Wolda Giyorgis was the most interesting and promising. No European had yet succeeded in penetrating south from Abyssinia farther than the northern boundaries of Kaffa, a powerful state which was closed to Europeans not long ago and which was conquered by the Abyssinians just in 1897.

A whole series of unsolved scientific questions stood before me. Where does the main river of southern Ethiopia—the Omo—flow to? Does it empty into Lake Rudolf, or, rounding Kaffa from the south, does it flow into the Sobat and then into the Mediterranean? If the Omo is not the upper course of the Sobat, but rather empties into Lake Rudolf, then where is the source of the Sobat?

No one had ever succeeded in going to Lake Rudolf from the north. Up until 1897, only four Europeans had visited its shores: 1) Teleki and Hohnel, who had discovered the lake, 2) Donaldson Smith, 3) Cavendish, and 4) Bottego.

The regions to the northwest of Lake Rudolf were until very recently "terra incognita" in the full sense of the term.

I was extremely interested in the solution of all these questions and in the answer to one of the numerous as yet undeciphered geographical mysteries on the globe: does the River Omo empty into Lake Rudolf or into the Nile? But before undertaking anything, I had to request permission from Acting State Councilor Vlasov, the head of our diplomatic mission in Abyssinia, to whose staff I belonged. Acting State Councilor Vlasov and the mission by that time had only reached Jibuti.

Because of the distance and difficulty of the journey and the brief time which remained at my disposal, it was very risky to rely on the accuracy of postal connections. So I decided to set out to meet our mission in person. I left Addis Ababa on November 27, having, at an audience the day before, received from the Emperor a letter from him to Acting State Councilor Vlasov.

On December 2, Menelik set out with all his troops, marched to Mount Managash and there, having appointed *Ras* Makonnen commander-in-chief of the first expedition, blessed him on his upcoming journey and returned to the capital.

The commanders of the other expeditions, *Dajazmatch* Tessema and *Ras* Wolda Giyorgis also set out to their lands, to the assembled detachments.

The departure of *Ras* Wolda Giyorgis from Kaffa, his main residence, was set for the first days of January. I had just a month and a half to get to Jibuti, return to Addis Ababa, organize a caravan, and arrive in Kaffa. In this time, I had to cover nearly 2000 versts [1400 miles]. (Jibuti to Addis Ababa— 750-800 versts x 2 = 1500-1600 versts; Addis Ababa to Andrachi in Kaffa—400-500 versts.)

I started on November 27; and on December 8, having changed men and animals in Harar, I arrived in Bayad (the first stop from

Jibuti with water; 50 versts from Jibuti.) I met our mission there, spent two days with them, got permission to take part in the expedition and, having again changed men and animals, on December 10 set out on the return trip. On December 20, I arrived in Addis Ababa, having covered nearly 1500 versts [1050 miles] in 23 days (from November 27 to December 20), including three days of stop-overs.

This "run," which only set the stage for the trip to follow, did not come easily to me. Equipped for cavalry-raid or reconnaissance conditions, I was constrained to content myself with only the necessities which one could take along on a saddle. Any convenience, such as a tent, was out of the question. The food was very scanty. Three times I had to change my numerous traveling companions and animals. Furthermore, it happened to be the season of cold spells[15] at night. These were particularly severe at the tops of the passes of the Chercher Mountains. Along with other difficulties of the journey, those cold spells gave me acute rheumatism in the legs. This illness caused me such suffering that, for a while, I was in no condition to sit in the saddle without outside help.

Having arrived in Addis Ababa in such a state, I presented myself to the Emperor that very day, then proceeded with the organization of the caravan, which took me seven days. Having bought 18 mules and some horses and pack-saddles, and having adjusted the packs, I began to recruit men.

For the traveler, the question of the personnel of the caravan is of the utmost importance: the outcome of a sometimes arduous expedition often depends on this or that choice of men. But this time my problem proved to be not particularly difficult. Many of my future traveling companions were already known to me, having taken part in my travels in Abyssinia in 1896-97. Having heard of my return to Abyssinia, they came and brought their relatives. I was particularly pleased with these recruits— most still quite young, 16-18 year-old boys, very obedient, diligent, still unspoiled by city life. From among them, I chose weapons bearers and bearers for the instruments and for a knapsack with papers and documents. At the same time, I note with particular pleasure that these boys never left me: in all the difficulties of the journey, they stayed with me, remaining faithful to their duty.

My retinue consisted of 30 men. There were 19 guns altogether, including my personal one.[16]

Over my *ashkers* (soldiers), I placed Wolda Tadika, a man extremely devoted to me. While still a soldier for *Ras* Makonnen, he had accompanied me on my first trip from Harar to Addis Ababa in 1896. Then, in the most trying circumstances, he showed great energy and resourcefulness. From the moment when he came to me for work, we didn't part, sharing together all the difficulties and dangers of the journey. I was also accompanied by Private Zelepukin of His Majesty's Life Guard Hussar Regiment, who had been attached to me.

Consisting of only the most necessary items, my baggage was not very large: I had two pack-loads of cartridges and two trunks (containing my clothes, linen, gifts, money and books) which also served me as a bed; a medicine chest adapted so it could be carried by hand if necessary; another similar chest with dining and cooking equipment and canned food ("Magi" dried broth), tea and sugar; a chest with wine; a chest with photographic equipment; and in addition, two packs with miscellaneous items. I provided for food stuffs for five days, counting on replenishing the stock on the way. Thanks to these measures, half of the mules went without packs, considerably facilitating the journey to Kaffa.

On December 26, I had a farewell audience with the Emperor. I set my date of departure for the next day.

My journey is of interest not only because of the actions of the detachment I accompanied and the final results it achieved, but also because of the ethnographic and purely geographical conditions in which the events took place. Beginning the description of the journey, I consider it my duty to note that, not allured by generalization, I confine myself to documentary truth—my diary, which I kept each day, noting all events, facts, and observations which, for one reason or another, seemed characteristic.

From Addis Ababa to Jimma

December 27 and 28

After long, but necessary musters, we finally set out. The mules, in high spirits, won't let themselves be saddled. One of them even breaks loose and dashes away with a pack on its back. With some difficulty, we catch the runaway and put it back in line. Everything is settled. The caravan is ready. With loud and joyful songs, at noon we leave the city. A little later, the city disappears behind us and, in front, boundless spaces spread. There, in the distance, lie unexplored regions full of unsolved riddles. I keep the aim of the trip a secret. I tell my *ashkers* that we probably have an elephant hunt in store for us.

We walk very quickly. The people sing, not falling silent. The animals are getting excited. The detachment is cheerful, happy, like a young thoroughbred horse which, when led onto first snow, breaks into the open with a neigh. The surplus of energy so overbrims. God grant that this state of mind last! I know by experience how you shouldn't count on these first invigorating impressions, how fast this energy abates, if squandered. The time is perhaps not far off when both man and beast will be counting every step. On this first day, we make a short five-and-a-half hour march, and set our bivouac at the foot of Mount Wochech, near a Galla farmstead. On December 28, we go down the valley of the Awash River; and after an eleven hour march with an hour and a half break on the bank of the River Berga, we camp for the night in the village of Gura.

The valley of the Awash is very beautiful and relatively densely populated. It is fertile, abounding in water, but completely treeless. Cow dung that is piled around each farmstead in regular heaps serves as fuel here. The inhabitants are Galla who, apparently, have recovered after their recent subjection. They stand up strongly for their property. For instance, one Galla raised a racket and came to me to complain that my cook, Ikasu, had taken three stones for our hearth from a heap that lay near his house.

The village where we stopped is called "Gura." There are about 20 farmsteads in it. The houses are large, round, with conical straw roofs. Near the houses are low, wattled-brushwood storehouses, slightly elevated above the ground to protect against termites, the dreadful enemies of all who live here.

In their way of life and in their clothing, the inhabitants are noticeably influenced by Abyssinian culture. The men wear trousers of *abujedi* (English shirt cloth) and *shammas*,[17] and the women wear long Abyssinian shirts. A black silk lace, a *matab*—sign of christening appears on the necks of all of them.

Twenty years ago, the beautiful wide plain of the Awash, on the horizon of which are visible mountains of enormous mass, was the scene of the bloodiest cavalry battles.

The Galla who inhabit it were famous for their horsemanship and bravery, and the subjugation of them cost the Abyssinians much trouble and sacrifice. Not so long ago, it was a rare and remarkable feat for an Abyssinian to water his horse at the Awash River. But blow after blow struck by *Ras* Gobana, Menelik's celebrated commander, broke the resistance of the brave tribe. *Ras* Gobana is by birth a Shoan: his father was a Galla, and his mother an Abyssinian. All the best fighting elements of Shoa thronged under his banners. Where *Ras* Gobana was, there too were success and plunder. At the call of Gobana, tens of thousands of warriors assembled. In the field, the celebrated *Ras* was courageous and indefatigable. His time was the epoch of the flourishing of the cavalry spirit and of mounted battle in Abyssinia. Firearms were almost unknown at that time. The lance, the ardent steed, the impact and the speed of the raid, numerical superiority—that is how Gobana triumphed.

He usually invited the Galla to submit, threatening to destroy them if they did not. Gobana sent such admonitions to all the neighboring tribes, but few of them submitted voluntarily. Then Gobana launched raids on the unsubmissive. He didn't take caravans of transport carts with him—these were raids of ten-thousand-man detachments. No one knew when the *Ras* would set out, where he would go, or when he would return. At night, the order was given to set out, and by morning all communications between the detachment that had moved into the field and the base was severed. Finally, after a long wait, those who stayed at home would see a column of dust on the horizon and say that Gobana was returning.

Approaching the domain of an unsubmissive tribe, the *Ras* surrounded the border by night. At dawn, his huge horde was already flying like the wind in all directions, destroying everything that fell in its path. This was the time of personal heroism, of epic warriors, when guns and smokeless powder had not depersonalized the soldier—when enemies met face to face to measure strength. Here each warrior sought glory and plunder for himself. The *Ras* was situated with the reserves, somewhere on a high central hill, from which a view of the horizon opened up. At the decisive moment, he set his reserves in Motion. The Galla used temporizing tactics. They retreated and escaped from the onslaught of the Abyssinians. But when the Shoans returned to the rallying point, burdened with plunder, tired, on exhausted horses, entire cavalry detachments of Galla, who had hidden in the rough terrain or in empty cattle pens, unexpectedly darted out of ambush. Singing *"Joli Aba Rebi"*—"I the son of Aba Rebi" (the leader of the tribe)—they attacked the Abyssinians, retaking the plunder from them. Many Abyssinian and Galla bones lie in this valley.

The essence of Gobana's style of warfare is expressed by his two favorite words: *"Hid bellau!"*—"Off with you, get going!"

This remarkable fighting cavalryman died several years ago, having badly hurt himself in a fall from a horse. With his death, cavalry activity in Abyssinia began to die away. However, there were other reasons for this. Everyone acquired guns; and, owing to the loss of livestock and constant wars, many no longer had horses. Meanwhile, the theater of military operations shifted: rocks and narrow, wooded mountain ridges replaced the plateaux and plains which formerly were the scene of mounted battles.

My guide, a participant in the expeditions of *Ras* Gobana, showed me the place from which the *Ras* unleashed his detachment in one of his many raids. This was at the foot of Mount Wochech. Many from the *Ras*'s detachment reached the Chobo Mountains that day and managed to return to the rallying point by evening. Fighting and seizing plunder, they covered 80-100 versts [53-66 miles] in a single day.

December 29

Crossing the Barbari-Medyr land, which is densely populated by soldiers of Menelik, we climbed Mount *Dendi*. At the summit of one of the spurs of this mountain huddles a small town, or rather, the fortified residence of the governor-general of this region—*Dajazmatch* Haile Maryam.

Strongholds of this type are very characteristic. They are usually built on some hard-to-reach hill which commands the surrounding area and on which the Abyssinian ruler builds his eagle nest. The strongholds are surrounded by a high palisade, in front of which is a deep ditch. The interior of the stronghold is divided into several separate courtyards, built up with all sorts of structures related to the household economy, and a large square where court is held. In the center is located the *elfin*, or inner chambers of the leader. On a neighboring hill, in the shade of huge fig trees is hidden a round church with a conical roof and a star made of reed sticks, with ostrich eggs stuck on the ends of the sticks. The low little houses of numerous clergy and soldiers are huddled around the church and the little town.

Governor-general Haile Maryam was away. He and his soldiers had taken the field with the detachment of *Ras* Makonnen. A significant part of the male Galla population had also gone with him.

By eleven in the morning, we climbed the crest of the former crater of Mount *Dendi* (3,000 meters above sea level), inside which is found the lake of the same name. The foot of the mountain is completely built-up with Galla farmsteads, buried in the verdure of banana plantations. Its very steep slopes are overgrown with huge coniferous trees *teda*—a type of cypress—and leaf-bearing *kusso* trees.[18] From the crest of the mountain there opens up a view that is rare in beauty and in the combination of colors. Far below sparkles the sky-blue, brilliant surface of the lake, surrounded by the dense green of huge trees. Around it, wild, plantless, forbidding gray rocks cluster. This lake seems to consist of two little lakes which touch each other at their circumferences. It may be that there used to be two craters here. From the southern lake flows the River *Uluk*, a tributary of the Blue Nile. *Dendi* in Galla means "great water," and *Uluk* means "passing through." Not far off from *Dendi* towers another mountain—Chobo—with a lake at the summit named "Wonch," from which flows Walga, a tributary of the River Omo. According to local inhabitants, Walga flows some distance under the ground then, piercing the crater, appears outside.

On the shores of the *Dendi*, stuck to the foot of a cliff, stands the farmstead of *Fitaurari* Abto Giyorgis, commander of the entire guard of Menelik II.

My path to Jimma went through his possessions; and, by order of the Emperor, Abto Giyorgis was supposed to give me guides. The General came to meet me and invited me to his home where dinner was already prepared for us. We sat on spread carpets and in front of us servants stretched a wide curtain that hid us from outside eyes. One of the *ashkers* brought a copper wash-stand of intricate form (with the brand of a Moscow factory), and we, in accordance with Abyssinian custom, washed our hands before the meal. One of the cooks, a beautiful young Galla girl, having washed her hands and having rolled the sleeves of her shirt to the elbow, kneeled in front of our basket and from little pots began to take out on slices of *injera* (a flat cake) all kinds of foods and to put them on the bread which was spread out on the basket. What an array of foods: hard-boiled eggs cooked in some unusually sharp sauce, and ragout of mutton with red pepper, and chicken gravy with ginger, and tongue, and ground or scraped meat —all abundantly seasoned with butter and powdered with pepper and spices—and cold sour milk and sour cream. In the corners of the fire in front of us, cut into little pieces, tebs meat was roasting. And the chief of the slaughter-house held over our basket a huge piece of beef. We ate with our hands, tearing off little petals of *injera* and collecting with them large amounts of all sorts of foods. My mouth burned from the quantity of pepper. Tears came to my eyes. My sense of taste was dulled. And we devoured everything indiscriminately, cooling our mouths, from time to time, with sour cream or by drinking a wonderful mead—tej—from little decanters wrapped in little silk handkerchiefs. They also invited Zelepukin to dinner. When we were full, they called the officers of the *Fitaurari* and my *ashkers*. They sat in close circles around ten baskets with *injera*, over which servants held large pieces of raw meat. Wine bearers served mead to the diners in large horn glasses. All ate decorously and silently. At the end of the meal, just as decorously, they all got up and left at the same time, not bowing to anyone. General Abto Giyorgis is one of the most outstanding associates of Menelik today. He is the son of the chief of a small tribe. When the Abyssinians subdued this tribe, in accordance with custom, they took the children of the best families of the conquered tribe to educate them. Among the pupils was Abto Giyorgis, who found himself at the court of Menelik. He spent all of his childhood and youth in the suite of the *Negus*. Here he went through the entire course of Abyssinian sciences, studied Holy Scripture and legislation; and, thanks to his intelligence, uprightness and knowledge of laws, Menelik made him one of the chief lecturers on judicial affairs. In the recent war with Italy, he distinguished himself at Adowa, and Menelik assigned him to replace a guards leader who was killed in that battle, *Fitaurari* Bobayu, and who is now glorified by bards as an Abyssinian hero. Abto Giyorgis now has the post of personal *Fitaurari* attached to the person of Menelik and commander of all his guard. Under his command there are an eleven-thousand-man regiment of *snayder-yaji* (i.e., bearers of "Remingtons"), and several several thousand of his own soldiers. These troops are deployed (due to the convenience of supplies) in a long band, from Chabo along the left bank of the River Gibye-Omo, then along the shores of Lake Abasi, or Walamo, southward to Lake Stephanie and the lands of Boran. The latter were conquered by Abto Giyorgis in 1897.

The origin of the armies of Menelik is interesting. At the beginning of his reign, the Emperor had a severe shortage of both guns and soldiers. The nucleus of his armed forces consisted of the armies of Emperor Tewodros, known as *gondari*—men of Gondar —that had gone over to his side. They are still called *gondari* and are stationed along the borders of the empire. They are about twenty thousand men strong. This army is divided into thousand-man regiments distributed among various leaders. Soldiers who mustered under the banner of Menelik at another later time were known by a name that corresponded to their armament. Those armed with muzzle-loaded guns were called *neftenya*. Those who had flint-lock guns were *tabanja-yaji*. Those with breech-loaded guns were *snayder-yaji"*

At first, Menelik supplied his personal guards with breech-loaded guns. They were subsequently divided into a separate corps and transformed into the Guard of Menelik. The *snayder-yaji*, as a picked army, is supposed to be in front of all the armies of the Emperor in campaigns and battles. The *tabanja-yaji* number over five thousand. They are under the leadership of *Likamakos* (adjutant general) Adenau. The *neftenya* number ten regiments distributed among various leaders. They are now all armed with breech-loaded guns although they keep their old names. Abto Giyorgis holds the very important post of "personal *Fitaurari*." In a march, he is always in front. In battle, he is obliged to attack the enemy first and always from the front. The men appointed to this high post are usually outstanding for their bravery.

December 30

At eight o'clock in the morning, we set out again. At parting, I gave the *Fitaurari* a good gold-hilted blade that he liked very much.

The morning was exceptionally cold. A strong west wind blew, and the temperature was only 5° Reamur [43° F], and clouds quickly swept past over the peaks of *Dendi*. Unaccustomed to this temperature, our arms became numb. To warm up, my bare-footed and half-naked, shivering *ashkers* ran in line with my mule.

The General gave me guides to Jimma: some soldiers and the son of the former Galla King Cholye-Byru, which means literally "ardent silver." This was an elderly, gray Galla of enormous build, with a masculine, but at the same time naive-childish face. In a picturesque white cloak, with a straw hat on his head, a small straw parasol in his hand, and a long spear on his back, he accompanied me on the back of a little mule. For him, a boy servant carried on his head a little bag with provisions.

The road followed the valley of the River Walga—along the region of Amaya, which is rich and densely populated by Galla, and which was recently subdued by the Abyssinians. The large number of streams flowing from Mountains Rogye and Tobo give this locale a rare fertility. The fields are completely under cultivation, and farmsteads stretch along the entire road, uninterrupted by any street.

The Galla of Amaya are very beautiful, of large build, well formed. Their women are especially beautiful—some have a perfectly Gypsy type of beauty. They dress in an ox-hide that girds the hips like a skirt, trimmed from above with little frills. Huge bracelets of copper and ivory are displayed on their arms and legs. Their pierced ears have earrings. Around the neck, they wear beads. Men wear trousers and *shammas*. In its domestic structure, this tribe differs very little from other Galla tribes. It surpasses them only by its trade and industrial development. Amaya abounds in markets at which one can get excellent cotton fabric.

Along the road, I killed a jackal. The bullet pierced both forelegs above the knee, completely breaking the bones. At this time, a Galla came up to me who turned out to be the son of the former king of Amaya-Moti—Bonti-Maya. The strong action of the small-looking bullet from my 3/8-inch-caliber rifle struck my new acquaintance and seemed supernatural to him. He looked over the gun for a long time with wonder, praising it.

Crossing the River Walga, which flows in rocky, sheer banks, we set up camp after a nine and a half hour crossing. At night there was a powerful storm. Two mules and a horse broke away from the convoy; and by morning, Galla from the neighboring village were already trying to steal them. My *ashkers*, however, overtook the malefactors and turned them over to the local judge. To my consternation, the judge considered it necessary to arrest not only the guilty parties, but also the animals, thus lessening my already insignificant caravan.

DECEMBER 31

We set out onto an almost uninhabited plain, which stretches in a wide band along the River Gibye and is overgrown with acacias of a type which is rarely seen in Abyssinia. These are small trees with light bark, almost without leaves. The upper part of their trunk is very branched, and the branches are studded with thorns which, at its base, are swollen into complete little balls, almost all of them with little wormholes. When the wind blows, these little balls give out a strange noise like a whistle. This plain, which is rich in game, bears the name *mocha*, which means "thicket."

At noon, we stopped for rest near a small Galla farmstead. A young good-looking Galla girl came out to meet us. She lived at the home of her parents, having recently run away from her husband.

I asked her, "But your husband can take you back. Didn't he pay your parents a ransom for you? What will you do then?"

"What's there to do? I am his slave... Against my wishes, I will submit myself," she answered. "Then I will run away again."

I cite this conversation because it seems to me characteristic of the position of women among the Galla.

Having thus accomplished a twelve-hour march, we bivouacked at the Galla farmstead. At this bivouac, Zelepukin killed a wild goat with a Winchester rifle. Thanks to that, we greeted the New Year with an excellent supper, consisting of soup, cooked from the dead goat, and good coffee with a glass of liqueur. However, having turned our attention to our future business, we meanwhile noticed on one of the pack animals a sore which my *ashkers* cauterized that very evening.

January 1, 1898

We for the second time crossed the River Walga, which in this place flows through a deep and narrow ravine. There was a lot of game on the plain leading to the river. Not leaving the path, I killed four wild goats.[19]

Along the River Walga stretches the settlement of Adale, bounded from the side of the *Mocha* by a wide thick fortification (abattis), built by the Galla for defense against cavalry raids from the Gurage.

This warlike tribe lived on a plateau, which lies between the Rivers Gibye and Awash, on the banks of several lakes. The Gurage are Semitic in origin and believe that they come from Gura in Tigre. The Galla invasion in the sixteenth century, when the Galla conquered the entire basin of the Gibye and the Awash Rivers, isolated the Gurage from other tribes who were related to them and forced them to wage for three centuries an unequal but desperate battle for independence with the Galla.[20]

They preserved their uniqueness, language, and Christian faith. Even today, subdued by Menelik, they have not lost their warlike spirit. During the war with Italy, when Menelik was in Tigre with his armies, the Gurage carried out a series of attacks on neighboring Galla, and among others, on the inhabitants of Adale. The people of Adale met them with the above described fortification, which is very awkward for mounted battle. The skirmish which took place here ended with the retreat of the Gurage.

The leader of the region, Basha Metaferya, was away. He is commander of a regiment of *snayder-yaji* which is posted here. The temporary commanding officer came to meet us, accompanied by a crowd of Abyssinians and Galla. With low bows, he begged us to take honorary gifts (*durgo*)—bread, honey, butter, rams, hens, eggs, milk and salt (customarily brought together by order of the Emperor as a gift to an honored traveler who is passing through)—and to stay at the home of Basha. It was much too early to stop for the night (there were still three hours of daylight left). So we had to decline this kind invitation.

Passing the village, we went down a very difficult path from a high steep plateau, rising 800 meters above the River Gibye. An inexperienced person could get dizzy from such steepness, which all the more seemed impassable for a loaded mule. But the mules demonstrated their agility and hardiness. For them, such slopes are an ordinary matter. Stepping quietly and carefully, only rarely squinting toward the abyss spread out almost under its feet, the mule confidently steps from rock to rock. But here it stops. An obstacle appears on the road. A moment. The mule makes a bold, strong jump and safely makes its way to an apparently unreachable spot. From the edge of the plateau, a remarkably beautiful view of the river opens up. Somewhere deep below, it twists among the enormous stone masses which press in upon it, framed with a thick green leaf-bearing forest, a narrow ribbon running away along its banks far, far. The valley of the river is uninhabited. Around it reigns a dumb silence, only rarely disturbed by the loud snorting, almost roar of hippotamuses playing in the water.

The Gibye begins in the Guder Mountains, which stretch across the left bank of the Blue Nile. Near the place where we passed, the Gibye takes, to the right, two of its main tributaries—Gibye-Enerea and Gibye-Kake, and to the left—the River Walga. Here, squeezed from both sides by mountains, it flows in a narrow channel. Farther on, as if digging through the mountain range, it runs to the south by a wide low-lying valley. Here already it takes the name not of Gibye, but of Omo.

We had to cross the river. The guides showed us the place, and we forded there. Here the Gibye has a width of 180 paces, and depth of one arshin [28 inches]. It flows at a speed of greater than eight versts an hour. On the other bank of the river we hunted large chamois-bulls (*orobo*), which from the mountain we mistook for buffalo. For the first time since my illness, I tried to walk and run during this hunt. My *ashkers* got very excited, shot quickly and therefore missed. Finally, only one *orobo* was killed, hit by two shots of mine from an express[22] rifle at a distance of 50 paces. The first bullet hit it in the thigh, and the wounded beast, making several steps forward, stopped, and turned halfway around toward me. I shot him with a second bullet, which pierced its cheek, and the *orobo* fell down.

There were many hippopotamuses in the river. Shooting them turned out to be a fine training exercise. This is because hippopotamuses commonly luxuriate themselves in the water, sticking their heads out of its surface. A bullet which doesn't reach a hippopotamus or that flies beyond it, falls in the water and throws up spray and, only if you hit the target do you not leave a trace on the surface of the water. Thus you get a clear indication of whether the sight of your rifle is true.

That evening, the leader of Adale came to our bivouac at the head of a long file of Galla, carrying *durgo*; and looking forward to an abundant dinner, my people rejoiced.

The place where we spent the night teems with predatory animals. As a precaution, we set large campfires for the night and placed sentries at the ends of the convoy.

JIMMA

Jimma is situated on a long narrow ribbon of land that stretches from the southwest to the northeast along the course of the Gibye-Kake River. It is surrounded by mountains, from which many streams and rivulets run into the Gibye. These streams irrigate Jimma and make it one of the most fertile regions. The tops of the mountain ranges are hidden by thick ancient forest. The climate of the valleys is particularly moist. (There are two rainy seasons here—one in March and April, and another in July and August). The equable climate even favors the growth of the coffee tree, which in the Ethiopian highlands is found only in the southwestern region, in places contiguous to Kaffa. These excellent natural conditions have made Jimma one of the most populous and productive regions of Ethiopia. In addition, its central position among other rich regions have made it a major commercial center. Arabs, Abyssinians, and Galla throng here to exchange their foreign merchandise (cloth, weapons, and beads) for coffee, musk, elephant tusk, honey, wax, bread and horses from Jimma and its neighbors Kaffa, Kulo, Konta, and Limu. From here, valuable merchandise is sent through Gojjam and Tigre to Massawa; and through Harar to one of the ports of the Gulf of Aden, on the shore of the Indian Ocean.

Jimma is well known for its cotton and iron artifacts. Their agriculture is very intensive. The area under cultivation is very extensive, because it is intended not only to meet local needs and to pay taxes but also for the export of bread. There is almost no fallow land. Contact with foreigners has had an influence on the development of industry and the prosperity of the region, as well as its mode of life and religion.

Unfortunately, along with the commercial-industrial growth of Jimma came the flourishing of the slave trade and the triumph of Mohammedanism. For three centuries, the reigning dynasty and the whole people have zealously professed Islam.

The population of Jimma belongs to the Galla or Oromo tribe. The people consider "Kake" as their ancestor—probably having come from Boranye, the cradle of all Galla. In general, by type or by morals, manners and customs, the inhabitants of Jimma are almost indistinguishable from their other fellow tribesmen. The Galla of Jimma are of large build, of exceptionally fine physique, with regular facial features. The women are renowned for their beauty. The color of their skin is chestnut. The men wear "*shammas.*"[22] A woman of distinction wears a leather skirt and a brown jacket. A slave girl wears just a small leather skirt. Women's hairstyles are very unique. Wealthy women wear wigs made of human hair, which resemble a large cap, plaited with parallel rows of horizontal slender braids.

Thanks to its wealth and commercial spirit, the people of Jimma do not distinguish themselves for warlike qualities. Prizing their prosperity, they have always been a tributary of their strongest neighbor—at first the King of Kaffa, then the *Negus* of Gojjam, and, finally, since 1886, the Emperor Menelik. Today, Jimma is autonomous in its internal government, pays tribute to the Empire, and observes the laws and edicts that are required for the whole empire. The highest court and the right of capital punishment belong to the Emperor of Abyssinia.

When the slave trade was suppressed by Menelik under pain of death, Jimma was one of the main centers of this business, and its prosperity was dealt a considerable blow. The Emperor likewise made it a criminal offense to turn convicts into slaves. (That used to be a wide-spread form of punishment in Jimma.) Formerly, those who underwent this punishment became the property of the king and furnished him with a source of considerable income. Now the continuation of prisoner-of-war status is limited to seven years, at the end of which the slave/prisoner-of-war becomes free. Thanks to these beneficial laws, slavery should be considered abolished, once and for all. But, in actuality, the descendants of former slaves find themselves still in a dependent condition today, analogous to the status of our peasants in the time of serfdom. Settled on lands of the king and obliged to work for him for eight days a month, the rest of the time they work only partly for themselves, and then their labor belongs to the local chief. Out of economic necessity, some former slaves stay at the court of the king, presenting themselves as a kind of manor serf.

At the head of the state government of Jimma is the hereditary king from the Kake dynasty, Aba Jefar, who inherited the throne from his father, Aba Dula.[23] The kingdom of Jimma used to be in feudal dependence to Kaffa. When Aba Jefar ascended the throne, he acknowledged himself first as a tributary of the *Negus* of Gojjam and then, eight years later, of the *Negus* of Shoa—Menelik.[24] Two years later, when Jimma was annexed to Abyssinia, Menelik punished Jefar (for inspiring excessive enthusiasm in his own standing army and trying to entice Abyssinian soldiers to his own service) by imprisoning him in Ankober for a year. When he was freed, Aba Jefar again received the throne of Jimma from Menelik, and after that lesson became one of the most obedient of vassals and one of the most regular in paying tribute to the Emperor.[25]

Near the King there is a high council made up of his relatives and representatives of prominent families. The King, with the elders, administers justice in all important matters, aside from serious crimes, which are scrutinized by the Emperor himself. But more or less minor offenses are decided by criminal courts or by local chiefs. From an administrative point of view, Jimma is divided into 60 small areas, governed by an *aba koro*—a duty entrusted to the oldest line of the oldest family in a given location. The *aba koro* names an assistant, aba genda, who has a small staff of lower functionaries, known as *aba langa*. It is interesting to note the special legal protection of merchants, who, by the way, control the king himself. Land is set aside for merchants, on which they erect their farmsteads—in short, for the development and maintenance of the commercial spirit in the country, merchants are given all imaginable privileges.

The duty to maintain the roads is considered very serious. Each landowner is entrusted, under penalty of serious punishment (in former times, that could even mean sale into slavery) with the obligation to keep the road in order. Thanks to this law, I never before saw any road like those there: wide, even, lined with trees, with bridges across ditches and swampy streams. On all roads that lead to Jimma, gates have been set up for surveillance of the movement of caravans, which are allowed free entry, but which cannot go back out without the permission of the King. After having arrived with his wares, a merchant informs the King of what he has brought with him, presenting gifts that are within their means.

Wishing to leave, a merchant requests royal permission for passage of his caravan. He is then escorted to the gates by specially designated people, armed with a unique spear with two blades. The tribute levied from merchants usually does not exceed ten percent of the value of the goods. At roadside bazaars, a passing caravan should bring as a gift several flat cakes made of bread, and boiled *gudera* (a kind of potato).

To the south-west of Jimma along the mountain range that divides it from the River Omo, resides the Janjero tribe, who formerly lived as an independent kingdom. On annexation to Jimma, the last king of this tribe acknowledged suzerainty to Menelik, but his successor in 1890 broke away from the Emperor. As a result of that, *Ras* Wolda Giyorgis together with the King of Jimma marched on the Janjero and annexed this territory to Jimma once and for all.

Janjero, both by its customs and its language, is sharply distinguished from neighboring tribes. Remarkable hunters and trappers, the Janjero are very brave, hardy, and extremely fierce. It is said that they even have human sacrifices.

January 2

We entered Jimma. Crossing the border forest, which stretches long the Gibye River, we climbed the high bank, on the steep ascent of which, in a ravine, was built an outpost, guarded by several Galla. The rock of Ali-Kela, a huge stone monolith, towers nearby, as if torn away from the high bank of the Omo River. Its sides are very sheer. On the summit is seen a small grove, in which the natives say there is a lake. Here, another rock rises almost in a row. This one resembles an obelisk and is called *Tulu-Saytana*, in other words "Mountain of the Devil."

Having on this day made a twelve-hour march with a short halt at noon, we made camp. It was already getting dark. Having stopped near the farmstead of a wealthy Galla, we hoped to obtain grain, hay, or straw for the mules from him. But the host, a Mohammedan, was not particularly friendly to us. He refused us grain, hay or anything else, claiming that he had nothing. The grass in the immediate vicinity had all been burnt, and only the grass on the bank of the stream was still intact. It was too dark to pick grass from among thorny bushes. I decided not to send my people to do this work. Anyway, they were exhausted from the march. The mules, consequently, had to stay hungry until morning. But my *ashkers* showed themselves to be fine fellows. On their own initiative, with the oldest member of the detachment at the head, they set out along the stream and gathered enough grass for the night. As was to be expected, this excursion did not turn out well. They returned bruised and badly scratched. But this action of my *ashkers*, better than anything, gave witness to the good morale in my detachment.

January 3

We went along a very beautiful, heavily populated and well cultivated area. The road went along the high right bank of the Gibye-Kake River, crossing its numerous tributaries. The surroundings differed sharply from the lands we had passed through earlier on the left bank of the Gibye River. In plant life, soil and in the wealth of nature it vividly reminded me of Leka, with which I had acquainted myself in my previous expedition (1896-97). Here I almost didn't see any mimosa or acacia, which are so often encountered in Shoa and between Addis Ababa and Gibye. A species of small trees, similar to peach trees, with bright green leaves, predominates. The soil is red clay; but in the valleys, lush black earth is found. As regards rocks, I most often observed reddish sandstone, and, here and there, granite. Basalt, which is often found in Abyssinia, I didn't see here at all.

On the way, we out-distanced and met commercial caravans, for the most part carrying cloth into Jimma and returning primarily with coffee. Heavily loaded mules[26] and horses walk in a herd, surrounded by drivers; behind them the owner, with an air of importance, sits on his mule with a felt hat, which he, on occasion, willingly sells to an Abyssinian, and with a straw parasol in his hands. Behind the caravan slowly walk the female slaves or wives of the drivers, loaded with all kinds of baggage. Caravans proceed very slowly, going not more than 12-15 versts [8-10 miles] a day. They set out early in the morning, and at noon set up bivouac, forming a picturesque scene. Somewhere in the valley, on the banks of streams, under a canopy of immense fig trees, the merchants' tents are pitched. The cargo is laid out in piles. Unsaddled and glittering with bright red padding on their backs, the mules graze on the sunny meadow. Here the drivers, half naked, their black skin and strong musculature shining, cut grass for the night with sickles. Around the campfires, women swarm, preparing food. For the night they take care of the animals on horse lines. The travelers, having dined on fresh flat cakes, seat themselves in a close circle around the campfire and spend the evening in endless conversation. Someone brings out a musical instrument that resembles a three-string harp, and, to the accompaniment of a monotonous rhythmic chord, draws out a sad and quiet song. The campfire is extinguished, and with it the melancholy melody dies down. The caravan arranges itself for the night's shelter. Here silence reigns. All that is heard is the regular chewing of the animals and the cry of a night bird.

Along the road small marketplaces are often encountered. A dozen women sit somewhere under the shade of a large tree and wait for buyers. They sell bread (small round flat cakes) and thick sour beer.

Among the sellers you run into very good-looking young women, but they all have an oppressed, sullen look, the like of which I never saw among the Galla girls of other tribes. Was this gloominess a result of Mohammedanism?

January 4

We forded the Gibye River and in the evening, having marched for eleven hours, reached the capital of Jimma—the town of Jeren.[27]

As we got closer to Jeren, the countryside became more beautiful and brighter. Trees, which were planted close together on both sides of the road, were in flower and filled the air with fragrance. Zelepukin, to his great joy, found in the bushes his old favorite—blackberry plants with ripe berries.

The town of Jeren lies at the foot of a mountain range that serves as the watershed of the Rivers Gibye-Kake and Gibye-Enareya. The palace of the feudal lord, Aba Jefar, stands in splendor on one of the highest hills. A wide street leads to the main gate of the palace. The farmsteads of relatives and retainers of the king, alternating with thick plantations of banana-like trees28 extend on both sides of that street. In the valley, several versts from here, you see dense settlements of local merchants and a large square, where twice a week is held the famous marketplace of Jimma.

The sun had already set when I arrived at the gates of the palace. On crossing the Gibye River I sent a rider to let Aba-Jefar know of my arrival, but the messenger somehow lingered on the way and got there almost at the same time we did. Our unexpected arrival caused some commotion. The chief *azzaj* (steward) ran out to meet us and apologized that because of the late news of our coming, he had not been able to prepare a lodging for us. In the name of Aba Jefar, he asked us to come and visit him.

Leaving the pack mules and some of the servants in the square, I and the other *ashkers* went to the palace, which was surrounded by a high and beautiful fence, made of split trunks of bamboo which were intricately interlaced, and divided into many separate courtyards. Each of these dwellings had its own special purpose: either for some section of the palace staff, or reception rooms of the king, or for his inner chambers.

Passing through a series of outer courtyards, we went into the inner chambers. Here we had to leave our mules and continue on foot. Finally, they led us into the courtyard where was located the sleeping chamber of Aba Jefar and the house of his harem— the place of incarceration of his two wives and two favorite concubines. The harem is a two-story building, of complex architecture, with narrow latticed windows and gaudily painted carved galleries. It is concealed behind a high wall and huge banana-like trees. Here I met Aba Jefar. The *Moti* (King) of Jimma sat on a folding chair near a large bonfire surrounded by several dozen of his retainers. Greeting me with a European-style handshake, he began to question me in broken Abyssinian about my journey, what I wanted to know, didn't I get tired, etc. Behind his throne, his body guards and suite sat on the grass, spread out in a picturesque group. My *ashkers* stood in a half circle behind my chair with their guns at their feet. (By

Abyssinian custom, servants should not sit in the presence of their master.)

Aba Jefar is still a young man—handsome, well-built, and somewhat in his prime. He has a typical face: a straight thin nose; bright, handsome eyes which shift suspiciously from side to side; a thick black beard; and black, short-cropped, curly hair. His hands are graceful. He wears large gold rings on all his fingers. Dressed in a white shirt and trousers, he has draped over his shoulders the thinnest white shamma. His feet are also very small and handsome, clad in leather sandals.

After a few minutes of conversation, Aba Jefar asked me to wait awhile, apologizing because this was the time for evening prayer. Accompanied by his suite, he walked a few steps to the side and started to perform the required ablutions. A slave boy brought a large silver pitcher with water, and Aba Jefar began to wash his hands, feet, chest, head, and shoulders in accord with all the rules of the Moslem ritual, at the same time uttering prayers in a low voice. Having finished the ceremony, he went up on a small white stone quadrangular patio, covered with a mat, and, turning to face the east, began to pray.

It was already quite dark... A marvelous, fantastic picture was presented by the prayer of a half-savage Mohammedan ruler in these circumstances so unusual to the eyes of European.

The blazing bonfire lit up with its changing flames the intricate and fanciful harem building, through the latticed windows of which the imprisoned beauties now looked out in curiosity. It also lit up a picturesque group of men draped in white *shammas*, and the huge shape of the king sharply prominent against the somber background of night. Aba Jefar zealously prayed, fingering beads and bowing down to the earth. There was total silence. Only random gusts of wind, rippling through the huge foliage of the banana-like trees and rustling their green garments disturbed the reverential silence that reigned around.

Having finished his prayers, Aba Jefar, apparently satisfied that he had had the opportunity to show off to a European his knowledge of all the Moslem rituals, once again settled into his chair.

We renewed our interrupted conversation. The king asked me about *Stambul* (Turkey) and *Mysyr* (Egypt). He wanted to know if it was true that *Stambul* was the most powerful state in the world. Of course, I had to, to some degree, disillusion him and refute the biased tales that Arabs had told him.

Servants brought a large earthenware pot of coffee and sat down near us on the grass to pour it. From a wicker straw basket in the form of a column embroidered with beads, they took out about ten small cups without handles, wrapped in red calico, and spread them out on a wooden tray. They offered coffee to us first; and then, in order, the whole suite and my *ashkers* were served.

Having drunk coffee, I asked Aba Jefar to order his suite to lead me to my house. I sat on my mule and, surrounded by the suite and by my *ashkers*, set out for the place that had been prepared for us. Our way was lighted by a torch made of a piece of bamboo trunk, the inside of which was completely filled with wax, with a thick paper wick.

At our house, a whole detachment of slaves was waiting for us, with the oldest housekeeper in charge. They had brought us as a gift from Aba Jefar abundant *durgo* (honorary gifts), consisting of 130 pieces of *injera* (bread), six buckets of tej (mead), four rams, butter, hens, honey, milk, salt, and firewood, as well as hay and barley for our mules. My boys forgot both their weariness and the pain of feet worn out by the long journey and rejoiced anticipating abundant refreshments.

January 5

A day's rest in Jeren. About nine in the morning, Aba Jefar sent to invite me to his quarters and sent along a guard detachment of 500 men to accompany me. Apparently, he wanted to compensate in this way for the ceremonial reception that had been planned for the day before but which hadn't taken place because of the suddenness of my arrival.

The detachment formed a front in several ranks before the gates of my house. Before it stood officers who had dismounted from mules. In response to my greeting, the detachment bowed to the ground and then quickly reformed in two units that took their places—one in front of me and the other behind. In this order we, quietly and with ceremony, headed toward the court, accompanied by a crowd of people and children. I was very pleased with the warriors—mainly Abyssinians—who served as my convoy. They were well dressed and armed. Almost all of them had signs of distinction in battle: gold ear-rings, sabers mounted in silver, shields decorated with silver, cloaks made of leopard skins, and ribbons on the head.

They led me to a large interior court of the palace which had two purposes: as the place of the main court of justice and at the same time as the reception hall. The court was built in a semicircle, which could easily accommodate several thousand people. A wooden pavilion, trimmed with various motley colored decorations and covered with a tiled roof, was constructed in the middle. Its architecture reminds one of Indian buildings. The pavilion was erected by foreign experts—Arabs and Hindus. Three sides of it, facing the courtyard, were open, and on the fourth, in a solid stone wall, a bay was arranged, curtained off with multi-colored fabrics. The throne of Aba Jefar stands here, all covered with carpets. A small wall clock stands near one of the walls of the bay, on a little table.

A long, low wooden colonnade, covered with thatch is erected along the side opposite to the pavilion. A crowd of people, who had gathered in the palace, ceremoniously sat on low stools made out of a single piece of wood.

Aba Jefar received me, sitting on the throne cross-legged, Turkish-style. An Arab mullah—the most influential person in the kingdom—sat on the step of the throne. Old men—chiefs of Galla tribes—were seated on each side of the throne, in two rows, likewise on low stools. A well-built Europe chair was set out for me, opposite the throne.

To my greeting, Aba Jefar replied in Arabic, imitating the guttural Arabic pronunciation and piously rolling his eyes. Then he very animatedly began to question me in Arabic, incessantly smiling for the whole time of the conversation. Aba Jefar translated my answers to Galla for the old men, who represented a complete contrast from their intelligent and progressive king. Wrapped up in their long cloaks (*shammas*), they sat majestically and silently, listening with distrust to the stories about ships, iron roads etc., which sounded improbable to them. They looked with complete indifference at the white man, who was brought by fate to their distant land as if from another world. It seemed that it was all the same to them whether the alien who was before them spoke the truth or lied.

Aba Jefar hurled me questions about European states that he knew of—about their comparative size, population, etc. The King had heard that the largest of them was Russia, and when I mentioned that in an entire year one would not be able to walk across it from west to east, he was startled.

Knowing that I had a medicine chest with me, the king asked me to show it and to share with him some remedies, and also to treat his sick mother. I fulfilled the first request: I gave him soda for heartburn, iodoform, and sublimate for treating wounds and copal balm. As regards his mother, I said that I had to examine her before I could treat her. They sent to warn the sick woman that I would be coming, and after several minutes I went, accompanied by the head eunuch, to the apartment of the harem which the mother of the king occupied. They led me by a narrow, little court, enclosed with high fences, past a whole row of low little houses which were covered with thatch and locked. At all the gates, menacing and silent guards of the harem stood— beardless eunuchs, armed with long whips. Here and there beautiful slave girls appeared. They looked at us with curiosity and then quickly hid themselves. The whole situation had the smell of some mysterious eastern bliss.

The house where the mother of Aba Jefar lived was found in a separate little court and was a little bit larger than the others. The entrance to it was hung with white cloth, which hid the mistress of the house from our view. A chair was set for me on this side of the curtain, and, at first, our conversation, with the help of a translator, took place through the curtain. The patient complained of heartburn, cough, and headache. I had to see her and listen to her, so I went beyond the curtain.

On a divan covered with carpets, the queen mother sat, dressed in a black silk burnoose embroidered in gold, thrown over it was a white jacket, decorated with silk. The color of her skin was quite light. The features of her face were regular. Her eyes were remarkably beautiful. Despite her 40 years of age, she still seemed like a youthful woman. Her forehead, neck and chest were tattooed. Her fingers were painted red. Arms and legs, on which were worn gold bracelets, were so small that any Chinese woman could envy them. The queen mother was heavily scented with attar of roses and sandalwood. A crowd of pretty maids of honor in original little brown leather skirts and white cotton blouses, adorned with silver links, necklaces, copper and bone bracelets and rings, surrounded the queen mother. Several of the maids of honor were positively beautiful. My unexpected appearance produced on them diverse impressions. Some stood, with downcast eyes and did not dare to look at me. Others stared with curiosity at the white man, the likes of which they had never seen before, and whispered to one another and exchanged looks among one another.

To the horror of all except the patient herself, I listened to the queen mother's chest. She had a little bronchitis, and I gave her some cough powder.

I had already made up my mind to leave, but the patient stopped me, proposing refreshments. They gave me honey mixed with water in a large horn glass. We began to talk. The queen mother surprised me with her intelligence, and the remarkable dignity and ease with which she conducted herself. It was evident that in spite of her closed life inside the walls of the harem, she did not remain a stranger to current events and, no less than her son, she knew both about the political position of nearby countries and also about distant European states. Animatedly and intelligently, the queen mother questioned me about our way of life and our governmental system. She was especially interested, of course, in the position of women. The freedom of women seemed to her quite incomprehensible, and the possibility of noble couples—husband and wife—appearing in public with uncovered faces surprised her extremely.

"Does this mean that in your country there are no budas" (werewolf, evil eye, who causes illness and bad luck), she asked, "since your noble people do not fear to show their wives to outsiders?"

I responded that among us the time has long since passed when we believed in budas. To that, the queen mother with a deeply convinced tone said, "But among us, even up until now, they still exist."

Taking my leave, I photographed the queen mother and her maids of honor, but the photo, unfortunately, did not come out.

In the evening of that very day, Aba Jefar visited me with his numerous suite, having arrived at a gallop on a marvelous gray horse, glittering with rich silver, densely gilded gear, with a gold chain on its neck.

The king asked me to show him instruments, photographs and such and asked about the significance and use of each of the articles he examined. Of course, above all he liked the weapons: 3/8" caliber rifle and saber, which he examined long and lovingly.

JANUARY 6

We set out into Kaffa. Aba Jefar gave me several bags of meal for the road and promised to send to Kaffa another ten, which should make up my food supply for the subsequent campaign. We went down from the hills on which was located the town of Jeren, and passing several thickly settled settlements of merchants and a large market square, went down into the valley of the Gibye-Kake River. At noon we halted on the bank of this river, in the shade of a huge sycamore, and toward evening, crossing the upper river, set up bivouac at the foot of the watershed mountain range between the Gibye and Gojeb Rivers.

A crowd of Galla cheerfully worked on the road near our lodging for the night. With a refrain that was inspired, and flying into a rage: *"Ashana, ada, kho, kho, kho"* ("Strengthen honey, ho, ho, ho.")—about ten strong Galla deeply dug the earth, with wooden pitchforks, with iron bound on the end. They chopped large clods of earth in time to the song. A woman with a large pitcher in her hands sat near the group of those who were working the earth. She poured beer from it into horn glasses for those who were present. When we came up to them, the Galla crowded round us, entreating us to drink beer. At first I, then my *ashkers* took a large glass, which contained more than half a bottle. One pitcher was not enough, so they brought another from the neighboring house; and only after they had treated all of us did they let us go, parting with cordial wishes. They seemed to me in the highest degree likable—these wild, half-naked, remarkably cordial and hard-working people.

January 7

We crossed a mountain ridge, overgrown with enormous, marvelous forest, inhabited by many birds and monkeys. Trees of uncommon size are interwoven with lianas and overgrown with white moss, which hangs from the branches in long threads. The natives call this moss *yazaf shebat*, which means "gray hair of the tree." The road was very busy. We met unending files of bearers—tall and strong Galla, carrying on their heads to Kaffa big skins of grain, or returning from Kaffa loaded with coffee and mead. Since a great shortage of grain has been felt in Kaffa after the recent war, all the surplus of bread from Jimma is now sent to there, where it is exchanged there for coffee and mead. For one piece of salt (20 kopecks) a bearer conveys a load of one to one and a half poods [36 to 54 lbs.] there and back. Going at a quick pace and making frequent stops, he easily goes 20 to 30 versts [14 to 20 miles] a day. The entire clothing of the bearers consists of a little leather apron on the hips. For weapons they have a dagger, which they wear on the waist. In their arms they hold long pipes, made of two hollow reed stems (the small one is filled with tobacco and the long one is the mouthpiece), stuck into a hollow little gourd half filled with water. I had observed this prototype of a hookah among all of the Galla tribes I had met up until then.

In addition to commercial caravans, we often passed soldiers of *Ras* Wolda Giyorgis who were going to the muster point. The most prosperous of them set out to war with their whole families. Several donkeys carry the household goods of the soldier and reserve rations. The wife carries field kitchen utensils in a sack on her shoulders. A boy who is a son or stranger is pressed under the weight of a gun that is one and a half times longer than him. And the master himself, with a straw parasol in his hands and a saber at his waist, who has probably already gone more than his first hundred versts [70 miles], light-heartedly and cheerfully walks toward troubles and deprivation, singing battle songs all the way. Soldiers who have assembled for the march treat the local populace rather impetuously. For example, they consider it their undisputed right to take everything edible from those they meet. So complained a Galla who had been robbed: Adera Menelik ("By the God of Menelik"), the soldier took from him a gourd of mead and a piece of bread—in a word, everything that caught his eye. And the soldiers' wives kept pace with their husbands in this behavior. I happened to see how one of them, a small and frail Abyssinian woman, for some offense hit in the face a big, strong Galla, who in response only mournfully lamented: *Abyet, abyet, goftako* ("Forgive me, forgive me, madam.")

Even my *ashkers* became imbued with this military spirit...

Finally I had to take strict measures to curb their impetuous outbursts, which were expressed, however, in rather harmless forms. For instance, I noticed that straw parasols had suddenly appeared in the hands of all my boys. In response to my question of where they got them, they answered me in the most open-hearted tone, "Galla gave them to us."

At about noon, we saw a large crowd of people at one house. It turned out that the brother of Aba Jefar, General (*Fitaurari*) Aba Diga, was carrying out an order of Menelik to the effect that prisoners who had been captured in Kaffa in the last campaign should be returned there.

Learning that I was passing by, Aba Diga sent to ask me to visit him, and I complied. The *Fitaurari* treated me to a good lunch, for which he ordered one of my slaves, a Christian, to slaughter the ram that had been designated for me.[29]

Aba Diga is already elderly, but he is a handsome and intelligent man. His whole figure has the imprint of aristocracy. The general conducted himself very simply and with dignity, conversing intelligently and the only way which nevertheless a savage appeared was in begging.

"What do you bring with you? Do you have a watch? I need a watch. Give me one! Do you have silk, perfume, soap? Give me some!"

He rained these kinds of questions and requests on me constantly, despite the fact that I answered negatively. Finally, Aba Diga was satisfied by my promise to give him a watch when we returned from the expedition. On his side, knowing that Europeans are interested in local articles which might have significance for an ethnographic collection, the general proposed on my return to collect some of the things which are known in Abyssinia in the simple style of the Italians by the name of "antiques." We parted as friends.

Having crossed the mountain ridge, we went along the northern slope, crossing, along the way, many streams and brooks which flow into the Gojeb. At first, the road went through a densely populated area, but the closer we got to the Gojeb, which constitutes the border between Jimma and Kaffa, we encountered settlements more and more rarely. Along the left side stretched a dense forest, which serves as a place reserved for the buffalo hunts of Aba Jefar, who built a hunting house near the road.

Having crossed the Gojeb River, we spent the night in a rather deserted place, on the bank of a beautiful brook, overgrown with date palms, the first of that kind of tree that I had seen in Abyssinia.

The Gojeb River begins in the mountains of Guma and flows into the River Omo. At this place its width is about 40 paces; its depth is one and a quarter arshins [35 inches]. Its current is so swift that fording it is very difficult. The valley of the Gojeb, surrounded by mountains of Kaffa, constitutes the border zone between these two regions and is uninhabited. It abounds in wild goats and antelopes. Leopards and lions are encountered here. Larger animals, such as elephants and rhinoceroses, stay lower on the river's course, near to where the Gojeb flows into the Omo.

January 8

Passing a series of frontier posts with various fortifications in the form of abattis, wolf-holes, and palisades, we entered the land of Kaffa.

From the Gojeb Valley, which was overgrown with high g*Ra*ss and sparse small trees, we climbed the mountains that surrounded it and entered a very dense forest, the trees of which are striking for their enormous size. At the summit of the mountain range, we saw bamboo groves; and in the foothills in the valley of rivers and streams, there were groups of beautiful date palms. The forest abounds in flowers which fill the air with fragrance. The sky was cloudless. The sun was almost at its zenith, but in the forest there was a cool breeze. The eye rested in the green of the surrounding thick foliage. In nature some kind of joy of living was felt—a surplus of strength hidden within it. The charming beauty of the place carried one off to some place far away, to a magical world. It seemed as if you heard and saw a marvelous tale while awake. It was as if in front of you stood the enchanted forest from Sleeping Beauty. All that was missing were the princess, her palace, and her subjects. But instead of the poetic circumstances of a fine story, before us appeared the dreadful signs of death and destruction. Amid the green grass, the white of human bones shone here and there. Settlements were nowhere to be seen—only thick weeds, growing on plots of recently cultivated earth, bear testimony of the people who once lived here. An evil fairy of war destroyed them, and scattered their bones across the fields. The closer we came to the capital of Kaffa, the more noticeable became the signs of recent battles. Near the town itself, clearings were completely strewn with human bones...

At five o'clock in the afternoon, we entered the town of Andrachi. The *Ras*, having found out about my arrival shortly before, sent soldiers, led by his chief agafari (gentleman in attendance), to meet me.

Surrounded by his retainers and commanders of units, the *Ras* received me with ceremony. Having exchanged the usual greetings, he reproached me for not having warned him of my arrival ahead of time, because he had no chance to meet me as he would have liked. By Abyssinian etiquette, it is considered impolite to weary someone who has just arrived from a journey with long questions. Therefore, after a few minutes of conversation, the *Ras* suggested that I go rest in the lodging which had been set aside for me. In the evening, the agafari (gentleman in attendance) of the *Ras* came to me to ask about my health, and one of his *elfin ashkers* (pages), Gomtes, a favorite of the *Ras*, brought me various dishes prepared in the European manner: chicken cooked in butter, and meat cooked in little pieces. For my *ashkers*, the *Ras* sent abundant *durgo*: a bull, several rams, bread, beer, mead, pepper sauce, etc. They slaughtered the bull immediately. Around the tent campfires shone, songs resounded and it was as if the 70-verst [49 mile] march had never happened.

Today, I finished my separate, so to speak, mobilization. We arrived on time. My men were cheerful and happy. Although the animals had lost weight on the way, they were still in condition to continue the journey. (By the way, their backs still seemed full). As for me, thanks to some conveniences I had managed to arrange for the crossing from Addis Ababa to Kaffa, despite the forced pace of the march, I had significantly recovered from the illness which I had come down with during the first difficult trek.

In the course of 42 days from the moment of my departure from Addis Ababa to meet our mission, I had traveled more than 2,000 versts [1,400 miles]. All this time, my strength was strained to the limit. Not to mention the physical weariness, illness, and deprivation, it seemed inconceivable to have arrived at the sea coast, returned to the capital, equipped myself and with full transport, and made a 500-verst [350 mile] crossing in such a short time. I had been oppressed the whole time by the disturbing feeling that all my work might go to waste if I didn't succeed in arriving at the mustering point on time. And only today could I fall asleep peaceful and satisfied...

KAFFA

Kaffa is located on the middle part on the eastern and western spurs of a mountain range that serves as the watershed between the Indian Ocean and the Mediterranean Sea.[30] The elevation of the mountain range makes Kaffa open to the southwest and northwest winds, which bring it abundant rain periodically twice a year (in February to March and August to September). However, rain also falls often the rest of the year, and in all of Ethiopia Kaffa is the place with the greatest abundance of precipitation. They never have droughts here like those in the northern part of the Ethiopian highlands. The rivers are exceptional for having such an abundance of water, and Kaffa itself is covered with rich vegetation. To the east from the mountain ridge flow the rivers Gojeb, Adiya, Gumi, Wosh and others which flow into the Omo, and from the western slopes the Menu, Bako, Baro and others, which serve as tributaries of the Juba or the Sobat.[31] All the numerous rivers are fed by a countless number of streams and small brooks that start in the main mountain range and its spurs. The water basin, serving as excellent irrigation, is distributed evenly across the whole expanse of Kaffa, which benefits the fertility of its soil, the like of which I have never seen. The moderate elevation of Kaffa above sea level—on the average not higher than 2,000 meters and not lower than 1,600 meters—also has a favorable influence on vegetation. However, separate summits, like Gida-Shonga, Gonga-Beke, Bacha-aki-Kila, Geshe, attain an elevation of 3,000 meters.

In the middle of rich black earth, clay is encountered in places. Whatever space is entirely free of cultivation is covered with forest, which grows amazingly fast and mightily. Just neglect some plot of ground, and in two to three years it turns into an impassable thicket. Here man must fight with the forest like those who live bordering on deserts must fight with sands covering the land.

The predominant kind of rock is a red porous sandstone. One rarely comes across granite.

With such an abundance of forests, one might presume that the country is likewise rich in their usual inhabitants—wild animals. However, there are almost no predatory species of animals here (which is explained by the standard of culture of the country and its former density of population). You rarely encounter wild goats, antelope, or chamois; and only in the crown forest reserves are buffalo and elephant found. It is strictly forbidden to hunt them. There are also very few birds in Kaffa. I never heard a single song-bird. They say that predatory birds appeared only recently, with the arrival of the Abyssinians.

Related to the Abyssinians and similar to them, the populace of Kaffa, represents a mixture of the tribes which originally inhabited Ethiopia with Semites. Undoubtedly, the percentage of Semitic blood in the Kaffas is less than that in the Abyssinians. However, all Kaffa people are not all of the same type. Rather, there are two varieties of Kaffa: the type which is purest and close to the Abyssinians—their aristocracy; and the lowest class of the populace—descendants of slaves from all the neighboring tribes, who resemble on the surface the Sidamo people, having mixed the least with other offspring of the generation of the original inhabitants of Ethiopia.[32]

Until recently, Kaffa was still a powerful southern Ethiopian empire; but in 1897, it was conquered by Abyssinia.

It is very difficult to reconstruct the history of Kaffa since, aside from several legends, there are almost no data. From Abyssinian sources it is known that the Ethiopian Empire was powerful, Kaffa formed with it one indivisible whole.

By legend, Kaffa was conquered in the fifteenth century by Atye (Emperor) Zara Yakob. The name of "Kaffa" is attributed to him. After his death, one of the sons of the Ethiopian emperor reigned in Kaffa.[33] Under Lyb-na-Dyngyl or David II, the king of Kaffa was considered the first vassal of the emperor of Ethiopia. At times when the King of Kaffa visited the court of the Emperor, he was shown the greatest honor: the Emperor himself went to meet him and the King of Kaffa sat on the right side of the throne.

The invasion of of the Gallas and the wars of Gran (sixteenth century) separated Kaffa from the rest of Abyssinia and for many centuries isolated it. Because of this, Kaffa preserved domestic and cultural relationships in the same form as there were when the Galla invasion occurred. However, much was lost, including the Christian faith, which they had professed before the invasion, and literacy.

Populated by a strong people, imbued with love for their fatherland and an enterprising, war-like spirit, occupying an advantageous central position, protected by forests and mountains, Kaffa subdued the neighboring states, and formed out of them a powerful southern Ethiopian empire, known formerly under the general name of Kaffa. This empire included the following six main vassal kingdoms: Jimma, Kulo, Konta, Koshya, *Mocha* and Enareya.

Jimma was populated by Gallas. In Enareya, also known as Lima, lived tribes which were a mixture of Gallas with the original inhabitants of the country[34] (kindred of the Kaffa). *Mocha* has the same origin as the Kaffa. In the kingdoms of Kulo, Konta and Koshya kindred tribes live, who are very similar in type, having a common language, culture and customs. Explorers of Africa called these people "Sidamo." (This name is unknown to they themselves.) I will adhere to this nomenclature.[35]

These subdued lands, however, did not lose their independence: Kaffa did not interfere in their internal affairs, demanding only payment of tribute and acknowledgment of their suzerainty. At the time of the death of Zara Yakob, his dynasty ruled in Kaffa. The kings of Kaffa—tato (from the word atye—"emperor" in Abyssinian)—styled themselves as Kings of Kaffa and Enareya. But discord, the time of which is difficult to determine even approximately, led to separation of their thrones. The ancient dynasty of Zara Yakob remained in Enareya, while in Kaffa the house of Manjo reigned. The disintegration of the empire did not destroy the ties between both states. On visiting Kaffa, the King of Enareya received honors even greater than its own ruler: for instance, the King of Kaffa rose to meet his guest and and had his guest sit with him on the throne to the right side.

After Enareya was subdued by the Limu Galla tribe, it lost its significance, having been made subject to the Galla prince who conquered it. But the dynasty of the king of Enareya continued to exist up until recent times, and up until the very end of the independent existence of Kaffa, Kaffa showed the kings of Enareya royal honors.

The dynasty of Manjo, apparently, does not differ from Kaffa in its governmental structure nor in court etiquette: as they are written in the ancient Abyssinian books Kobyra Negest, so exactly they remain. In its structure, culture, and class distinctions, Kaffa is indebted entirely to Abyssinia.[36] At the head of state stood the autocratic tato (king, emperor), who had unlimited authority. His person was considered holy and inviolable. He surrounded himself with great honors and was inaccessible for his subjects. At his court, the strictest etiquette was observed. With the exception of his seven advisors and several retainers, none of his subjects dared look their sovereign in the face. When he appeared, his subjects prostrated themselves, snapping at the earth with their teeth, and in this manner literally fulfilled the common salutation, "For you I gnaw the earth."

Special roads were built for the king, along which no one else could go. The tato had several residences in various places and lived in them for those times of year which for that particular place were considered the healthiest. The main capital was the town of Andrachi, in which an enormous palace was located: the span of each of the columns that support it was several times the reach of both extended arms. The Abyssinians, having torn the city asunder, had to spend a long time trying to destroy this colossal building, until they finally succeeded in burning it down. In front of the palace, there was a large open space. Those who came to court had to dismount here and go the rest of the way by foot.

Sometimes the tato would appear in the court of justice. There he sat silently, with his face covered, up to the eyes, with a shamma. Those who were being tried stood with their backs to him.

The dinner of the king was accompanied with great ceremonies. The only person allowed to go behind the curtains, where the tato made himself comfortable, was the one who had the responsibility to feed him and give him drink. The sovereign himself would not exert himself at all. The gentleman carver brought everything to him and placed it in his mouth. This post was considered very important in the court hierarchy. This dignitary had to be distinguished for the best moral qualities so as not to in any way harm the king. During the time when he was away from his main duties, his right arm was tied in a canvas sack, in order that this arm, which fed the king, not contract some illness or be bewitched.

Originally, the tato was Christian. But the last six kings formally renounced Christianity, having banned Christian priests from the palace and having replaced them with pagan priests. Each week the tato locked himself up in the temple together with the head priest of Merecho and spent several days there with him, telling fortunes and conjuring.

For discussion of the most important matters, the king appointed a high council, for which only representatives of five families could be selected: Hio (two people), Amara, Argefa, Machya and Uka.[37] From among the seven councilors (usually from the Hio family) one, named *katamarash*a, was the main spokesperson and announced the will of the king. This council served as the highest court of law.

For administrative purposes, the whole country was divided into 12 regions: Bimbi, Gauta, Beshe, Bita, Oka, Dech, Adda, Kaffa, Gobe, Shashi, Wata, and Chana. Each of these was entrusted to the management of a governor—waraba or *Ras*ha (this name derives from the Abyssinian word *Ras*), who had an assistant—guda. Warabas were appointed by the king, independent of what family they belonged to. Their responsibilities included administering justice and inflicting punishment, and, in time of war, assembling and supplying provisions for the militia.

The regions, which derived their names from the families which inhabited them, were, in turn, divided into smaller parts or parcels. The eldest man of the eldest line in the family was considered the local chief. Consequently, at the foundation of the state there lay a tribal, aristocratic origin, on which class distinctions were also based. After the first subjugation of Kaffa by Abyssinians (in the fifteenth century), to consolidate his realm, the reigning king distributed to his fellow fighters both the conquered lands and the inhabitants, who had been turned into slaves. Those native families who voluntarily submitted or who performed some service for the Abyssinians kept their freedom and privileges. Thus the descendants of the Abyssinian new-comers who had settled in the country and the privileged natives formed a class which enjoyed the advantages of freedom and landownership, but which in return was obligated on the one hand to defend the state from external enemies and on the other hand to keep the subdued region in hand.

The closest advisors of the king were selected from several families who perhaps had blood ties with the ruling dynasty or whose ancestors distinguished themselves by some special outstanding deeds. As a consequence of the tribal nobility that emerged in this manner, the older lines constituted the ruling class, and the younger lines were free nobles, obliged only for military service.

My assumptions are confirmed by the existence up until now of a dependent populace which is conditionally free, which is not exempt from military service, and likewise the fact that among the names of the clans are found family names of Abyssinian and non-Abyssinian origin. For instance, "Amara" is undoubtedly an Abyssinian name, and "Hio" is probably local.

As a consequence of new conquests, captive slaves, merging with the subdued populace, increased the number of the dependent class.

In Kaffa, aside from these two basic classes, there also exist free merchants and pagan priests. The first are former local merchants and new-comers; the latter, in view of the strict succession of their religious order, also constituted a separate class. However, only one of the sons of a pagan priest was obliged to succeed to the profession of the father—the remaining children of this priest had free choice in this regard. Similar to Abyssinians in all other respects, the Kaffa are only lower than the Abyssinians in the level of their culture: letters are completely unknown to the pagans.

The Kaffa dress the same as Abyssinians. Men of the higher class wear the shamma—a wide piece of thick cotton material which is thrown over the shoulders, and the free ends of which fall back. They also wear short, very wide trousers which do not extend to the knees and are made of thick cotton material with beautiful patterns woven on the edges.

The lower class does not have the right to dress themselves in cloth and wears only leather. The entire costume of a man consists of a leather apron on the hips, and, in cold weather or rain, they throw over their shoulders a cape made of huge half-leaves of a banana-like (musa enset) tree, laid upon one another. The wide part of the banana-like tree leaf is like fringe attached to the main stem of the leaf and falls in long ribbons.

Women of the higher class wear long shirts, and those of the lower class wear leather skirts. Headgear is the same for both classes. In addition, cone-shaped caps made of those same banana-like tree leaves are also seen.

Men, as well as women, adorn their arms and legs with bracelets, rings, ear-rings, and beads.

The Kaffa differ from other tribes in their hair-style. Men grow long hair which, for instance on the king, stands up in a shock or is braided in plaits that hang down to the shoulders. Women have the same kind of hairstyle.

In former times, the food of the Kaffa consisted of meat, milk, and porridge made of the seeds of various bread-grain plants. Nowadays, they eat almost exclusively bread made from the roots of a banana-like tree (that same musa enset), since that is the only food stuff they can obtain after the general destruction.

This bread is prepared in the following manner: once a tree has attained four years of growth, they dig it up and strip off the leaves; then they bury the thick lower part of the trunk in the ground and leave it there for several months. After this time, it begins to rot and turn sour. Then they extract the buried tree from the ground, clean off the spoiled outer layer, and scrape and grind the part which has turned sour and soft. Then they bake it in large earthenware pans. This bread is not very nutritious. It is unsavory and has an unpleasant sour smell. If you add flour to it, then the bread is somewhat improved.

As a supplement to this food, they serve various roots, cooked in water, and also coffee, which they drink several times a day, up until and after eating. They boil coffee in earthenware vessels and pour it out into little cups made of ox horn.

The favorite drinks of the Kaffa are beer and mead. The beer is very thick and strong, but prepared without the stupefying leaves of the gesho, in only one malt. The beer is also very thick and sour.

Household utensils are the same as those of the Abyssinians—except for earthenware jogs, which are oblong and similar to ancient Greek vessels, and are of a more beautiful form than those of the Abyssinians.

The buildings of the Kaffa are very similar to those of the Abyssinians, but they are made more carefully and more elegantly.

The Kaffa bury their dead in very deep graves at the bottom of which they make a cave. They usually wrap up the corpse in palm branches, and, at the burial, lower coffee, money, and ivory together with it into the grave. Close relatives of the deceased, mourning his death, dress in rags, scratch their faces until they bleed, and tear out hair. They stay in mourning for a long time.

The Kaffa are bold, dashing horsemen. Their horses are rather tall and, judging by those which I saw, cannot be called bad, even though the climate and character of the place do not favor horse breeding. Only the upper classes have horses, and horses serve exclusively for military purposes. The Kaffa saddle differs from that of the Abyssinians in that it is smaller, covered with leather, and the pommel is much lower. The bit is the same as that of the Abyssinians. The saddle is adorned with metal decorations, but differently from the Abyssinian.

The weapons of the Kaffa include a throwing spear, which has a very beautiful form and is sometimes decorated with an intricate point; and a dagger worn in the belt. Round leather shields serve for defensive armaments. There are no bows and arrows.

Women in Kaffa are in a more dependent position than in Abyssinia. Wives are bought and become the slaves of their husbands, and do not have the right to divorce.

Although the Kaffa language differs sharply from the Abyssinian, it has many roots in common with it.

Their religion is a strange mixture of Christian, Jewish, and pagan beliefs—a conglomerate of all possible superstitions. The highest deity is called *Iero* or Ier (in all probability, this name derives from the Abyssinian word *egziabeer*, which means "god").[39] *Deontos* is honored in parallel with *Iero*. They make sacrifices to both deities. According to the beliefs of the Kaffa, Christ, Mary, and Satan (the devil), and simply a *kalicha* or *bale* (pagan priest) can help in case of misfortune.

Very few traces of Christianity remain here. They only left a few churches whole. Priests who came from Abyssinia sometimes served in them. And up until most recent times several fasts were observed by the king and the aristocracy. For example, they had a 50-day fast which coincides with the time of our Lent, and a thirty-day fast which falls in autumn. Of the Christian holidays, the Kaffa honor Holy Cross Day, which is *Mashkala* in their language (*Maskal* in Abyssinian) and *shanbat* (sanbat in Abyssinian)—Sabbath [Saturday]. Friday is considered a holiday. And with that is exhausted all connection of the religion of the Kaffa with Christianity.

From Judaism, they adopted the ceremony of circumcision of babies and the method of slaughtering cattle (which, as is well known, Jews perform in accord with strictly defined ritual). The paganism of the Kaffa appears most strikingly in the fact that, from their point of view, all success and failure in life, all disasters and averting of disasters depend on a deity who is in each separate case either merciful or inflicting punishment. In order to dispose this deity favorably toward oneself and to propitiate him, one must make sufficient sacrifice. The mood of the deity and the answer to the question of which of the gods to address oneself to is only known to a pagan priest, a sorcerer—*bale*. He sacrifices an animal supplied to him for this, then tells fortunes by its innards and... gives advice. But there are other means as well at the disposal of the *bale*: various incantations, medicines, etc. If prayers do not succeed, the pagan priest is never to blame, but rather the client was not able to propitiate the deity sufficiently, or did something contrary to the deity or was "bewitched" again by some evil man after the sacrifice.

Formerly, sacrifices were frequent and national and done in mass. These sacrifices were performed on days which corresponded with several of our holidays (for example, Holy Cross Day, etc.) and also on especially important occasions of state life. The place of sacrifice was Mount Bonga-*Shanbat*a, i.e. Sabbath Bonga, on the summit of which a temple was built. According to old-timers, on days of national sacrifice, hundreds of bulls were slaughtered. Their blood flowed from the mountain in a stream, and tens of thousands of men ate the sacrificed animals.

However, despite the fact that Christianity is almost completely forgotten, there remain here several families who still firmly adhere to it and who therefore received with joy the missionary Massai who visited the capital of Kaffa and the surrounding area. This missionary succeeded in converting several hundred people to Catholicism.

In the far distant past, before its destruction and conquest by the Abyssinians, Kaffa was the industrial and commercial center of Ethiopia. Thanks to its wealth, to the fertility of soil etc., it had the reputation of being an almost fairytale country. It abounded in bread, mead, cattle, and horses, and with its tributaries, it gathered a huge quantity of ivory.

A large part of the musk exported from Ethiopia was obtained in Kaffa. Excellent cloth and the best iron articles—spears and daggers—were made in Kaffa. But circumstances changed, and the once flourishing and busy state is now completely destroyed and an almost deserted country.

During the time when Kaffa, isolated by the Gallas, did not change its internal structure at all and got hardened in the old forms of life, Abyssinia recovered from the blow the Gallas had struck, quickly grew, got stronger, and developed. In its wars, Abyssinia acquired guns. Abyssinia subdued one after the other the peoples who surrounded it, under whose power it had temporarily fallen. Finally, expanding its borders, it became a neighbor of Kaffa. Having gone through so many revolutions in this time, tempered in heavy conflict both with external and internal enemies, once it had gotten stronger, Abyssinia really couldn't stop on the way to fulfillment of its cultural-historical mission—the union and development of the Central African tribes who inhabit Ethiopia.

The collision of the two tribal states became inevitable, even though all the chances for victory were, evidently, on the side of Abyssinia. To Kaffa, as the weakest, there remained only to submit voluntarily or be subdued. But Kaffa decided to defend its independence to the very last. Wars began which struck a terrible blow to the prosperity of the country, gradually reducing it to complete collapse and destruction. Despite the desperate resistance, it ended in the complete subjugation of Kaffa and the annexation of it to the Ethiopian empire (1897).

The first campaign against Kaffa was carried out by *Ras* Adal, the ruler of Gojjam, in 1880. He ravaged one of its districts. At the same time, Kaffa lost one of its vassal states—Jimma—the king of which recognized the power of *Ras* Adal over him.

The campaign into Kaffa, a warlike country which was inaccessible due to mountains and forests, was considered by contemporaries as an outstanding feat. As a reward for this success, Emperor Yohannes made *Ras* Adal the *Negus* of Gojjam and Kaffa. He has reigned in Gojjam up until the present time, under the name of Tekla Haymanot. In 1886, conflict arose between Shoa under Menelik and Gojjam under Tekla Haymanot, over the division of southwestern Ethiopian lands.

Having utterly defeated the king of Gojjam in a battle at Embabo, Menelik took in his hands all the land to the south of the Abbay River, despite the fact that they were at that time independent. Kaffa was among the regions seized by Menelik. It was then that began the gradual conquest of the Kaffa empire by Menelik's leaders.

Hard times now ensued for all the states which made up the southern Ethiopian empire. A new phase in their history began.

Up until this time, they were isolated and closed off. Now they gradually merged into a continuous whole with the entire united Ethiopian highland. Such revolutions don't happened easily.

Regions that did not want to submit voluntarily Menelik turned over to his most talented commanders, whom he let have the opportunity to conquer them and "feed off" them. However, once these regions had been completely destroyed by war, they could not supply provisions for all the troops that had conquered them, which gave rise to the conquest of neighboring lands which were still free. Thus, little by little, the domain of Menelik grew, and the borders of Abyssinia expanded.

On the southwestern outskirts, three Abyssinian leaders operated: *Dajazmatch* Tesemma, *Dajazmatch* Beshakha, and *Ras* Wolda Giyorgis (at the time still a *Dajazmatch*).

In 1887, Menelik turned over Goma to *Dajazmatch* Tesemma, Gera to Beshakha, and Lima to *Ras* Wolda Giyorgis. The tribes who inhabited these lands, especially the Goma, put up a desperate resistance against the Abyssinians. More than once, Tesemma had to turn to Wolda Giyorgis for help, and he quickly gave that help. Once when Tesemma, with an insignificant detachment, was besieged in his fortress by superior forces of Gallas and his military and food supplies were exhausted, only the timely arrival of Wolda Giyorgis with his army saved Tesemma from inevitable destruction.

In their military actions, these leaders stuck to a single tactic. When they arrived in a new land, each of them would choose the most advantageous strategic point and build a fortress or, more correctly, a camp there. Then they would begin to carry out raids on the surrounding area until the inhabitants who were bravely defending were finally convinced that further defense was unthinkable and useless, and submitted. Those who submitted retained their self-government and ruler. But the Abyssinians took the ruler's children and those of prominent families to raise as hostages. The area was divided for "feeding" among units of the army. They allotted land to those soldiers who wished parcels of land, and gave them some of the defeated inhabitants as serfs.

For the sake of popularity with the troops, the military leaders, in times that were free of military action, arranged endless, abundant feasts. Bulls taken from the enemy were slaughtered daily by the tens, mead flowed in rivers—the fame of the leaders grew with each day; and together with their fame, the quantity of their troops increased... Of course, the means of the conquered region were drained.

The most popular of these commanders was the *Ras*, at that time still *Dajazmatch* Wolda Giyorgis. Having received from Menelik permission to conquer Kulo and Konta, which are found on the other side of the Gojeb River, he carried out his plan in a single campaign, as follows. He smashed the feudal Kaffa states of Gofa and Kyshya, then crossed the River Omo and conquered Melo, Boko, and others, having extended his domain almost to Lake Stefanie.

At the same time, *Dajazmatch* Tesemma subdued all the lands which border Kaffa on the north, and likewise its ally *Mocha*. As a result, at the beginning of 1896, out of the large Kaffa empire only Kaffa itself still remained independent. And it was already surrounded on three sides by the domains of its bellicose neighbor. On the southeast was *Ras* Wolda Giyorgis with a fifteen-thousand-man army, half of which was armed with guns. On the east was the feudal king of Jimma. On the northeast was *Dajazmatch* Demissew, who after the Italian campaign had been made commander of the 8,000-man corps of men from Gondar who were stationed in Leka, Gera, and Guma, and who were armed with guns. On the north was *Dajazmatch* Tesemma with an 8,000-man army, also armed with guns.

These three leaders repeatedly tried to take possession of Kaffa, but, acting separately, did not have any success: the first campaign of *Ras* Wolda Giyorgis against Kaffa ended without result, and failure befell both *Dajazmatch* Tesemma and *Dajazmatch* Demissew.

Due to the stubbornly held belief in the impregnability of Kaffa and the desperate bravery of its people, the Abyssinians set out on these campaigns reluctantly. The difficulty of mountain roads and the humidity of the climate had a disastrous effect on the health of people and horses. In addition, little plunder was expected there: dense forest and mountainous country served as an excellent means for concealing both livestock and property, as well as the inhabitants themselves.

Having decided to break the resistance of Kaffa and annex it, once and for all, to the Ethiopian empire, Menelik in 1896 gave orders to attack it from three sides at once. He entrusted the overall leadership to Wolda Giyorgis, to whom he had granted the right of ownership of all the lands he conquered.

The King (Tato) of Kaffa at this time was Chenito, who had ascended the throne in 1887 on the death of his father, Tato Galito.[40] Young, brave, energetic, he, knowing the people's love for the fatherland and devotion to him, decided to fight to the bitter end.

Foreseeing all the burden of the upcoming resistance, Chenito thoroughly prepared for it and actively took measures for the defense of the country. Along the borders he built a series of frontier posts in order to get advance notice of a surprise attack. He considered the destruction of grain supplies to be the main means of fighting. Knowing very well that the

Abyssinians during campaigns supplied themselves exclusively with the provisions of the region under attack, Tato Chenito issued an edict which prohibited producing any crops, even planting. He hoped that the lack of provisions would force the Abyssinians to retreat, and that only the Kaffa, who were used to it, could nourish themselves. To this end, word was spread among the people that a revelation had come to the high priest that by exactly this means the Kaffa would defeat the Abyssinians.

The fact that in the upcoming war the king intended to hold to an exclusively defensive form of action was also from the fact that he himself taught his beloved wife to ride on horseback in case of flight.

The character of their main enemy, *Ras* Wolda Giyorgis, was well known to the Kaffa. And they didn't entertain any illusions with regard to the battle that was in the making and its possible outcome. The anxiety which reigned among them gave rise to several different rumors. For example, it was said that, at one of the dinners in the presence of Menelik, *Ras* Wolda Giyorgis solemnly swore that he would subdue Kaffa and take its king prisoner. And as if to confirm his oath, he in one swig drank a huge goblet, which he then threw up with such force that it broke into smithereens when it struck the ceiling.

But, nevertheless, neither the evident inequality of forces, nor the insignificance of the chances for success, nor the undoubted destruction of the country in the unlikely case of victory could stop the king and his people in their unshakable determination to fight to the very end.

In November 1896 *Ras* Wolda Giyorgis, the first of the three participants in the campaign, marched into Kaffa from Kulo with 10,000 men and, putting to fire and sword everything on the way, arrived at the city of Andrachi, the capital of Kaffa, where he built a fortified camp. Tato (King) Chenito retreated, continually ha*Ras*sing the rear and flanks of the Abyssinians with his cavalry detachments, such that the first days were marked by continuous skirmishes of small parties, in which the Abyssinians, thanks to fire-arms, always had the upperhand.

Having consolidated his position in Andrachi, *Ras* Wolda Giyorgis divided his army into large detachments, and sent them out in various directions. These detachments laid waste the country, ravaging it for a radius of many tens of versts [seven miles], taking prisoner the women and children who were hidden in the forests, and setting fire to everything that could burn.

But the destruction of the country by far still did not lead to its submission: as long as the king was alive and free, the Kaffa cause could not yet be considered lost. The Abyssinians had already destroyed parts of Kaffa many times, but in the end almost always the conquerors retreated, forced to do so by the fatigue of the of the troops, the lack of provisions, and the bad climatic conditions (two rainy seasons per year). When the enemy left, the king, who had been hiding, again appeared in the capital; women and children came out of the dense forest and caves; and the cattle were driven home again. The people made sacrifices of thanksgiving, rebuilt houses that had been burned down—and... Kaffa healed as before.

In order to avoid this, *Ras* Wolda Giyorgis decided to exert all his force and use all possible means to either kill the King or take him prisoner. With this aim, he organized secret reconnaissance and espionage, mainly by means of prisoners. They paid the spies large sums and, by order of Wolda Giyorgis, set the prisoners free.

As soon as he received word of the location of Tato's sanctuary, Wolda Giyorgis quickly set out towards there with significant forces. The king fled to another place, but Wolda Giyorgis found this place as well and pursued him in this manner, indefatigably, five times.

The position of the king became even more difficult when the detachments of Tesemma and Demissew appeared and began to take action on the western and northern borders. Demissew entered Kaffa from Guma in February and in March joined forces with Wolda Giyorgis and set up camp in the town of Bonga.

The forces of Tato Chenito soon were completely shattered. Scattered and deprived of their main leader, finding themselves in complete ignorance regarding his fate and not knowing where he was, the Kaffa could not rally for his defense. Each of the survivors could only think about saving himself.

Staying in the center and moving from there in all directions with "flying detachments," Wolda Giyorgis with part of his army surrounded the area where the King was located, having seized with separate detachments all the main routes to the south, to the Negro lands, and having put a series of guard posts in place on all paths and tracks. Each guard post set up an abattis at the narrowest place on a protected route—narrow gates and beside them a small fortification in the form of a high fence surrounding a guard house. This system gave fine results.

The wives of the King, all his property and regalia fell into the hands of the *Ras* at the very beginning. The only one who was still free was the favorite wife of Chenito, who had not parted from him; but in the sixth month of the blockade she, too, was taken prisoner.

The King did not give up his freedom easily. The rest of his suite was scattered; he even lacked horses, but, in spite of this, he continued to skillfully hide himself, accompanied only by several faithful servants.

Now the life of the King was not at all like the pampered and luxurious life he had led up to that time. Surrounded on all sides by secret and obvious enemies, forced to suffer all possible deprivations, with difficulty obtaining scanty food for himself, not having even shelter for several months (and that at the very worst time of year), Chenito, however, displayed such will power and such courage, amounting to daring, that he astonished his enemies. According to stories, he sometimes appeared in the very camp of the Abyssinians in rags, dressed as a simple Kaffa, and successfully went through their hands.

But the *Ras* did not easily give up the pursuit. When at the end of February, the first rainy season started, mud became deep, and roads impassable, the troops began to feel the absence of provisions and as a result of poor food an epidemic of dysentery began, which claimed many victims, especially among the irregular forces, consisting of Galla and Sidamo. To all this was added still the loss of livestock, and the fact that corpse flies appeared in abundance in the vicinity of the camp.

A murmur arose among the troops, and all surrounding the *Ras* began to insist that he go back to Kulo. They demonstrated to Wolda Giyorgis that hope for capturing the King was lost and that to stay longer in the plundered and finally drained region was pointless and disastrous. The *Ras* gave evasive answers, promised to leave, delayed fulfillment of his promise from week to week, but strongly, in his soul, decided to not leave Kaffa until it was completely subdued. In order to in some way entertain the troops, he undertook a small raid on Geshe, a Kaffa region which was previously untouched (which lies on the summit of a mountain ridge that rises up to 3,000 meters above sea level). And *Dajazmatch* Demissew decided to move against the southern Gimiro territory. But the guard posts and a small reserve stayed in place to continue to blockade the place where the king was located.

This was the time of the spring rainy period, and the troops strongly suffered from the cold.

The invasion of Geshe had a positive effect on the situation, since it raised the spirits of the soldiers which had previously been falling. It also made it possible for them to obtain some food supplies. Returning to Andrachi, the *Ras* took pepper seeds and cabbage sprouts and ordered the soldiers to plant them.

After Easter, which arrived in the most difficult circumstances, the summer rainy season arrived, when there wasn't any talk either about the pursuit of Chenito nor even about leaving. The king was still free. The troops of the *Ras* were totally worn out by hunger and disease. There arose an intolerable stench from the quantity of corpses in Andrachi. It appeared that the *Ras*, despite his strength of spirit, would have to give up his well-conceived plan; but fate decided otherwise. On August 14, 1897, in the main camp of Wolda Giyorgis a message was received from *Fitaurari* Atyrsye[41], who occupied the southern guard posts with his regiment—they had taken Tato Chenito prisoner.

Chenito, for whom staying among the Abyssinian guard posts was becoming every day more dangerous, had intended to flee to the southern lands belonging to the Negroes. He decided to break through the guard posts, at night, dressed as a simple Kaffa, accompanied only by a single servant. They noticed him and raised the alarm. Chenito ran into the nearby forest, which the Abyssinians quickly surrounded. In the morning, they passed through it several times in a chain, but did not find King; and only at night, one soldier, searching in a thicket for a missing mule, accidentally stumbled upon Chenito. The king threw two spears at the soldier—silver and copper—but missed, and having no hope for being saved, gave himself up. The *Ras* ordered the captured Chenito to dress in his best clothes and showed him royal honor. The first meeting between the conqueror and the conquered was remarkable. Both bowed to the ground to one another, and Tato Chenito, having taken from his arm three gold bracelets, asked the *Ras* to accept this gift, saying the following: "I give this to you, man among men. Neither *Ras* Gobana, nor *Negus* Tekla Haymanot, nor Tesemma, nor Demissew ever succeeded in subduing me; but you have done so. If you refuse to wear these bracelets, then I will despise you."

News of the capture of the King was announced to the scattered people, and the war ended of itself. Captured Kaffa were set free; and through them the word was spread that all, not fearing for their lives, could return to their lands; and that the elders should assemble in the town of Andrachi. For the most part, the leaders of regions remained as before, and individuals who were well known for their services to Abyssinia were named to prominent posts. On the restoration of peace, the *Ras*, together with Chenito as prisoner, set out for Addis Ababa, having entrusted to his wife and a small detachment the job of guarding the territory. The other troops were given furlough.

Andrachi

January 8-22

Andrachi is located at the confluence of the River Guma with the River Gichey, which below that town turns to the south and flows into the River Omo.

The town is at a height of about 1,800 meters above sea level. It is surrounded on all sides by high mountains. It is spread out picturesquely on several hills. The climate of the locale where Andrachi lies is very humid, due to frequent rain, abundant dew, and thick evening fog.

Andrachi, which was formerly the capital of the Kaffa kings, has now been made the residence of the *Ras*. The palace of the Kaffa king, erected on top of one of the highest hills, was burnt down on orders from Wolda Giyorgis. In its place now a new one now rises, which occupies a circular area, about 200 sagenes [426 meters] in diameter, enclosed from all sides by a high fence. The courtyard is partitioned by lower fences into several separate plots, each of which (with the buildings found within it) has a special significance: reception rooms, or inner chambers, or rooms for household necessities. Several gates, of which some are considered the main ones, lead inside the palace.

A rather large courtyard lies behind the main gates. Here the *Ras*'s leaders come daily and leave their mules. Only officials have the right to enter the courtyards which follow—officers or those who come to the *Ras* on some business, or, finally, those who bring gifts. In the second courtyard there is only one building (I pitched my tent next to it. Earlier there was a cannon here which was taken away on my arrival.) The third courtyard, which is called *Adebabay* serves as a throne room. A tower is situated along the wall opposite from the entrance. It is two-stories tall, and the *Ras* sits on it in state during trials and ceremonial receptions. In the little courtyard after that one is located Aderash—a large dining room of the *Ras*. Here on Sundays, Thursdays, and holidays, the *Ras* gives large dinners—*gybyr*—and entertains his officers and soldiers.

The dining room with three doors, which can easily accommodate a thousand people, is somewhat like a large barn without windows. The walls are made of connected rings. Inside, a colonnade of thick posts supports a thatch roof. The alga—the throne on which the *Ras* sits in state during ceremonial dinners—stands near one of the walls, under a canopy made of white cotton cloth. Not far off are a large sofa (one and a half arshins [70 inches] high), and another small one (three-quarters of an arshin [21 inches] high) covered with carpets. The area where the sofas are located is separated from the rest of the premises by a white curtain, which is lowered when the *Ras* eats and raised when invited guests enter. The inner chambers of the *Ras* and his wife are located in the next courtyard beyond the Ade*Ras*h. On both sides of the main courtyards are small courtyards, with buildings in them. These courtyards have economic significance, as for example: gymja-byet, the storerooms where the money and belongings of the *Ras* are kept; wot-byet, kitchens; *injera-byet*, bakeries; *tej-byet*, places for cooking honey; *sega-byet*, slaughterhouses; etc.

Doorkeepers, armed with long sticks stand at all the gates of the palace. Guards are posted around the *elfin*ya (bedroom) at night.

Of the old palace, only the chapel of the Kaffa king was left whole. Near the palace of the *Ras*, it is sheltered in a grove of huge sycamores. It has now been turned into a church.

The slopes of the hill on which the palace was built are covered with cabins of soldiers of the *Ras*. On the neighboring hills rise the large houses of his leaders, likewise surrounded by the low cabins of their soldiers.

On the large area in front of the palace, a market assembles twice a week, to which the natives of the neighborhood throng. For bread from Jimma, they exchange coffee, which today constitutes the only wealth of the region.

It is very difficult to determine the number of inhabitants of the town, since Andrachi is nothing more than a permanent camp of the Abyssinians, not having in it a settled form of life. A local permanent population simply doesn't exist.

I stayed in Andrachi for 12 days, form January 8 to 22, 1898, waiting for the muster of the operational detachment.

The first three days we rested and stayed in bed after the journey. People slept almost all day and only in the evening, having dined, became animated: sat around a campfire and sang songs. I didn't see the *Ras* those days. By Abyssinian custom, it is considered a special courtesy not to disturb with invitations someone who has just arrived from a journey. Each day in the morning and in the evening the *Ras* sent to find out about my health; and, in turn, I sent my ashker to convey to the

Ras my gratitude for his consideration and to ask about his health and that of his wife. For dinner and supper, an *elfin* ashker (page) of the *Ras*, Gomtes, brought several dishes prepared for me on orders of the *Ras* and marvelous tej (mead) in small decanters wrapped in a silk cloth. In the evening, they gave me *durgo*. A long file of women with baskets filled with bread, pitchers with honey, earthenware pots with sauce etc., came to my tent. One of the kitchen shums (leaders), bowing low, entered my tent and showing the gifts that had been brought, had those who were carrying them file before me. My *ashkers* took the *durgo*, and the bread, according to custom, had to be counted again. One of the baskets, covered with a red calico coverlet and chosen for its size, was usually stuffed with the most delicate *injera* (bread flat cakes), intended especially for me.

I spent these days plotting my route to Kaffa on a map and took solar observations.[42] Several retainers of the *Ras* came to me to make my acquaintance. The deputy of Konta[43] Beleta-Menota even appeared with gifts—two chickens and some talers (silver rubles), which I, to his deep chagrin, refused. However, he brought the gifts not entirely unselfishly, counting on rich return gifts on my side, and from his first words began to ask me to give him a hat, a silk burnoose, a gun, a saber, etc. Not at all embarrassed by my refusals, he confidently said, "Well, if not now, bring them to me next time."

Incidentally, here's some information about Beleta-Menota. By birth, he is from the Konta tribe and fulfills there the duties of regent until the king comes of age. Neither in clothes nor in appearance did Menota differ from the average Abyssinian; only his eyes, which were wild, always moving, curious and narrower than those of Abyssinians, drew attention to him. He tried to conduct himself with dignity and in general noticeably imitated the Abyssinians, but naive curiosity and greedy begging betrayed the savage in him.

Beleta came to the *Ras* with tribute and after two days went back to his land. Before leaving, he came to say good-bye to me, and invited me to come to his place as a guest. "Come see me," he said. "I will give you a beautiful wife. I will slaughter for you my fattest bulls and rams."

I likewise became acquainted with the king of Kulo[44]—Haile Tsion. He is still a very young man, of large build, with regular facial features. He has the same savage, shifty eyes as Beleta-Menota, and, also like him, Tsion differs little in appearance from Abyssinians. On the death of his father in 1892, Haile Tsion fled with his mother to the neighboring land of the related Walamo tribe. Soon, however, he successfully returned there and expressed submission to the *Ras*, who confirmed him in his legal throne, on condition that he recognize the authority of the *Ras* and pay him tribute.

When Wolda Giyorgis erected his residence in Kulo, Haile Tsion was with him the whole time. The *Ras* christened him and stood as his godfather. Living at the court of Wolda Giyorgis, the king adopted Abyssinian customs and manners, studied the Holy Scripture and after several years, thanks to his aptitude, became a thoroughly educated Abyssinian aristocrat. During the Italian war, when the *Ras* went in a separate expedition against the Aussi Sultan, Haile Tsion stayed to govern the country. The people, thinking to take advantage of the absence of the Abyssinians, rebelled and forced their young king to take part in the uprising. On his return the *Ras* himself put down the uprising, and the people again expressed their submission. Not having been able to keep the country from the uprising, the king was shackled and sentenced to a fine of 10,000 talers.

Haile Tsion was very interested in everything European. He often visited me, asking about our way of life, and in turn willingly answered questions about what interested me about the life of his people, which up until this time was still very little known. Previous explorers (Massai, Antoine d'Abaddie) called all the tribes who inhabited the banks of the middle course of the Omo and who composed at one time several separate states—Kulo, Konta, Kushya[45], Walamo, Goma, and Gofa[46]—by the general name "Sidamo."[47]

As I already said above, up until the conquest by Abyssinians, those of these the states who populated the right bank of the River Omo were tributaries of Kaffa.

January 11. Sunday

At dawn, I set out to church for mass. The church—a large round building, covered with thatch—was sheltered a few hundred paces from the palace, on a hill in a grove of huge sycamores. When I arrived there, the *Ras* was already inside, and the church was filled with people. It was dark inside. Only after a while did the eye become accustomed to the surrounding objects. High thick wooden columns supported the building. The altar was located on the eastern side, separated from the rest of the room by a bamboo partition, covered with a white curtain. There were three gates in the altar, one of which was the king's. There were no icons at all. Two priests and three deacons performed the religious service. One of the priests was a tall old man with a severe, handsome face, overgrown with a long white beard; the other, who was still a young man, was thin and short. Their robes were threadbare—wretched silk chasubles, faded from age. The chasubles were worn above the same kind of silk shirts. Their feet were bare. Their heads were covered with large white muslin shawls, which draped over the shoulders and the back.

The deacons, 10-12 year old boys, were dressed just the same as the priests, only their heads were not covered. They all read together quickly (for the religious service they use the Geez language) and sang the exclamations and songs prescribed by regulation (14 of them in the whole mass). The tunes are very difficult to discern because of the continual transition from one tone to another. Those who were conducting the service stood in front of the altar several times to read the Gospel or to spread incense, in which case large censers, hung round with bells, rang pleasantly. When the time came for the consecration of the holy gifts, one of the deacons went out in front of the king's gates and, bowing in a characteristic pose to the altar and hanging his head low, began to ring a small copper handbell for a long time. Then the mourning began for the suffering and death of Christ. The melody of this mourning was amazingly sorrowful and sincere. I noticed that tears actually flowed from the eyes of the priests. After those who were conducting the holy service received the Eucharist, they brought the holy gifts for the Eucharist of those who had come to offer prayers. One of the priests carried the holy body on a large wooden disk, which was supported on the sides by two deacons; and another priest brought the holy blood in a glass chalice,[48] over which a third deacon held an open parasol. First, the men took the Eucharist, then the priests went to the southern part of the temple, separated by a curtain, behind which stood the women, and having given them the Eucharist, returned to the altar. They first gave the holy body, which the priest broke off from the lamb with their fingers and placed in the mouths of those who were taking the Eucharist, and then from the imitation of the holy blood. At the end of the communion, prayers began, during which the priest and the deacons went out with crosses and censers to the chancel, and a choir of *debtera*[49] sang prayers of praise.

One of the *debtera*, who had a high voice, sang, apparently improvising, and the choir continued the refrain, hitting copper rattles[50] in time, and another debter, sitting on the ground, accompanied him, striking a long drum with his palms. Little by little, the slow tempo of the song began to speed up, the singers became more and more inspired, the beating of the drum became more frequent and stronger, the rattles were silenced, and hand clapping resounded in rhythm. The group of singers, who at first had been motionless, began to wave. The inspiration turned to ecstasy. The singers squatted in time to the song. Some went out to the middle of the church with their staffs, which were as long as a man is tall and which they had leaned on during the holy service, and began a holy dance. The dancers rose up on tip-toe, dropped down in time to the song, again rose up, and stretching out their hands, moved smoothly. Their eyes, turned toward heaven, sparkled... The inspiration reached the extreme limit and was transmitted to the crowd; even the calm, severe face of an old priest became animated; and he, too, began to squat in time to the singing. Finally the choir stopped. A priest read a prayer. One of the *debtera* began to quickly go around among those who were praying and to assign them, in groups, a saint to whom they would pray. In this manner, he went around among those who were praying several times, until all the saints had been enumerated. Then on the reading of the concluding "Our Father," all kissed the cross and left the church.

The holy service made an indelible impression on me. The dark church, which was similar to a barn, the wretched beggarly conditions, but there was such ecstasy, such strength of faith among these black Christians. Such sincere prayer, such deep and touching feeling shines in the faces of people whole-heartedly devoted to their religion!... Imagination involuntarily carried me to the first centuries of Christianity...

I sat on a mule and, surrounded by a crowd of my servants, slowly went home. It was a marvelous, quiet morning. The sun shone brightly. Trees were in blossom and filled the clear thin mountain air with perfumes. So beautiful were the huge mountains which surrounded us, and which were lost in the clear-clear blue sky!.

No sooner did I return home than Gomtes came and asked me in the name of the *Ras* to come to the great dinner and to lend him my folding table, chair, and dining set. I answered that I accepted the invitation with pleasure, but I asked that he not trouble about obtaining European conveniences for me, since I know the customs of the country and was used to them. At nine o'clock, the agafari (gentleman-in-waiting) came for me, and I ceremoniously set out to the *aderash* (dining room), accompanied by all my *ashkers* with rifles on their backs. When I entered the dining room, the curtain had already been lowered. The *Ras* sat on his divan and washed his hands. Beside him on the carpet to one side sat *Dajazmatch* Balay, and on the other side a chair was prepared for me. The *Ras* was surrounded by his closest servants. Behind the divan stood Ilma, the chief sword-bearer of the *Ras*— a handsome Galla of enormous build, with a thick black beard. Opposite, picturesquely leaning against columns which supported the roof, *Azzaj* Gebra (the *Ras*' marshal of the court) and several agafari (leaders of guards) made themselves comfortable, having artistically draped themselves in their white *shammas*. They held little whips in their hands—as an emblem of of power during receptions. In front of the *Ras* and in front of me were placed two large baskets, covered with red calico cloth. A file of cooks, dressed in shirts clasped at the waist, carried in a great number of earthenware pots of various sizes, with foods. The chief cook, a rather beautiful woman, dressed more neatly than the others, with silver ear-rings and a silver necklace on the neck, removed the cloth from our baskets. The Asalafi of the *Ras* (a special post which in translation means "he who serves the food") dropped down on his knees in front of the basket and, having tasted each dish brought to him by the cook, began to take them out on chunks of *injera* and place them before the *Ras*. The Asalafi, a strikingly handsome young man of the pure Semitic type, is a descendant of a Tigrean family: he was raised at the court of the *Ras* and, probably, will receive some more important appointment, i.e., a company or a regiment.

For me, the *Ras* prepared a special dinner, which, in his opinion, should satisfy the taste of a European. Here is the menu: 1) fried chicken, 2) thin slices of meat fried in a pan, 3) beef ribs grilled on hot coals, 4) afilye[51]—an Abyssinian national dish, 5) meat that was scraped and boiled in butter, and 6) soft-boiled eggs.

With an air of great importance, Gomtes, page of the *Ras*, carried these dishes in small enamelled cups, hiding them under his skirt, in order that some evil eye not spot them. He placed them before me on a basket. I was hungry and, to the great satisfaction of the *Ras*, I ate everything with great appetite: both the boiled and the fried meat, and the soft-boiled eggs, and the rest.

When we had eaten half our dinner, other honored guests began to be admitted behind the curtain—commanders of regiments and senior officers. Finally, they gave us coffee in miniature china cups without handles and then opened the doors, through which an endless file of other guests began to enter. They appeared decorously, not hurrying, having wrapped their clothes around their waist and legs. Holding the free end in their left hand, they gracefully dropped to the floor, distributing themselves in tight circles around baskets, on which were laid in piles breadless flat-cakes of *injera* (some slices of it were soaked in a pepper sauce). Soon the dining hall was filled with a motley crowd of banqueters. Above each circle of diners, one of the servants, leaning over from the weight, held a large piece of beef. They passed to everyone a long knife mounted in ivory. Having selected a piece of meat, each, in order, sliced it and ate, very adroitly slicing pieces at their very teeth by a motion of the knife from below upward that was so fast that I positively did not understand how their lips and teeth remained in tact.

A line of wine servers adroitly gave the banqueters huge horn goblets of mead through the whole room. A traveling singer appeared, and standing in the middle of the room, sang heroic songs and improvisations in honor of the *Ras*, with the accompaniment of an instrument similar to a violin[52].

Zelepukin was among those who were invited. They had him sit near the divan of the *Ras*. In front of him stood the basket from which I had eaten before. But, regarding the black foreigners skeptically, he only distrustfully glanced at the dishes placed before him, not touching them at all. With his thickset build and muscularity, Zelepukin produced a strong impression on the Abyssinians. In particular, the *Ras* took a liking to him, calling him nothing other than zokon or "elephant." Looking on Zelepukin with unconcealed pleasure, the *Ras* asked me if all the soldiers in Russia were such fine fellows as this. It is necessary to mention that the Abyssinians formed a rather unflattering opinion of European soldiers from their acquaintance with the Italians—namely that they are all feeble and weak.

As soon as the first set of diners had satisfied themselves, they got up on at signal from the agafari and left. In their place, their immediately appeared another set, and after it a third, and, finally, a fourth. The *Ras* himself and his honored guests continued sitting in their places the whole time, carrying on pleasant conversation among themselves and draining small decanters of tej (mead) one after another. They also served red wine—"Bordeaux"—as the *Ras* called it—and a local vodka distilled from mead.

Conversations for the most part touched on military matters and hunts. The *Ras* and his military comrades remembered "by-gone days and battles, where side-by-side they fought with sabers."[53] With captivated interest I heard about the battle at Embabo in 1886, during the war with the Gojjam *Negus*. Not holding out against the first onslaught of the Gojjam, Menelik's whole army fled, and only the Emperor himself, then still a king, stayed calmly in his position on a high hill. Suddenly, he opened up on the Gojjam with the only 200 rifles he had at that time, with such a murderous fire that they wavered. At that moment, *Ras* Gobana, who had just arrived in time, attacked the Gojjam from behind, and the enemy turned in flight. The *Ras* personally took 40 men prisoner. I heard about the Aussi campaign of 1895, and about the attack of the Danakils in the Battle at the Awash River. That day so many Danakils died, that the Abyssinians, having pitched camp for the night on the very field of the battle, fastened the tent ropes to bodies. They also told about the horrible return of the *Ras*'s detachment from this campaign, marching at a run, but not from the enemy, rather from terrible Awash fevers, which every day claimed masses of victims.

The *Ras* also asked me about our army and about methods of conducting war. As I already mentioned before, the Abyssinians had formed a very unflattering opinion of European armies. In their eyes, European armies although disciplined, were in the highest degree just a stationary mass, and in battle their whole action consisted exclusively of gun-fire. I found it necessary to refute that opinion with regard to the Russians. That astonished him.

"We attack with bayonets on "Hurrah!"; and the cavalry, likewise, with sabers," I told the *Ras*.

"I thought," he noted in reply, "that 'foreigners' only fire their guns; but if you attack with side-arms in hand, that means that you are truly good soldiers."

He asked me, among other things, about whether we drink tej in our country and whether we put on feasts like they do.

I told him that among us, in the distant past, almost all was rather similar to their style of life now. I told him about Saint Vladimir, about his feasts, the baptism, about his answer to the Mohammedan ambassadors: "The joy of Russia is drinking."[54] The *Ras* liked my story so much that he soon retold it to his retinue, who unanimously decided that Russians, truly, must be true Christians.

Only at two o'clock in the afternoon did we leave the dinner which we had sat down to at 9 o'clock in the morning.

JANUARY 12

The regiment (2,000 men) of *Fitaurari* Imam arrived in Andrachi. Previously, they had been stationed in the far regions of Dime and Melo, on the left bank of the River Omo. The *Ras* invited me to watch the arrival of the regiment. We made ourselves comfortable on a tower in the *adebabay* (law court), looking out for the appearance of the army on the road. Finally, on the summit of the mountain opposite us a detachment appeared which stretched four columns along the narrow path bordered on each side by thick bushes. It slowly drew nearer, gaudily displaying a great number of flags, snow-white *shammas* of the soldiers, and weapons and armor shining in the sun.

Through a telescope, Wolda Giyorgis recognized the majority of the officers and many soldiers, and not even the slightest details of their dress and equipment escaped the notice of the alert eye of this military-leader. Frequently, he even seemed to know the mules and horses. The *Ras* expressed his impressions in characteristic exclamations, "There is so-and-so," he quickly said. "Look, the gray mule which I gave him last year seems to be exhausted... There so and so has ribbons on his head. Truly, he has killed an elephant." And so on.

Going down from the mountain and crossing a stream which flows at the base of the hill on which sits the court of the *Ras*, the detachment went to the square in front of the palace, forming a front in two lines. In the first line—behind the leader, all the mounted troops stood in several ranks (2-4); all the infantry stood about 25 paces behind them. The regiment stopped in front of the gates. the mounted troops dismounted. Servants and younger soldiers took the mules and horses; all the rest quickly and loudly ran into the *adebabay* and formed a front 4-5 ranks deep in the room in front of the tower of the *Ras*. The first row consisted of all the officers and distinguished soldiers of the lower ranks.

This army presented a remarkably beautiful spectacle! You could see in each soldier his awareness of his own dignity and pride. How manly were the expressions on the faces of these warriors hardened in battle! How natural and majestic was their bearing!.

These barefoot men, dressed in white linen trousers, wore rich silk shirts and gold-embroidered multi-colored velvet *lemds* (cloaks) or *lemds* made of the skins of lions, leopards, snow leopards, or, finally, of long-haired rams. The shields of many were decorated with silver. Those who had killed elephants displayed on their heads green, yellow, and red ribbons. Others, who had killed Danakils in the Aussi campaign, displayed on their heads little silver crows—kalecha—military distinctions or silver helmets with silver chains hanging in the face. Several officers had their heads wrapped in ribbon cut from a lion's mane —this amfara[55] corresponds to our order of George. For the act of picking up wounded in battle, many have sabers with silver tips. For having killed some of the enemy, others have sabers with silver rings.

When the regiment had formed up, the commander, *Fitaurari* Imam, calmly and with deep awareness of his own dignity, appeared in front of the regiment, with his senior officers. From the tower resounded the greeting of the *Ras*:"Endyet Sonobatatchukh!" The *Fitaurari* and the whole regiment in answer bowed low: like one man, they laid their rifles in front of themselves and going down on one knee, bent their heads to the very ground and lightly, quickly rose up again. In this bow, you sensed not humility before an unlimited ruler, but rather devotion to their beloved leader. After the first bow, the commander of the regiment made several steps forward and on the second greeting of the *Ras* he answered with the same kind of bow. Finally, when he came close to the tower itself, there followed yet another greeting and a third bow, and the official part of the welcome ended.

Troops mingled with those they had met. Old friends and acquaintances found one another and kissed one another three times. It produced quite an impression, as if an entire compact crowd were kissing. The *Ras* went into the aderash (dining room), where a feast had been laid out for the arriving troops, just the same as that described by me above.

Fitaurari Imam represents a characteristic type of Abyssinian leader. He is still young, remarkably handsome, energetic, well-known for selfless courage and adored by his people. As a 14-year-old boy he found himself at the court of the *Ras*, and having made himself the *Ras*'s *elfin* ashker (page), accompanied him on all his campaigns. At first, he only followed behind the mule of the *Ras*, carrying a Psalter or a saber or a goblet for water. When he was older, he got himself a spear and began to take part in battles himself. Finally, they gave him a gun and ten cartridges; and from that time his military career began. Soon the *Ras* made Imam his agafari (gentleman in attendance) and commander of his person guard, and several years ago promoted him to the rank of *Fitaurari*. Imam received as a command about 300 soldiers, several hundred guns and several thousand cartridges; and for the feeding of the detachment he received one of the outlying districts. From this moment, he was permitted to recruit for himself whatever size detachment he deemed he was in a position to maintain. Of the 300 men in his command, Imam selected the most capable and outstanding men and made them leaders of a thousand, leaders of a hundred, and leaders of fifty men, dividing the remaining soldiers among them; and he let them fill their units as they wished. At the present time, his regiment has grown from 300 men to 2,000.

The formation of the detachment of Imam as described by me is the prototype of the origin of all Abyssinian units.

January 13

I spent the morning with the *Ras*, examining a map of the theater of future military action. The *Ras* received me in the courtyard of his *elfin*ya (inner chambers) under a small awning, resting against a fence and covered with straw. This place was the favorite working office of the *Ras*. From there one had a wonderful view of the mountains surrounding Andrachi. When I entered, the *Ras* was occupied with current business with his secretary Aloka-Melke and sitting on a divan, dictated some document to him. Aloka-Melke is a handsome young man, who some years ago was a deacon. Having settled himself on the floor, he quickly wrote on a paper placed on his knee. The scratch of his reed pen resounded almost uninterrupted. From time to time, he dipped it in an inkwell, made from a cartridge case, which was placed between the toes of his right foot. When the document was finished, the secretary moved away, and the *Ras* and I were left alone. I spread out on the floor a map I had obtained which was marked in Abyssinian, and we began to consider it. Recognizing where Andrachi and Addis Ababa were located, the *Ras* himself oriented the map and tried to determine for himself the relative distances between points that interested him and to understand the concept of "degree" which was then completely unknown to him -- meeryg as the Emperor Menelik calls it. The *Ras* showered me with questions. How far was Lake Rudolf? How many degrees? How great is the distance from the line of operation of *Dajazmatch* Tesemma? Where is the second degree? Why did these two degrees appear so big? From where are they calculated? It was necessary to deliver a lecture on the spherical shape of the Earth, to explain the concept of the Equator, the latitude of the place where we were, etc.

"Why is there neither words nor rivers there where we will go?" the *Ras* asked me.

I answered that this place still hadn't been explored. The *Ras* shook his head and thought. Really, a difficult problem lay ahead: he had been ordered to subdue and annex to Abyssinia the huge territory which lies among Kaffa, Lake Albert and Lake Rudolf from 2° north latitude, and, while doing this, to oppose any other force which might have a similar intention. The region which the *Ras* had to conquer was completely unknown to Abyssinians. They only had information related to the region that is closest to Kaffa and to the Shuro tribe which lives there. It remained a complete riddle to them what territory the Shuro occupied, who their neighbors were, whether there were any neighbors, and, finally, what kind of country lies beyond the borders of this tribe, and whether it is rich in bread grain.

Provisions for the troops could only be supplied by way of requisition, i.e. by the doubtful capabilities of a completely unknown regions. In view of the large numbers of the corps that was setting out on the campaign and their shortage of lifting power, it seemed unthinkable that they could bring enough provisions with them, all the more so since there wasn't enough time to prepare for the campaign and to reconnoiter the theater of action. Due to political considerations, The Emperor Menelik, demanded that the *Ras* complete the task given to him this very year, and there were only five months left before the rainy season.

16,000 men were supposed to go in the expeditionary corps. Of those, 10,500 regular soldiers had guns; the rest—volunteers from Galla and other tribes—had only spears.[56]

One part of this army was posted at the center of the *Ras*'s domain, another at its outskirts. All soldiers received provisions from the location in which they were stationed, and the commanders of units were at the same time both administrators and chief justices in their regions. In the interior provinces, which were completely pacified, soldiers were allotted plots of land and several enslaved natives. In time of peace, they dwelled on their allotments and made a living from them. In the outlying districts, which were not yet pacified, the system of military settlements was inapplicable, all the more so because the troops were almost always under arms and in raids against neighboring lands. They lived in fortified camps. Native leaders obtained the necessary quantity of provisions for them, gathering them from their tribesmen, under threat of requisition in case the quantity was insufficient.

In monetary and material prosperity, the outlying units were quite equal with the ones in the interior. Each soldier received annually from the treasury of the *Ras* from 5 to 15 talers to purchase a donkey, horse, or mule. The amount depended on the merit of the warrior. Each also received one outer garment—a shamma—and linen for two pairs of trousers.

Five of the regiments were called *waruari* and were considered the Emperor's troops. The rest were the *Ras*' own troops. In each of these regiments, part of the soldiers were mounted and part were on foot. The more well-to-do soldiers and those who had already served for some time bought themselves a horse or a mule. The young soldiers and also the poor ones did not have them. The troops were not subdivided by type of weapon.

The origin of the *waruari* is interesting. On the accession of Menelik to the throne of Shoa, eleven-year-old Wolda Giyorgis went to serve the *Negus* as his *elfin* ashker (page). He accompanied Menelik on all his campaigns and soon made himself one of Menelik's favorites. *Ras* Makonnen, cousin and great friend of Wolda Giyorgis, had the same kind of job. Together they endured all the burdens of their position: they froze at the entrance to Menelik's tent; they were happy when one of the senior men let them drink from a half-drunk decanter of tej or to eat what was left of the meat.

In 1870, it was reported to the emperor that three young soldiers who had formerly served King Tewodros had arrived and wanted to join his army. Menelik gave the order to invite them in. Pondering over who he should assign them to, he asked Wolda Giyorgis who, at that time, was blowing on the campfire in front of him.

"Well, Wolda Giyorgis, advise me—who should I give them to?"

"Give them to me," he answered.

These three soldiers were the nucleus of that 15,000 man corps which the *Ras* now commands.

Wolda Giyorgis quickly promoted his first soldiers to commanders of fifty men, obtained for each of them a leopard skin for battle dress, asking his older relatives for them, and let his subordinates recruit their own half-companies. Soon about 20 men were assembled. Money obtained in raids was used to acquire pack mules, which, on the march, carried provisions of the entire detachment and the tent of the commander. The newly formed unit began to occupy a separate bivouac, marked by this tent.

Little by little, the number of soldiers of Wolda Giyorgis increased, and his property and fame grew. Distinguishing himself with outstanding courage and enterprise, he could also elicit these qualities from his men. Thanks to rare talents as a regimental commander, Wolda Giyorgis created from his soldiers, who were still almost children, such fine fellows that during the war with Wollo they were the talk of the whole detachment of the *Negus*. A day did not pass without them participating in a raid and without one of them returning to camp with trophies taken from the enemy. Menelik took notice of the feats of these daring fellows. Once, talking about the ever more famous soldiers of Wolda Giyorgis, the Emperor said: "These are not mucha (unfledged youths) but *waruari* (spear throwers)." And he kept affirming this name for them. As a reward for his feats, Wolda Giyorgis received a small portion of land, thanks to which he was able to increase his small detachment.

In 1883, Menelik named Wolda Giyorgis chief agafari and *elfin*-askalakay-ishaka—head of the *elfin ashkers* (pages) and of the personal guard of the *Negus*, and then made him gerazmatch (lieutenant colonel).

In 1887, Wolda Giyorgis was promoted to *Dajazmatch* (full general) and received independent control of the region of Limu. At this time he already had five regiments with a total strength of about 3,000 men, which were considered soldiers of the *Negus* and were called, as before, *waruari*. The units newly formed after Wolda Giyorgis was named governor-general of Limu consisted of troops of the *Ras* himself and became called byet lyjog (children of the house).

At the time of the announcement of the mobilization, the troops were at the places where they were stationed. Because of this, several units were 400-500 vests [300-375 miles] from the town of Andrachi, which was the mustering point for the whole detachment. The mobilization order was sent from Addis Ababa at the end of November and could be received by the farthest units no sooner than after 16-20 days, that is in the middle of December. The troops were supposed to assemble in Andrachi in the middle of January. Consequently, they had at their disposal only one month for muster and concentration, and remote units, in this short interval of time had to allow not less than 15 days just to get to the mustering point. However, despite the mass of difficulties, the whole 15,000 man detachment was already at muster by January 15, and January 24 was set as the departure day. It was decided to use the nine days (from January 15 to 24) to rest the animals of the units that had come a long way and to organize the feast that is customary before a campaign.

The order of the *Ras* which announced this mobilization is interesting. I will present it in translation. It begins with the customary introduction to all orders that are announced nationwide: "Listen! Listen! Listen! Whoever does not listen is an enemy of the Lord and of the Mother of God! Listen! Whoever does not listen is an enemy of the Lord and of the church! Listen! Whoever does not listen is an enemy of Menelik! Warriors! I am setting out on a campaign against the Shankala (Negroes). All of you, assemble on the first on the Holiday of the Baptism in Andrachi. Whoever is late will not go on the campaign and will miss this unique opportunity to win fame and get livestock and prisoners."

Soon after town criers had announced this order in all bazaars and in all the places where troops were stationed, first individual soldiers from interior regions, who made a living from allotted parcels of land, began to gather at the mustering point. Then the farther units began to come. Natives also responded to the call and assembled, as said above, in the number of about 5,000 volunteers.

By the designated date, the mobilization and the concentration of the detachment was completed. Now it only remained to the *Ras* to set in motion the 16,000-man force which was dependent on him in order to carry out the mission that was assigned to him. The assignment was dreadful, because of the absolutely unknown conditions which he would have to take into consideration and the responsibility to his state and to the people who followed him which the *Ras* took on himself.

Wolda Giyorgis was aware of all of that but did not show the least hesitation or indecisiveness. At the end of our conversation, he, in saying good-bye, told me, " It's a difficult task ahead of us, but I set my hopes on the God of Menelik who will help me. To strengthen the throne of Menelik (na Menelik alga), I will use all my strength; and with joy I will sacrifice my life."

These words clearly express the determination of the head of the detachment and how he looked at the expedition. The subordinates of the *Ras* regarded the campaign in a way that was not far from that.

Feeling an innate love for war and having full faith in their leader, they dutifully gathered under his flag and were ready to set out on the campaign, but it was noticeable that the soldiers were worried about the unknown conditions in which they would have to operate. The troops felt that there lay before them something more difficult than the usual raids.

"Where are we going?" There was no simple answer to this question which all were concerned about, and rumor excelled at finding every possible answer. The soldiers were startled by the large transport of cartridges (about 10-16 mules per regiment). My presence in the detachment also troubled them, arousing many rumors.

"It's a bad sign that a *frenj* (foreigner) goes with us," said some.

"In the south they say there are Europeans. We will be led to fight against them," observed others.

"The English took land from the *frenj* and took away his wife and children. He complained to Menelik, and Menelik ordered the *Ras* to go punish the English and to return to the *frenj* what was taken away from him. Only they say that this is very far. In that place there are people who are like dogs. It will be bad for us to go so far," added others.

The soldiers of the *Ras* beset my men with questions which in their opinion should have been known for a certainty—where we are going and for how long, etc. When my *ashkers* answered that they themselves knew nothing, the soldiers observed, "Sure, for you it's good! You will go straight home. But how hard it is for us."

The soldiers held onto such hearsay very stubbornly. As for the officers, while they did not believe all this gossip, they did foresee a long campaign and difficulties, and showed ill-will toward the expedition. The aim of the campaign—to go to some distant region which was unknown to anyone—seemed quite pointless to them. All the more so because in the immediate neighborhood there was still an abundance of forage and land rich in food-stuffs.

The *Ras* knew about both the rumors that were going around among the soldiers and also the frame of mind of the officers. He listened tactfully to these rumors and countered them by starting new favorable rumors, for example that in one of the lands where they were going there are horses and cattle. He tried to influence the officers through his closest supporters who gathered in a military council where he impressed on them his way of thinking.

January 14

In the morning, the *Ras* had to hold trial court in the *adebabay*, and I received an invitation to attend. The *Ras* sat in the tower, and a place was prepared for me beside him on the carpet. Below, on the square, sat two judges—the "right" and "left" judges, and a group of leaders, several priests and scholars, *debtera*. In front, facing the *Ras* stood a crowd of people. Here were the litigants and witnesses and simple spectators.

The first matter heard was essentially administrative in character. A local judge and the leader of a small detachment which had settled in his district disputed the competence and right of the court over local residents in matters regarding administrative infringements of the law. The litigants got very angry and argued endlessly, citing decrees of the *Ras* which had been published at various times. The judges showed great interest in the debate: apparently, the resolution of the question being examined infringed on their interests. The *Ras* silently and patiently listened. He already, for a long time, knew the main point and all the evidence brought by the parties, but he didn't interfere with the debate, at this time looking through a telescope at the neighboring mountains. Finally, the disputes began to abate; the evidence of the one and the other side ran out. No one convinced anyone, and all awaited the decision of the *Ras*, which he decreed in a clear and brief formulation. The litigants bowed to the ground to the *Ras*. The next defendant was accused of having sold his military prisoner, under the guise of a gift. The crime was obviously proven. The guilty party was subject to the death penalty, but the *Ras* did not have the right by his own authority to impose that sentence because the criminal was an Abyssinian. The *Ras* ordered him put in chains and sent to Menelik.

"Ass!" he concluded his resolution. "He only needed three talers for a slave, and as if he does not understand now all Europe is watching Ethiopia..."

The third case before the *Ras* was a Kaffa accused of murdering an Abyssinian with a fishing line. The criminal was interrogated through an interpreter, and Kaffa officials took part in the trial. The murder was committed by two Kaffas, who fell by surprise on an unarmed Abyssinian. But one of the malefactors escaped from the place of confinement. The remaining one asserted that it was not he who killed the Abyssinian, but rather the man who fled, who before this had succeeded in bribing the chief judge. The judge, against whom the criminal brought the charge of accepting a bribe, was present. He stood right beside the Kaffa and energetically protested.

"He lies!" he said. "I didn't do that!"
"He did," he said. "What will you stake on it that you don't lie?"

"Your head!" answered the judge.

Thus, the matter took quite a new turn. A new investigation would be necessary. This was entrusted to one of the Abyssinian judges together with the Kaffa *katamarash*. After the investigation, one of the accused would be subject to the death penalty.[57]

Then several more, somewhat less interesting cases were examined. Last one of the priests of the town of Andrachi who was accused of blasphemy appeared before the court. He asserted that the Holy Trinity consists of nine persons and did not yield to any arguments of the pastors, and finally they accused him, before the *Ras*, of heresy. The court sentenced him to fifty lashes with the *jiraf* (whip). They took the priest off to the bazaar and, after forty strokes on the kettledrum, delivered his punishment. I, by this time, had already taken leave of the *Ras* and was in my room at court. My *ashkers* were keenly interested in the outcome of the punishment, which was often fatal; and even took bets among themselves: would the convict survive the flogging or not? They took off the outer clothing and the shirt from the convict, placed him with his stomach on the ground, and began to carry out the sentence. The hands and feet of the priest were tied with ropes, which the executioners pulled. The kettledrummers performed the duty of executioners. The lashes were delivered with a long, thick belt whip with a short whip-handle. They beat him with wide, infrequent strokes, which the officer designated for this counted. With each stroke of the whip, a noise resounded that was like a pistol shot. The convict endured the punishment very patiently, and those who had bet on his death lost. After the flogging, they lifted the priest, dressed him and, supporting him under the arms, took him home. His back was completely blood-stained.

January 15

The last troops that the *Ras* was waiting for arrived—the regiment of *Fitaurari* Damti, who were stationed the farthest away, namely in the lands of Aro, Bako, and Shangama, on the slopes facing Lake Stephanie. The meeting of the troops was exactly the same as what I described above, and then followed a dinner which I attended.

Fitaurari Damti is still a young man. He began his service, like *Fitaurari* Imam, as *elfin* ashker (page) of the *Ras*. He now already has the rank of *Fitaurari* and commands a regiment which made an excellent impression on me. A large part of his soldiers are adorned with military armor obtained for distinguished services. Among the officers, there were typical veterans. Quite incredible stories were told about one of them, Aba-Ilma, stories that I could only with difficulty have believed if I had not heard them from Aba-Ilma himself, and also from other people who are worthy of confidence—for example, from the commander-in-chief. (Subsequently, I became very friendly with him and came to know his absolutely truthful character.)

Aba-Ilma is a representative of an interesting, obsolescent type of Abyssinian warrior from the time of Emperor Tewodros. He is a gray, lean, muscular old man, with a remarkably lively temperament, who doesn't know fatigue, is always happy, who encourages his comrades. He has waged war his whole life; and if you were to gather all the blood he has shed, he could, I believe, swim in it. But there is not a trace of cruelty in him. Aba-Ilma is pure of heart, simple, and naive like a child.

Aba Ilma is from the Agau tribe. His father ruled an insignificant principality in the neighborhood of Tigre, and was, at the accession to the throne of the Emperor Yohannes, one of the feudal lords who had revolted and taken the side of Yohannes. In one of the battles, Aba-Ilma—then still a young man—was wounded with a spear. This happened when, after charging at his opponent, he threw a javelin at him, but missed, and turned his horse back in order to gallop away. The spear hit him in the neck, somewhat to the left of the spine, came out his mouth, cut through his tongue, and broke three upper front teeth... Aba-Ilma fell from his horse, but was not lost: with quick action, he pulled the spear from the wound and at the very moment when his opponent having dismounted, intended to finish him off, Aba-Ilma, with a pistol shot put him in his place. A comrade of the dead man rushed on horseback to the rescue. Ilma lay still, and as soon as the enemy drew close, inflicted a serious wound on his leg with a saber stroke. Finally, he fell senseless; soldiers, having recognized him as son of the prince, took Ilma prisoner; and, in spite of the serious wound, put him in shackles. When he recovered, Ilma went into service for Menelik, took part in all his wars, and was repeatedly wounded, including once when a bullet passed right through his chest.

Aba-Ilma is a passionate hunter and killed many elephants. While hunting, quite improbable adventures happened to him. For example, pursued by a wounded elephant, he with a saber cut off a piece of its trunk. When that elephant turned back, with a second stroke Ilma cut off a piece of its tail.

Aba-Ilma has been rewarded with all the distinctions attainable at his rank. He has a lemd (a cape for the shoulders, made of a lion's mane), and a silver shield, and silver gilded manacles, worn on the arms from the hands to the elbows; and gold ear-rings in both ears, and silk ribbons to decorate the head, and a silver head-dress (kalecha) of filigree work, similar to a crown.

After dinner, I received as guests Abyssinian officers and natives who came in order to become acquainted with me. Among them was the first high official of the Kaffa king—a retired *katamarash*. He limped from a recent injury and, long before reaching my tent, taking off his rags, which covered his emaciated body, he bowed low.

I called him into my tent and, through an interpreter, asked him about the Kaffa way of life before the land was conquered. But I learned little from him. Parting with him, I gave him several talers. This touched the old man so much that he fell on the ground. And (it must have been as a sign of gratitude), he hit himself in the chest for a long time.

January 16

Today, they held another large dinner, one of those which Abyssinian military leaders hold to entertain their troops before setting out on a campaign. These dinners bear a special military imprint and are very lively. Veterans, with some embellishment, reminisce about by-gone battles, tell about outstanding feats and so forth. Tej (mead) flows in rivers. At the end of the dinner, the lifting of spirits attains its highest level. One after the other, the banqueters jump up and, hoarsely crying out, enumerate the feats they have performed and vow fidelity to their leader.58 "I am a killer!" cries out some soldier with foam in his mouth. He seizes a saber by the hilt. His eyes wander wildly; he shakes all over nervously and seems positively insane. "I repelled a spear in battle! I repelled two spears in battle! I repelled three spears in battle! I killed in the Aussi campaign, and in Tigre and among the Negroes. I killed everywhere where I waged war! I am your slave, your dog! With you I will conquer! With you I will die! I am Kaytimir! (His personal name)." And in conclusion, he bows to the ground to the *Ras*.

The talking subsides. All listen tensely: one person follows another to deliver *fokyr*. Only the commander-in-chief keeps his composure and each time quietly utters, "Name a guarantor." The person vowing fidelity finds himself a guarantor among his comrades and, having received a large goblet of mead, sits at his place.

From the Gimiro tribe, which borders on Kaffa, a deputation arrived in Andrachi, consisting of the prince of this tribe, the chief priest and three elders. They brought ivory to the *Ras* as a gift and asked him to take them under his protection. The *Ras* showed much kindness to them, gave them presents, and let them go home.

Before leaving, they came to me to have a look at white people. Entering my tent, they looked at me and my things with childlike pleasure and curiosity. These savages were very original in the bright red cloaks bestowed on them, worn on the naked body, and the red bandages worn on the head.

I asked them if they had ever seen white men before. They answered no, and added that they had heard that last year white men, from where they didn't know, had entered the neighboring land. They had pitched a sparkling silver tent and the following day vanished without a trace.[59]

From the point of view of geography and hydrography, the Gimiro knew very little about the territory neighboring them. They had not heard of the existence of a large river (Omo), about which we then assumed that it flows to the west, to the Sobat, passing Lake Rudolf. They also knew nothing about this large lake, but talked about some other lake—Bosho, into which flow the streams of their country.

I also asked them about their way of life, and with one question made them very embarrassed. Wanting to find out if they practiced polygamy, I asked the priest how many wives he had. The priest looked at me suspiciously, evidently at a loss for understanding why I needed to know this and perhaps suspecting that I wanted to demand them for myself as a gift. He slowly answered, "As many as God sends."

At parting, I gave them several talers. In gratitude, they kissed the ground and hit themselves in the chest with their palms. Leaving, they crowded at the exit to the tent, as if expecting something more from me. It seemed that they wanted to see how one got fire by hand (matches)—a wonder about which they, correctly, had heard from the Kaffa. To their fascination, mixed with terror, I showed them this trick, and they left completely satisfied.

January 17

I visited *Nagada-Ras* Vadym-Aganokh60 He lives 10 versts [7 miles] from the town of Andrachi, in Bonga, what used to be the second capital of the Kaffa king.

The *Nagada-Ras* is a young, very energetic and lively man and belongs to that class of smart dealers that is coming into being in Abyssinia, who present a complete contrast to the type of leading Abyssinian personality which has dominated up until now. These "new men" have become acquainted with Europeans, and have adopted from them many good things, learned their energy, their openness in address, not considering it necessary, as people of the old stamp, to strike an important pose and shorten their speech to the minimum etc. in order to maintain their authority. I encountered such people mainly among the merchant class, but noticed the same tendency also in other strata of the population. The Emperor Menelik himself and his foremost associates belong to this new type.

I sent my foot servants ahead, and myself went on horseback accompanied by two mounted *ashkers*. I sat on a horse for the first time since my bout of rheumatism. Having rested for those days, Defar (my horse) left my fellow travellers far behind me. At full gallop, we jumped off steep banks and again clambered up rising slopes and at a wide gallop rushed across plains... Thick bushes, completely covered with flowers grew along both sides of the road. The multi-colored tents of the assembled troops appeared in all the clearings.

My *ashkers* and all the soldiers of the *Nagada-Ras* were in formation to meet me near the house; and he himself went to the gates to greet me, wearing his parade clothes as a sign of special respect to his guest. His home is located on the site of the burnt-down palace of the king of Kaffa. From the previous building there remained only a palisade made of enormous trunks of palm trees and, sticking up from the high grass, several charred ends of columns which had supported the roof of the palace. The dwelling of the *Nagada-Ras* was built in the Abyssinian manner: inside a court, enclosed by a high palisade, rises a large house (aderash) intended for receptions, and several other buildings, such as the bedroom of the host, the kitchen, etc. Behind the palisade, around the perimeter, several groups of low cabins took shelter. The soldiers of the *Nagada-Ras* live in those cabins. The court was full of merchants who had come on business with their leader. Here were Kaffa, Gallas and Abyssinians. The Kaffa and Gallas were sharply contrasted in their appearnace from the Abyssinians. As Mohammedans, they wore turbans on their heads; and on their necks they wore long beads. Vandym-Aganokh led me into the aderash, which was this time covered with carpets and filled with the smoke of incense. There behind a cane partition, sat his elderly mother, who had recently become a nun, and his eighteen-year-old wife. His wife was very shy and hung her head low and only at the end of the dinner did she decide to now and then glance at me in curiosity.

They gave us an excellent dinner, and the hospitable civilized host entertained me not only with local mead, but also wine and absinth ("abusent" he called it), and even liqueur. He gave all my men enough to drink to get them dead drunk, and when I went back, they ran in front of my horse, not letting me outdistance them. They cried out heroic recitatives, fired their guns, etc.

Two of them—Ambyrbyr and Aulale—even fought, arguing which of them was braver.

January 18

I received the *Ras* at my place and showed him how to develop photographs. He was especially interested in the moment when the figures of people known to him (whose pictures were taken) begin to appear and to become clear on the white plate.

January 19

Ras Wolda Giyorgis introduced me to his wife—*Woyzaro* Eshimabet. Because of ill health, she had been unable to receive me earlier. The reception took place in the *elfin*—the bedroom of the *Ras*—and was very ceremonial. The *elfin* is a large round building about 15 arshins [12 yards] in diameter and 8 arshins [6 yards] in height. The walls are coated with clay and whitened. The floor is covered with carpet and strewn with freshly picked fragrant grass. Inside, a series of high thick hewn posts support the roof. The rafters and concentric bamboo hoops, with the attached-to-them bamboo foundations of the roof, are wound with multi-colored calico cloth. There are two doors to the house which are located diametrically opposite one another. There are no windows. In the middle of one wall stands a high bed under white bed curtains, alongside which stands a small divan, and in line with that was placed a chair for me. At the opposite wall is another small divan. That's all the furniture. In line with the bed, there rises a bamboo partition. On the walls are displayed guns and sabers of the *Ras*, several shields and his library, which consists of books on spiritual subjects, each of which, in a large leather case, hangs on a strap on a separate peg.

The *Ras* and his wife sat beside one another on the low divan near the bed. *Woyzaro* Eshimabet is already aging, but she is still a rather beautiful woman. The color of her skin shone strikingly for an Abyssinian woman. She was very richly dressed, and all of her absolutely glittered with the brilliance of a mass of gold and silver. Her black silk burnoose, draped over a colorful silk blouse, was richly embroidered with gold. On her head, she wore a silver diadem, hung round with silver chains and spangles. On her ears, she had large gold earrings, and on her hands rings.[61]

Behind her, with their arms around one another, stood several maids of honor—pretty Galla and Abyssinian girls, dressed in white blouses which extend down to their heels and tied around the waist with sashes. Here were also several little pages, and near the door, turned away from his mistress, not daring to look at her, stood the agafari who had led me there. Behind the partition were the rest of the female staff of the *elfin*, and through cracks there sparkled several curious eyes. These others included two daughters of the *Ras* from his first wife, two daughters of Eshimabet from her first husband and also two daughters of the *Ras* and Eshimabet.[62]

Having shaken hands with the hostess, European style, I sat on the chair opposite her; and interrupted with long pauses, the ceremonial conversation began: "How are you? How do you like our country?" etc.

The *Ras* very much wanted to have a portrait of his wife, so I sent for my photographic equipment. But the *Woyzaro* flatly refused to go out into the courtyard, saying that she was afraid of the sun, and I was forced to take her picture inside the room, having opened wide both doors.

The appearance of the equipment put an end to the solemn ceremonialness of the reception. The *Ras* sprang out of his place, dragged out from behind the partition four young women who were hiding there and sat them beside his wife. He was such a likeable bustler at that moment! How much he, apparently, wanted the portrait of his beloved wife to come out as well as possible! He ran from her to the apparatus, and then again to her, this time adjusting the decoration on her head, that time smoothing out the wrinkles in her clothes. Finally, the procedure of taking the picture was finished. The former boring stiffness and coldness did not return. The young ladies did not go back behind the partition. We, sitting at a small decanter of white *tej* (mead), conversed enjoyably until evening.

No sooner did I return home when, in the name of Eshimabet and the other women, *ashkers* came and brought me several baskets with the most delicate *injera* and several large jugs of aged mead. In reply to this, I sent them my last bottle of champagne.

In the evening, as usual, I developed the photographs I took during the day, wrote in my journal, and chatted with Zelepukin. We lay—I on my bed and he on a tarpaulin on the floor, and, lending ear to the unusual animation which prevailed in the camp of the *Ras*, we reminisced about our distant homeland...

Having raised high the flaps of our tent, we admired the marvelous picture of Andrachi around us. On these nights, no sooner did it become dark than in the cloudless sky there appeared a myriad of stars. And against the black background of mountains which surround the city, these innumerable little stars burned, shining much more brightly. Those were the soldiers' campfires which burned at their bivouacs... On all sides resounded songs, accompanied by sparse, but uninterrupted gun-fire, with which those who were feasting expressed their warlike frame of mind. The falling bullets sometimes buzzed over our own tent.

My *ashkers* kept up with the soldiers of the *Ras*. Having dined and drunk their portion of mead, they sat around the campfire and struck up songs. For the most part, these were military improvisations, and their contents amounted to praise of themselves and of their master. Liban sang in his clear, beautiful voice, and the chorus joined in the monotonous refrain, "*Gedau! Berekhanyau!*" ("Killer, killer, tramp of the desert!"). One of the *ashkers*, in a form of accompaniment, beat in time with his palms on an empty water tin. Women's voices joined in the chorus. The longer it went on, the more lively became the merriment. Finally, someone jumped up with a loaded gun in his hands and cried out a full self-praising recitative, a *fokyr*, at the end of which he fired into the sky. Comrades calmed the warrior who had lost his self-control, telling him: "Don't burn ("ayzokh")! Don't burn! Everything that you say is true!" And the interrupted singing continued. Military songs were mixed with satrical ones, sometimes very clever. Then they struck up merry dance songs. Men and women at the cheerful refrain "Chi-chi-ko! Chi-chi-ko!" portrayed rather unambiguous pantomimes and this black "flirt" provoked outbursts of laughter.

The excitement which had seized Andrachi was aroused by the upcoming war. The Abyssinians got themselves ready for it as if for the most joyous festive occasion. It was evident that craving for military exploits entered the flesh and blood of this people and that in spite of all the troubles and deprivations they had experienced in previous wars, the Abyssinians, although they foresaw great burdens, still worshipped war. The Abyssinian connects his idea of war with glory and spoils. He dreams about having killed several enemies, returning home, proud of his success. His wife would smear the hero's head with oil; and friends and relatives would hold a feast for him. He would let his hair grow long and braid it in plaits—the irrefutable sign of his valor. And how great would be the joy of his whole family, if moreover he brought home a fat cow or a female prisoner who would fetch water and go into the forest for firewood, or a captive boy who until he grew up and became a solider himself, would carry for him his rifle and shield and pasture his mule...

January 20

In the morning, I again took pictures of the *Ras*'s whole family —this time with better success. Today the shipment of meal that I had long awaited arrived from Jimma. It was supposed to serve as the basis of my food supply, which I hoped to replenish on the march. Altogether there were about 50-60 poods [1800-2160 pounds) of meal, and that could be enough for the whole detachment for 30 days, figuring two pounds of meal per day per person.

In addition to the meal, Aba Jefar sent me a cow as a gift. It turned out that on my first bivouac from Jimma, when I was going to Kaffa, the local chief was ordered to give me *durgo*, and since he for some reason did not do this, he was fined one cow, which was now sent to me as if in compensation for the losses I had suffered!...

The departure of the detachment was set for January 24. I decided to leave a little earlier, namely January 21, in order to freely make as exact a map of Kaffa as possible. The interpreter Gebra and the Kaffa Kata-Maguda (assistant of the *Katamarash*) were assigned to accompany me.

We made preparations in the evening and on the following morning my transport set out. I stayed in Andrachi until noon, printing the photographs I had taken in the *elfin* the day before. The *Ras*'s whole family took an active part in this. *Woyzaro* Eshimabet fixed the prints; her stepdaughter then placed them in the bath. Even the permanent staff of the *elfin*—a stern monk (a former colonel who had taken orders at the death of his wife) and another young monk (from a sect of celibates) got excited and crowded around the bath with curiosity. By eleven o'clock, the printing was done. *Woyzaro* Eshimabet treated me to lunch; and after long farewells, I finally set out. I spent the night in Bonga at the house of the *Nagada-Ras*.

THROUGH KAFFA AND GIMIRO TO THE ABYSSINIAN BORDER

JANUARY 22

I spent the whole day in Bonga as a guest of *Nagada-Ras* Vandym-Agnaokh. Here I finally formed the caravan for our subsequent movement.[63]

The order of movement was as follows. We set out at about seven o'clock in the morning, when the dew had fallen and it became warmer. While the tents were being taken down and the mules loaded, Zelepukin and I ate our breakfast. Then the transport set out. First went two herdsmen with *tarads* (poles from the tents), measuring their pace with the full pace of the mules. After them went one or two mounted *ashkers*, and after the horses obediently went the herd of loaded mules, after which followed *ashkers*. At the end, rode Aboye, the head of the transport. And behind everyone went Zelepukin, his broad-shouldered bulky figure and sunburnt crimson-colored face making a complete contrast with the light, well-proportioned, black-skinned Abyssinians.

Some time after the transport set out, I sat on my regular mule and started, accompanied by weapon bearers, who carried my guns,[64] a knapsack with writing implements, a theodolite, and photographic equipment. With me also went Gebra the Kaffa language interpreter and Katama-Guda my guide. We usually went very fast, but I often stopped along the road to observe the azimuth and to plot the location on a surveying plane-table. At noon, if the weather allowed, I made solar observations. In a day, we marched 20-30 versts [13-20 miles] and by 2 or 3 o'clock in the afternoon, we made camp for the night. On arriving at the bivouac, the mules were let out pasture; and in the evening, they were brought to tether. Quickly, the tents were broken out. Some of the *ashkers* set out for water, wood, and grass. The rest, together with my two cooks, prepared the food. For this part of our march, we ate excellently. The men each received each day a large cup of meal which they used to cook themselves very tasty flatcakes—kita—and ate them dipping them in crushed red pepper or pepper sauce. Each day they received mead, which they drank with water. And every two days, they got meat... Zelepukin and I, having meat and meal in abundance, all but feasted.

JANUARY 23

In the morning, we left Bonga. The transport having set out first, I ascended Mount Bonga-Shambata, which in translation means "Holiday or Festival Bonga." It was given this name because at its summit there once was located a temple to the god Dento or *Deontos*, where several times per year were held massive sacrifices. The summit of the mountain, which is overgrown with high g*Ras*s and, along the sides, with thick forest, attains a height of 2,075 meters above sea level. I made azimuth observations from there. From there, we went down to the River Gicha, crossed it by a bridge made of the trunks of date-palm trees, and climbed the mountain ridge that stretched out to the west of us. Here the country is picturesque. It seemed as if we were going through a marvelous park. On both sides of the road were encountered beautiful groves of date palms, coffee and huge deciduous trees of various types, mixed sometimes with clearings overgrown with grass. In times gone by, all these clearings were inhabited, as evidenced by the planations of banana trees which had escaped destruction.

We set up our bivouac at the foot of Mount Bonga-Beke (in translation "To see Bonga"), on the banks of a swift, shady stream.

JANUARY 24

The transport having set out on a straight road to the southwest, I climbed Mount Bonga-Beke. The chief of the region of Dake (Dake-*Ras*ha*)[65], a handsome young Kaffa, accompanied me to these places. Lightly and elegantly, he sat on an excellent chestnut-colored horse and with ease, adroitly controlled it. His white cloak fell down in artistic folds. Short wide trousers left bare from the knees his lean, muscular legs. By the Semitic features of his face and his whole primeval figure, he resembled an ancient biblic warrior. Behind him ran several servants, one of whom, a typical Kaffa of enormous size, blew the whole time on a horn made of a small elephant tusk, to notify the populace that their leader was passing through.[66]

The road was gently sloping, rising amid dense forest. In intervals between huge trees, it was overgrown with dense thickets of bamboos and ferns. The ferns looked similar to small palms and attained a height of several arshins [arshin = 28 inches]. The summit of the mountian was densely populated. Small huts, constructed soon after the war, were hidden in groves of banana plantations and were surrounded by fences of intricately interlaced splintered bamboo stalks.

In one of those framsteads, the wives of the imprisoned Kaffa king, Tato Chenito, lived under strict surveillance. I wanted to meet them and sent in advance to notify them of my coming. Past narrow gates which were protected by guards, we went into a small tidy courtyard. On a spread out oxhide in the shade of banana trees, a young, rather beautiful woman sat, and behind her stood the chief guard of the captive harem—a large beardless eunuch.

Having exchanged greetings, I began to converse with her through an interpreter. She answered my questions quite naturally, and behaved reservedly, and with extraordinary dignity.

She is the daughter of the king of Kusho[67], one of the former tributaries of Kaffa. She got married at the age of 12. She is now 25, and the 13 years of her marriage were for her, in her words, continuous happiness. The king loved her more than all his other wives and adorned her and dressed her more richly than them and more frequently than any of them summoned her to himself.[68] She loved her king, was depressed without him, and asked me if I had seen him, if he was healthy, if he had already died in confinement...

She spoke with amazing simplicity, remembering her former life with regret. The whole time, there was an imprint of deep sadness on her face. Two other wives were with her, as well as four concubines of the king and his bold beautiful twelve-year-old sister. I asked that these others also come out, and I took their photograph. Among the concubines was one "rising star," an amazingly good-looking Galla woman, who was remarkably cheerful. She was never bored anywhere, even in captivity, and at a time when all were sad, she smiled and even flirted.

Having taken leave, I set out for the summit of the mountain in order to take observations there. But the noon solar observation was unsuccessful since clouds obscured the sky. I just took azimuths on the surrounding mountains, and after long examinations finally determined their names. From Mount Bonga-Beke, all of Kaffa was visible—divided by natural boundaries into 12 regions. On the northwest rise Mountains Bacha-aki-Keli and Gaua-Gunga in the Kaffa region of Gauat, which borders Geroy. A bit further south, along spurs of the mountain ridge, is located the region of Gimbi, with the summits of Gida, Shonga, and Goli located there. And to the west of that, on the crest of the mountain ridge is the region of Geshe. To the southwest of Gimbi, along the courses of streams which flow into the Gumi River, are seen the forested regions of Bunta and Opa. Further south along the same crest of the main mountain ridge, heading to the southeast lies the region of Chana. To the northeast, along valleys of streams which flow into the Gojeb River are the regions of Shasha and Shara. South of those lies Kaffa itself, with the town of Andrachi. East of Kaffa lies the region of Buta, and the region of Adiya lies on the crest which serves as the watershed of the Gojeb and Gumi rivers. On the southwest appears the mountainous region of Goa. Mount Bonga-Beke itself is located in the region of Deche. From here, the system of the Gumi River is clearly delineated. Among mountainous ravines, it flows from the northeast of Mount Buty and at the foothills of the mountain at the town of Andrachi, it joins with the Gicha River. The Gicha River flows from Mount Bonga-Beke and skirts the mountain to the west. Having passed Bonga-Beke, the Gumi goes through a wide low plain. Here the realm of Kaffa itself ends and the Negro settlesments of Shuro begin. To the northwest is seen the valley of the Gojeb River. From Mount Bacha-aki-Kela, a river that the natives call "Tira" flows into the Gojeb. On the northeast, the Adiya River flows from Mount Adiya into the Gojeb River. Waters of the southwest slopes of Gauata to the west from Opa form the Menu River, which flows into the Juba and the Sobat. From here is visible how the main maintain ridge from Gera stretches out to the southeast. The height of Mount Bonga-Beke is 2,615 meters above sea level, and the summits of Bacha-aki-Kela, Gaua-Guno, Gida and Shonga exceed 3,000 meters. On the east, on the crest which serves as the watershed between the Omo and Gumy Rivers, stands the pointed peak of Mount Wadibalo, likewise probably exceeding 3,000 meters above sea level. The mountain ridge gradually and significantly gets lower to the south.

 Only at five o'clock in the afternoon did we arrive at our bivouac, which was laid out on the banks of the Wosha River in the region of Deche. A crowd of Kaffa were waiting for me, with the leader of the region at their head. By order ot the *Ras*, they brought provisions (*durgo*) for my detachment. I took a ram from the *Ras*ha and gave him five efimks. I refused the rest and returned the *durgo* brought by his half-starved Kaffa. In addition, I gave them several efimks to buy seed. The Kaffa were very touched by this and beat themselves in the chest and kissed the ground as a sign of gratitude.

January 25

We set out after noon. Completely naked hungry Kaffa children wandered around our bivouac, picking up any garbage. It made you feel sorry to look at them. They had lost the appearance of humans and were terribly thin; more precisely, they were skeletons covered with skin. On their thin legs, which were almost devoid of meat, the joints at the knees were sharply delineated. The cheeks and eyes were sunken, and the stomachs were distended.

The morning was cool (10o Reaumur [54° F]). The grass was covered with abundant dew, and the unfortunate children, shivering from the cold, looked for bones in the grass, fought among themselves for the internal organs of a ram, and if they found its foot, then gnawed on its skin and flesh.

I had a confrontation with one of my *elfin ashkers*, Ambyrbyr, a young hot-tempered Tigrean. He got into an argument with Haile; and despite the fact that Haile invoked Bulatovich by his God—"Ba Bulata Amlak"—to leave him alone, Ambyrbyr started a fight with Haile. All this took place right in front of my eyes, and consequently it was an encroachment on the authority of my name. In view of this, I had to intervene personally in this matter. In spite of my command, Ambyrbyr did not stop. Then I struck him, but he got even more enraged from this and was ready to throw himself on me. I had to act decisively. I pushed him in the chest, and he fell down unconscious. After several minutes, he came to. With this, the incident ended. On the day after this unruly conduct, I dismissed Ambyrbyr from the *elfin ashkers* and replaced him with Aregau.

We made a short march and stopped in the land of Bunta. Along the road, they showed me the burial vault of the Kaffa kings. The graves were completely level with the earth and were not marked in any way.

January 26

We entered the region of Chana. Going along the road which led past Kaffa settlements along the crest of the mountain ridge, and having passed an outpost, we went over the boundaries of Shuro. The boundary is separated from Kaffa by a wide uninhabited strip, which on the west was adjacent to land reserved for elephant hunts of the Kaffa kings. Along the road we now and then came upon signs of elephants. The Shuro, knowing that a campaign was being launched against their side, guarded their borders with reinforcements and watched this road. In the dense grass and on the edges fo the forest, here and there, their black figures appeared in passing.

Having proceeded through this area, we passed an outpost and again entered the rather well inhabited region of Chana. We set up our bivouac right beside the detachment of the newly named head of the border Kaffa regions—Ato Kassem. He soon came to greet me and brought as a gift several pitchers of mead. Ato Kassem, a 60-year-old man, frail and smooth-tongued, was formerly a judge in Kulo. He received these regions which were under his leadership as a pension for long service.

The house of a well-known priest (*bale*) of Chana was located not far from our bivouac. I ordered someone to send for him. The *bale* soon came and sat at the entrance of my tent, deciding not to go in so as not to defile himself by being present in a dwelling of a man who uses the meat of unclean animals as food, which is what he took Europeans for. The *bale* was a young, very handsome Kaffa, who by appearance did not differ at all from his other fellow-tribesmen. He is from the Gossa clan, and all his ancestors as far back as he remembers were also priests. I asked him about many matters, but got very little information from him.

January 27

We went down from the mountain ridge to the Uka River (from a height of 2,400 meters to 1,700 meters above sea level) by way of a road that is skilfully built along the crest of a spur. The road went through dense forest in which the trees attained dimensions the like of which I had never seen before. Even the kolkuala cactus contended with the most colossal trees in height. In the forest, we came across many monkeys, but almost no birds. We cross the Uka River by an extremely well constructed bridge. The Uka constitutes the southern boundary of Kaffa itself, and beyond it begin the lands of tribes that are subject to Kaffa.

We stopped with a bivouac near the river and on the following day again climbed the mountain ridge. I went up to a summit located near Mount Boka or Bokan, from which, at a height of 2,714 meters, a distant horizon opened to the south and southeast. From here it could be distinctly seen how the crest of the main mountain range stretches to the east and then turns south. Far in the haze are seen its sourthern summits, which I later became familiar with and got to know by name—Kastit, Say, Uyta, Shashi, and others. Still farther to the east rises the pointed pyramidal summit of Mount Dime, which Donaldson Smith gave the name "M.I. Smith." To the north of it appeared another, even larger mountain, having the shape of an obliquely truncated sugar loaf. We called this mountain Ya-Menelik-Saganeyt.[69] These two mountains were located on the other side of the River Omo. The evident direction of the crest of the main mountain range gave rise to my first suspicion of the possibility that the river might skirt it from the south and turn west. (The further journey finally confirmed that this newly discovered mountain range deflects the Omo to the south, forcing it to flow into Lake Rudolf and that it constitutes the watershed of the Nile and Omo Rivers). The crest of the mountain range is covered in several parts by forest, and its gently sloping western inclines and the valleys of many westward flowing tributaries of the Menu[70] River were densely populated. Here dwelt the Gimiro tribe, which is divided into small principalities dependent on Kaffa: Kaba, Shevo, Isheno, Yayno, Duka, Benesho, Shyaro, and Shyako.

This people differs in type from the Kaffa. The skin of the Girmiro is darker, and the facial features are more coarse. The language is completely different from the Kaffa and very difficult to pronounce. It abounds in whistling and dental consonants. Its syllables are pronounced as if swallowed. It also differs from the language of the Sidamo tribes: Kula, Konta, and others; but the mode of speech of these languages is similar, and you encounter common roots in them. The Gimiro believe in God, calling him by a name taken from the Kaffa—*Iero* or *Iero*chi. However, there exists another deity—Kiy—to whom they offer sacrifices. The Gimiro do not recognize the rite of circumcision. The culture of this people is the same as that of the Kaffa in both weaponry and clothing. In character, they are peaceful and hardworking rather than warlike. Their houses are built very skillfully and simply. Their household utensils include washtubs—the first that I had encountered in Abyssinia. These tubs are made from trunks of kolkuala cactus. The Gimiro dig their fields deeply with pickaxes and sow them with bread grain of all kinds, depending on the altitude of the location. Cattle breeding flourishes. Their cattle are very good. There are no horses. They hold bees in large quantities. The rich vegetation and moist climate favor beekeeping.

On the summit of Bokana, I conducted the noon solar observation and took azimuths on the surrounding mountains. A crowd of natives who gathered around me examined me and my instrument with curiosity. I asked them about the names of the surrounding mountains, but they knew only the nearest area and couldn't tell me anything about the mountains visible in the south, except that Shuro, i.e. blacks, live there. When I asked them for water, they brought it in an enormous bamboo stalk.

Having gone down into the valley of the Wayna River, which lies at an altitude of 2,000 meters above sea level, we entered the densely inhabited region of Shevo. The Wayna River, which flows in marshy banks, we crossed by an extremely well-made bridge, covered with palm branches. Along the other side of the river, the inhabitants had cleared the road for the passage of the *Ras*. Catching sight of us, some hid in a thicket; the rest, bowing low, greeted me with the words "Saro, saro!"[71]

We stopped on the bank of one of the tributaries of the Wayna River, on the site of the future bivouac of the *Ras*. A whole palace was built for him on the bank of the stream. It consisted of several houses built in the form of enormous cabins, surrounded by an intricate fence. In the palace, active preparations are being made for the reception of the *Ras*. The Gimiro are bringing meal wrapped up in banana leaves and honey; and soldiers of Ato Kassema are making tej from it. Some of them chop gesho leaves into fine pieces (a stupefying remedy added to tej). Others add honey to water in huge pitchers and tubs, separating wax from it.

Ato Kassem and Prince Shevo came to my bivouac and brought me a ram and honey and meal. The honey was remarkably fragrant and completely white, but to eat it in the afternoon seemed impossible. As soon as they brought the honey into the tent, the tent filled with bees, which clung to the plate and spoon and flew at my mouth. The bees here are very good compared to ours, and you can brush them away from you. Nevertheless one of them, having sat under the spoon at the very moment when I put it in my mouth, stung my tongue and made me put off eating dessert until evening. My tongue swelled up, and for two days I could talk only with difficulty.

JANUARY 29 AND 30

We stayed in this place for two days. I made solar observations, determined the latitude, checked the chronometer, determined the declination of the magnetic meridian, and entered on the map the recent stages of my journey. The rest period was very opportune for me, since the rheumatism in my legs had not yet gone away, and after two climbs on Mounts Bonga-Beke and Bokan, the pain had increased significantly, furthered by the damp and cold weather in the mornings. On January 29, I rode out to photograph two hanged men I had seen the day before. They had hung already for more than a year on an enormous sycamore and had completely dried out.

In our bivouac, great excitement reigned. In the afternoon, the *ashkers* practiced throwing javelins at a target. As a sign of victory, he who hit the mark the greatest number of times walked to the target on the backs of his player-comrades who were lying face-downwards on the ground. In the evening, songs and dances were organized, during which the Kaffa showed us their war dance—a very beautiful dance reminiscent of the lezginka [Caucasian dance]. They dance in twos, armed with spears and shields. One of the dancers, wildly calling out in time to the song, attacks. Having aimed his spear at the chest of his opponent, he advances at him and shakes the spear the whole time. The opponent backs up and parries the blows with his shield, and then, in turn advances. The motions of the dancers were very smooth and graceful. They described circles, as in the lezginka. When the dance was in full swing, they accomplished amazing steps, jumping high, throwing themselves against one another, sometimes squatting as in the Russian prisyadka.

JANUARY 30

An incident occurred which showed how far the spirit of comradeship had grown among my *ashkers*. One of them, Damye, suffered from syphillis, and his legs were covered with sores. He hid his illness from me from fear that I would exclude him from the campaign; and, suffering silently, he was doing the same 11-hour marches on foot as the others and did not do any less than his comrades. Here the opportunity presented itself to buy a horse from one of the soldiers of Ato Kassem. Since Damye did not have the money, his comrades formed a pool and collected the 30 efimks necessary for this.

JANUARY 31

We entered the land of Isheno, which on the east and south borders on domains of Shuro Negroes who still do not recognize the authority of Abyssinia. The western boundary from here is ten versts [seven miles] in all, and the eastern is twenty versts [thirteen miles]. This place is just as rich in vegetation and abounds in water as much as the land we had just passed through. The road stretches along the western slopes of the mountain range, crossing many streams with excellent bridges built across them.

We laid out our bivouac beside the house which was built for the *Ras*; and soon after our arrival, Prince Isheno appeared. A typical Gimiro of enormous stature, he brought me meal, honey, and a ram as gifts.

FEBRUARY 1

My detachment spent the following day resting, and I climbed the mountain ridge which constitutes the western border of Isheno. A whole detachment of Gimiro accompanied me—a hundred men under the command of a prince. Of my servants, I brought only the gun bearers, to the great chagrin of the other *ashkers* who probably supposed that we were undertaking a raid on neighbors.

From the altitude of the crest, there appeared the low-lying valley of the Uka River, which flows to the east, and which joins in the distance with another river (according to the natives, the Gumi).

Many settlements were scattered along the slopes of the crest. My fellow travellers were seized by a passionate desire to go down there to enemy land and finally give vent to their warlike aspirations. With dificulty, I succeeded in holding them back. Having looked around the place, I returned.

On the return trip, we went past a market at which a mass of people crowded—men and women—who, at our appearance, rushed to run away. Prince Isheno with difficulty succeeded in stopping and calming his subjects, and they continued their interrupted commerce. Here bread, beer, hens, rams, and various kinds of cloth were sold. The merchants and buyers seem to be mainly women. For the men, the market serves as a club. They thronged here with long pipes in their teeth, chatting and exchanging news. I bought a large wooden pipe from a Kaffa nobleman and ordered him to come to my bivouac for the money. At the designated time, he appeared. I invited him into my tent, served him honey, and conversed iwth him. My interlocutor seemed to be pagan. Formerly, he was very rich, and owned many cattle. He had two wives, seven slaves, and three children. But they all died during the war. He spoke of this with genuine sadness. "I asked God for death," he said, "but he didn't give me it."

"Who is God?" I asked him.

"*Iero*!" he answered me. (He knew about the other Kaffa deity—*Deontos*—but could not explain to me what the difference was between them. He also knew about the devil—Saytana.)

I asked him if he had heard about Christ. He answered no.

"And about the Mother of God?"

"I have heard about Mary."

"What do you think will become of you after your death?"

This question evidently touched one of the most sensitive and lively places of his soul, and he decided to share with me what had for a long time burdened him.

"It is the absolute truth," he began enthusiastically. "What I say is the absolute truth! We have heard that good people will be in a state of bliss after death, and the evil will be racked with pain. We have heard that to get the first, we should fast: meat is tasty, butter is tasty, but we do not eat them. There are many beautiful women; we are attracted to them, but we restrain ourselves. I heard all this as hearsay, and for a long time this has hurt my soul (literally, "my stomach hurts"). But what all of this means and how it happens, I do not know."

I briefly told him the foundations of Christian teaching. He listened with great attention, striking himself on his chest with his fist from time to time. In conclusion, he asked, "What must I do?"

"Be baptized!"

"And who will teach me fasts and rites? And can I be baptized when my ancestors were not baptized? Will I do well?"

I again advised him to be baptized, after which he thanked me; and, evidently sincerely agitated by our conversation, he went away...

In the evening, a courier arrived at a gallop with a letter from the *Ras*. He informed me that he would arrive in Shevo on the following day, and asked about my health and about how successful my work was. "Did you see many lands?" he asked in the letter. I answered him that, thanks to God, I was healthy; I had seen many lands; and that on the following day I would come to visit him in Shevo.

February 2

In the morning, I took a short stroll in the land of Yayno, to the southern Gimiro border. After dinner I set out to the *Ras* on horseback, accompanied by two *ashkers*, also on horseback. His camp was spread out wide. For several versts from the headquarters of the *Ras*, the road was studded with tents on both sides. Soldiers, soldiers' wives, children, mules—all were mixed together here in disorder. Only where the terrain allowed, I rode with a wide gallop. At the sight of me, some of the Abyssinians we met respectfully made way for us. Others looked around contemptuously, crying "Ali." That's what the Abyssinians called Italians and, together with them, all white men. This name is insulting in the highest degree, and Menelik forbade calling Europeans that, under threat of punishment with the *jiraf*. But this time I did not pay attention to the offensive calls, not wanting to begin my acquaintance with future comrades on the campaign with reprisals. However, I also heard approving exclamations relating to my horse and my riding, as for example "*Ay faras! Ay faras! Frenj* farasenye!" ("There's a horse! There's a horse! The foreigner is a cavalryman!").

I found the *Ras* in the little courtyard of his headquarters, surrounded by officers. He sat cross-legged, on a carpet in the shade of a branchy tree and light-heartedly cleaned his teeth[72] with a little stick. The old warrior, hardened in battle, apparently felt fortunate to find himself once again at the head of his army, in a campaign, under the open sky, on the border of enemy land, on the eve of crossing into it. To this feeling of pleasure must have been mixed some nervous alarm before a new fight, such as a fast horse feels at the start of spring after having passed a peaceful winter.

The *Ras* and I met heartily, and I stayed with him until sunset. In the evening, I returned to my bivouac.

February 3

From eight o'clock in the morning, the continuous file of the *Ras*'s soldiers began to arrive. About ten o'clock, the clear sound of flutes was heard from afar, signalling his arrival. In front, drummers in little red fezzes rode, sitting on the sacrum of mules, loaded in the front with the drums. Swinging their sticks high, they beat the drums in a beautiful joyous rhythm. Behind the drums, two mules carried the enormous tent of the *Ras*; and bearers carried the long bamboo posts for it. Then his horses in silver gear and his mules were led. The stable-man of the favorite war horse of the *Ras* carried two spears—silver and copper. Then a long file of pages and bearers followed with property of the *Ras*: a well-made wooden armchair in a red calico cover, a medicine chest, two small water-skins, a library, a telescope, etc. The *Ras* takes these things with him during his journeys and his campaigns. Behind the bearers walked the flutists and, finally, surrounded by all the officers and soldiers of his guard, rode the commander-in-chief. Immediately behind him followed weapons bearers, carrying ten guns of the *Ras* in red woolen covers and so many ammunition belts, thrown around their necks. The mule of the *Ras* in a heavy silver collar had an Abyssinian saddle, covered with velvet trappings, embroidered with silk.

The *Ras* wore a thin white shirt and trousers. A black silk burnoose was worn over the thinnest shamma, thrown over the shoulder. With the free end of the shamma, he covered his face up to the eyes. The *Ras*'s feet were bare, and his head was covered with a wide felt hat. His armaments consisted of a small revolver and a saber mounted in gold (a military distinction, received from Emperor Menelik).

The *Ras* settled down and waited for dinner in one of the houses, where his camp-bed was set up and carpets were spread out. Deputations greeted the *Ras* by bowing to the ground; and, as a sign of joy at beholding their lord with their own eyes, they kissed the ground and beat on their chests with their palms. Prince Isheno brought several marvellous bulls as a gift, one of which the *Ras* gave to me.

Prince Isheno and his subjects, as inhabitants, were invited to take part in the campaign; and they with joy accepted this offer. A special detachment from them was formed under the command of Gebra, who had until then served as my interpreter.

It was decided to cross the Shuro border the following day. The Shuro lands were separated from the Gimiro by a dense border forest, through which only difficult foot paths led. The *Ras* issued orders to quickly dispatch workers to clear a road ahead and designated a combined detachment of a hundred soldiers as a guard.

I wanted to set out with the advanced detachment, and after a big dinner with the *Ras* to which all the officers, the most senior soliders, and his whole guard were invited, I crossed the border.

At five o'clock in the evening, we reached the edge of the frontier forest and set up our bivouac in a small clearning. I rode ahead to acquaint myself with the neighborhood. Going several versts along a scarcely discernible trail in a very dense forest, we ran up against Shuro scouts, who hid themselves as we approached; and, finally, we climbed to the crest of the mountain spur, which went down by a precipice to an unknown river. As far as the eye see, the valley and hills were densely settled. Smoke arose from the houses. Evidently, food was being prepared there. Cattle were returning from the pasture, and the sight marvellous white cows aroused the appetite of my travelling companions, who exclaimed the whole time, "Look how many cows! So white! And cows! Those are such cows!..." The field around was cultivated. The quiet hardworking life of a peaceful people was evident in all, and it was sad to think that tomorrow all this would be destroyed... The picture will change: the inhabitants will flee, driving their livestock and carrying their goods and children. They will, most probably be killed, wounded, and captured. Their houses will go up in a blaze, and all that will remain of them will be the hearths. Didn't the Shuro foresee this? *Ras* Wolda Giyorgis more than once passed on to them through their Gimiro neighbors the advice to voluntarily submit. They know that the Abyssinians are close: scouts watch over all trails leading into their country. Disaster draws near. Evidently, sorrow is close by and unavoidable. But despite this, on the eve of disaster, they prepare their food without a care.

It had already gotten dark when I returned to our bivouac. Along the road, we came upon my *ashkers* who had set out for food. On their own initiative they took all military precautions, and the two who were carrying water were convoyed by two others armed with rifles.[72]

In the evening, we slaughtered the bull which had been given to me by the *Ras*, and I treated the combined detachment to dinner. I invited 14 officers into my tent, and we ate raw meat, dipping it in red pepper. My guests appeared with their own knives or daggars. (Some had little knives inserted in the scabbards of sabers.)

During dinner, we established the procedures for the night watch, in view of the probability of an attack by the Shuro. Campfires were set at the four corners of the bivouac, and eight guards lay down in front of each of them. They were strictly instructed to shoot only in extremity and never inside the bivouac. In case of alarm, they were ordered to muster at my large tent. Our precautions, however, were not justified, and the night passed peacefully...

From the Borders of Abyssinia to Lake Rudolf

February 4

In the morning, a light rain drizzled. The Gimiro cleared a path with axes, cutting down trees that stood on both sides. And Abyssinians stationed in front of the workers chopped the densely interwoven lianas with sabers. The work proceeded so slowly that I decided to go ahead with several of my gun bearers and, having managed to get to an open place, to conduct some observations.

We advanced with difficulty along a narrow trail in the dense forest, time and again moving past huge trees which had been deliberately felled by the Negroes. For nearly half an hour, we went quietly, not disturbed by anyone, when suddenly, on crossing one of the abattises, right beside us, the loud warning sounds of a horn resounded, which forced us to stop and grab hold of our guns. Our bolts clicked. Holding our breath, we waited for the attack. Straining our sight, we peered into space to see the enemy in a thicket of the forest. In response to the first horn, others resounded in the distance. Finally, all fell silent, and all we could hear was the sounds of some people almost beside us, who had penetrated into the bushes. We cautiously moved farther ahead, and in an hour and a half got to the forest's edge. The whole time, we were followed by Negroes; but they did not decide to attack us. The valley of the Oyma River, which I had seen yesterday, now unfolded before us. Its populace was at this minute in full flight. Women came out of the houses loaded with every kind of goods and supplies, and hurriedly left, driving their cattle with them. Some of the men followed their wives. Positioning themselves along the crests of mountain spurs, others watched us. It was evident that the exhortations of the *Ras* to submit voluntarily had had almost no success.

By 11 o'clock, the road was cleared, and the *Ras*'s army poured into the valley, where they scattered in various directions, rushing to replenish their supplies. Any prohibition would be unthinkable and fruitless, since the whole provisioning system of the campaign depended on such commandeering. The ground was covered with Abyssinians jumping in all directions; and in the farmsteads the real work was in full swing: from little granaries raised on piles over the ground, the soldiers threw off sheaves of *shef* and *mashella*, and here in the courtyard threshed them with sticks on spread out *shammas*. Several lucky ones found meal in houses, and rejoicing in this find, triumphantly carried it to the bivouac. Soon all trails that led to our stopping place were covered with soldiers who were heavily loaded down: one carried grain, another hay for mules, another a hen, another drove a ram. The soldiers were contented and threw jokes at one another.

The bivouac of the *Ras* was located along the crest of a mountain spur which towers above the Oyma River. My tent was in front of the headquarters of the *Ras*. On returning, I went to visit him and to congratulate him on the border crossing. He was surrounded by senior officers and was composing the order of the day—*auaj*.

The order began with the usual formula and said the following: "Do not separate from your unit without permission of the commander. Do not go far to comandeer goods. Do not kill if you are not attacked. Try to take prisoners in order to obtain guides. If you come upon a mule that is lost, do not unsaddle it, but rather present it to me, along with all the property that is found on it. I will cut off the hand of anyone who is guilty of stealing lost, loaded mules. Quickly bring prisoners and cattle to me."

With 40 strokes on the nagarit (kettledrums), the detachment was notified of the upcoming announcement of the order of the day, after which the order was read before the assembled officers and senior soldiers. The prisoners and cattle that were taken that day were presented to the *Ras*.

There were three prisoners in all: an old woman and two young women, one of whom was pregnant. All of them were extremely ugly. Their facial features were typically Negro. In punctures made in their thick lips, they had inserted small wooden sticks. Their teeth stuck out in front. And their lower incisors were knocked out. The slit of their eyes is narrow. The whites of their eyes are reddish. The hair, cut short around the crown of the head, was let grow above and was curled in hanging locks, abundantly smeared with a mixture of clay and oil. On arms and legs, they sported iron bracelets; and in the ears, they wore small wooden ear-rings. They were dressed in two large ox-hides, of which one was wrapped around the waist, and other was fastened by the lower end to the first, and by the upper ends was tied across the shoulder. On the back, in an upper skin in the form of a sack, they put infants, for whom the bosom in front serves as the storehouse of all good things. We only found on the captive women the following items: provisions, various household utensils, iron arm and leg bracelets, and iron ornaments twisted in a spiral shape which they wear on a string tied around the hips. This waist decoration probably serves for them as a kind of "decollete manches courtes" and is worn during dances and feasts.

The women were interrogated in the presence of the *Ras*, but we succeeded in learning very little. They replied stupidly and disconnectedly, dragging out their words and speaking repulsively through their noses. The *Ras* ordered that the prisoners be fed. One of them he kept as a guide, and the others he let go, having ordered that they be turned over to their fellow tribesmen in order that they would express support for submitting to him. In case of submission, he promised full inviolability of property and freedom. The prisoners thanked the *Ras*, kissing the ground and striking themselves in the chest with their hands, and left, swearing to carry out his will. They were led outside the limits of the camp with the cattle which had been taken that day, and they left in all directions.

After the prisoners left, I stayed alone with the *Ras*. Realizing the gravity of his position, the *Ras* did not consider it necessary to hide it from me. Now he had crossed the border and he had under his leadership a 30,000 man army, completely cut off from its base. And besides, his army possessed only the most scanty means and had to count exclusively on provisions from an unknown region. We definitely could not guess in advance what awaited us ahead: our future was as unknown as was little known the goal of our operation—Lake Rudolf—which we wanted to reach.

"From worry, I do not sleep, eat, nor drink. Reading the Psalter serves as my only comfort," the *Ras* told me. Suddenly, after a short pause, he forcefully announced, "But however difficult it may be, I will fulfill my duty or die!" And he asked me to help him choose the route of the detachment.

I agreed, with pleasure, and on the following day had to set out with the regiment of Fituarari Atyrsye and with Ato Bayu for the first reconnaissance mission. Atyrsye commands a regiment of *waruari* and is the chief *Fitaurari* of the *Ras*. His place both on the march and in the bivouac was always in front of the whole detachment. Atyrsye is a descendant of simple peasants, and advanced through the ranks thanks to his personal military service. He took part in almost all the wars and was wounded several times. I can see him now riding a small white mule, with a long javelin in his hands and with a soiled felt hat on his head; always cheerful, cracking jokes and filling our whole column with ringing laughter, with which his fat figure shook.

In complete contrast to him, Ato Bayu is a typical contemporary Abyssinian courtier—young, handsome, restrained; subtle in speech, and elegant in manner. In his childhood, he served as an *elfin* ashker (page) of *Ras* Dargi and, at court, learned various crafts from Europeans. Once he made a gun with his own hands and presented it to Menelik. Struck by the talent of the boy, the emperor took him to himself; and from that time, Ato Bayu became a favorite of Menelik, accompanied him on all campaigns, brilliantly carried out secret missions which were assigned to him, and finally received authority over the Wollaga territory, a land rich in gold, which is located on the western boundaries of Abyssinian domains and borders on Emir Abdurakhman's Beni-Shangul. Having established relations with Abdurakhman, he convinced him to send an embassy to Menelik, with gifts as a sign of recognition of his suzerainty over them. But the timing for the embassy was unfortunate since Menelik was then preparing for war with Italy, and the question of Beni-Shangul was set aside.[74] The appointment of Bayu to a country rich in gold and ivory aroused envy toward him. Many began to say that Bayu gave himself airs, that he is friends with Europeans, that he enriched himself at the expense of the Emperor, etc. The slander produced its effect, and the Emperor deprived Bayu of the region, under the pretext that he gave refuge in his house to a relative who had fled from imprisonment. Too confident of his influence on Menelik, Bayu was impertinent and unrestrained when the *Negus* announced this decision to him, and for this he was subjected to definitive disgrace. He spent a year in shackles, confined in Ankober, but then was freed and sent in exile to *Ras* Wolda Giyorgis. He has now been with the *Ras* four years. And in this time, he has succeeded in getting close to him and becoming his closest advisor in all matters.

February 5

I was still lying in bed when Ato Bayu came into my tent and told me that it was time to get started. I quickly dressed; and having called my gun bearers, I rushed to the mustering point. Day was just breaking. It was fresh and damp (+6o Reamur) [45o F]. The detachment was still sleeping, and soldiers, having wrapped their heads in their *shammas*, lay like mummies on the dew-covered grass. Someone who was cold was busying himself at the night's campfire, which had died out. He was trying to reignite the fire. Among the general silence, the distant doleful song of a sentry chasing away sleep and the loud repulsive roar of a donkey resounded. We passed the headquarters of the *Ras* which was surrounded by a ring of tents of his guard, then passed the bivouacs of the vanguard regiments, and finally went beyond the limits of the camp. The regiment of *Fitaurari* Atyrsye was already at the mustering point. The soldiers crowded in a little clearing, impatiently awaiting their departure. In a motionless authoritative pose, leaning on a long walkingstick, the Fituarari stood in front of his soldiers and, having turned his face to them, he held back his troops who were striving to surge forward.

No sooner did we succeed in starting out than they were each seized by a desire to be in front of the others in the first battle of their unit. All of them dashed forward irrepressibly. This was some kind of spontaneous, mass motion; and orders to stop would have been useless. The *Fitaurari* and his officers galloped to a narrow passageway in the dense forest, and standing here across the passageway, stopped the unit. The noise and uproar at this minute were inconceivable. The *Fitaurari* and officers restrained their soldiers and blows of the officers' sticks rained down on the shields of the foremost soldiers. Senior soldiers helped the officers in this matter and with the butts of their guns held back their coomrades who were straining forward. When order was reestablished, we went farther. In front were ten men, who consituted our vanguard. Behind them, under guard of several soldiers, the guide who had been captured the day before walked submissively. Behind her followed: me, the *Fitaurari* and Ato Bayu and, finally, the regiment. They put a rope around the neck of the guide. It was held by the translator, Gebra Maryam, a huge, typical Negro. As an eleven-year-old boy, he had been captured by the Abyssinians, brought up and educated by them. He completely assimilated the Abyssinian customs and now feels deep contempt for his former fellow-countrymen, considering them animals and savages. Therefore, very often when I wanted to ask prisoners about their way of life, Gebra Maryam made the most disdainful grimace and told me:

"Geta! (Lord!) Why do you ask them about this? As if they were people; they are animals!"

Gebra Maryam was the only interpreter of the Shuro language in the detachment. Therefore, he had to accompany me on all my reconnaissance missions, which he really didn't like. He wept bitterly, feigning that he was lame, and kept asking for a mule for himself.

We went toward Mount Kayfesh, which was seen not far away, in order to look over the territory from its height and plan the path of our reconnaissance. At 7 o'clock in the morning, we reached the summit of the mountain. The terrain which was opened in front of us was a system of mountain spurs, descending to the west of the main mountain ridge. In the southwest was seen the valley of the Sebelimu River, which probably flows into the Menu River. According to the native, the large Shorma or Shorum River (probably the River Omo) was found to the east of the mountain ridge.

The mountain and the closest crest located to the north of us were covered with very dense forest which constituted the border between the Shuro and the Gimiro. In the farthest parts of the border forest, the trees had been felled and the bushes burned[75], apparently for sowing or for settlement. To the south of Mount Kayfesh, the land is densely populated. I took azimuths on the mountains that were visible, and wrote down the names of the closest of them, which the guide named for me, and selected for myself the path from here for the reconnaissance. We went down from the summit and, going to the southwest, went into very densely settled territory. Near the border, the farmsteads of the natives were close together and surrounded by high wattle fencing for defense against incidental attacks by their Gimiro neighbors. Farther to the south, there were no such fences. The houses here are low, covered with thatch, and look more like temporary shelters than permanent dwellings. Beside the houses are overhangs into which they drive their cattle at night and small granaries raised above the ground for protection from termites. The fields are cultivated, but not so thoroughly as among the Gimiro, and they are sown with *mashella*, maize, tef and dagussa. In elevated places, kogo [banana-like tree] and barley are found. Near the houses tower enormous sycamores, covered with beehives. The inhabitants had abandoned their dwellings. The women and children went to the south, and the warriors, having spread out along the crests of the surrounding mountains, vigilantly watched us, sometimes attacking Abyssinians who had separated from the detachment and parties of soldiers who were returning with booty. The Shuro retreated before us, and alarm sounds from their horns informed the populace of our approach. At 9 o'clock in the morning, they unexpectedly attacked us. We had just begun to enter the dense forest at the bottom of a narrow ravine, when suddenly war cries of the natives resounded and shots from our vanguard detachment answered them. The troops who were closest to them quickly ran to their aid, and *Fitaurari* Atyrsye, having assembled several dozen soldiers, sent them off to attack in the forest. Then having selected a glade on a hill from which the place of battle was visible like the palm of your hand, he stopped there and the regiment which had been stretched out along the narrow trail began to assemble at that place. To support those who were attacking, The Fituarari gradually sent new units. About 10-15 minutes after the first shots, the Shuro were already retreating, energetically pursued by Abyssinians.

The road in front of us was now free, and there was no need for further bloodshed. But to stop the pursuit was now not so easy. The *Fitaurari* and all of us shouted to the pursuers who had gotten carried away, telling them not to kill the natives and to try to take them prisoner and return to the detachment. But it was very difficult to take alive a naked Shuro who was remarkably adept at going through thickets. And the feeling of competition, which seized the pursuers, was great—to kill or to take an enemy prisoner in the first battle—especially since very often several Abyssinians were chasing after one Shuro, none of them wanted to give up the "prize" to a rival, and they raced one another to shoot the man who was fleeing.

To hide from Abyssinina bullets, the Shuro climbed high trees; but the bullets found them there, and the Negroes, like shot birds, dropped from there to the ground; and the victors, with penetrating joyous cries, proclaimed their victory to their comrades. One old Shuro man also climbed a tree, but having seen that they noticed him, he quickly came down to the ground and started to run. Several Abyssinians rushed after him in pursuit, but the old man, with remarkable adroitness, managed to go through the dense thorny bushes, jumping over the trunks of fallen trees... We shouted to the soldiers not to kill him, but to take him prisoner; however, the question of who exactly would kill or capture the old man was so important for the Abyssinians that they, paying no attention to our shouts, shot at him and, fortuantely for him, missed. Finally, the old man got tangled in lianas and fell, and Abyssinians piled on top of him. There wasn't anyone left to pursue, since, as is usually said in Abyssinian reports "who was killed, was killed, and who ran, ran." And one after the other, the victors began to return to us. In heroic recitatives (*foky*rate), they recounted their victory to their leader and, expressing their devotion to him, bowed to the ground, at which the *Fitaurari* replied indifferently, with the usual congratulatory phrase: "Ekuan kanykh," "Finally, you have had a stroke of good luck..." The captured old man shook from his recent agitation and looked at us vacantly with his narrow reddish eyes. He must have been perplexed that he had not yet been killed. He was completely naked. His body had been heavily scratched by thorns. We calmed the old man and promised him freedom if he would faithfully serve us and tell the truth. And we began to interrogate him. The old man only knew the nearest territory and revealed that there is a big road in the east which leads to the southwest. We gave him something to eat, tied his hands to the hands of the woman guide, buried the dead soldier, and having made slings for the two wounded, set out to find the road. In this action, we had lost one man who was killed and two wounded.

The old man belonged to that nationality which the Kaffa call "Shuro", i.e. blacks. They themselves do not call themselves that and, in general, I did not succeed in finding a common name for all these tribes.

By type, language, religion and culture, the Shuro differ from the tribes that were known to me up until that time. The facial features, the shape of the skull, the sharp facial angle,[76] curly hair, narrow eyes with a vacant expression and reddish whites of the eyes—all of which testifies to their Negro origin. But the color of their skin, although darker than that of the Kaffa and Gimiro, has a chestnut tint which makes one think they are not completely pure representatives of the Bantu race, but rather have mixed, to some degree, with another non-Negro race.

The Shuro language differs completely from the langauge of the Sidamo and Gimiro. They speak in an amazingly ugly manner, pronouncing words as if through the nose. They believe in the god Tumu, but do not sacrifice to him. Circumcision is unknown among them. They bury their dead in a sitting position, with knees bent to shoulders, in shallow graves. They buy wives, paying relatives their redemption fee. The wealth of a Shuro is expressed in the number of his wives. The culture of this people —thanks to laziness, which is the main attribute of their character—is on a rather low level of development. The manufacture of cloth, for instance, is completely unknown to them. Women dress in skins, and men do not cover themselves even with skins, except that some of them wrap the small skin of a young goat around their waists. They are armed with javelins, small round leather shields (some of which are only 5-6 vershoks [9-10 inches] in dimater) and heavy wooden clubs.

The Shuro are divided into many separate tribes, ruled by independent princes, but the beginning of a state system is still in a rudimentary stage among them. Their way of life is extremely simple. The Shuro engage in cultivation but also keep livestock. They eat primarily a vegetable diet, and also use the meat of domestic animals and birds. But they do not eat the meat of elephants, hippopotamuses, and other wild animals, and in this way differ from other tribes who are related to them by type and language and who are not squeamish about any kind of meat. Therefore, the Shuro call these others by the contemptuous name of "Idenich"—"sons of non-people."

We soon found the road which we were looking for. It was a rather narrow trail, very well placed along mountainous territory and trampled down by running inhabitants and livestock. At 11:30, we went down into a deep stone ravine and stopped on the banks of the Kilu Rivulet.

The sky was cloudless. It was nearly noon. I sent a file of soldiers to the side where natives had been seen following us on the ridge, in case they might unexpectedly attack. And I began to carry out solar observations. Looking with curiosity at the actions which were unintelligible to them, the remaining Abyssinians clustered around my instrument. Seeing foreign sorcery in this, several old men turned away with disgust and spat. When I finished the observations, we went back; and at four o'clock in the afternoon, we arrived at the bivouac. The *Ras* was very satisfied with the results of this first reconnaissance. The prisoner was presented to him. The *Ras* ordered him to wear a shamma, to wrap his head in a red band and to be fed. The old man was delighted with his fate. He closely scrutinized his clothes and all the time kept repeating: "Byshi! Byshi!" ("Good! Good!") The anxiety he had recently experienced was expressed in him only by his unquenchable thirst. On the road, he drank at each stream and now didn't stop asking for water. The old man stayed with the detachment as a guide. The *Ras* let the captive woman go free, having given her a shamma and having repeated to her that she should pass on to her fellow tribespeople the invitation to voluntarily submit.

I went to bed quite sick. Bees had stung me badly during the reconnaissance. Going down from a steep mountain by a narrow rocky trail, I suddenly noticed that the people who were walking ahead for some reason fell to the ground and covered their heads with their *shammas*. Not understanding what was going on, I continued to ride farther; but I no sooner succeeded in going a few steps, when bees swarmed around me and my mule; and the mule, like a lunatic, galloped down the trail. I beat the bees off as best I could, but nothing helped. Finally, I pulled my helmet over my ears, put my hands, in my pockets and let the mule go as it pleased. The mule at full gallop carried itself away from the mountain and, at the bottom, literally flew into a crowd of Abyssinians who had gone down there at the appearance of the bees. They covered me and the mule with *shammas* and killed the insects. By evening I had a high fever, my head ached, and my face was very swollen.

FEBRUARY 6

At 5 o'clock in the morning, the sharp sound of a signal horn from the *Ras*'s headquarters woke me. Twenty minutes later there followed a second signal, indicating that the *Ras* was setting out. Along the path that went right by my tent, a crowd of people surged. Leaving Zelepukin with the transport, I jumped on my mule and, together with my gun bearers, rushed to join the *Ras*. Feeling better, I rode beside him. His marvellous mule ambled, and the cavalry went at a trot, and the infantry ran to try to keep pace behind him.

Along the way stood regiments that had formed up with their officers and with those soldiers who were free from duties, to meet the commander. In answer to the greeting of the *Ras*: "Endyet walatchukh?" ("How are you?"), pronounced by his agafari, they bowed to the ground and then quickly joined the moving column. Where the terrain allowed them to walk in formation, they formed a reserve column. Or they stretched out on trails in a long uninterrupted file.

Having sent scouts (salay) ahead, the regiment of *Fitaurari* Atyrsye went in the vanguard. Behind the vanguard went the main forces, and behind them followed the transport, under guard of soldiers who did not have units. Finally, at the tailend of the column, went the rearguard—the wobo.[77]

We went very quickly long the road we had reconnoitered the day before. By the pace of the march, the vanguard shortened the time required for stretching out the whole column, which was made difficult by the long-accepted Abyssinian custom of the whole army breaking camp at the same time.

With piercing cries of "Hid! Hid!" "Go! Go!" officers who were riding behind urged the foot soldiers ahead, and the seemingly indefatiguable soldiers ran easily, without tiring. Their lean, well-proportioned figures were remarkably warlike and beautiful. In this apparently undisciplined army, an astonishing rise of spirit and energy was felt!

Having come alongside one of the hills which rise not far from the road, I separated from the column and climbed it to examine the territory. I spent a short while on the summit, and the vanguard of the column did not go far off. But when I went down from the hill, I found myself amid such a dense mass of people and animals that I couldn't get out of it; and only at the bivouac, did I connect with the *Ras* again. Like an endless worm, the transport, wriggled quietly, following the detachment. Dust rose high over the column. Soldiers, women, children, horses, donkeys, and mules went alternately in a dense mass, and an unimaginable groan—in which were mixed the roar of animals, loud laughter, cries, and swears—hovered above this crowd...

Spontaneously, by an irrepressibly powerful flow, this human sea rushed forward, following its leaders. Imagination involuntarily carried me to the distant times of the emigrations of peoples.

How various are faces and types! Here is an old experienced warrior, with a thick black beard, with a large scar on his face from a saber blow in some battle, who drives in front of him a small heavily loaded donkey. And what hasn't he loaded on it!

Here is the soldier's felt coat "burnoose" and his little tent, and two skins filled with grain, and a skin with meal and every kind of household article—a wooden bowl in which to knead bread, an iron pan, etc. The little donkey quietly trudges along under its burden, and the owner urges it on from behind and, driving it, calmly repeats: "Hid, vandyme, hid" "Go, brother, go!"

But the donkey is tired of going. It is hot, stifling, dusty. Here it sees on the side of the road a branchy tree and, abruptly turning, runs under its shade and stops—to the complete vexation of its owner, who now rewards his recent "brother" with strokes of the cane, and at the same time runs through the entire lexicon of Abyssinian swear words. Behind the soldiers walks his wife—a young, beautiful Abyssinian woman who carries on her back a gourd in which dough for bread is soured. A boy—a relative or the son of the soldier—carries on his shoulders a bunch of stakes for the tent, a gun and a shield.

Beside this group walks an enormous solider—a Galla with a manly, but savage expression on his face. He has no baggage. He wears all his property on his person. His clothing does not hide his magnificent musculature. He wears only trousers. He rolled his shamma up into a ball and placed it under a skin full of grain, which he carries on his head. From his cartridge belt, one or two cartridges stick out. Behind his belt is a small dagger. On his shoulders is an old Remington, which the Abyssinians call "Snayder."

Here come the tej-byet, the people who cook honey for the *Ras*. A whole file of women carries fermenting tej on their backs, in pitchers, wrapped round with red shawls. The women who carry the pitchers merrily flirt with the soldiers, sometimes get into a squabble with one another, crack jokes about friends, and burst out in ringing laughter. The head of the honey-cooks rides behind them, having covered his nose with his shamma, and has such an important look about him as if he were the commander-in-chief.

Here too is the wot-byet—the kitchen crew of the *Ras*. Several mules carry various utensils and the cook tent, which is made of black woolen material. The head of the kitchen and the chief cooks ride on mules, silently, with dignity. The female cooks act like the greatest dandies. They adorn themselves with silver necklaces, rings, and bracelets. Close by them walks a file of women of the *injera*-byet—the bakery. They carry on their backs dough, fermenting in large gourds. They are just as merry as their friends in the tej-byet. Here is the baggage transport of the *Ras*—a whole herd of mules loaded with all kinds of provisions, surrounded by teamsters, under the supervision of the head of the transport—chincha-shuma. Having reached the edge of the heights, the road narrows and goes down along a very steep rocky slope, winding along ledges, which only allow passage by one person at a time. A whole sea of people and animals is backed up before the descent. And behind them more and more masses arrive. The growing crowd becomes an impetuous, deep river, which has suddenly been dammed. It seemed that calamity could not be avoided. In other words, it would only take for those behind to press on those in front to clear a place, and those waiting on the edge of the precipice would fall headlong into the abyss. But to my great astonishment, this didn't happend, and the crowd seemed to discipline itself. They made a lot of noise, but order stayed exemplary and each tried to support the other. If someone tried to push ahead, cries and incantations immediately poured on him from all sides: "Ba Wolda Giyorgis Amlak! Ba gora!" (In the name of the God of Wolda Giyorgis! In the name of the ravine!"). And the guilty party stopped, because otherwise his comrades would use force against him. The difficult descent was traversed safely, without any misfortune. I, for exmaple, was not even once pressed. This was the first time I had ever seen such intelligence and judgement in a crowd, which struck me and forced me to more deeply consider the seeming disorder of the Abyssinian army.

We forded the little Kila River, and the sound of a horn informed us that the head of the column was setting up camp. In one of the clearings, the tent of the *Ras* shown white. The front sector of the bivouac was oriented to the side toward which the entrance was turned. Orienting themselves by that, the commanders of regiments laid out their headquarters. And based on that, the order of their units was established. My tent was laid out in front of the tent of the *Ras*. To the left of me was *Dajazmatch* Balay; to the right was Geta-Wali; in front was the head of the guard, AgafariMentyr; and beside him were the kettledrummers who immediately on their arirval at camp had begun the beat which corresponded to that event. Behind the first large tent of the *Ras*, which served him as dining hall and reception room, stood a second smaller tent with a double roof, in which was located the bedroom. Behind those were spread out various deparments of the on-the-march housekeeping of the *Ras*: tej-byet, *injera*-byet, wot-byet, sega-byet, gymja-byet (honey cooking, bread baking, kitchen, butcher, storeroom), his mules and horses at tethering posts, etc. Here was stationed the secretary of the *Ras* and Ato Bayu. The headquarters of the commander-in-chief was surrounded by tents of his guard. At the entrance of the camp, a unit of soliders was deployed in the vicinity, searching for forage or provisions, and at the same time finding good places for pasture and watering of animals.

The mules, as soon as they were unsaddled, were let to graze, and commanders designated the units to be on duty, who were stationed at some distance around the camp. When I arrived at the bivouac, the *Ras* in his tent read the Psalms and prayers which had been determined in the morning by the occasion of a fast day (Wednesday). Around his headquarters sat officers who were waiting for dinner time—"when the shadow of a man is the length of seven steps"—since during a fast one is only permitted to eat after noon. The commander-in-chief asked me through his agafari to set out quickly to scout the road for tomorrow; and before I set out, he invited me to come and drink a glass of vodka. I entered the tent. The *Ras*, sitting cross-legged on the bed with a book on his knees, read the Psalter aloud quickly. Not interrupting his reading, he acknowledged my arrival with a bow. Gerazmatch Zemadenakh gave me a glass of vodka ("turpentine" is what Zelepukin and I called it); and when I drank, he covered me with a flap of his clothing. Then the *Ras* and I said good-bye in the same silent manner that he had greeted me, and I set out on reconnaissance.

At 11 o'clock in the morning, we got started and began to go up the crest of the heights. When I stopped here to take the noontime solar observations, beside me a battle started between our soldiers who had gone off to the side and Shuro who suddenly attacked them. The Abyssinians soon fought back the attack, losing one dead and two wounded. A spear pierced the throat of the dead one, and the others were hit in the chest. We left several men to bury him, and moved ahead ourselves.

The territory farther along seemed even more thickly settled, but the inhabitants were not at all visible. They went away to the depth of the country, driving their cattle; and only warriors followed us from a distance. At 5 o'clock in the evening, we returned to camp.

The *Ras* met me with questions: "Did you find a road? Did you screw up the sun?" (That's what he called solar observations). And "Do we have many degrees left to go?" To the last question I had to answer that we had as much a journey ahead of us as we had the day before. Actually, we had traversed in today's march no more than 10 versts [six miles] to the south. Indeed, with such a large army, it was impossible to move any faster. A 30,000-man army with 10,000 animals had to move along a narrow trail which only allowed them to go one at a time, which meant the journey had to stretch out for five to seven hours. The most we could go would be 20 versts [12 miles], but in that case the rearguard would only arrive in the evening. Evidently, in such circumstances it would take us a long time to get to Lake Rudolf.

The sun set, and the time came for evening prayers. In front of the entrance to the tent, on a spread out carpet stood the commander-in-chief, who had turned his face to the east. Beside him stood the priests of the detachment. And behind him in a semicircle stood his retinue. One of the boys—a page who was standing in front of those who were praying—took an icon out of a leather case and carefully took off the red silk shawl in which it was wrapped. This was an icon of the Mother of God, made in Moscow. At the sight of it, all bowed down to the ground. A public prayer service began. This service is called "Udasye Maryam", which means "glorification of the Mother of God." The priests read the prescribed prayers to themselves, Most of those present knew them by heart and, in a whisper, repeated them after the priests. This hour was the time when the next night's watch came on duty at the headquarters of the *Ras*. They arrived in the middle of the prayer with their full complement and armed for battle. Having bowed to the ground before the *Ras*, the watch stood opposite him in a front. The stern faces of the soldiers, the inspired look of the *Ras*, the quiet rustle of the wind in the thick leaves of an enormous sycamore, were mixed together with the whisper of his prayer... At the end of the prayer service, one of the debters several times went round those who were praying, giving each group the name of a saint to whom it should pray. Then a priest read the recessional "Our Father," and the prayer service ended.

This prayer produced a magical impression. With the detachment in the midst of unknown lands, we were like on a ship, lost in a boundless ocean. Who of us will be left here and who will return?...

The *Ras* went into his tent and, after several minutes, sent his agafari to ask for me. Abyssinian etiquette requires that the host go into his house before the guest.

The prisoners taken that day were interrogated and then let free. Our guide recognized one of the prisoners as his grandson. Their meeting was remarkably moving. When the *Ras* gave him the boy, the old man tenderly hugged his child, cried from joy, and beat himself on the chest. They were both fed and taken away to camp.

One after the other, military leaders of the *Ras* entered the tent to take their leave and say good-bye to the commander-in-chief. The agafari gave them their orders and duties for the following day. Finally, the tent became empty, and we were served dinner. The official day of the *Ras* ended. Evening was dedicated to conversation with his friends and to rest. For dinner, the usual guests of the *Ras* gathered: *Dajazmatch* Balay, Geta-Wali, and the detachment's monastic priest, the confessor of the *Ras*, Aba Wolda Madkhyn. We were given a handwashing. The female cooks brought several baskets with *injera* and little pots with food that had been prepared for us. Aba Wolda Madkhyn read a prayer, and we began our modest meal.

I remember these minutes with pleasure. I vividly recall now the tent of the *Ras*—long, round, covered over inside with green cloth, supported by one internal post. On one of the sides stands the camp bed, and over it stands a small canopy made of white canvas. Here a gnarled pole stuck into the ground serves as a rack for all the guns and ammunition belts of the *Ras*. On one of its twigs hangs a pocket watch. The host sits on the bed, crossing his legs under himself. We arrange ourselves beside him on the carpet. Leaning against the supporting post of the tent stands one of the pages of the *Ras*. He holds in his hands a long wax candle which throws its dim light on the handsome face of the page, who time and again thoughtfully removes the candlesnuff, and on the group of those standing around nearby— *elfin ashkers*, agafari and others of the *Ras*'s retinue. The light did not penetrate in the corners of the tent.

The lively talk did not stop. Everyone, even the youngest, took part in the conversation. The commander-in-chief and his comrades-in-arms seemed to me like a large family, united by strong bonds of comradeship in battle.

I also remember the *Ras*'s entourage. Here is Ilma, a black gun-bearer of enormous size, whom they tormented for his Galla origin. Here is the elegant secretary Ato-Melk, whom they force to tell about his love affairs. Here is little feeble Gerazmatch Zemadyenakh, who is devoted like a dog to the *Ras* and doesn't take his eyes off his host. No one can serve the *Ras* as he does. He knows how to lay down a pillow, and how to stretch weary legs... The Gerazmatch is deaf. They make jokes at his expense, laugh at him, but he doesn't hear it. The brave Kanyazmatch Alemnekh serves as the reference book for all historical stories. He remembers everything; and when the *Ras* begins to tell some story, he turns constantly to Alemnekh for him to tell the details... Agafari Mentyr is a very meticulous veteran. He always stands in the same spot at the entrance to the tent and holds in his hands a long staff. Conversation doesn't interest him. He is involved in fulfilling his duties and waits until the *Ras* finishes eating and the time comes to call the others who have been invited to dinner. Two boy-pages stand hugging one another. They evidently want to go to sleep. One of them, without doubt, is a future hero. I observed today how he at the campfire proved his manhood to his contemporaries by burning his hand with a smoldering rag. On the burnt spots, bright black marks will remain, and the skin will look like the pelt of a leopard...

And the friends of the *Ras* were also interesting: *Dajazmatch* Balay, Geta-Wali, and Aba Wolda Madkhyn.

Dajazmatch Balay was deprived of his estate for a civil war with the neighboring sovereign of Wolo—the *Ras* Wali (cousin of the Empress Taytu)—and was sent to Kaffa to *Ras* Wolda Giyorgis. Before this, he spent a year in fetters at the court of Menelik and only on the insistence of Wolda Giyorgis, whose wife was the Emperor's cousin, was Balay's punishment softened. *Dajazmatch* Balay is well known for his bravery, and Menelik calls him his most courageous Tigrean. Balay is lean, with rare beauty, a typical Abyssinian aristocrat. The color of his skin is remarkably light for an Abyssinian. For this he is indebted to his descent from some *Ras* Ali, a newcomer from Arabia. The manner of the *Dajazmatch* is always distinguished by unusual dignity, and in all his conduct you sense a natural gentleman. The *Ras* is amazingly delicate in his relationship with Balay, who is under his power. The *Dajazmatch* is by rank lower than the *Ras*, on whom he is by his present position completely dependent. Almost the same age as the *Ras*, the *Dajazmatch* is quite ruined. The *Ras* fed him and his servants, lent him money, clothed him, and showed him, in view of his former glory and the misfortune which had befallen him, honors the likes of which would not be shown to one's equal. The *Ras*, for example, rose when the *Dajazmatch* entered and answered the greeting of the *Dajazmatch* by bowing to the ground.

Geta-Wali is an old friend of Wolda Giyorgis. He is chief of one of the most warlike Mohammedan tribes in Walo, renowned for his despearte audacity and horsemanship. This man is fifty years old, of tall stature, with a thick black beard and whiskers cut short, which gives him a rather fierce appearance. The *Ras* got to know him during one of the wars of Menelik gainst *Ras* Mikael. They became friends despite the difference of their religions, which in Abyssinia is a big obstacle to intimacy. Now setting out on the campaign, the *Ras* let his old friend know about it; and Geta-Wali left home and family and rushed to his call-up.

One of the most sympathetic personalities was the priest of our detachment—Aba Wolda Madkhyn. An idealist and dreamer, quiet, gentle, tolerant toward others, but strict with himself, he represented a complete contrast to the lawyers found among the Abyssinian clergy, who with blind devotion to ritual call to mind the ancient scribes and Pharisees. All withered, having turned into a mummy from strictly observing fasts regardless of circumstances; with all his seeming frailty, he displayed remarkable powers of endurance and never showed signs of weariness.

When our dinner neared its end and the treasurer of the *Ras*, the head of the gymja-byet (storeroom), gave us coffee[78], the retinue of the *Ras* sat down to dinner. First came the most senior of the suite: Ato Bayu, Kanyazmatch Alemnekh, Agafari

Mentyr, Gerazmatch Zamadyenakh, and others. After them came the rest of the retinue, and, finally, the *elfin ashkers* (pages).

Not far away, kettledrums were beat, using the customary rhythm for the evening. In the distance there resounded muffled gloomy sounds which the Abyssinians through should frighten the enemy. The entertainment ended. We finished drinking our decanters of dull unfermented tej, which to us on the march seemed like the height of perfection. Then having heard the after-dinner prayer read by Aba Wolda Madkhin, we said farewell to the *Ras* and went to our own headquarters.

Near the exit from the tent, *ashkers* who had come for me were waiting. Escorted by them, I returned to my camp. One of the pages, by order of the *Ras*, lighted my way by torch.

Work was already awaiting me at home. I had to write down my observations in my journal, to plot today's route on the map, to unload and load again my photographic apparatus. Only at 11 o'clock did I manage to go to bed.

February 7

At 5:30 in the morning, we set out and stretched out in the usual marching column. Having gone 15 versts [9 miles], we set up camp on a plateau which constitutes the watershed of the Sebelimu and Kilu Riveers, near Shuro settlements. They set up the tent of the *Ras* in the shade of a huge sycamore. They built a platform. On its branches and fit a ladder to it. From there, the *Ras* examined the countryside with a telescope. As soon as I arrived at the bivouac, I set out, by order of the *Ras*, on reconnaissance with the regular regiment of Kanyazmatch Alemnekh. Like on the day before, I was accompanied by Ato Bayu, Gebra Maryam, and the old prisoner. This time the prisoner carried his grandson, with whom he didn't want to be parted for anything. The countryside was the same as what we had seen the day before. It was just as densely populated, but we didn't see inhabitants anywhere. We only came across one dead body—a completely naked, huge Shuro, who had died of a gunshot wound while running away. There were copper and iron bracelets on him, and beside him lay a spear and a shield.

At 4 o'clock in the afternoon, we returned to camp. As usual, some sick and wounded were waiting for me. One who was very seriously wounded was brought on a strechter. He had set out the day before looking for booty, and with several comrades he had gone off to the side from the camp. The Shuro had attacked them from ambush and killed one of them. A spear went through the back of this one and came out the abdomen near the navel. The wounded man, however, did not lose consciousness. He took the spear out himself and continued to defend himself by firing back until help came to him. The wound looked very bad. Intestines hung out from a hole about the size of a fist, by which the spear had exited. The intestines were so squeezed at the edges of the wound that to put them back in place I would have to extend the cut. But this would be completely useless and could only lead to censure if the man were to die from my operation. I covered the wound with iodioform and bandaged it. The wounded man suffered badly, but did not moan nor complain. Evidently, he had no doubt of the outcome of his wound and peacefully awaited death. He died the following day.

That day we captured several women. They were just as ugly as those captured earlier. Their lips were also pierced. One of the captives was wife of a local prince, and in her bosom they found some kind of flatcake, similar to a piece of hardened cinder. It turned out that this is salt which the Shuro exchange for cattle with the Dulume tribe which lives near the Shorma or Shorum (Omo) River. Here salt is very valuable, and is owned only by the wealthy, who use it as a great delicacy. The Dulume prepared these flatcakes with cinders of some kind of grass, mixing it with water.[79]

Before sunset, I made solar obsevations to determine the angle of the hour. The *Ras* was curious to see how "to screw up the sun," and his escort crowded around my instrument. I showed Wolda Giyorgis the sun, which amazed him by its quick passage across the hairline. And I even gave him a short lecture on astronomy, explaining setting up the instrument by levels, the meaning of the calculations, the annual revolution and daily rotation of the Earth, etc. He listened to me very attentively; and most of what I said he retold in his own way to his entourage, who in amazement only quickly clicked their tongues, "Ts, ts, ts, ts!" Others spread the word, expressing astonishment with the exclamation "Oyyougud. Ytjyg!" etc., making urgent jerky movements toward the instrument to see how it happened that the heavens shone in a tube.

After sunset was over, there was the usual evening prayer, after which I, having eaten at home, occupied myself with developing photographs.

For dinner, the *Ras* sent me some marvelous white fragrant honeycomb honey. This served as the occasion for Zelepukin to formulate in the following manner thoughts which had probably interested him for some time.

"Here, your Honor, in this country they go too far: they cut honeycombs in February!"

February 8

It was the last day before Lent[80], which is strictly observed by Abyssinians both at home and on the march. Abyssinian military leaders wait with impatience for the beginning of Lent, since at this time soldiers do not use raw meat and therefore are more protected from illness.

On the occasion of the day before Lent, the *Ras* held a great feast. All officers and the most senior soldiers were invited, as well as Zelepukin and my *ashkers*. The bakery was busy the whole night. In the morning, several dozen bulls and rams were slaughtered. Both tents of the *Ras*, joined as one, formed a room where about 200 people could assemble at once.

At 9 o'clock in the morning, one of the *elfin ashkers* came to call me to the feast which was proceeding in the usual order, not differing from those which the *Ras* gave his troops at his place in the capital. Among the soldiers, there was a singer who delighted us with his voice during dinner. Only at 3 o'clock in the afternoon did we go back to our headquarters.

Returning home, I noticed that someone had been in my tent in my absence, since some of the negatives which had already been developed and some of the ones still in the bath were ruined. I conducted a strict interrogation, and it turned out that the guilty party was Adera, my second cook. He wanted to drink. There wasn't any water in the camp, so he drank the contents of the bath. Adera stubbornly denied that he did it, but Faison saw him drink and confirmed his testimony with an oath on his gun. By the way, the ritual of this oath is interesting: they stuck Faisa's loaded gun in his belly, cocked, and he, pronouncing an oath, licked the barrel of the gun with his tongue. Adera could not say anything against such testimony and was severely punished.

February 9

At 5:30 in the morning, we set out and by 10 o'clock set up camp on the banks of the Sebelimu River, having gone down from an elevation of 1,600 meters above sea level to the altitude of 1,000 meters. The descent was steep and rocky. We began to come across granite and gneiss rocks.

The Sebelimu River flows into the Menu River. At this place it is a rather sizable little river (25 paces in width), with a very swift current. Among the numerous kinds of acacia which overgrew its banks, I for the first time saw a tree which subsequently, further south, I came across more frequently. Similar to the acacia in appearance, it differed from the acacia in its enormous fruit, which from a distance looked like large elephant tusks. Each fruit, by its basic structure, calls to mind the cucumber, and is an average of one to one and a half arshins in length and up to a quarter arshin in cross-section, [arshin = 28"]. Its shell is rather strong, and the core is soft with small white seeds, like a watermelon.

From camp, I set out on reconnaissance with two regiments, those of Gerazmatch Zamadymakh and Kanyazmatch Wolda Tensae. With them, I went across the uninhabited valley of the Sebelimu River and climbed the mountain. The countryside seemed rather densely populated, but not concentrated in a definite center—rather in small groups.

In one of the ravines, we came across two women. One of them, who was young, rushed to run away with a scream. The other, an old woman, was quite peaceful and not at all confused. She came to us. She was terribly ugly. Her few teeth stuck out, and in place of knocked-out lower incisors a black breach was seen. She was called Belemusa. She was a market woman; and, therefore, she knew the surrounding territory extremely well. She agreed to serve us as a guide. We let the young Negro girl go and brought the old woman back to camp with us. It turns out that all trade among these people is conducted by old women who go freely over all the lands of the various tribes. Men are not allowed inside the boundaries of another tribe.

On my return, I had a meeting with the *Ras* about the rationale behind our daily reconnaissance. To me, these missions didn't seem to be accomplishing their goal, because we were only checking out a very limited region—not more than four to five hours of the route ahead of the bivouac. Besides, this reconnaissance involved a very large and wasteful outlay of troops. In addition, in recent days the regular members of the reconnaissance—I, Ato Bayu and our *ashkers*—had been setting out at 5 o'clock in the morning and not returning to camp until 4 to 5 o'clock in the afternoon, going all that time without food. According to the Abyssinian way of thinking, it would be absurd to take food with you on a military enterprise if you would have to bring it back with you to camp at night.[81]

Moreover, the regiments assigned to reconnaissance were worn out pointlessly, forced to do in one day at least a triple march. In other words, they set out together with the troops of the *Ras* and went with them to the next bivouac, and from there they immediately went further to find a new bivouac site, and then went back again. Longer-range reconnaissance would, in my opinion, be more useful. Then we could report better regarding territory lying farther ahead and select a more convenient route for the detachment. In that case, people would not have to make a double trip there and back, but rather, having fulfilled their mission, they would stay and wait for the arrival of the main forces or of new orders.

I told the *Ras* these ideas, and he agreed with me. Having gathered his *Fitaurari* in a military council, he told them the following:

"Yskynder Bulatovich finds that our present close-range reconnaissance isn't of much use. He advises that we undertake more distant ones. What do you say to that?"

The majority approved of my proposal, but since separating oneself from the main forces by a significant distance was against the spirit of Abyssinian tactics, it was decided that tomorrow we would only move ahead two days' march and, having reconnoitred the road and chosen a camp site, we would send a message to the *Ras* and would wait there for his arrival.

February 10

At dawn we set out on reconnaissance with the regiment of *Fitaurari* Imam. We left our whole transport with the main forces and only the leaders took with them by mule, a tent, and some provisions. Zelepukin rode with me. We sat the guide Belemusa on a mule owned by one of the soldiers of *Fitaurari* Imam. The old woman, who before this had never seen a mule, was afraid to sit on it. Several soldiers picked her up—some by the legs, some by the arms—and, to general laughter, lifted her onto the animal. At this moment Belemusa was a pretty sight: she was all bent over forward, clutching hold of the front arch of the saddle, her naked legs dangling helplessly. The soldiers laughed and made fun of her, but this didn't offend her. Making a disgusting grimace, she tried to smile.

Along a trail that had been trampled down by fleeing Shuro, we went up a mountain spur which stretched to the south of the main mountain ridge. At about 10 o'clock in the morning, we went up to the summit of Golda (1,800 meters above sea leve). From there I took azimuths on surrounding mountains, and Belemusa told me the names of the nearest of them. Mount Golda is covered with grass and bushes. Its slopes are quite densely populated by Shuro. The *Ras* set his bivouac on the banks of a stream, at the natural boundary of Gornu. Having gone down from the mountain, we moved farther to the southwest and soon arrived at the steep edge of the spur. Below began the wide valley of an unknown river which Belemusa named very inconsistently: either Chomu or another. In the southeast towered a mountain ridge about which she, likewise, did not give me any information, pleading complete ignorance both of its name and of who and how many people lived there.

We went down into a valley from an elevation of 1,600 meters to 1,000 meters above sea level and set camp at the natural boundary of Shabali, at the foot of the mountain spur.

While we were climbing Mount Golda, our soldiers had a little skirmish with the natives, killing several of them; and on the way down, we captured a Shuro who had hidden in bushes near the road. This was an old man of 60 to 70 who was barely moving, and who looked quite unlike a Negro. The color of his skin was lighter. The features of his face were rather regular. His clothing, in contrast to others, consisted of a long, excellently worked oxhide, thrown over one shoulder and the ends skillfully set in iron rings. Several iron and copper bracelets and one belt adorned his arms. On his neck, on a small strap, hung a snuff box made from a small tusk of a wild boar. His spear was also distinguished by more elegant decoration. The prisoner cursed the whole time and did not want to answer questions. He didn't seem to be an ordinary Negro; so we, having lifted him onto a saddle, took him with us to camp. There, after we had fed him, he became more gracious and answered several of our questions. The old man turned out to be the prince of this territory and was named Komoruti-Geda. In the west, according to his words, Shuro also live along the mountain spur, in the territory named Jiri. He was friends with their prince, and sometimes he went there to drink beer with him. But he couldn't tell us anything definite about the southeast of this mountain range.

"That's not our land, and I don't know it."

He also said that over there, in two to three day's journey, lies a land which is abundant in bread grain, and that, on the contrary, on this side, except for elephants and other wild animals, there is nothing. We asked him again, dozens of times, and still could not get a definite answer. The interpreter, Gabro Maryam, was worn out repeating all these questions and hearing the same negative answer: "Y, y, y."

For the time being, we had to be content with suppositions and guesses. Taking into account that the mountain range seen in the south wasn't so far distant from us that the climatic conditions could be different or that on it there would likely be less water than on this spur, we decided that it must be populated like this one; but that its populace probably belonged to a different nationality. The main direction of our journey should go through these mountains, and it would be necessary to reconnoitre them. In this spirit, the *Fitaurari* sent a report to the *Ras*, and we stayed to wait for his arrival.

On all the trails, we saw fresh signs of people and animals. In the vicinity of the bivouac, time and again there resounded gun shots of our soldiers who had gotten into fights with Shuro.

This day a few dozen Negroes were killed and one Abyssinian. One Negro attacked my ashker Wolda Markyn from ambush. While Wolda Markyn was pulling up grass for the mules, the Negro threw a spear at him, but, fortunately, missed. The opponents grappled hand to hand, and Wolda Markyn knocked the native out with a dagger. Evidently, all the populace who had fled was concentrating in this valley and was getting ready to desperately resist the Abyssinians. We, therefore, expected an attack. We laid out our bivouac more compactly and posted a strong guard, and at night set out large campfires along the edge of the camp. However, these precautions turned out to be unnecessary. The night passed quite peacefully.

FEBRUARY 11

At ten o'clock in the morning, the *Ras* arrived with the head of the column and conducted a second interrogation of Komoruti-Geda, after which, at council meeting, it was decided to go with the whole detachment farther west to the foot of Mount Jasha on the following day, and to set up camp there. The regiments of *Fitaurari* Dameti and *Fitaurari* Gebra Maryam, together with me and Ato-Bayu, would set out to investigate the mountains to the south; and the regiment of *Fitaurari* Chabude would move to the west with the same goal. The *Ras* would wait in place for definitive results from both reconnaissance missions. For that time, the troops would replenish their reserves of provisions in the mountains.

The *Ras*'s prohibition against entering into battle with the natives now seemed unfeasible. The natives evidently had no intention of submitting; and, on the contrary, they attacked first. Just as the day before, the surroundings resounded with gun shots and in camp, time and again, you met victorious soldiers singing victory songs, with trophies, prisoners and livestock taken by force.

Several dead men were carried in, and comrades loudly mourned the deceased. Several wounded were brought to me for bandaging. One of them was suffering very badly. A spear had passed through his chest, going in the right shoulder blade and going out around the middle of his chest, at the level of his nipple. In the back, the width of the wound was five and a half centimeters; and in front, it was three and a half. In addition, the palm of his right hand was badly cut, having caught the point of the spear, which was sticking out, at the moment of impact. The flesh between the middle and index fingers was severed to the bone. I washed the wounds and covered them with iodoform and stitched them.

Out troops did not distrub the women and children. Only Galla soldiers brought in livestock since the Abyssinians could not use meat during Lent. Therefore, the Galla ate their full that day. The area around our bivouac was littered with ox innards and the chopped off heads and bones of animals killed the day before. Struck by their quantity, I couldn't help but ask myself—how many pounds of meat did each man need?

FEBRUARY 12

We went to the foot of Mount Jasha. The detachment set up camp there, and two regiments (*Fitaurari* Gebra Maryam and *Fitaurari* Faris) set out on reconnaissance. I rode with them. We left all the transport with the main forces and only took with us provisions for ten days.

We went down into the low-lying valley of the Chomu River (which is at an elevation of 800 meters above sea level) and went in the direction of the spur of the mountain range seen on the horizon. The terrain here is very rocky, overgown with short grass and occasional trees. Among the stones are found granites of the most diverse coloring, flints and mica shales.

The valley of the Chomu River is completely deserted. The water is held in holes, in dry river channels, the vicinity of which abounds in wild life. We came upon elephant tracks, but we did not see the animals themselves.

At four o'clock in the afternoon, we crossed the riverbed of the Chomu and took a short break on its banks. Here we found water in a deep hole and watered our mules. It was very hot. My head and eyes ached from the blinding light of the sun, which reflected in myriad beams in the bright rocks scattered around. I felt very weak—probably the old fever was coming back to me.

But *Fitaurari* Gebra Maryam—a cheerful, carefree soldier, a fine swordsman who never let pass an occasion to drink with a good fellow—drove away my weariness. He gave me a large horn cup of his strong tej, which one of the *ashkers* always carried for him in a huge ox horn. The mead made me a bit intoxicated, but it also cheered me up.

We went farther. When it had become quite dark, we set up camp for the night in a hollow near a small water hole. Fires shone on the mountains opposite us. Evidently there were people there. But our former guide, Belemusa, did not know what people live in those places. In that day we covered 58 versts [35 miles], and we were still about 15-20 versts [10-13 miles] from the mountains.

FEBRUARY 13

We didn't set fires at night, and we got up before dawn and quickly set off toward the mountains. The regiment of *Fitaurari* Gebra Maryam went first, at the head of which rode the commander of the regiment, Ato Bayu, and I. Behind us, in a front several files wide, went the officers and mounted soldiers. Fifteen paces behind them, also in a front several files wide, advanced the foot soldiers of the regiment. Behind the first regiment, at a distance of 50 paces, went the second regiment, in the same order. They were commanded not by *Fitaurari* Faris himself, who because of illness stayed behind with the main forces, but rather by his most senior officer.

At about eight o'clock in the morning, we saw huts of natives not far off. And near them, we saw a herd of cattle peacefully grazing. Natives noticed us and raised the alarm. The mountains resounded with cries. Warriors ran in small groups and rushed to meet us. We moved ahead without shooting, having made the translator call out that they should calm down, that we wanted peace with them. But they evidently didn't understand the Shuro language in which the translator was speaking, and little by little, they surrounded our detachment from all sides. One javelin and another flew at our side. A stone thrown from a sling whistled past my ears. It would have been senseless to hold back our men any longer, since we had not come this far just to sacrifice soldiers. The long awaited command of *Fitaurari* Gebra Maryam resounded: "Belau!" ("Go ahead!") And our whole mounted detachment threw itself at the enemy at full gallop. The natives did not stand up to the onslaught, and scattered in all directions. But not a single man from our regiments stayed in place. Having for a long time thirsted for battle, our soldiers rushed in a frenzy to take advantage of the situation which presented itself and to finally obtain the laurels about which they had been dreaming from the first days of the campaign. Each sought a victim for himself...

A whole series of individual skirmishes now took place in front of us. Here an Abyssinian jumps on a mule and urges it forward with all the strength of his legs, pursuing a naked young native who is running about twenty paces ahead of him. The Abyssinian lifts a saber high, perparing to strike, but the native dodges. He has two spears and a shield in his arms, but he doesn't even consider defending himself, but rather rushes to the nearest house. Another soldier on a small frisky horse, his shamma fluttering in the wind, cuts off the path of the fugitive. Now the first soldier overtakes him. The saber flashes; and the native falls, spilling blood. With victory cries of "I am zarraf!" ("killer"), the winner seizes his victim by the hair and slits his throat with the customary dexterous *moti*on of the saber. The eyes of the victor look senseless, wild. He is drunk with blood, and at this moment he seems insane.

Here an Abyssinian foot soldier overtakes another native. The soldier shoots and misses. The man he is chasing quickly turns around and throws a spear at the Abyssinian. The Abyssinian is now in a helpless position. He doesn't have a saber, and he couldn't reload his gun... But now nearby resounds the obliging shot of a comrade, and the native falls—the full length of his enormous body—dead.

One of the wounded managed to hide in a house, but the trail of blood on the sand gave him away. A soldier throws himself headlong after the tracks, but falls dead on the doorstep, pierced through with a spear... Comrades of the brave man surround the house, which is dark inside. No one decides to go inside, and the soldiers crowd around the lair where the fox has just hidden. One of them finds a match, and after a few moments, the house goes up in flames. Like a madman, the native jumps out of the flames, but a well-aimed shot from an Abyssinian kills him on the spot. His wife runs out after him, and the soldiers take her prisoner. The unfortunate woman shudders from the terror she had just lived through and, stretching out her arms with the palms of the hands up, she mutters something disconnectedly, probably begging for mercy. She is rather pretty. On her completely naked body, iron trinkets are attached to a small strap at the waist. Her hair is smeared with yellow clay. A large stone earring is displayed on her ear... Over there, two young soldiers pursue two natives. Despairing of escaping, the natives who are fleeing throw themselves on their knees and lower their heads to the very ground, submissively awaiting death. I see this scene from afar and cry out to the soldiers, "Do not kill! Do not kill! Do not kill! Take them prisoner!." But the soldiers had recently received guns, and they very much wanted to test the effect of their new weapons. Now they take aim, hurriedly fire two shots, and miss. At that moment, I succeed in catching up with them, and we take the natives prisoner.

On one of the hills, the tent of the *Fitaurari* shone white. It was supposed to serve as a beacon and muster point for the scattered detachment. The soldiers little by little began to gather there. Most of them returned with trophies of victory. All were excited and seemed drunk with killing and with the sight of human blood: nervous jerky movements, feverish brightness of the eyes, unnatural speech. Each told of the events that had befallen him. Several quarrelled and came here to the *Fitaurari* for judgement as to who actually killed such-and-such a native.

More than a hundred men and women were captured. All of them totally did not understand the Shuro language. We had no means whatsoever to talk to them. Finally, we let them go free.

At about 12 o'clock noon, when the detachment had assembled, we moved ahead, intending to climb the densely populated crest of the mountain ridge, which rose steeply several hundred meters above us. Scouts reconnoitered the trail which the natives used to drive their cattle down. Having stretched out in single file, we began to climb cautiously. The way up was very difficult, and the natives could easily have made it completely impassable by blocking the only trail which meanders along the ledge. Letting loose a landslide on us, they could do us great harm. But the morning battle which they saw from the height of their mountains had stunned them. It was as if new, never-before-seen people had fallen from heaven—people who dress in some kind of white clothing and jump on wild animals and kill enemies with puffs of fire, the bang from which resounds like the thunder of a spring storm.

We climbed the mountain ridge unimpeded. Its summit was completely built up. As in other settlements, each farmstead was fenced in. Inside the fence there was a house and excellently cultivated fields. Among the farmsteads went a little road lined with trees. Not far away, on a hill, we could see a small grove of high trees. Beside the grove stood a large house, near which natives crowded. We advanced on them without shooting; and when we got within several hundred paces of them, they threw down their weapons and, raising their hands to the heavens, apparently asked for mercy, crying out to us, "Halio! Halio!"

Our detachment stopped. With signs, we invited the crowd to come near. To definitely convince the natives of our peaceableness, I ordered everyone to sit. I tore up a little bunch of grass and began to show it to the natives. Then some of them, having placed their arms on their chests, and others, having grapsed one hand with the other behind their shoulders and holding it suspended, indecisively came toward us, repeating the whole time "Halio!" At fifteen paces in front of us, they squatted.

Then began negotiations the likes of which have probably occurred only very rarely in military history. Perhaps the situation was similar in the time of Christopher Columbus and Cortez in America. The natives did not understand the Gimiro or Shuro languages and only mumbled in answer to all our questions.

The large house on the hill probably belonged to the chief of the tribe, and I wanted to find out if he was here in front of us or if he had gone. I tried to express this thought in many different ways, but my attempts were in vain. Beside me, separated from the rest of the crowd, stood four negotiators, shaking from fear and depicting the shape of a grape leaf with their hands. Finally, I stood up and set out for the large house. The negotiators became agitated and stood up in front of me as if to ask me not to go there. Now it wasn't difficult to make them understand our wish to see the person who was in this house—the big man himself. The natives understood, mumbled something cheerfully and, asking me to sit, ran to the house. After a few moments, a file of people came from there, carrying on their heads several large gourds filled with a very thick beer (turcha), a small elephant tusk, several hens, several little parcels of honey wrapped in banana leaves, bundles of tobacco and, to crown all, they dragged after them a dog. These gifts were sent to us by Koys, as one of the negotiators kept calling him, while giving us the gifts. We accepted the offering, but to the horror of the natives, the dog broke free and ran away. They threw themselves at it to catch it, but failed; and in place of the runaway dog, they brought us two puppies from the house. Finally, the prince himself made his appearance. He was a tall, fat, bald old man. Like his subjects, he was naked and adorned with a large number of bracelets on the arms and legs. He approached us calmly, filled with a sense of his own dignity, and squatted opposite us. He ordered the negotiator to kiss my hand. The negotiator, approaching me, first clapped his hands and having taken my hand in both of his, turned the palm upward and kissed, opening his lips wide while doing this. The prince said, "Halio! Halio!" The Abyssinians slapped the natives on the shoulders and soon a close friendship was established among them. They brought additional gifts from the house of the prince: several packets of ginger (probably one of their favorite delicacies). I took a little piece, bit off half and gave the other half to Koys. We explained, as best we could, that they should supply us with provisions at our camp; and we went down from the crest of the hill to our previously laid out camp.

The Abyssinians were delighted with the natives. "What kind of Shankala (Negroes) are these?" they asked. "Even though they are naked, this is a civilized people. They respect their king, and their houses are well built, and they were able to submit to us. Real Shankala would run away like animals and would perish to the last man, not realizing that it would be better to submit voluntarily. But why did they give us a dog? Either they are scoundrels and think that we eat dogs or, perhaps, they themselves eat them." This circumstance surprised me as well. Maybe there was some symbolic significance in the gift of a dog, or maybe they really do use them as food. I didn't succeed in finding out.

The inhabitants of these mountains do not resemble any of the tribes that I know. I noticed almost nothing that they had in common with Negroes. Their facial features were beautiful and regular. They had a high forehead. The shape of the skull was oblong. Their eyes were expressive and intelligent. All were of large stature, of strong build, with strongly developed musculature. The large calloused hands of tillers-of-the-soil testified to the industriousness of this people. The hair of some of them hung down to their shoulders and was twisted in small locks. Others had their hair cut short or fluffed up above and sprinkled with ashes. Completely naked, as I already said, the men were adorned with large bracelets made of iron, of ivory, and, rarely, made of copper. I noticed that one of them had on his elbow a large iron bracelet to which was attached a small elephant tusk that stuck out behind. The warriors had the right part of their chest and their arm tatooed, for which several deep incisions were drawn in the form of straight parallel lines with a border, below which was a decorative pattern. This operation must be very painful and is carried out, as I later discovered, with a scorching hot knife. I saw one warrior who had been recently tatooed. His incisions were bright red, and it looked like they had torn all the skin off his arms... All of them had the end of their ears pierced and in them they had put large wooden or stone earrings in the form of a disk, one and a half inches in diameter. Some had bands made of skins wrapped around their heads. Others wore hats made of the skin of some animal. I noticed that many had a special decoration in the middle of their forehead: in the hair in the front, a wooden hairpin stuck out, to which was attached a red pelt, taken from the head of a pretty bird. Perhaps this is some kind of military distinction.

Their armament consists of a large spear and a round leather shield.

The language abounds in whistling dental sounds: t, ts, s. The pronunciation resembles the Gimiro language, but they did not understand one another and even did not know of one another's existence.

The culture of these natives is much higher than that of their Shuro neighbors. Their dome-shaped houses are excellently built. The fields are very deeply dug up and well cultivated. For the most part, the fields are sown with bread grains which are well-known in Ethiopia. Their iron articles seemed extremely well made. We found blacksmith's tools in almost every house.

Their food is for the most part liquid. The preparation of bread, either leavened or unleavened, is apparently unknown to them. In place of bread, they drink a very thick sour liquid, made from meal and seeds of various bread grains. It is not similar to Russian kvas nor to beer. They call it turcha. It is very tasty, remarkably nourishing and is not intoxicating.

At night, from the bivouac *Fitaurari* Gebra Maryam sent a report to the *Ras*. One of the officers carried it with a mixed command of 20 men. We surrounded our camp with an abattis and took precautions in case of a night attack.

I did not have a tent with me and shared quarters with Ato Bayu, whose tent was in the very middle of the camp. Having thrown an Abyssinian shamma on the ground, I laid my head on a saddle, covered myself with a cloak and fell sound asleep, full of the impressions of my recent experiences.

FEBRUARY 14

We climbed the mountains to reconnoiter the lands that lie farther to the south. Part of the detachment stayed in the bivouac and part went with us. Inhabitants met us, squatting along our route. There were no women. We climbed a hill from which the countryside opened up beautifully to us. Here I stopped to carry out some observations. Soon, Koys came and brought some gourds with turcha. He treated our soldiers and then his subjects. His subjects very guardedly took from the their prince a little scoop in both hands and drank from it, two at a time, mouth to mouth. (It is surprising: the rule that you must use two hands to take things from those who are senior to you also exists in Abyssinia). Together with the prince appeared a small clever old man—the one who the day before had been the first to understand me during the negotiations. His face shone with intelligence, and I began to try to find out from him what this land and the surrounding territory is called. Naturally, I had to express myself with signs. I stamped my foot, touched the ground with my palm, then cried out questioningly, etc. I repeated this performance many times, but the old man still did not understand me, but rather just imitated me in all my motions and mumbled like a monkey. Finally, he became awfully happy and cried, "Beru! Ko-Beru! Beru!" He repeated this ten times, touching the ground with his palm and he pointed to the settlement. The most difficult task was done. Now I could find out other names.

The old man called the densely populated hill to the south of Beru "Ko-Kassi." He named the surrounding mountains one after the other: Ko-Garo, Ko-Dami, Ko-Kanta, Ko-Moru. When I didn't know which one he was refering to—the near one or the far one—he cried "i" sharply and with his finger pointed down; when the mountain was far, he snapped his fingers, stretched his arm forward and pronounced "cho-lo-lo-lo-lo-lo..."

February 15

Sunday. The detachment rests. In the morning, I was engaged in a rather original activity—conducting war on the multitudinous inhabitants of my underwear. Ato-Bayu did the same. We sat side by side in light clothes and carried out our work. An old aunt of Ato-Bayu, his constant companion on all his campaigns, bashfully turned away and prepared a drink of honey and water at the other end of the tent. When one of us succeeded in catching a very large specimen, we boasted to one another and showed it to the old aunt. She got embarrassed and cried with horror, "Ere Ba Egziibeer!" "Ah! For God's sake!"

At nine o'clock in the morning, I set up the universal instrument for solar observations. On the day of the battle, I had forgotten to wind up the chronometer, and now I had to determine the moment of true noon by the corresponding heights. In the meantime, I measured the latitude and even managed to eat lunch. My *ashkers* cooked a hen for me on a spit and baked unleavened bread. Already, by this time, I had run out of salt several days before.

After noon, Kira came. (That was the name of the old man who told me the name of the place the day before.) He brought turcha, a small elephant tusk, some packets of coffee, and a large copper bracelet. Kira kissed my hand, laid the gifts down in front of me, and explained that Prince Koys sent them. Then he leaped up and began to mark time, as if he were walking and repeated, "Goro, goro, goro." Finally, he cried out "e" interrogatively. I understood from this that Kira, as a subject of Koys, was asking us to take the gifts and leave their lands. Then I helped Kira sit down, and I myself stood up. Lifting the canvas of the tent a little, I expressed with signs that there at Mount Jasha are found still many more Abyssinians and a very important man who is sending all of them here, and then we would all go south—"goro, goro, goro." At first Kira listened very sadly; but later, when he understood, it pleased him. He jumped up and began to mark time side by side with me and to recount the lands where, according to what he knew, we should go: "Beru! E? Kassi! E? Bais! E? Menu?" At the word "Menu," he mumbed in a long drawn way that probably indicated that Menu is the farthest limit of the lands known to him.

The more we talked, the more Kira and I understood one another. Finally, we even worked out our own language, which consisted of basic gestures and of several words of the Shuro language which were known to both of us. Kira even managed to express to me his position with regard to the king. He came from another land and when he was an infant his mother brought him here. When I asked him if there is a very large river to the south, Kira said that not far away to the east there flows a large river named "Kibish," in which the water is thigh deep; and farther off there is a very large river named "Shorum" in which hippopotamuses swim. In saying that, Kira depicted how they dive and snort. Apparently, Kira did not know about the existence of a large body of standing water to the south—Lake Rudolf.

He sat with me in the tent until evening, entertaining us with songs and dance, and went away only when it had become dark. I asked him to come see me the next day, as soon as the cock crows. Kira understood and promised to appear.

February 16

Kira came early in the morning. I took with me part of the detachment and climbed the mountain, going in the direction of Kassa. We crossed streams which had banks overgrown with dense forest and which served as the boundary between the lands of Kassa and Beru. The inhabitants raised the alarm when they saw us, but Kira called out to them that they should calm down, throw down their weapons, and sit on the ground. Without a shot, we went through their settlements and, having reached a hill from which the surrounding territory was visible far to the south, we stopped. The prince of Kassa came to meet us, accompanied by a crowd of his subjects, and brought us a gift of some gourds, turcha, tobacco, and a large elephant tusk.

I set up my universal instrument and began to carry out solar observations to determine the latitude, and then began to take the azimuths and to ask Kira about the lands to the south.

Below us flowed a stream named Kora, and beyond it lay the land of Balis. To the southeast stretched a high mountain ridge on which rose the three pointed peaks of Kanta. To the southwest of the mountain ridge was seen its rocky spurs. Kira pointed to the west and said that there lies the land of Menu or Men. By his words, in that land there was so much bread grain, that to them it was just something to blow your nose at. To explain that, he took a handful of seed and, throwing it on the ground, blew his nose. But I wasn't able to determine exactly where this Menu lies—whether near or far. There could hardly be fertile land on the pointed rocky peaks we saw. I tried to get Kira to say how many times we would have to make camp for the night before we could reach Menu. But Kira, evidently, did not know very well and gave very inconsistent answers. Maybe three days, maybe five...

February 17

At night there was a violent storm which nearly tore away the tents. In the morning, a messenger from the *Ras* arrived to congratulate us on the successful outcome of our reconnaissance. The *Ras* sent me as a gift a large fish, similar to a sheat-fish, which he had caught the day before in the Choma.

At eleven o'clock, the tent of the *Ras* appeared below us, about seven versts [four miles] away. I set out with Ato Bayu to see him. We took Kira with us. Kira immediately understood who was the commander-in-chief and kissed his hand, made him laugh with songs and dances, and went away having completely charmed the *Ras*.

My boys greeted me joyfully. Some of them with heroic exclamations boasted to me of their victories. Liban sang of how he stabbed a Shuro with a dagger. While we were gone, the army had carried out several requisition raids in the mountains of Jiri. The natives resisted stubbornly, suffered significant losses, but also inflicted losses on us...

Several of my *ashkers* were sick. Zelepukin also suffered from a fever.

February 18

At night there was a storm with rain. In the morning, the detachment crossed to the foothills of the mountain ridge and set up camp near the land of Garo. At noon two princes from Beru arrived—Koys and Kiyas—with several thousand of their subjects. Among them was an old priest. Kira called him "Dormoro" and, pointing to the sky said, "Dadu" ("God"). Around the neck of the priest hung the "white fat"[94] of a ram which had just been sacrificed.

The princes brought the *Ras* a large elephant tusk as a gift. A dense crowd of natives squatted in front of the *Ras*; and in the name of both princes, Kira kissed the hand of the commander-in-chief. The ceremonial reception was silent: we couldn't express ourselves.

The *Ras* gave Koys and Kiyas red woolen cloaks. (However, they looked on them rather suspiciously and were not especially willing to put them on). Then the *Ras* let them go home. He intended to keep Kira with the detachment as a guide and ordered that he be detained. At first, Kira was very displeased with this, but then he seemed to resign himself to his fate. And after dinner, in the tent of the *Ras*, Kira entertained us with his tricks. He was supposed to be shackled to prevent him from running away, but I felt sorry for him and asked that he be given to my custody; and the *Ras* agreed.

In the evening, shots rang out on the right flank of the camp. The inhabitants of Garo, on the boundary of whose settlements we now stood, attacked some Abyssinians who had gone far from camp, looking for firewood and grass. The commander of the regiment on the flank, having heard shots, went to help. The Garo were beaten off, but the Abyssinians lost several men killed.

I let Kira sleep in my tent, beside my bed, and posted a guard at the entrance. Kira took with him the trousers the *Ras* had given him; and rolling them into a bundle, he put them under his head. He covered himself with the shamma which had been given to him, and, after a few minutes, he was snoring...

FEBRUARY 19

When I woke up in the morning, I saw only the trousers and shamma in the place where Kira had slept. Kira had run away! With my misplaced sentimentality, I was responsible for his escape. In any case, without Kira, the detachment was in a very difficult position. So I decided to try to find Kira and bring him back. Most likely, he was hiding at the house of Koys. I had to go to Koys and demand that he turn Kira over. The detachment had still not yet set out when I climbed up Mount Beru. Behind me went my three gun bearers. When Ato Bayu saw me going past his tent, he joined me, together with his gun bearers. The sun still hadn't risen when we climbed the mountain ridge and arrived at the house of the prince. Despite the early hour, a mass of people were already crowding around, and it was strange to see that, to a man, the peaceful, friendly Beru people were now armed with spears and shields. Had Kira already aroused the whole populace with some fable concocted by him? Late-arriving warriors rushed by all the little roads to the house of the prince. Seeing us, they hid behind houses and trees. I went straight toward the crowd. From the crowd was heard the exclamation "Halio! Halio!" and those standing in front started to hide their weapons. Koys ran out to meet me. I began to explain the purpose of my visit and demanded that he hand over Kira right away. Koys mumbled something in reply and quickly ran into the house. After a few minutes, he returned dresed in the clothes which had been given to him the day before. He must have thought that this was what I had asked him to do. After lengthy explanations, he finally understood me. Pointing to the east, he said that Kira was at the house of Kiyas, the other king of Beru. Then I demanded that they bring me Kira, and I went into the house of the prince and sat there, indicating that I wouldn't leave until Kira appeared.

The courtyard consisted of a round area about 40 paces in diameter, surrounded by high wattle fencing. On its south side was adjoined a high house with a roof that hung over to the ground, and a low, solidly closed door. In the middle was built an overhang for cattle and under it stood several excellent cows. The right side fo the house was set aside as a place for sacrifice, as testified by a pile of ashes, in which was buried a large elephant tusk. Along side lay a large rectangular stone slab, on which were preserved traces of beer poured during sacrifices. Evidently, the dwelling place of the prince was considered holy. There was no one in this place aside from several old men. And my presence here, apparently, defiled the supreme rights of their leader and horrified the people.

The natives made loud noises behind the fence and talked animatedly about something. Several old men came up to me, explaining something, but I persistently repeated the word "Kira," demanding that they bring him to me. They pointed to the east, evidently saying that Kira and Kiyas were there and that they themselves could not bring Kira from there. Then I decided to go to Kiyas and, taking the prince by the hand, ordered him to take me there. He obeyed. I sat on a mule. Koys walked ahead with ten natives. Two hundred paces behind us, stealing behind bushes, went all the warriors who had assembled at the house of their prince. Several of them more openly dared to show themselves in front of us with weapons in hand. I personally disarmed them or ordered my *ashkers* to take away their spears. Ato Bayu and my weapons bearers were amazed at the behavior of the natives and kept telling me not to trust savages. Each minute they expected an attack. Just in case of this, their guns were loaded and cocked, and between the fingers of the left hand, they held several cartridges in readiness... I, no less than them, understood the danger of the situation; but I felt that the natives would not dare to touch us despite the fact that there were so few of us...

Kiyas lived down in the valley, about five versts [three miels] from the house of the prince, but we couldn't go there because at this time, our main detachment of troops, having climbed the mountain ridge, got into a heated battle with the neighboring Garo tribe. Suddenly, not far away, their shots rang out. Koys was terribly frightened, trembling all over from fear. he suddenly broke away from the *ashkers* who were holding him and broke out in a run, and all his followers went with him. This was a signal for general panic of the natives. It was now useless to try to catch the fleeing prince. It made no difference if he fell into our hands now. And I had no intention of killing him. Therefore, when one of my *ashkers* was aiming at him and ready to pull the trigger, I (fortunately, in time) stopped him. Now, of course, hunting for Kira was pointless. As sad as it was, we had to abandon that intention and return to the detachment. I set out for Kassa, where a bloody battle was going on.

Already on the day before, I had had a feeling that if we joined battle with the Garo, then the Abyssinians, in view of the indefinite boundaries, would cross over into the peaceful and in no way guilty land of Kassa. I had alerted the *Ras* of this and had urged him to take measures. He actually guarded the way to Beru with fences, but he thought that it seemed possible to cross Kassa without causing harm to its inhabitants, if he first assembled the whole detachment in Garo. But, apparently, he hadn't succeeded in doing that. The border forest, in which a mass of natives was hiding, was surrounded by Abyssinians who had literally massacred their enemies. Shots rang out from all sides. Bullets whistled by our ears. Over here lay the bloody bodies of savages, among which were also found Abyssinians. The sight of the bodies with enormous wounds was horrid. There were practially none of them which did not have the gaping wounds of saber strokes, since natives who were shot almost always also had their throats slit by saber. At times, we chanced upon wounded. I still remember one of them well. With stomach ripped by a spear and intestines pouring out, he was still conscious and silently watched those going by. It was evident how terribly he suffered, but he didn't let out a single sound...

In the clearing where we such a short time before had drunk turcha and where I had shown the savages the shining compass and watch and had amazed them, now lay the dead prince of Kassa and the chief representatives of his tribe. They probably had gone to meet the Abyssinians, but the Abyssinians had misunderstood their peace-loving intentions and had shot them all...

Now the *Ras* was in no position to stop the bloodletting. A thirst for blood and murder had taken possession of the troops. They showed no mercy, not only to men, but also to animals.[82] The corpses of animals with slit throats lay all about the road in masses. Only women and children escaped death, and they were taken prisoner.

The commander-in-chief was deeply grieved by what had taken place. He practically wept from compassion and rode silently, covering his face with his shamma. The officers who were accompanying him were also upset. It was distressing and disagreeable to all of them.

We made the difficult descent to the Kori River and set up camp on its banks. Little by little, the detachment began to assemble. They brought some wounded whom I bandaged. The soldiers drove livestock and prisoners ahead of them.

When all of them were already at muster, they beat the nagarit and informed the army that the order was being announced. The kettledrummer shouted the usual introductory formula for an order, and then the secretary of the *Ras*—Ato Melke, who was standing beside the confessor of the *Ras*—read the contents.

"Are my words the words of a cook?" the order announced. "Why kill unarmed men and for no purpose waste cartridges? I do not consider heroes those who killed today. I consider them mice. Let them not smear their heads with oil, and let them not braid their hair for today's killings. Whoever was with me in Aussi[83] knows what real courage is and demonstrated his bravery. Let all know that with those who kill without being forced to do so, I will act as I vowed to my confessor today. Gather all livestock and prisoners. Let every true soldier tell me if he finds out that another violates my orders by killing natives or livestock and slitting their throats."

When the order was read, all bowed down to the ground and silently went away. About a thousand men had been taken prisoner. By order of the *Ras* they were led behind the bivouac and set free. I took several photographs. Among others, I took some of one rather beautiful woman prisoner. When I aimed the camera at her, she started to scream, probably thinking that I was getting ready to shoot her. The only way I could take her picture was to have a soldier hold her behind the arms.

February 20

The detachment crossed the land of Balis. We now had no guide and no interpreter. Kira had told me about the land of Menu, but where was it and how could we pass through it? The commander-in-chief decided to stop here and ordered two regiments —those of *Fitaurari* Damti and *Fitaurari* Chabude and me together with them—to reconnoiter the territory and find Menu.

At twelve o'clock noon, I set out on reconnaissance from the new bivouac. Zelepukin, my gun bearers, and several *ashkers* went with me. We left our transport with the main forces, taking with us only enough provisions for a few days. We set out toward the south and soon were beyond the limits of inhabited lands. The temperature was 27° Reaumur [93° F] in the shade. We went along a deserted rocky plateau. The soil was covered with sharp rock fragments. In the gaps between them grew scraggly grass and sparse low thorny trees. The channels of streams were dry. Only in one did we find some very foul water. Rarely, we came across dilapidated huts and small open enclosures for livestock. But judging by the dried manure, one could conclude that the settlements had been abandoned by their inhabitants. Natives probably migrate here with their herds during the rainy season.

At 5:30 in the evening, we reached the cliffs which Kira had pointed at and called "Menu." However, near at hand, there were absolutely no traces of population. The sun went down. Our soldiers had been moving almost non-stop since five o'clock in the morning, and they hadn't had anything to drink since noon.

It was time to set up camp, so we sent out mounted soldiers in all directions to look for water. For a long time, the searches were in vain, and only at 7:30 did one of the scouts gallop back with the message that water was found. Then we fired our guns to get the others to return.

We set up camp near the water. My *ashkers* quickly put up the tent, made the camp fire and cooked coffee (the last handful I had). Both *Fitauraris* and Ato Bayu came to visit me. I served them coffee. Here they put together a report and sent it to the *Ras* with one officer and 20 soldiers.

February 21

Our reconaissance detachment divided into two units and, early in the morning, we set out to reconnoiter. Ato Bayo and *Fitaurari* Chabude went north. I went southwest with *Fitaurari* Damti. To guard the camp (against wild animals, but not against men), we left several dozen soldiers.

The farther we went, the more barren the territory seemed. The countryside was gloomy and bleak, but at the same time remarkably beautiful. All around were granite rocks of the oddest shapes, and some stones of all possible hues—from rose to dark gray—were seen. After several hours we found water in the channel of a stream, and near it, we found fresh traces of men and animals. Probably, the inhabitants who were fleeing from *Bale* were hiding here. Nearby rose a high hill. Having climbed to its summit, we began to check out the vicinity with binoculars and a telescope. Fifteen versts [ten miles] to the southwest was seen the valley of some stream. A band of green trees bore testimony of the existence of that stream. The river must flow to the southeast and into it flowed all the channels of all the dried up rivulets which we had just crossed. Farther to the west rose rocky mountains, and on the horizon in the west was seen the gently sloping inclines of mountains that were unknown to us. Their gentle outlines were similar to the outlines of Beru and Kassi, which provided some basis for supposing that they might be inhabited. If Menu really exists, then in all probability, it should be there.[84] In my opinion, we should go down into the valley of the rivulet seen in the southwest and, on the following day, look for Menu in the west. But my travelling companions energetically protested. It seemed to them that the mountains which I indicated were too far off; and that if we were to go there, then we would not be able to return to the main forces within a week, and the *Ras* had not ordered us to go that far. The nearest mountains were evidently uninhabited. And they thought that nothing more remained for us but to return to the *Ras* and communicate all to him for his judgement. I was a guest, and it was not fitting for me to push my opinions on them... We returned to the bivouac, loaded the mules, and set off toward the main forces.

The reconnaissance was unsuccessful. We did not fulfill the task that had been given us, and the question of whether inhabited land was more or less near to us remained open. This was all very disappointing to me. In my soul, I blamed my travelling companions for indecisiveness; but now, coolly considering all the circumstances of the recent expedition, I was forced to regard this failure more tolerantly. Really, the conditions of the campaign were most unusual. This wasn't so much a military campaign as a geographical expedition by a fifteen-thousand-man detachment in absolutely unknown territory. Outstanding Abyssinian troops were completely unprepared for this activity, which was new to them.

The sun had already set when we returned to camp. The commander-in-chief invited me to visit him in his tent and began to ask me about the reconnaissance. I candidly expressed my dissatisfaction.

"You are right," he told me. "But I foresaw that this would happen in this way. My soldiers are brave. They love war. But they do not tolerate deserts. Now they are convinced that there are no people farther off; and wherever I would send them, they would return with one answer: 'It is impossible to go farther.' Only following behind me will they go forward. But where are we going? How should we act?"

"Our position is not so hopeless," I reported to the commander-in-chief. "Not far off, behind us, is a land rich in bread grain. We can leave there all the sick and the weak and a large part of the detachment. Then we can go farther with selected men, following the course of the Kori River, which apparently heads to the northwest. It must have tributaries both on the right and on the left, and along one of them we could then go south. We will be well provided with water, and we will take with us provisions enough for ten days. When those provisions run out, we will find wild game in abundance, if not bread grain. Perhaps Menu is not so far off as it seems. If to the south we find a densely populated territory which is rich in bread grain, we will pull part of the detachment over to there, will build a second strong point, a second base, and then will go farther."

The commander-in-chief listened to me with great attention, and when I finished he said, "Your words go through me and into my heart."

He decided to hold a military council the next day.

February 22

The military council was held in the morning. The *Ras* opened it with a speech in which he described our present situation, having shown both the necessity of going forward and the fact that such was the will of the emperor. In conclusion, the *Ras* proposed that those present express their opinions, but all were silent.

Then the *Ras* said, "Tomorrow, we return to the mountains. There we will leave part of the detachment, the sick, and the weak. We will replenish our provisions, and then I will go ahead with the best men."

The day before, we had found traces of the presence here of the Italian expedition of Bottego—some iron fasteners from pack chests, spent cartridge cases of the Veterli system, ten-caliber paper cartridge cases, and some miraculously intact pages from "Theory of Probability" in the Italian language. The astronomical position of this place is 6° 48' north latitude and 35° 26' east longitude from Greenwich.

Prisoners taken in this vicinity belong to a nationality which is completely different from the other neighbors (the mountain dwellers of Beru and Kassa). They more closely resemble the Shuro Negroes, but they also do not understand the Shuro language. The men and women are very ugly. They all have their lower front incisors knocked out. The women are especially unattractive. Their lower lip is pierced wide and hangs low, uncovering the rare teeth which stick out, with a gap in the middle in the place of the knocked out front incisors. They place a wooden disk about two vershoks [three and a half inches] in diameter[85] in the hole that is pierced in the lip. The prince of the tribe—Jufa—was found among the prisoners.

February 23

We went back to the Kori River and made camp on its banks to the southeast of our former one. In a large water hole in the channel of the river, we found a lot of fish, which the soldiers caught with their *shammas*. The commander-in-chief also went fishing and caught 14 of them and sent them to me as a gift. In addition, Zelepukin and my *ashkers* caught a saucepan full. On this day, one of the colonels gave me what couldn't have been a more opportune gift—a piece of salt. Zelepukin and I cooked ourselves a marvellous ukha [fish soup] and ate it.

In the time after supper, I took care of medical treatments and bandaging. Around my tent, as always, there crowded a mass of sick people. Above all, the troops suffered from bloody flux, and our supply of bismuth and castor oil was quickly exhausted. They also suffered from fevers and inflammation of the eyes. The eye illnesses I very successfully treated using eyedrops which are still unknown to medicine (a secret of I.S. Dzhevinskiy, my landlord in Tsarskoye Selo). I often treated the wounded. Some of the more lightly wounded recovered very quickly. Today, for example, I removed a splint from a soldier who on one of the first days after crossing the border had had his arm broken by a rock thrown from a sling. Another had been hit by a spear several days before. It had pierced through the muscles of his chest, missing the chest cavity. Today, I removed the bandage and poured collodion on the healing wounds. But one poor fellow whose chest was piered by a spear at Jasha Mountain did not recover. He got terribly worse. The wound, which had been sewn by me, opened; and when he exhaled, a white liquid flowed from it, and stinking pus and air bubbles came out.

February 24

At night there was a violent storm; and all morning it rained, accompanied by the strongest wind. With incredible efforts, we climbed the mountain along a steep slippery trail. The mountain ridge was densely populated with the same kind of people as Beru. Their buildings were the same, and their fields were just as carefully cultivated. The whole population ran away on our arrival and not a single soul could be seen. The head of our column arrived at the site of the bivouac at nine o'clock in the morning, and the rearguard only at six o'clock in the evening. The transport marched past in front of our tents all day long. The tailend of the column was a melancholy sight. The sick and wounded stretched out quietly in a continuous file. Some were carried on stretchers; some went on foot, supported by comrades; others rode on mules and, so they wouldn't fall, they were held behind the shoulders by those who were walking beside them. They led one dying Galla on a mule, having placed him on the saddle, with his legs bent behind and all fastened to the saddle with straps. The poor fellow had no one to carry him on a stretcher; but all the same, he couldn't sit on a saddle. Those suffering from small pox were an awful sight. For the most part, those were Galla soldiers, or male and female servants of Abyssinians. The Abyssinians innoculate themselves against small pox, taking it for the most part when they are still children.[86]

Half naked, covered with large gray boils, with terribly swollen faces on which you almost couldn't see the eyes, the small pox victims languished in the rain and the wind. Already at five o'clock in the morning, the unfortunates who were riding had started their journey, enduring all the suffering and misfortune with amazing patience.

After noon, the *Ras* personally conducted reconnaissance and selected the site of our future fortress. This was a hill which rose at the end of a mountain spur and was a very strong and convenient location. A stream flowed at the foot of the mountain, and there was fuel and also an abundance of grass for mules.

FEBRUARY 25 TO MARCH 4

The detachment went to the site which had been chosen and set up a compact bivouac, grouped around the tent of the *Ras*. Immediately on arrival, they began to build a palisade around the bivouac and to build a house for the *Ras*, into which he moved that very evening. The order was announced to the troops: they were forbidden to leave garbage in the camp, and they must maintain special cleanliness. Each soldier had to dig his own latrines and each time fill it up with earth.

We stayed at the bivouac in Kolu from February 25 to March 4. These days were passed in daily foraging and in work on strengthening the fortress, which they surrounded with a high palisade and a moat. The soldiers built cabins for themselves and houses for their leaders. The hostility of the populace among whom we now found ourselves called for strong defensive measures on our part. In the daytime, we sent out guards from one of the regiments, in order, and posted them in raised and open places in front of the watering places, pastures, and sites of wood-chopping; and almost all day long, they waged war with the natives. The natives used every opportunity to inflict casualties on us, and attacked from ambush not only soldiers, but also women and our mules, donkeys, and horses. They committed outrages on the dead. I saw, for example, the body of one woman whose stomach they had ripped open, whose breasts they had cut off, etc.

A military council was held on February 27. At this meeting, they finally determined the compositon of the detachment that would go with the *Ras*. In all, 5,664 guns were chosen. This number included almost all the officers and a large part of the mounted soldiers. In the fort, under the command of *Fitaurari* Faris would stay all of his regiment and about three thousand men from the other regiments, the sick, the weak, and also all of the transport and all of the women. If any of the officers wanted to take a cook along with him, he was obliged to give her, without fail, a mule. With the detachment went only part of the transport of cartridges and provisions. Each soldier had to take with himself enough for not less than ten days. Responsibility for provisions was laid on the soldiers themselves. A soldier would ride on a mule and carry the provisions with him or load them on a pack mule. Others carried the provisions on their heads.

February 26, 27, and 28, they commandeered provisions in the neighborhood. For this, the regiments were divided into three shifts. The commandeering took place in the following manner. The regiment whose turn it was, having received the direction in which it was supposed to act, set out with its full complement. Going to a rich populated territory, the soldiers scattered, drove out the natives, and loaded their mules and horses with provisions. Part of the regiment served as a reserve in case of unexpected attack and was stationed in the center of such a territory. On the way back to the bivouac, the reserve followed at the tailend of the detachment and served as the rear guard.

In those three days, they gathered a month's supplies for the detacment which was staying behind and fifteen days' worth for the detachment which was leaving.

I rested during this time. Part of the day, I usually occupied myself with marking the route on a map, making some observations, and tending to the sick. But all my free time I spent with the *Ras*. These days flowed quietly and peacefully.

Early in the morning, the commander-in-chief went out to his favorite place, from which the whole camp was clearly visible. Seeing the commander-in-chief, the commanders of regiments, the officers, and soldiers rushed to bow to him. With a light, gracious movement, they threw their *shammas* off their shoulders and bowed to the ground. Then they sat down in a close circle and, in this manner, the *Ras* was soon surrounded by a crowd. The commander-in-chief sat here from morning until dinner and from dinner to sunset. They took care of business or amused themselves with conversation or games. Officers and men came to be judged. Often, serious matters were decided. Here are two typical cases and their amazingly simple resolutions: The Emperor Menelik, having changed the distribution of his troops, took away from *Ras* Wolda Giyorgis his estates on the left bank of the River Omo and gave them to other leaders. In exchange, he granted the *Ras* all the lands to the southwest of Kaffa. When the troops evacuated the regions that had been taken away, many soldiers joined the service of the new ruler. Because of this, the number of soldiers in many companies of regiments previously stationed in those territories had diminished to the point that the companies only existed nominally. In several companies all that remained were the commander and several officers. However, all companies received an equal allowance. In view of this, several companies of one of the regments complained to the *Ras* about the abnormality of this situation. The *Ras* acknowledged their complaint as completely well-founded. Commanders were responsible for the numbers of their units and, consequently, were guilty if their companies were not fully manned. On the basis of this, the *Ras* ordered men from incomplete companies to transfer to other, fuller ones; and the officers were demoted to soldiers... The other case arose from the fact that the commander of one of the companies had evaded going on campaign for a second year, under pretext of illness, and his sergeant major commanded in his place. Before the present campaign, this company was supposed to receive twelve new guns, but Tuki declined to take them since the responsibility for them would then lie on him as the commander. The sergeant major was well known as an excellent soldier.

"You don't want to take these twelve guns?" asked the *Ras*.
"I can't. I'm poor."
"You are commanding in place of your sick leader for the second year?"
"Yes, for the second year."
"Then take the company and become a captain (*yamato alaka*)!"
So the sergeant major became a captain.

They also brought to the commander-in-chief soldiers who had been found guilty of taking livestock from the natives and having slaughtered them, which was forbidden by the *Ras*, under penalty of strict punishment. These were for the most part Gallas, because the Abyssinians were fasting and didn't eat meat. The guilty were punished with ten lashes of the *jiraf*, which like pistol shots resounded through the camp, accompanied by plaintive cries. One soldier was guilty of wanting to kill a native when he wasn't forced to and of having shot at him with a gun. He was sentenced to 40 lashes. It was fortunate for him that his shot had missed; otherwise he would probably have been executed.

In the intrevals between these cases, people talked to one another, recalled interesting true stories, or simply cracked jokes with one another. As in any gathering of comrades, here there were some natural wits, among whom one kanyazmatch particularly distinguished himself. I have forgotten his real name, but everyone called him Kanyazmatch Yanye Wadaj ("my friend") because that's what he called everyone. A Gojjam by birth, he was lean, with a remarkably comical face, with a small beard that stuck out and with legs so long that when he rode on his little mule they seemed to drag on the ground. He was always cheeful and joked constantly, making fun of one or another of his comrades and provoking a friendly outburst of laughter.

They played gebeta with enthusiasm or looked through a telescope at the surrounding mountains. The *Ras* had two telescopes which he took with him here, and his favorite pastime was to look through them. (However, a telescope is one of the attributes of every Abyssinian leader. In their paintings, the Abyssinians depict the military leader standing on a hill and looking through a telescope during battle.) First the commander-in-chief himself looked through the telescope. Then it passed from one to another; and little pages waited impatiently for the moment when they too would finally get a chance to look. The *Ras* knew all the subtleties of the construction of telescopes. With special love and even pride, he dismantled and polished not only his own telescopes, but also those of his officers.

Gebeta took up a lot of our free time, and I eventually took a great liking to it.[87] We enthusiastically squandered hours at the board. All who were present showed the most active interest in the game. All seniority disappeared while they were playing. The commander-in-chief and his fellow players laid on their stomachs at the board and sometimes argued heatedly. The best player and the invariable partner of the *Ras* was his ashker—the one who carried his parasol.

When evening fell, the carpets were removed, and we stood for prayers. Then the *Ras* invited me to his small, comfortable little home, and entertained me with a scanty dinner and a little decanter of tej with water or a little glass of home-made vodka. He himself did not dine during Lent and ate only once a day, after noon, making an exception to this rule only on Sundays. He didn't even eat fish during Lent.

The little home of the *Ras* was divided into two halves. His bed was in the one half. In the second, stood his two war horses and two mules. The horses were outstanding. One was a gray mare —the well-known Sougud. The other was a dark-bay mare. Abyssinians are very superstitious and distinguish between lucky and unlucky horses. Both of these horses were lucky. Gougud— the Bucephalus of Wolda Giyorgis—formerly belonged to Menelik and was considered wild. But the *Ras*, according to his retainers, asked the emperor for him and completely tamed him. When the *Ras* rode Gougud during the Battle at Embabo[88], he had the good luck to take 35 men prisoner that day, after which this horse became the main battle horse of the *Ras* and accompanied him in all his campaigns. The dark-bay horse was likewise in high esteem. On it the *Ras* made war with Gomu, and from it he killed three rhinoceroses in one day.

Our rather extended stay had good consequences. The natives, seeing that the strong forces which had arrived did not go away but rather built themselves houses and, by all signs, would stay, decided that, whether they liked it or not, they had to submit. On March 1, the first deputation from the land of Duk arrived with an expression of submission. At its head was the prince, an old man named Muruta Babus. He brought the *Ras* a large elephant tusk as a gift. Muruta was a lucky find for us since, being of the same nationality as the Beru, he also knew the Shuro language and could serve as an interpreter. This circumstance extracted us from the helpless position we had been in before of not being able to communicate with a nation which had submitted. They treated Murutu Babus with affection, gave him gifts, dressed him in a red woolen cloak and kept him with the detachment as an interpreter, keeping him shackled at all times so he would not make off as Kira had. They promised him that if he would faithfully serve us, they would subsequently make him the chief ruler of all these lands.

Now we could converse with the mountain-dwellers, but we still needed another interpreter who would know the language of the captured Jufa. We found one the next day. The inhabitants of the land of Kanta, who are from the same tribe as the Beru, also came to express their submission, and one of them knew the language of Jufa. A deputation also appeared from the inhabitants of nearby Dami Mountain, relatives of the Kassa, Beru, Kolu and Duka. Their prince was two archins and 12 vershoks tall [six feet five inches]. Their tatoos were deeper and larger than those of their fellow tribesmen, and their adornment was more elaborate as well.

Having treated those who arrived with affection and having given them gifts, the *Ras* let them go, telling them through Murutu Babus, that they should let the surrounding tribes know that the Abyssinians fear nothing, that they do not wish to harm anyone, and that they only require submission.

The interrogations of all prisoners carried out that day gave us some information about the stay here of an Italian expedition and about the territory which lay ahead.

The "Guchumba" (which is what the Jufa called the Europeans), arrived, by his words, from the southeast. They set up camp beside a Jufa settlement, and stayed there several days, demanding, under threat of their fire-breathing weapons, that they deliver bread free of charge. Then they went away to the northwest. As we found out later, all the tribes from here to Lake Rudolf call Europeans "Guchumba." "Guchumba" literally means "tramps."

The Jufa also let us know about the territories lying to the south and west. Menu or Meun, a region rich in bread grain, was found, by his words, in the west, at a distance of three to four days' journey. Another land rich in grain crops—Murle, which lies somewhere to the south—was far off, and he didn't know how to get there. (This land, as it later turned out, is located on the banks of the River Omo, at its mouth). The Jufa had heard nothing about the existence of a large lake in the south, but he was familiar with another lake several days' journey to the northwest into which flowed the Kori River. He called this lake Kiy and agreed to be our guide, saying that along the way to it there is a land rich in bread grain. The banks of the lake, by his words, do not have a settled population, and along it wild hunters wander, armed with bows and arrows. I asked Jufa what their nationality is and whether he knew their language. "They are all Idenich," answered Jufa. Telling me this, Gebra Maryam turned away from Jufa with scorn. Muruta Babus and Kanta did the same. I was amazed by this scornful attitude of savages to savages, and I asked them to explain to me about the Idenich. "Inhuman children!" said Gebra Maryam. "They are wild animals. they eat the meat of elephants and of lizards. They almost do not sow grain. They are Watu," Gebra Maryam finally added, spitting with disgust. Watu are the pariahs of Abyssinia, scorned by all the other inhabitants of Ethiopia. They are probably the remnants of some tribe which belonged to a lower race. The Watu dwell in the dense forests and low-lying unhealthy river valleys. They occupy themselves mainly with hunting. They kill hippopotamuses and from their skins make alancha whips which are widespread throughout Abyssinia and also shields. They use the meat for food, like the Idenich, not being squeamish, in general, about any kind of meat. I saw several Watu in Abyssinia and saw that, on the exterior, they had much in common with the Jufa and with those of their fellow tribe members with whom I was then acquainted: they were just as unattractive, with just as indeterminate facial features and the same vacant, stupid expression in the eyes. Might the Watu and the Idenich belong to one and the same race? They appear to be the northern and southern representatives of the same race, and living either in deserts with little water or in dense forests, they have preserved themselves by having mixed very little with other tribes.

The plateau to the south of the main mountain range is populated by Idenich nomads who in the territories nearest to the mountains live a more or less settled life style and till the soil. I also met them in the forests on the banks of the River Omo, where their main occupation consists of hunting and fishing. Everywhere the Idenich were equally despised by other tribes. In this territory, they speak a language which is close to the Shuro. They call God "Tuma," but have only the most vague conception of Him. They perform no sacrifices. A distinctive feature of this tribe is the knocking out of the front lower incisors, the ugliness of their women and their using all kinds of meat as food. I could not explain the reason for this disfigurement. Could it be that they consider it beautiful or do they do it so their brave neighbors won't want to take away their women?

...

On the basis of the testimony of the Jufa, we made the following plan of action: on March 4 (March 3 was a major

Abyssinian holiday), the *Ras* and the select detachment would set out to the west. We would follow down the course of the Kori River to its confluence with the lake, if there really was such a lake. From there, we would choose a route to the south or southwest through Menu or another region abundant with bread grain which we might come upon along the way.

During our stay in Kolu, I happened to observe rather unusual meteorological phenomena. Each evening before sunset, in a cloudless sky, little storm clouds appeared from the west. At about nine o'clock, a violent storm rose in the mountains which intensified to nearly the strength of a hurricane. First it swooped down on us with terrible force in several gusts and was accompanied by rain. By midnight everything had quieted down. This phenomenon took place the first time on February 15 and from that time was repeated daily, only with varying force, depending on the altitude of the terrain. After we went down to the Beneman plateau on February 20-21, I no longer observed such storms, but then in Kolu they began to be repeated with even greater force, so that they blew away our tents. The first time I experienced such an unpleasant event was February 26. We did not suspect the approaching calamity and calmly went to bed. On the little table beside my bed lay my open notebook and barometer. Photographic prints were soaking in the bath.

At nine o-clock in the evening, we heard from afar noise in the mountains and the earth shook, and the first terrible gust of wind that swooped down on us ripped the edge of the tent from its pegs, lifted the table, like a little pen, and threw it across my bed. The next gust, which was even stronger, took away the inner post of the tent, the lower part of which fell on my head; and the tent covered me and Zelepukin. Several intact ropes didn't let it fly away, and it beat against the ground like a wounded bird, now being raised by the wind, and then again flopped down again, and the slapping of its ends against the ground resounded loudly. How terrifying that moment was, but there was no point in thinking about calling servants and setting the tent up again. I could only lie under a felt cloak, protecting my head from injury with my arms, and waiting to see what would happen next. When the storm calmed down, the soaked roof pressed down on us, forming like a solid hot compress, under which we gasped for breath from the stuffy heat. When it had grown quiet, Zelepukin and I tried to make an account of the damage.

"Zelepukin, you weren't knocked out?"

"Not at all."

"Where is the knapsack (with documents)? Is it near you?"

"It's near me."

"And where is the instrument (theodolite)?"

"Yes, your worship. It's here."

"And where is the photograph?"

The photograh was gone. It was taken away together with the table. But I had managed to hide the barometer under the cloak. A new gust of wind that swooped down on us at that moment drowned out our conversation.

On the following day, in the evening, I took measures to strengthen the tent, but my efforts turned out to be futile and again it blew down. On the third day, I surrounded it with a fence—again it blew down. Only when we beat the pegs deep into the ground, attached double ropes to them and covered the whole tent in the middle with a long pack strap, in order to restrain the flaps, did it stay standing. Having learned by experience, we took precautions at night, like a ship expecting a storm, and when the sun set, we gave orders to reinforce the rigging. Everything that could be soaked or carried away by the wind was put away in packs. We hid guns under a tarpaulin. Then we lay and waited for the storm, wondering uneasily if it would blow down the tent.

From Kolu to Lake Rudolf

March 4

At 5:30 in the morning, the select detachment of 5,664 men under the command of *Ras* Wolda Giyorgis left the fortress at Kolu. I accompanied him.

Since we were travelling light, I only took 11 *ashkers* and several pack mules. Of course, Zelepukin came with me.

Before I set out, the sick and wounded who were staying in Kolu asked me to give them medicine in reserve. A heavily wounded man, with a puncture through his chest was desperate, saying that now he would be helpless and most likely he would die...

Finally, we got started.

All four interpreters were led in front of the *Ras*. The old man, Muruta Babus, rode, wearing the red cloak he had been given. His legs, which were too long, dangled helplessly since he could not rest them in the short stirrups. Jufa boldly ran ahead and led the detachment. Along a steep slope strewn with rocks, we went down to the Kori River and headed west, following its course. At four o'clock in the afternoon, after a ten-hour march without a break, we reached the inhabited and cultivated territory of Lessi and set up camp here. The natives ran away when we got close. Nonetheless, soldiers succeeded in capturing several women who were from the same tribe as Jufa and who were just as ugly as those we took prisoner in the land of Balis.

It turned out that they too know Guchumba—Europeans. They said that Europeans crossed their lands last year and that their prince brought the Europeans gifts of grain, hens, and rams. From here the Guchumba went north. The natives really didn't know about the existence of a lake. But they said that nearby there is "a place where water lies."

The stream on the banks of which we set up our camp abounded in fish. On our arrival, the commander-in-chief set off with a fishing rod to go fishing. I went along to watch. The officers sat on the shore of a little pond surrounded by steep cliffs.

The air was stifling, so I began to climb up one of the cliffs, hoping that up above it would be cooler and also hoping to take photographs from up there of this unique group—the commander-in-chief fishing, surrounded by his whole staff. My undertaking nearly cost me dearly. At a height of two sagenes [4.26 meters] above the water, the rock on which I stepped broke away and after it toppled a boulder, several armwidths in girth, which must have rested on the small lower one. I, too, slid down the cliff. Seeing this, the *Ras* and his officers cried out in horror. The boulder slid down at the same time over me, and it seemed like it was unavoidable that it would crush me. But I somehow luckily jumped aside; and having flown past right beside me, it fell into the water with an uproar and raised a whole column of spray. In general, this day was rich in adventures for me. 1) On jumping across the rocky channel of a stream, my mule stumbled and fell on its head, carrying me along with it. 2) While climbing a very steep mountain, overgrown with thick bushes, when striking against a thorny branch, I leaned back, a twig caught my pistol cord, and before I could succeed in unhooking it or catching by the reins the mule which was quickly clambering up, I was pulled off the saddle and fell on my back, with my head down, under the feet of another mule which was immediately following me. Luckily, both times I got away with just bruises.

March 5

We passed the settlement of Lessi and went into the low-lying uninhabited valley of the Kori River, which is a wide rocky plain, at an elevation of only 700 meters above sea level, with scanty grass and mimosa and acacia trees. The air here is remarkably dry and motionless; and as a result, the heat was extremely strong. In the shade it was 29-30° Reaumur [97 to 99° F].[89]

On arrival at camp, we set out to the river to go fishing, and our soldiers accidentally dragged out a little crocodile.

At the camp itself, we caught two Idenich natives. They knew about Europeans who had passed through last year (Bottego), and one of them had even brought them a ram for sale. They denied the existence of a lake nearby. The land of Menu was two days' journey from here.

The old man Jufa continued to affirm that the lake was near. The women who had been taken prisoner yesterday said today more confidently than the day before that in one days' journey there is water of a river that "lies." We decided to go down the river a bit further in order to make sure of whether there actually is a lake there.

March 6

We found the place where the water "lies." It was the confluence of the Meru and Kori Rivers and, actually, the current here was very still—not more than four versts [two and a half miles] per hour. The width of the river is 40 to 60 paces.

We set up camp a bit below the confluence of the Meru and the Kori; and I set out, accompanied by my gun bearers, to a small rocky summit, which was visible about seven versts [four and a half miles] from camp. Exhausted by the difficult climb in the scorching heat, bathed in sweat, I clambered up it.

I was rewarded for my work by the marvelous view and distant horizon which opened up from here. In the northeast arose the mountain ridge which we had just left. It had the shape of an enormous row which disappeared in the haze of the horizon. In the north, as far as the eye could see, there stretched the low-lying valley of the Kori River, and lines of mountain spurs, to the right and left of it, marked the tributaries which flow into it. On one of these spurs arose Mount Jasha, at the foot of which we had set up camp February 10-12; and beyond it was seen the valley of the Sebelimu River, which flows into the Kori.

Here, evidently, all the streams which flow down the western slopes of the mountain range we had passed through must unite and form the high water level Sobat or Jubu which serves as the western boundary with Abyssinian domains. The mountain range to the east constitutes the watershed of the Omo and Sobat Rivers, which undoubtedly demolishes the former assumption which found many proponents among people interested in this question. Those who were of that opinion included the Emperor Menelik and the Europeans who were close to him. Count Teleiki and Hohnel, who discovered Lake Rudolf, found at its north end the mouth of a large river and first expressed the thought that this was the River Omo. Their assertion was for the time being unsubstantiated and was soon refuted by Donaldson Smith, who went a few dozen versts up the river. However, he mistook one of the tributaries for the main river, and in view of how little water it contained, confirmed the hypothesis which d'Abaddie had first put forward. Bottego attested by his journey that the Omo flows into Lake Rudolf, but at the time of my journey, the work of his expedition was still not elaborated and was unknown to me.

Setting out on the present journey, I, along with the majority, held the opinion that the River Omo skirts the Kaffa Mountains on the south and is nothing other than the beginning of the Sobat River, which flows into the Nile. On January 28, when from Mount Boka, I saw the moutain range which stretches from Kaffa far to the south, a mountain range which up to then was not marked on any map, I had my first doubt of the truth of that assumption. Now it was definitively refuted. The mountain range discovered by me separates the basins of the Omo and the Sobat and drives off the waters of its western slopes from what seems to be its natural basin—Lake Rudolf—to the distant Nile and the Mediterranean Sea. This mountain range is named, with the permission of the Tsar and with agreement of the Emperor Menelik, the "Nikolas II Mountain Range."[90]

But where could the lake I had heard about from three completely different sources have disappeared? Even in the town of Andrachi, Benesho natives had told me that to the southwest of them there is some Lake Bosho into which their main rivers flow. The guide Belemus said that in the west there was some lake with hot water, on the shores of which her fellow-tribesmen extract salt. And finally, the Idenich Jufa pointed to the northwest and definitely said that there is Lake Kiy, on the bnaks of which wander savage hunters who are armed with bows and arrows.

If the lake really exists, then it must be found in this low-lying, fog-covered valley of a river. The elevation of the river above sea level—attaining 700 meters—convinced me of this, in addition to the indications of natives. With very little fall and the very slow flow, the river had a huge area ahead of it before it could unite with the Nile.

The main goal of our campaign was to the south, and therefore I, unfortunately, could not verify whether my assumptions were correct.

Returning to camp, I saw a crowd of people surrounding my tent. They were waiting for my return. It seemed that they had brought a soldier who had just been bitten by a crocodile. The wounded man was so frightened that his face looked greenish. He had been swimming with comrades, and the crocodile grasped him in its mouth across his whole body, and began to drag him under the water. At the sight of this, the soldiers cried out and the crocodile let his victim go. On the soldier's shoulders and chest, there were 12 deep wounds, as if made by the sharp teeth of a saw. The wounded man complained that his heart hurts, and he thought that the bite of the crocodile was poisonous. I sewed up his wounds with 32 stitches. (After several days, he recovered). At this point on the river, there were quite a few crocodiles. One of our soldiers was killed while swimming; and after that, we decided not to go swimming any more.

March 7

The detachment moved southwest in the direction of Menu. Two Idenich, who we had taken prisoner on March 5, led us. The steppe where we were going abounded in wildlife. Sometimes, wild goats shot out from under foot, as if insane, and galloped along our whole column. I killed one large gazelle. It was comparable in size to a small ox, but it galloped with the ease of a chamois, with the long wide stride of a thoroughbred race hose. Its hair was light yellow. Its snout was like that of an ox, as was its tail. Its horns were spiral and rather straight. I chopped off one of the back legs of the gazelle with my saber, and one of my weapons bearers lifted it on his shoulders and set out to catch up with the detachment, which had gone far ahead while I was hunting.

At about 11 o'clock in the morning, we found water in the channel of a dried up river, digging a little hole in the sand. From here the terrain begins to rise. We crossed several mountain spurs and finally, at about three o'clock in the afternoon, entered the first settlement of Menu. Houses here are arranged in groups, and each farmstead is surrounded by a low fence. The intervals are sown with *mashella* and corn. In the valleys, herds of goats and rams grazed. The inhabitants fled as we approached. Soldiers scattered through the farmsteads looking for meal and grain, replenishing the supplies of provisions which we had used up over those days. Several natives were captured, and were taken to the *Ras* for interrogation. They belonged to the Idenich tribe, the same as in Jufa, and differed from them neither in type nor in language; only the women weren't as disfigured and their lower lip, although pierced, was not cut widely, as with women in the land of Beneman.

The prince of this territory—Besela—was among the prisoners taken. He was a large decrepit old man, dressed in an oxhide thrown across his shoulder and with heavy iron bracelets on his arms. The surrounding territory was completely unknown to him, and he had never heard about a lake to the northwest or to the southeast. Farther to the south, the terrain was, by his words, completely deserted; people didn't live there. When we asked him if he had ever seem Europeans—Guchumba—he, to our great surprise, answered they are quite close to us on the southern boundaries of his land. The women prisoners had also seen them, and one of them just yesterday met one there, bartering meal for strings of beads. To the question of how many of them are white men, they answered that they are all white men, probably because they are all dressed in white clothes. And to the question of whether there are many of them, they pointed at the bivouac of one of our regiments.

This news was so important that the commander-in-chief called his unit leaders in order to tell them. It was unknown who these Europeans were. Perhaps it was Major MacDonald's detachment of the English army, which from Uganda was suppposed to go north to meet Kitchener, (at this time we still did not know about the failure of that expedition), or some scientific expedition. In any case *Ras* Wolda Giyorgis had been given quite definite instructions by Emperor Menelik about how to act in case he ever met with any Europeans. Therefore, it was decided to go the next day to the place where the Europeans had been seen. Today it was already too late, and the army was too exhausted from a non-stop ten-hour march and from requisitioning provisions after that, for them to undertake further reconnassiance right away; and it seemed too risky to rely on a captive at night in compeletely unknown territory.

Besela agreed to recognize the authority of Menelik and together with all the other prisoners was set free. He designated one of his subjects to stay with us as a guide.

March 8

At dawn the signal horn of the commander-in-chief awoke us. Scouts were sent ahead. The detachment was constituted as a reserve column. All the regiments had a full complement of files and detached only the most essential men and transport. The regiment of *Fitaurari* Atyrsye went in front of all. Behind it, at a distance of 25 paces, the regiment of *Fitaurari* Gebra Maryam went in file. Then at the same distance, went the regiment of *Fitaurari* Chabude. At 100 paces behind it, surrounded by two regiments of *Azzaj* (marshall of the court) Gebra followed the commander-in-chief, directly protected by men of his own gurad. Up front, inside a ring formed by them, they carried the banner of the *Ras*. They carried his tent and drums, and led his war horses. His weapons bearers brought his guns. Behind the regiments of *Azzaj* Gebra went the regiment of *Fitaurari* Ubye. To the right of the *Ras*, at an interval of 200-300 paces, went the regiments of *Fitaurari* Imam and Kanyazmatch Alemnekh. To the left, at the same distance, went the regiment of *Fitaurari* Dubye and *Fitaurari* Damti. Behind the reserve column followed the transport, and after it went the rear guard, consisting of the next regiment. Each regiment was constituted as a front in several files. In each regiment, the foot soldiers went in front in 6-10 files. Then at a distance of 15 paces went mounted soldiers (in 204 files). In the interval between foot and mounted soldiers rode the commander of the regiment. The depth of the front of each regiment was about 40-60 paces. Its width was 50-70 paces.

I admired their balance, order, and ability to adapt themselves to the terrain.

The units passed through a ravine with remarkable skillfulness: the front units ran through it at some distance and formed up again. They did this so adroitly and quickly that the middle of the column went almost without delay.

At about 9 o'clock in the morning, we climbed to the summit of the ridge, at the foot of which, according to our guide, the camp of the Europeans should be. But when we reached the summit, we only saw the abattis which surrounded their camp. The smoke of their extinguished campfire bore witness to their recent presence.

We stopped on the ridge. Below, on the edge of a grove, on the banks of a stream, the natives who had fled from us crowded. Through an interpreter, we began peaceful negotiations at a distance of 500 paces. We called out to them to go back to their houses calmly and that they shouldn't fear us since we would not do them harm and that their king Besela had become our friend the day before. For a long time our assurances were unsuccessful, and only after a rather extended period of time did several bold spirits dare to approach to within 200-300 paces of us, hiding behind trees. In their hands they carried twigs—symbols of peace. We also took branches and leaves; and by this act we definitely convinced them of our peaceableness, and they began direct negotiations.

These completely naked natives belonged to the Idenich race, but the features of their faces were much more regular, with a much more intelligent expression than that of their fellow tribesmen. Being a settled people, they evidently surpassed the nomads in culture. Their spears and shields seemed excellently made. On their arms they displayed numerous iron bracelets. They decorated their heads with ostrich feathers.

Our envoys reported that the Guchumba left today at night and that their camp was very noisy. By the light of torches made of dry grass, they loaded their animals and hurriedly went east—to Belu or Balis—to the place from which they had come seven days before.

I rode into their camp, which was arranged very well, on the boundary of a settlement, near a shady stream. A round area about 60 paces in diameter with two gates was enclosed by a rather high abattis made of trees which had been cut down and piled up one on the other. Inside there were places for two tents, a place for a kitchen strewn with hen feathers, a place for storing provisions (raised a foot above ground on a stone area), 13 small cabins where servants probably lived, and 11 little pens. Judging by the manure, five of the pens were for mules and donkeys, and six were for cattle. The broken fence testified to the haste of their departure. Probably, it seemed too slow to drive the cattle through the gates; so to speed up the procdure, they broke the fence. Many of the cattle were left along the raod, and, in general, the exodus resembled a panicky flight. The *Ras* was amazed by the fear the fugitives displayed. Judging by the size of the detachment, they constituted a scientific expedition which had nothing to fear from us. With this in mind, the *Ras* sent a letter after them, expressing bewliderment about the cause of their flight.

Objects found in the abandoned camp led to the conclusion that the expedition consisted of Englishmen.

Our detachment set up camp a bit below the camp of the English expedition, on the banks of the same stream. I climbed one of the nearest hills in order to orient myself. The ridge of the height, covered with dense forest, shut off the horizon in the south. Farther in this direction there were no more people. The natives said that only elephants and other wild animals are found there.

From Menu the *Ras* had to make a rather difficult choice of route. It seemed impossible to go farther to the southwest. According to the natives, there were no inhabited lands; the time was already late; and the rainy season should be coming soon. Therefore, the *Ras* decided to postpone farther movement to the southwest to the following year and to take possession now of the mouth of the Omo River, the most important strategic point in these regions; and then return to Kaffa to finally conquer all the tribes found on the route which we had followed, and to station garrisons in their lands.

I very much wanted to investigate to what degree the territory to the southwest of Menu actually is uninhabited and impassable. I thought about separating from the *Ras*, with my own little detachment; but yielding to the request of the *Ras*, I gave up this intention and decided to go together with him to find the famous Lake Rudolf.

March 10

We rested... Since the natives did not know where to find Lake Rudolf, our natural guide was now the compass.

I determined the geographical position of Menu approximately, and showed the *Ras* the direction in which the northern section of Lake Rudolf should lie. He decided to lead his detachment straight to there. I did not fully approve that decision.

After reconnaissance on Feb. 20 and 21, I doubted the possiblity of a large detachment going across a rocky plateau with little water, straight to the lake. Besides, it seemed to me it would be necessary to thoroughly reconnoitre the territory lying to the southeast and southwest before leaving Menu.

Ras Wolda Giyorgis understood the morale and strength of his soliders better than I did. He considered it useless to undertake reconnaissance now with units of the detachment, since he was already convinced that they would yield no results. It was necessary to move ahead, not losing time and to use that inertia of strength which the army still had, rather than risk it by delay. As an experienced warrior, the *Ras* knew the laws which apply to human masses. He felt the degree of intensity of energy of his detachment and foresaw that stopping threatened much greater danger for them than the uncertainty of the desert.

MARCH 11

At dawn, the signal horn woke us as always. We left the settlement and set out to the southwest into the desert. Near the settlements, we came upon cattle left behind by the English expedition which had passed through here two days before. And at several hours journey from Menu in one ravine, which caught our attention because many predatory birds were flying over it, we found fresh bones and the innards of rams. The English expedition must have here rested during the day, after their night march of March 8 to 9.

At 11:30 we found water and set up camp. I conducted solar observations and marked our approximate astronomical position on the map.[91] Because he was extremely interested in the results of these observations, the *Ras* sent his *elfin* ashker (page) with the usual question: did I "screw up" the sun? How many numbers (i.e., minutes or degrees) had we gone? And he asked me to show him on the map the place where we were going.

I sent him the map. I wasn't in any condition to go myself. I lay on my bed in complete exhaustion. I was beginning to get a fever. To this was added severe diarrhea from disgusting food. The wheat meal had run out several days before. My *ashkers* had used a small stone bar to thresh meal from some grain they had obtained. This was, strictly speaking, not meal but rather shattered grain. From it we baked unleavened and unfermented flat cakes in iron pans, and that constituted the basis of our food. We only ate meat on days of successful hunts or in inhabited lands if we succeeded in catching a goat or ram. I no longer had any salt.[92] Because of this we could only cook meat on coals, pouring some bile over it for taste. Cooked unsalted meat and the soup made from it were too disgusting. Instead of flat cakes, we sometimes ate *mashella* grain cooked in a pan. This is a remarkably fine dish. Each grain is split into several pieces, fastened at the base, and resembles a snow white miniature rose. It is tasty but bad for the stomach, since the skin irriates it.

For a long time, I had neither tinned goods nor wine nor coffee. There remianed several little boxes of broth (Magi), in case of illness, which I now ate, and a little bottle of essence of cognac, several drops of which I added to boiling water, which, together with saccharine, I drank instead of tea. In camp, Zelepukin and I drank several saucepans of this beveridge, avoiding unboiled water. We restrained ourselves from drinking on the march.

In general, it is unpleasant to be sick; but on the march it is immeasurably worse, especially in such circumstances. The long marches then seem endless, each step of the mule seems a torture, but arrival at camp is no easier. You have no beds, and you can't get grass nearby. You lie on a tarpaulin spread out directly on the rocky ground, accommodating yourself to rocks that stick out under it. The sun shines through the poor quality material of the small soldier's tent. The temperature is 28-29° Reaumur [95-97° F] in the shade. The stuffy heat is terrible. You pour with sweat and wait and wait for evening. Finally the sun sets. Camp fires blaze. They are our light and heating. The camp grows quiet. It becomes colder and there is a new misery. A violent storm swoops down and brings down the tent; and under a downpour of rain, you are soaked to the bones...

That day we made a seven-hour march and set up camp at the foot of Mount Bume, which I had noted from the cliffs on February 21.

March 12

We set out at dawn and the *Ras* sent ahead reconnaissance to find water. The terrain we were going through was very rocky. Here and there among the stones there was some scanty grass, scorched in places, and low little mimosa and acacia trees. About twelve o'clock noon, we took prisoner several women of the Tirma tribe who live in the mountains which rise in the east. They were gathering beans here from a tree which is similar to the acacia and which the Abyssinians call komora or rok. The fruit of the komora looks like pods, inside which there are paired seeds with a meaty covering. These fruits are used in the preparation of a fermented drink; and the women, having gathered them here, take them to Menu where they barter these fruits for grain.

The prisoners had heard about Guchumba (Europeans) who passed through their lands 8-10 days before. The Europeans had bought bread from their tribe for beads and had taken a guide to Menu.

They did not know of the existence of a lake to the south. The land of Murle, about which our guide Jufa had spoken, was also unknown to them. According to them, there was no water nearby. Fortunately, we found some puddles with water, which had collected in the channel of a dried up river after the night's cloud burst. Our mounted patrols returned late in the evening and by campfires told the bivouac that they had found only desert.

The temperature during the day was 28° Reaumur [95° F] in the shade and at night was 18° Reaumur [72° F].

After a completely calm and clear day, a violent rain storm arose at night.

I felt better and recovered somewhat from my illness.

MARCH 13

The commander-in-chief continued to persist in his intention to go straight to Lake Rudolf, despite the absence of water.

We left the Tirma mountains in the northeast (where the prisoners had come from) and began to go down a little along the gently sloping inclines of the plateau, moving along the channel of a stream on the banks of which we had stayed the day before.

The countryside here is just as threatening as it is beautiful. In places there rise cliffs arranged like decorations. Their outline is in the highest degree distinctive.

In the southeast there stood out a high rocky mountain, similar to a truncated pyramid, which looked like it had another pyramid of smaller dimensions placed on its upper surface. I had first seen this mountain on February 20 and now beginning on March 8 it rose all the time on the horizon in front of us, serving as our beacon. Then I saw it March 24-30 from the valley of the River Omo, and finally in the month of April from Mount Kastit. Its local name remained unknown to me. Very often I had to plot it on my plane-table and when during the long tedious hours of lengthy non-stop marches, suffering from intense heat and thirst, I was carried away in thought to my distant homeland, this mountain reminded me of the Tsar's Cylinder at *Krasnoye Selo*. This plateau seemed to me like a huge military exercise field, and it was as if we were maneuvering our detachment over it, and ahead was the Tsar's Cylinder with a tent pitched on it as on parade days...

Therefore I named this mountain "Tsar's Cylinder" both in my journal and on my map.

About noon, after long searches, we found a puddle of water in one of the dry channels. The territory where we had come is a realm of animals, in the full sense of the word. The flat steppe, at an altitude of 1,000 meters above sea level, is covered with short unscorched white grass and rare trees. The whole animal population crowded near water. Herds of zebras roamed alternately with antelope and wild goats, and looked with astonishment on humans who unexpectedly appeared. They did not rush to go away from us. In the sand of the channel were seen the deeply pressed tracks of rhinoceroses and elephants.

Around the camp, uninterrupted gunfire resounded: the soldiers, the majority of whom had exhausted their supply of provisions, were hunting to get themselves food.

Our soldiers had left Menu with a very small quantity of provisions, hoping that a new land abundant in bread grain was no farther from Menu than Menu was from Kolu; and for those who had to carry all their supplies on their heads, it had all run out already. These soldiers, who usually observed fast strictly and were squeamish about eating the meat of wild animals, now killed whatever kind of game came their way and were not squeamish about any kind of meat; and those who did not go hunting bought meat for themselves from their more fortunate comrades. For example, two soldiers came to me during dinner and, bowing low, entreated me to sell them, in exchange for cartridges, a piece of an antelope I had killed... The old man guide Muruta-Babus said that in two marches to the north there is Kira a land rich in bread grain. The women prisoners taken the day before likewise confirmed this and on the following day the *Ras* decided to once again climb the mountains.

It was quiet and joyless in our camp. Neither songs nor laughter nor jokes, nor the humorous sayings which Abyssinian soliders so much enjoy.

This goal of wandering in uninhabited desert with little water and suffering deprivation was incomprehensible to them. Fantastic rumors spread among them. Of course, they blamed the foreigner—me—for all their troubles and gave my *ashkers* an extremely hard time.

"Where are we going?" they asked. "Are we soon going to be able to go home? Your *frenj* wants to destroy all of us! To him this is child's play. He's enchanted. He can go without eating and drinking and doesn't get tired..."

Sometimes fights even broke out between soldiers and my *ashkers*. However, in relationship to me, both the officers and the soldiers were courteous.

Incidents of people making insulting statements about me no longer occurred (as they had in the first days of my acquaintance with them), and although their feelings toward me were hostile, at the same time the soldiers respected me. Malice toward me grew in recent days and began to reach such proportions that some of my firends felt it was their duty to warn me so I would be careful...

March 14

We turned north and began to climb the mountain. I hunted antelope and zebra, killed several but, unfortunately, could take neither the hide nor the horns of the antelope and only loaded on my saddle one leg of a dead zebra for dinner. From an altitude of 1,000 meters above sea level, we climbed the mountain range to a height of 1,500 meters and by a difficult, steep descent, clearing a road in dense thickets of thorny bushes, went down to the Demu River at an altitude of 600 meters above sea level. There was very little water in the river. It sufficed only for the men. The animals were prohibited from drinking. To maintain order, a guard was posted at the water. We had gone non-stop for eleven hours that day, at a temperature of 26° Reaumur [91° F] in the shade; and during the entire march we had only found water once, at nine o'clock in the morning, in a small hole at the top of the mountain range.

In the territory where we found ourselves, nomad Idenich of the Tilay tribe wandered with their herds. The soldiers captured one of their herds and drove it to our camp. This was a lucky find for our hungry soldiers. With a cry, forgetting their weariness, they chased oxen, goats, and rams, taking them from one another.

One Tilay fell captive to us. He was two arshins and 12 vershoks tall [6 foot 5 inches], armed with two spears. A seventeen-year-old soldier caught him.

The prisoner knew the territory to the north and that to the west, including Menu. He had see Guchumba (Europeans) when they crossed through his lands, and he had sold them a goat. Regarding the existence of Lake Rudolf, he had not heard. He only knew that the Kibish River, into which the Denu River flows, flows in turn into the large War River, which was east of us about seven days' journey.

Of the tribes living to the south, he mentioned the Bumbi, who came from far to take their livestock.

MARCH 15

We crossed to the Kibish River by a valley thickly overgrown with bushes, and set up camp on its banks. The Kibish River goes down the southeast slopes of the mountain range and flows into the Omo. Its sandy channel was widely eroded as a result of the abrupt variations of the level of its water. Its current near our camp was about 6 versts [four miles] per hour. Its width was about 30 paces. Its depth was no more than an archin [28 inches]. Its altitude above sea level was 900 meters.

Near the bivouac itself, our soldiers found fresh traces of the presence of Europeans: on the banks of the river several campfires smoldered, near which lay pieces of meat, thrown away during a hasty exit, clothing of servants, and some articles such as knives with English brand names.

Apparently, they still hadn't gotten over their panicky fear of the Abyssinians and, taken unawares, had hurriedly fled. It would not be difficult for the *Ras* to pursue them now, if there were any need to do so; but, of course, there was no need for any kind of aggressive action, and the *Ras* let the Europeans go away peacefully.[93]

In the low-lying valley, closed in by mountains, it was even hotter. At noon it was 31° Reaumur [102o F] in the shade. I, as usual, "twisted the sun" and determined the astronomical position of our bivouac.

The afternoon weather was calm, but at sunset there were gusts of strong northwest wind which reminded me of the violent storms in Kolu.

March 16

We entered the land called Kira and set up our bivouac among dense settlements at a height of 1,400 meters above sea level. Near Kibisha, we stumbled upon a female rhinoceros with her young and killed them. Entering a populated land, the soldiers spread out to get provisions for themselves. The inhabitants retreated before the Abyssinians, attacking only when they got the most excited. Individual fights, which broke out rarely, cost us several men killed and wounded. Among those killed was one officer, whom the soldiers carried into the bivouac and loudly mourned.

My *ashkers* also went to get spoils and brought several skins full of grain, several pounds of coffee and a ram with a large fatty tail. I was delighted to get the coffee. We melted down fat from the fat ram's tail. From its "white fat"[94] we made candles, which for two days served as my substitute for what up until then had been my only light—the flame of the campfire.

Several prisoners were taken who belong to the same nationality as the mountain dwellers of Beru, Kasi, Dami, etc.

March 17

On the occasion of a holiday in honor of the Mother of God, the detachment was given a day of rest. Foraging was prohibited.

March 18

We went east, following along the summit of a densely populated mountain spur which stretched in this direciton. In the north, arose the rocky peak of Muy, and from both sides of the mountain ridge, streams, flowing in deep valleys, fell into the Kibish.

The natives left their dwellings and, sitting on cliffs several thousand paces from us, looked at our marching column, and sometimes pointing at the road with their spears expressed their wish that we quickly go away. The settlements were just as dense, the houses as well built, and the fields as well cultivated as in Beru. On the hill were seen the farmsteads of the tribal leaders, and near them were holy groves.

Going up to the mountain spur, we went down by a steep difficult cliff to the Karka River and set up a bivouac on its banks.

We left the populated territories behind, and ahead of us again stretched low-lying hot, and almost uninhabited space with little water.

Our march was of short duration. We had only gone for 12 days up until now, from the time when we left the fort at Kolu. We hadn't gone very many versts over that time, wandering in unknown places. But, in spite of that, our soldiers were exhausted and our animals were worn out. In such circumstances, however, it is not the distance nor the time which determines the expenditure of strength of the detachment, but rather the obstacles of the march.

Not finding water very often from bivouac to bivouac, we moved without stopping, sometimes going for ten or eleven hours under scorching intense heat, without a road, breaking a path along rocky desert strewn with sharp stones or among dense thickets of thorny bushes, which turned our clothes into rags. How much these marches made the men lame and crippled the animals, and how little time the soldiers had for rest in these conditions!... No sooner did the detachment arrive at bivouac than some soldiers went to tear out grass for mules (but there was very little of that on the rocky plateau), to fetch firewood, to fetch water, to grind meal on field millstones for flat-cakes for dinner, and others were assigned to details and guard duty. Only in the night did the detachment quiet down, and even then people who had lost their mules during the day roamed about calling out in monotonous cries "in the name of Abo" (Abyssinian saint), "return it or show me where it is."

There were also a good number of sick people in the detachment.

Now new difficulties lay ahead of us. Soldiers were ordered to supply themselves with provisions enough for not less than ten days. The *Ras* explained to his officers that we would go to the lake which is located ten days' journey away, and on the shores of which we would find provisions. But who in the detachment was confident that this lake actually exists and that the *Ras*'s words were justified? Up until this time, prisoners had talked very indefinitely about some river to the east—Shorum or War—a very large river in which, judging by the chuckles which they made when saying this, hippopotamuses swim. The water of this river becomes very great farther on and then "lies." But where the river "lies" and who inhabits its banks remained unclear; and relative to anything regarding this lake in general, the testimony was extremely contradictory. The only one who knew for certain about the existence and location fo the lake was I, and the commander-in-chief had complete faith in me. The officers were very unsympathetic toward the new march. When the *Ras* explained his decision to them at a military council, many of the leaders protested, pointing out the condition of the detachment. The commander-in-chief was unshakeable; and in refutation, he answered with the following words: "Let cowards and old women perish or clear out! I will not return without having reached the shore of the lake. And if you all leave me, I will go there with Iskyndyr Bulatovich and with the men of my guard."

I do not know if another leader could have succeeded in moving his immense weary army, who felt immediately ahead of them the horror of hunger, in a new unknown and seemingly endless desert. But Wolda Giyorgis, in the highest degree, had the gift of a military leader to control the will of his subjects and to carry them along behind him.

MARCH 19

We left the bivouac at the Karka River and went southwest. There had been a rain storm at night, which made our route very difficult. We crossed several mountain spurs of Mount Say and, finally at three o'clock in the afternoon, set up camp on the lower reaches of the Karka River. For the first time our guides were two young natives of the tribe which inhabits the western slopes of Mount Say. They had arrived the day before and had brought as a gift to the *Ras* two rhinoceros horns. These natives had heard that there is a lake to the south. They called it "Boru." Near our very bivouac was found the stopping place of the English from a month before. According to the natives, the Europeans stayed here a rather long time and then went west. These two mountain dwellers were remarkably good looking women. They had a bold open expession on their faces, and regular features, large expressive eyes, and straight noses. They led us to the southwest until we had gone a significant distance from their lands. Then when we went into a dense thicket, they quickly hid in it and ran away.

Our bivouac was at an elevation of 920 meters above sea level. The temperature was 32° Reaumur in the shade [104° F].[95]

I was beginning to feel very sick. Feeling an attack of fever approaching, I swallowed strong doses of quinine.

March 20

We went across low-lying, black-earth steppe, which was boggy from rain that had poured at night, to the Kibish River, and set up camp on its banks. Here a mass of wild game appeared. There roamed herds of wild goats, antelope, and zebra; and I shot at them without leaving the trail. Hunting the wild goats was the most fun. Frightened, they rushed at a gallop back along our whole marching column, sometimes, like crazy, bursting into our ranks. The men raised a cry, shot at the goats, threw spears, chopped with sabres and then ceremoniously divided the booty. I killed one he-goat with horns nine inches long. In the thick forest which stretches along the banks of the river, a rhinoceros attacked us. Unexpectedly, it threw itself from the bushes on the very middle of our marching column and having killed one mule (the Abyssinian who was sitting on it saved himself by some miracle), it hid in the bushes on the other side. This happened so quickly that no one even managed to shoot at it. It was remarkably hot that day, even though the thermometer only registered 28° Reaumur [95° F] in the shade. It was really a steam bath. When I arrived at bivouac, I lay in total exhaustion under my tent, having raised its side, having taken off absolutely all my clothes, and having drunk weak warm coffee. At noon I still had enough strength to conduct solar observations.

In the east, according to our guides, a large river should be found at a distance of one or two days' march. (In all probability, that would be the River Omo). But what the natives understood by one or two days' journey and whether there would be water along the way, remained unclear. It was necessary to conduct reconnaissance, but who could you rely on now? The commander-in-chief decided to do it himself. Not far away there rose the height of a mountain ridge from which one could see the river valley well. The *Ras* and I climbed one of the peaks, and in front of us in the east opened the low-lying valley. About 30 versts [20 miles] from us, at the foot of the mountain ridge which stretched out on that side of the valley, was seen a dark ribbon of trees and here, evidently, must be the water surface. The Kibish River turned to the northeast. We did not notice any other tributaries of the supposed river to the east. And the commander-in-chief took the bold decision to go straight to the east. The way along the Kibish River would take a lot of time, but, evidently, we could cover in about seven hours, without much trouble, the 30 versts [20 miles] separating us from the other river to which the Kibish aimed its path.

Not far from the hill from which we were examining the countryside arose a higher mountain which promised me a more sizable horizon. I separated from the *Ras* and headed to it, accompanied by one of my gun bearers. However, the mountain turned out to be much farther than I had guessed, and was at least 10 versts [7 miles] from the bivouac. At an altitude of more than 1,000 meters above sea level, the crest was overgrown with low grass and rare trees. On the summit, I saw several holes with water collected after the rain. Near them the ground was completely trampled by the hooves of zebras and antelope. Here went fresh trails laid by elephants, along which they, probably, crossed the mountains, wandering from the River Omo to the Kibish River. Despite such an abundance of signs of wild animals, I only chanced to see one antelope. The sun had already set when I reached the summit. I was mistaken in my expectations: nothing new could be seen from this mountain, and having taken from here azimuths on the surrounding mountains, I rushed back to the bivouac. Only at nine o'clock in the evening did I return, delayed by complete darkness and by the difficult descent.

The locale where we were now was remarkable from a minerological perspective. The bed of the stream was strewn with fragments of every possible kind of granite and gneiss. In the mountains, you encounter micaceous shale, veins of quartz, and rock crystal. Here the natives, as we later learned, mine iron and copper ore.[96]

March 21

This day was one of the most memorable of the whole expedition. At four o'clock in the morning, by the light of campfires, we loaded our mules and went beyond the Kibish River, to the southwest, toward where we presumed the River Omo lay. Having passed dense bushes along the banks of the Kibish, and having left behind us the mountain ridge on which we had climbed the day before, we entered a wide smooth steppe. Here the soil, having reverted to a swamp in the rainy period, now was strongly cracked, and in fact, our mules stumbled. The road became still more difficult thanks to the sticky mud of a night shower.

Our detachment went spread out along the steppe in a wide front.

At ten o'clock in the morning, the terrain began to change its character, and we came upon rare bushes in clumps which stood along the steppe. Here there was a lot of wildlife, but we didn't disturb it because we had such a long crossing ahead of us. Only for a giraffe was an exception made. The commander-in-chief very much wanted to kill this animal—the only one which he, up until this time, still hadn't killed. The advance guard was even ordered to quickly report as soon as giraffes were spotted.

At 10:30 in the morning, a soldier from the advance guard galloped back with the report that a herd of giraffes was near. The *Ras* jumped on his horse, and all of us who were riding mules or horses galloped in the indicated direction. We quickly overtook the herd. The fleeing giraffes made a very humorous sight. They held their long necks high (so that their snouts rose above the bushes which grew around). The short hind legs hopped as if in a gallop, and their long front legs, not bending, ran ahead of us in some sort of Spanish trot. Our horses and mules seemed faster. On my marvellous little mule, I soon caught up with one large giraffe and galloped beside him. I very much wanted to chop with a saber along its long thin neck, but the damned mule did not by any means want to get near to such a strange animal, which it had never seen before. I finally laid low the giraffe with several shots from a Mauser revolver and, having chopped off its tail as a trophy, hastened to return to the detachment, which had already gone off rather far to the side.

Passing occasional bushes, we went into dense thickets of thorny trees which the Abyssinians call "kontyr". This is a low little tree almost devoid of leaves, with branches covered with long (about a vershok [1-3/4 inches]) thorns, turned to the base. There were occasions when these thorns literally took you prisoner. One soldier caught by the shoulder and wanting to free himself, caught himself by the sleeve. With his other arm he tried to free the first, but it did not escape the same fate. The soldier tried to free it with his teeth, but the thorns caught his lips in several places, and the poor fellow began to yell with foul language.

Salt marsh replaced the black-earth steppe. Our column stopped. With sabers, we hacked a narrow trail in the bushes and slowly entered it. The heat became intolerable. The sun was almost at its zenith and scorched us with its perpendicular rays. Air in the thickets was completely motionless and was made even more stifling by the multitude of people crowded together. After a fast walk by a difficult muddy road, an intolerable thirst tormented all of us, and especially pained those of us who had gone hunting giraffes and had taken part in the 20-minute gallop after them. But we still didn't come across water, and all the water that we had had with us had already been drunk.

All our thoughts and striving concentrated on the expected river, but almost each step brought us new disappointments. Here the terrain begins to drop steeply. You strain your sight to see through the trees the water you are wishing for; but, alas, this is just a dry riverbed. Beyond that follows a second and a third... Time passes, and the torment becomes even more unbearable. Many Abyssinians—people who, it would seem, are accustomed to the heat—began to collapse, to fall from sun stroke or exhausted by heat and thirst.

It was already four o'clock in the afternoon. More than three hours, which seemed to us an eternity, had passed since we found ourselves in such completely agonizing uncertainty. Dry river beds followed one after the other. There wasn't even a sign of the presence of a river nearby. These were painful minutes... The thought oppressed us that we could be mistaken in supposing that there is a river in these thickets. Perhaps it really doesn't exist. Perhaps it's still several dozen versts away from us. Perhaps it is even located on the far side of the ridge ahead of us, and along here go only dry riverbeds of its tributaries... Perhaps, finally, I had made a sigificant mistake in determining the longitude of our bivouac, and we were actually much farther west than I thought? If this was in fact true, the detachment was threatened by certain destruction. My head became foggy from these thoughts. A moment seemed like an eternity. You count each step of the mule. You continually look at your watch, but the hands haven't moved. It's as if your watch had stopped.

Suddenly, up ahead, a cry resounded: "Water!" It was 4:30 in the afternoon. Under our feet, there began to glitter a wide band of water on the surface of which, here and there, shone the black drówsy forms of crocodiles, stretching the full length of their enormous bodies.

The commander-in-chief ordered that horns be blown—the signal to stop and camp. Along the whole column, like electrical current, went the news that water had been found. The forest resounded with joyous cries. What a feeling! What incomparable joy we experienced at this minute! Water was found! The detachment was saved!

We rushed to the river and endlessly drank its warm water. I scooped with my helmet, and the more I drank the more thirsty I became. My body, which up until then had been completely dry, was soon completely covered with sweat. One of the officers wanted to drink so much that, having arrived at the water, he felt very dizzy and fell into the river.

Only at seven o'clock in the evening did the rearguard arrive, having buried on the way four soldiers who had died from sun stroke. In all, on this day, more than ten men died, and in addition, several dozen lost their way and were missing.

Near the river itself, an Idenich woman fell captive. In the forest, she had been gathering some kind of grass which they use for food. Kelemis was the name of our prisoner. She called this valley "Kelese," and the river "War." Kelemis belonged to a tribe of savages who roamed these woods and lived by fishing and hunting. The only place which was abundant in bread grain which she had heard of was a land, according to her, about five or six days' journey away. She also knew Europeans—Guchumba. By the testimony of Kelemis, they had gone through here four days ago and had crossed the river at some distance south from our bivouac.

The river is 657 meters above sea level. Its banks are sandy and steep, rising about 30 meters above the water. The width is 200 to 300 meters. The current is about eight versts per hour.

We kept Kelemis as a guide.

MARCH 22

As usual, we set out at dawn and went south, following, at some distance, the riverbed of the War.

At about 10 o'clock in the morning, we set up camp.

I used the early stopover and hurried to one of the nearest hills to conduct noontime solar observations.

In his descriptions of his journeys, Donaldson Smith or Hohnel (I do not now remember which of them) said that those who think that travel is just a pleasant way to pass the time are very mistaken. And, actually, if the traveller only wants to get some favorable results, he would make a mess of the work. I am thoroughly convinced of the truth of that. Apart from a whole series of trouble, apart from the constant strain of attention, of cares, and long wearisome marches, how much time it takes to put together maps of the route, and make every kind of osbservation, and to choose the route, etc. On arrival at camp, instead of the wished for rest, new work awaits us: we have to mark the route on the map, write in a journal, conduct astronomical observations and calculate them approximately, take photographs, etc. If you take all this into account and also the fact that there was almost never a day's rest in recent time, and that we were on the road every day for not less than six hours, and that our transport arrived only two to three hours after arrival at the bivouac of the head of the column, then actually my whole day was filled with work. The hardest task for me was conducting solar observations at noon, especially in the low-lying valley of the River Omo. As soon as we arrived at camp, if it was before noon, I rushed with my instruments to some high hill, from which I could observe the territory. Out of breath, bathed in sweat in the 60° Reaumur [167° F] heat, I tried to get to the desired summit. Noon was already approaching. There was no time to rest. You rush to set up the instrument but somehow, out of spite, the level doesn't want to stay still for long. From the heat and the rapid walk, my heart beats quickly, my fingers refuse to handle the micrometrical screws with the necessary care. My gun bearers spread out around the little hill where I am conducting observations, protecting me in case of unexpected attack from natives lying somewhere in ambush. It is difficult to sit motionless in the full heat of the sun. The sun burns mercilessly. Sweat pours in a torrent from my forehead, onto my eyelashes, and prevents me from looking in the eye-piece of the instrument. My temples throb. My head spins... But I had to observe with my full attention. With effort, you observe the moment when the sun touches "the edge of the hairline." You must not make a mistake regarding the second on the chronometer and regarding the vernier[97] in the "vertical circle." What torture all this is and how much patience it takes!

Making use of the fact that in these latitudes the sun is almost at the first vertical, simultaneously with observations of the least zenith distances, I conducted observations of the moment of greatest height of the sun by corresponding altitudes. At the same time, I observed the place of the meridian and, with the universal instrument, took true azimuths on salient mountains.

On this day, several Idenich women fell captive to us. They were extremely ugly and gave the impression that they were complete imbeciles.

After sunset, a violent storm flew down from the northwest, bringing rain.

March 23

The detachment continued to follow along the course of the river, just as the day before, blazing a road in the dense thickets with sabers. The river turned west, and its salt-marsh banks were eroded by rain stroms in a rather large space, forming an intricate miniature mountain system. We went zig-zag, following the turns of the river and thereby, to no purpose, lost strength and time. It would have been much better to follow at a greater distance from the river, straight to the chosen bivouac site on its banks.

The *Ras* stopped and began to personally interrogate Kelemisa about the location of Murle[98] and the closest way to get there, avoiding the bushes which were holding us back. But Kelemisa, who only two days before had said she knew Murle and the road there, now flatly renounced her words and announced that she had not heard anything about Murle. Probably the other captive interpreters, wanting the detachment to quickly turn back, got her to say that. This evident lie produced an enormous impression on the soldiers who were crowding around the *Ras* and who were attentively listening to the interrogation. And because of the speed with which this news spread among the Abyssinians, it could have had dire consequences for us. They all at this point believed the *Ras*'s words that the land of Murle, abundant in bread-grain, was just a few days' journey away. Now, suddenly, the promised place had not been found, and our guide even denied its very existence. Fortunately, I was with the *Ras* at that moment and hurried to intervene.

"You lie," I told her through a translator. "Here, for this lie, I am now going to give you a medicine from which you will quickly die as soon as you tell another lie."

I ordered soldiers to open Kelmisa's mouth, and staring fixedly at her eyes, I squeezed a dose of quinine in between her teeth. Kelemisa looked at me with horror.

"Where is Murle?" I asked her after that.

She pointed south with her finger.

"Liba ie unto? Is there bread there or not?" (In the Idenich language.)

"Ie. There is," she answered.

The *Ras* and I triumphed: we had avoided a major calamity.

After this, we went further, and toward noon came to water. Kelemis now obediently carried out our orders.

At about 11 o'clock we set up camp. On the opposite bank of the river, native farmsteads were seen close together, surrounded by fields of *mashella*. On our bank, the fields were also cultivated in some places, but there were no settlements. The natives probably crossed to this side in dug-out canoes for field labor. Two men and several women fell captive to us. By outward appearance and dress, they differed from the Idenich. And they didn't understand the Idenich language. They were much better looking than the Idenich. The lower lip was pierced and into it was placed a small stick, several centimeters long, decorated with copper plates. The edge of the ears, from top to bottom, was threaded with several copper rings with red beads on them. The men were completely naked, and the women on their hips wore a short apron, embroidered with little shells, and had an oxhide thrown across their shoulders. Their hair was cut short and let grow only on the crown, in curled locks.

I "twisted the sun" and then dispensed medicine and made bandages for the sick and wounded who had come to me. The medical condition of our detachment became worse each day. Many soldiers had cut their legs on rocks or gotten splinters from thorns, and the hot tropical climate was very injurious to even the smallest wounds, subjecting them to virulent putrefication. In addition, many suffered from abscesses. Many were sick with diarrhea and fevers. There were some who were wounded during recent foraging. These men were amazingly patient. I had never seen such powers of endurance.

I spent the time after dinner with the commander-in-chief on the bank of the river, in the shade of an enormous tree. We watched the inhabitants on the other bank through a telescope and shot at crocodiles and hippopotamuses when they appeared on the surface of the water. The crocodiles were amazingly bold and did not fear men at all.

MARCH 24

The river turned east. The detachment followed its flow and about 12:30 the head of the column set up camp on the shores of a small lake, formed by flooding of the River Omo. The low-lying part of the bank was overgrown with dense forest, in which the trees attained gigantic dimensions. I "twisted the sun" and since we had gone first to the southwest and then to the southeast, and were almost not getting any closer to the celebrated Lake Rudolf, Wolda Giyorgis despaired when I showed him the location of today's bivouac on the map. He had begun to doubt that we would ever reach the lake, and today he expressed his thoughts to me in private. Evidently, the strength and energy both of the detachment and of the commander-in-chief had fallen. A characteristic indicator of this was the extent to which the marching column had stretched out: the head of the column arrived at the bivouac at 12:30 and the rear guard only at about 7 o'clock in the evening. Mules withstood the heat very badly and, going daily with packs, from seven to thirteen hours a day, with each day they became weaker and weaker. The men also were terribly exhausted—especially those who because they didn't have pack animals carried their provisions on their heads.

I acknowledged the justice of the *Ras*'s misgivings, but the lake should be quite close. And we should find provisions there! "We mustn't lose spirit," I told the *Ras*. "You know that no great deed is easily done; yes, even a woman, when she gives birth, suffers."

The commander-in-chief liked these words. Laughing, he replied, "God grant that we soon give birth to your lake."

At eight o'clock in the evening there was a violent storm, but a weaker one than the day before.

MARCH 25

The day of the Annunication was very lucky for us. Going through hilly salt marshes, we came to a level steppe overgrown with succulent grass and bushes. At eight o'clock in the morning, we sighted the farms of natives, ripening fields of *mashella* and corn and numerous herds of cattle and donkeys. How gratifying this picture was for our hearts after the barren salt-marsh hills and impassable thickets of thorny bushes! Soldiers forgot their weariness and, with a whoop, scattered over the plain. They took cattle and went into houses, looking for milk and bread. The inhabitants fled and only rarely did shots resound, bearing witness to individual skirmishes. At nine o'clock in the morning the detachment set up camp in the very center of the settlement.

I climbed one of the hills which rose not far from camp and from there conducted solar observations. Several paces from me lay an Abyssinian officer, face downwards, having buried his face in the ground and having put *matab* to his lips (a silk cord with an amulet sewed onto it, for which the Abyssinians have now substituted a cross). He had just been killed. On his back and on his neck gaped enormous wounds caused by a spear...

Having returned to camp, Zelepukin and I dined marvelously on ram cooked in butter, and drank a pitcher of milk... Soldiers returned to camp weighed down with grain and drove before them them livestock and prisoners. The prisoners were interrogated, and they indicated that the lake was just two days' journey away. For the whole detachment this day was a great holiday. For the first time in three days of marching we could go to sleep without heavy worries about the following day.

The camp didn't settle down for a long while this night. After dinner, the joyful beat of drums which rang out—*gybyr*! *gybyr*!—as the Abyssinians called it, was drowned out by the bleating of sheep, the moaning of cows, and the he-haws of donkeys newly captured by soldiers. Somewhere people were singing. Joyful laughing was heard, along with lively stories about today's battle episodes. And among all these noises resounded the usual long drawn-out cries of soldiers searching for their lost mules. Near each tent was a campfire; and by its light, soldiers busied themselves with their just-acquired donkeys, training them to carry packs. The donkeys break loose and fight, but finally submit.

MARCH 26

At five o'clock in the morning, the signal horn resounds, and we set out. A captive who was taken yesterday leads us straight along the smooth steppe which is covered with grass and rare trees. The Murdu settlements[99] were left behind. Near the banks in some places are seen fields of *mashella*, but houses are not noticeable. About eight o'clock in the morning, the surface of the lake shows in the distance. Here, finally, is the cherished goal of our expedition! Soldiers greet the long-awaited lake with joyous cries. Our marching column is again just as noisy, impetuous and joyful as it had been before. With laughs, the soldiers repeat sayings they have made up during the march, expressing in a humorous vein the hardships they have undergone.[100]

We set up camp on the shore of a small lake, among small settlements of the Masai tribe[101] and took several inhabitants prisoner. The majority of the prisoners were lame as a result of damaged tendons under the knee. I didn't succeed in determining the cause of this circumstance. Did they go lame in a fight with comrades, armed with bracelet-shaped knives, or was it a punishment for vagrancy, and a way to attach them strongly to the land?...

THE MOUTH OF THE RIVER OMO AND THE RETURN TRIP TO THE RIVER KIBISH

••••••••••••••••••••••••••••••••••••

After the uniting of three rivers named Gibye into one, the Nyanya River (what the natives who live near its mouth call the Omo) is pressed on the east by a high mountain range, which constitutes the watershed of the basins of Lake Walamo (Regina Margherita) and Lake Rudolf. On the west, it is pressed by the high Kaffa Mountains—spurs of the Emperor Nikolas II Mountain Range, which is the watershed of the basins of the Omo and Sobat Rivers. Hence it goes south from six degrees north latitude, from mountain ravines into a wide valley. Then one of the spurs of the eastern mountain range, rising in the shape of a rock ridge above the left bank of the river, deflects its flow westward, and the river skirts the southern end of these mountains at 5° 20' north latitude, flows from there south, and then at 4° 59' north latitude and 36° 14' east longitude from Greenwich falls into the Rus or Yrus Bay of Lake Rudolf. The bay is separated from another bay to the east, by a narrow belt, overgrown with half-submerged, high trees.

Along the right bank of the river, which was several dozen versts from us, a high mountain steppe stretches parallel to its flow. On the southern end of the steppe is found the pointed stony summit of Mount Kuras. To the west of these mountains, from a rocky plateau, a stream, which from time to time dries up, flows down to the lake. It flows into the wide Labur Gulf. From the east, a sizeable tributary flows into the River Omo at a latitude of 5° 20' north latitude. (Donaldson Smith climbed along its left bank during his journey and mistook this river for the Omo). The river valley is a smooth low-lying salt-march steppe, covered with grass, and along its course are found dense thickets of thorn bushes and a narrow strip of dense virgin forest. During rainy periods, the terrain near the shores of the lake is flooded to a significant extent. High fantastical column-like structures built by termites are scattered all across this space.

The banks of the Nyanya River are populated only at its mouth. The tribes who dwell here—Murle, Rogo, Murd or Murutu, Masai, and others—are related to Idenich savages, judging by type and language. The typical signs of the Negro race are noticeable in them, but they are more cultured, the expression on their faces is much more intelligent than among the savage hunters and nomads who are related to them and who dwell higher on the course of the river, and who roam in its dense riverside forests and on the rocky plateau to the northwest of the lake. This people startled the first Europeans who discovered them both, by their appearance and by the dignity with which they behaved. They are all well-built. The women are far from ugly. The men don't wear any clothing. The women wear around their hips a small crescent-shaped skin which is sometimes sewn with shells; and across their shoulders they throw a large, excellently made oxhide which hangs to the knees. The men and women adorn themselves with iron bracelets, copper ear-rings which are threaded seven in each ear, and small sticks a vershok [1-3/4 inches] in length, which are pulled through the pierced lower lip. Sometimes they replace the stick with a stalk of dry grass and whistle with it. The women, in addition, wear a necklace in several rows, made of finely sawed-up bird and crocodile bones or from clay beads, among which they flaunt blue and white European beads. For the most part, the men cut their hair short. Some have their hair fluffed high and form two separate tufts of hair, front and back. The women have their heads shaved around the crown, on top of which they grow several locks which fall downwards.

The armament of the warriors consists of long spears, the cutting edge of which is stuck on a horn handle, attached to a long cane. Spears are well sharpened and covered with leather hair-pieces. Defensive armaments consist of shields, decorated on top with ostrich feathers. Warriors adorn their heads with helmets, made from felt put together from human hair, sewn above with shells or from braided dry grass, richly decorated with ostrich feathers.

A characteristic belonging exclusively to this tribe is a small low stool which the men always carry with them. The men sometimes tatoo their right shoulder and right arm with spots and their forehead with several little vertical lines. The lower incisors of both the men and the women are usually knocked out.

Their language, judging by those words which I gathered, differs very little from the Idenich language.

Their culture is at a comparatively high level. Their dome-shaped houses are excellently built. Settlements are arranged in groups, farmsteads are surrounded by fences. The land is excellently cultivated. They raise cattle and, in addition, breed donkeys, the meat of which they use for food. Donkeys here are much larger than Abyssinian ones, light-bay in color, and excellently formed.

Most of their settlements are arranged on the left, higher bank of the Nyanya, and only the Murdu or Murutu tribe, who are distinguished for their warlikeness, spread out on the right bank, not fearing attacks of the warlike Turgana steppe inhabitants/nomads, who dwell to the west of Lake Rudolf.

MARCH 27

At seven o'clock in the morning, we set up camp on the very bank of the river, in the shade of high trees, where the Nyanaya flows into the Rus Gulf. Our detachment in part scattered through the vicinity searching for booty, while part built cabins in the camp. I took advantage of the early stopover and having set up the universal instrument on a small hill on the shore of the lake, carried out solar observations. About two o'clock in the afternoon, having finished the observations, I set out for camp. Along the way, I passed soliders returning with booty. Some carried on their heads corn or *mashella* packed in a cloak; others carried huge gourds, full of sour milk; some lucky ones drove ahead of them herds of donkeys, oxen, goats, and rams and carried on their shoulders shields, spears, and military helmets— today's victory trophies—taken from the natives. The rich booty made the Abyssinians forget their recent troubles and deprivation. They sang war songs and threw one another witicisms and jokes. They met me now with special respect and bowed low to me. Several kissed my knees and naively thanked me for having "led them to a good land," as if I were the one who had initiated this...

I no sooner succeeded in returning and dining on a piece of meat cooked in donkey oil, when the *Ras* and his confessor, surrounded by a crowd of soldiers, came to my tent. They brought me a small boy, abandoned by its parents and terribly mutilated by our blood-thirsty Kulo.[100] By the look of him, he was about three years old. A priest found him in the reeds, where he lay in a helpless state near the river itself. The priest picked him up and took him to the *Ras*, who now brought him to me asking that I help.

The boy stood silently before me, with his legs spread wide. He was terribly covered with blood, but the blood for the most part had dried. The little sufferer did not moan and did not cry, but just looked at all of us meekly. When I laid him on his back so I could bandage him, he, seeing scissors in my hands, began to defend himself with all his strength and to plaintively cry, "Ay! Ay! Ay!"—pounding his chest with his palms. Stern soldiers, who had shed much blood in their time, out of pity could not look at the innocent boy who had spilled his blood and was suffering. One after the other, they left. The first to go was the *Ras* himself. I cleaned the wound, washed it with a mixture of mercuric chloride and cocaine and, having made a bandage, laid the boy in my tent.

Vaska, which is what I called him, turned out to be a good, healthy, big-bellied, little boy. The hair on his head was cut short. Only on top did two bunches of hair stick up. His two lower incisors had been knocked out. He had iron bracelets on his arms and legs, and on his neck on a string were fastened two small crocodile bones and were strung beads made of clay. Zelepukin wanted to take them, but Vaska caught hold of them and wouldn't give them up for anything.

I spent the rest of the day in a "dolce far niente" [pleasant idleness] on the banks of the river. In my soul, above all other feelings, the feeling of uncommon peacefulness and "satiation of energy" predominated, if one could express oneself that way—a state which only occurs after completing some difficult protracted task which you have been given. It is pleasant to realize that it is finished, but at the same time you feel some emptiness... The *Ras* lay on the high bank of the river on the spread out shamma of one of his pages, having laid down his head on the knees of a colonel. The other officers sat or lay around. We looked at the quietly flowing, turbid waters of the river and took shots at crocodiles and hippopotamuses which appeared here and there. Through a telescope, we observed what people were doing on the opposite bank, and, now and then, exhausted from the heat and stuffiness, ran down to drink the warm water of the Nyanya...

MARCH 28

The detachment was given a day of rest. The troops were ordered that each rank of the detachment get two stones for the building of a monument in commemoration of our arrival here. One of the colonels was ordered to get men and prepare for the crossing of a small detachment to erect the Abyssinian flag on the other bank.

In the morning I ordered Gebra Maryam (the soldier-interpreter of the Shuro language) to bring all of the prisoner-interpreters, and each of them came accompanied by the soldier to whom he was entrusted. I spoke to Gebra Maryam in Abyssinian and he tanslated my words into the Shuro language for the old man

Murutu-Babus, who translated them into the language of the mountain dwellers for the captive of the land of Kanta, who in turn translated them for the Idenich, who had been captured several days before near the River Omo, and who, finally, communicated my question to the latest prisoner, the one from the Masai tribe. This wasn't an easy matter. At first, each interpreter repeated several times to his neighbor "Listen well!" and translated my words for him only after the listener had, as requested, answered several times: "I hear well." In this manner, my question travelled to the Masai and back and, of course, underwent all kinds of distortions. Therefore, it was necessary to begin again, with the risk, however, that the mistake would be repeated, since it was not known at which link of the chain it had occurred. Even what would seem to be the most simple pieces of information—for example, the names of the land and the tribe of the new captive—could only be obtained after long interrogations. To satisfy myself that they were really answering the question, I had recourse to all possible ways of verifying it; otherwise you could obtain phenomenal distortions. In a word, I refined my sensitivities, like an investigator during a difficult interrogation.

Finally, I succeeded in learning something. I put together something resembling a dictionary.[103] The languages of the Masai and Idenich tribes seemed so similar that I suspect that a mistake occurred, and that the captured Masai answered with words of the Idenich language which he knew.

Regarding the tribes which live nearby, I found out the following: to the west from the mouth of the river is the land of Lomodok, the inhabitants of which are rich in livestock, but who do not do any cultivation. To the south of them, along the western shores of the lake live the warlike Turgana, who have many herds of livestock and many camels. The Turgana do not sow bread grain, but gather on the shores of the lake some kind of grass which they use as food. (Our soldiers found supplies of grass with many of the women whom they took prisoner near the lake; but not knowing its use, they threw it away). Many of the prisoners had light blue beads on their neck, some had copper cartridge cases, which, they said, Guchumba (Europeans) had given them. Actually, near the very mouth of the river traces of a demolished European camp could still be seen. A low abattis surrounded a small area in one of the corners of which was built a watch-tower. Around the abattis lay many fish and ram bones and, among them, a human skull. The Guchumba were here three months ago, and from here they went into the land of Naruga, up along the course of the River Omo. Apparently, these Europeans were those whose traces we encountered in Menu. The natives, according to their words, had never seen any other Europeans.

Worn out by the interrogation, I went to rest on the bank of the river, where, at this time, soldiers were getting ready for tomorrow's crossing. The *Ras* requested interpreters for himself for negotiations with natives on the far side of the river.

Several naked black figures sat on that far bank on low stools, under the shade of a branchy tree.

"Come submit to us," the Masai cried out to them, on order of the *Ras*.

"We don't know you," they answered from the other bank. "You Guchumba (vagrants), go away from our lands."

"If you don't surrender voluntarily, we will shoot at you with the fire of our guns, we will take your livestock, your women and children. We are not Guchumba . We are from the sovereign of the Amhara (Abyssinians) Menelik."

"We do not know Amhara-Menelik. Go away! Go away!"

These talks brought no success, but when a dug-out canoe, found higher on the course of the river, arrived at our bank, the natives became more tractable and began to ask:

"Who is this Amhara-Menelik to whom we are supposed to submit?"

"We are Amhara, and Menelik is our great king."

"You will kill us if we come to you."

"No, no. We will not kill you. Come. Bring tribute."

"Good. We will have a talk about that..."

At this time, several Abyssinians moored to the opposite bank in order to bring across to our side another dug-out canoe which was there, and the natives hid.

Before evening I performed some operations. I lanced the abscesses of three sick men: one on the hand and two on the soles of the feet.

In our camp, despite the fact that we have been here such a short time, the stench of the mass of innards of slaughtered animals lying around had begun to spread. The Galla literally stuffed themselves with meat. The Abyssinians cut it up into thin ribbons and dried it in the sun for the future, for the first meal after their fast. In particular, processing water-skins corrupted the air. To do this, they moisten the just-taken animal hide and hold it until it begins to rot so much that the animal hair begins to come off easily. Then they take the hair off, inflate the skin and press down on it with their feet. There was almost no soldier who didn't stock up with water-skins. At almost every tent you see either moistened water-skins, set out to rot in the air, or ones fully inflated with air and drying in the sun. You see soldiers dancing on other such skins, holding onto the branch of a tree with their arms and jumping high on a tightly inflated water-skin.

Vaska lives, and today I gave him a bandage. Today one of the *ashkers* went past the tent where Vaska lies, going to slaughter a ram. As soon as Vaska saw the knife in his hand, Vaska grabbed a stone and raised it threateningly at him. Such spirit in a three-year-old boy! I completely agree with those explorers of Africa who confirm that here there are no children, or, better said, that all—old and young—are equally children.

March 29

In the morning, everything was ready in camp, and volunteers were already beginning to cross to the other side of the river in the two canoes obtained yesterday. They were dug-outs and were very unsteady. The people sat six to a canoe, holding their arms overboard and clasping the person in front of them with their legs. On the stern, stood experienced boatmen of the *Ras* from the Kulo tribe, who lived on the banks and of the Omo. They rowed with long oars. From the lake there blew a strong wind which raised waves on the river, and the waves washed across the low sides of the dug-outs. About a hundred men crossed over, and from this side a thousand guns supported them. The last to cross were Ato-Bayu and I, with a flag attached to a long pole. We tied the flag to the top of a large tree, and from the other side, the troops saluted with a volley of gunfire and the beating of drums.

After having erected the flag, Ato-Bayu and I went back, but the other soldiers scattered along the densely populated bank; and the shots which resounded from time to time showed that they, with deeds, were confirming the words of the *Ras*, when he was trying to convince the natives to submit willingly. The volunteers assembled for the return crossing only at sunset and returned to our side in the same order in which they had come. The *Ras* did not undertake any more serious operations on that side, since his domain ended at the right bank of the River Omo.

In the evening we ceremoniously erected a flag at the mouth of the river. On a signal from the *Ras*, the detachment came forward, as a reserve column, to the shores of the lake. Each rank of the detachment, including the *Ras*, carried two stones on its shoulders. We stopped on one of the hills at the very shore and made a high pile from those stones. In the middle, we fixed a column (12 arshins [28 feet] high), made by connecting several tree trunks; and on the end of it rustled a silk green, red and yellow Abyssinian flag. Then the detachment formed up in the shape of the letter pi in front of the flag, with their backs to the lake. On the opposite side, with his face to the lake, stood the commander-in-chief and his suite, and behind them the drummers and flutists and pipe players. The *Ras* took a gun in his hands. All became quiet. All eyes were directed at the commander-in-chief, and the army with tension waited for his first shot. This was a moment of celebration. In front, the lake glistened, that same long-wished-for lake, to which we for so long and steadfastly had striven. To the right, stretched out the low-lying steppe, and there the far mountains; to the left lay the dense forest along the banks of the River Omo. And against this background the front of the Abyssinian army stood out brightly. The silk shirts shone, the animal hides, the gold and silver decorations; and Abyssinian flags fluttered. Finally, a shot rang out, and five thousand Abyssinian guns saluted the new domain of Menelik and again erected his flag. They beat drums, blew on pipes, blew on flutes, and broke out in military songs. Moved, *Ras* Wolda Giyorgis embraced me, and I, warmly and with feeling, congratulated him.

March 30

The detachment set out on the trip back. I separated myself from it, intending to climb Mount Kuras, which rose on the southern end of the mountain range, and which stetched out at several dozen versts from the right bank of the river. I wanted to conduct observations there and to make connections with the summits of the mountain range in the north which should be visible from there. Because the detachment was overtired, only two of my gun bearers accompanied me—Ababa and Aulale. I didn't forewarn the *Ras* of my intentions, knowing that he would not agree to let me go alone without a convoy. We set out at four o'clock in the morning and went quickly along the plain. At first, the terrain was very even, and I, in an amble, rode on my marvellous little mule. Ababa and Aulale, the first with the three-eighths inch caliber rifle and the universal instrument, and the second with the tripod, rushed after me at a run. The sun soon rose, and it became hot, and the road became more difficult. The loose soil, which had become soaked during flooding, had deep cracks. The mule stumbled every minute. We went more gently. At about nine o'clock in the morning we heard, not far from us, conversation in the bushes. My boys rushed there and stumbled upon about ten natives with their families. They had just slaughtered a large ram and were skinning it. Taken completely unawares, the natives fled in all directions, and my *ashkers* rushed after them. My mule, which could not run quickly because of the cracks in the soil, fell behind the *ashkers*. However, this was for the best since soon the natives, having noticed that the there were only two Abyssinians, stopped and began to go up to my *ashkers* from behind; and only when I appeared did they definitely run away. Ababa finally caught a native who was armed with spear, shield, bow and arrows, and Aulale caught his wife with an infant. In this case, my *ashkers* showed themselves to be fine fellows, since only a brave man could capture an armed man, even if he was fleeing. It was much easier and more tempting to shoot him with a gun... As for Aulale, he was completely unarmed, with only the tripod for the instrument on his shoulders, when he pursued the natives. The prisoners were in complete despair. The man plaintively bellowed and stretched his arms out forward, having turned them palms upward; and the woman pressed several drops of milk from her breast on her palms and stretched them out to me, begging for mercy. The baby howled. A little dog, who had stayed faithful to his masters, twirled around us and inundated us with barking... I had the idea of using our captives as guides, and I began to calm them down as best I could, pointing at the mountain which was seen up ahead and expressing with signs that I wanted to go there and then would let them go free. They understood, it seemed, and stopped trembling. My boys lifted their burdens onto them—the instrument and the tripod—and we went toward the mountain.

The prisoners were from the Turgana tribe. The man was of tall build, with rather regular facial features, a straight nose, not at all similar to the Negro. His lips were not especially thick. His eyes seemed intelligent. The expression on his face was open. He was circumcised, and his hips were tatooed with small spots. Over his shoulders was thrown the black hide of a little goat, which hung from the shoulders backward and constituted his entire dress. His hair was plaited and long, hanging down to the shoulder in a chignon, somewhat resembling the hairstyle of one of our seventeen-year-old women, who wear their hear in silk nets. The end of the chignon is twisted in a tail with sticks out behind. On the crown of his head was an ostrich feather.

His travelling companion was a young, very well-built and comparatively beautiful woman. By type, she was similar to a Somali. Around her hips was wound an oxhide. She had iron bracelets on her arms. Her hair was cut short, and only on the crown of her head was there left a tuft of hair. Her lips were not pierced, as is the case with Idenich women; and her front incisors were not knocked out. At about ten o'clock, we reached the foot of the mountain and began to climb up by a way strewn with hardened lava and rocks. Soon I had to get down from the mule and, leaving one of my *ashkers* with it, I went ahead on foot.

The sun was particularly scorching that day. The ascent seemed difficult and very steep, strewn with small stones. Its inclines were overgrown with dense thorny bushes. We clambered up with difficulty; all the same, stumbling and falling... Half-way, the prisoners refused to go farther and lay down, hugging one another. No kind of threat helped. They, probably, decided that it was better to die than to go farther. The captive man was very necessary to me because only he could tell me the names of the surrounding mountains. Therefore, I decided to force him to go at any cost. I shot my revolver right above his ear and, making use of his fear, I picked him up by the hair. I lifted his burden onto my shoulders and went forward. He followed me mechanically. The woman continued to lie, and we left her. The father took the baby in his arms. At 11:15, completely worn out, we reached the summit of the mountain. Its height above sea level is 1047 meters. The height of the climb was 500 meters. The temperature of the air at the foot of the mountain was 34° Reaumur [108° F] in the shade, and at the top was 28o Reaumur [95° F]. Noon was approaching. In addition to the least zenith distances of the sun, I also had to observe the moment of its greatest height and the place of the meridian. There was no time left for rest. I, despite complete exhaustion, hurried to set up the instrument and got to work. Having finished the solar observations, I began to draw on the plane-table the territory which opened up from the height of the mountain, and to take azimuths on salient points and to try to find out from the captive the names of the surrounding mountains. Because I didn't know his language, of course I had to express myself with signs.

From here, all the northern part of the lake with its three bays is seen as clearly as if it were on your palm: two narrow and long on the east, into one of which, Rus, the Nyanya flows; and a wide bay in the west—Labur, surrounded with mountains, like an amphitheater. This bay ends in the south with a high rocky cape, on which there rise three peaks. I could not determine the local name for it and therefore in honor of Vaska, whom I had found that day, I named it the "Cape of Vaska." This cape ends with the mountain range of Moru and Nakua which stretches from the west to the east.[104] Separate from these mountain ranges and somewhat north of them, rises a cone-shaped summit, like an extinct volcano, which the captive called Erek. Farther, in the northwest, was seen the high mountains of the mountain range which was already known to us, and in the west towers the sharp peak of the mountain I called the Tsar's Cylinder. In the northeast, scarcely noticeable in the haze of the horizon, were the summits: Mount Dime (M.O. Smith) and Mount Ya-Menelik-Saganeyt, which were first seen by me from Mount Boka. To the south of them was a high mountain range with several sharp-peaked summits, hidden away in the southeast.

Into Labur Bay, on its northeast end, there flowed an unknown river, and along its course there wound a ribbon of green trees.[105] This river unites in it those beds of dried up streams which were crossed on March 11 to 13.

The water in the bay had apparently risen to a higher level than usual, since part of the trees at the mouth of the river were half-submerged.

It was already 1:30 in the afternoon when I finished my observations and we began to go back down the mountain. Standing on our feet or squatting, we slid down the steep descent, strewn with crushed stone. And at two o'clock in the afternoon we reached the spot where we had left the mule. The captive also went behind us. Plaintively repeating "Dulole! Dulole!" he called his wife. But Dulole did not respond. We were tormented with thirst. In a gourd, there remained still a few mouthsful of water, and we divided it equally. The Turgana, for his part, gave several drops to the baby.

Up until sunset there now remained only three and a half hours. And until water, there were no less than 20 versts [13 miles], and to the bivouac it was still much farther. We had been on the move since four o'clock in the morning and had gone more than 30 versts [20 miles], not counting the climb up the mountain. We did not have any provisions with us. Water, of which we needed to have only two cups per man, was all drunk up. And up until the Nyanya itself we would not have any more. Having left the captive with his baby, we just barely pushed forward. Auiale had colic. I sat him on the mule and went on foot. After an hour he felt better, and we went farther, taking turns on who sat on the mule. On the horizon, the forest along the river bank, toward which we were stiving, shone black. But it didn't seem to get any closer, but rather seemed to get farther away from us. At five o'clock in the afternoon, we took a five-minute break; and I no sooner succeeded in sitting on the mule again, when, not far off, a herd of goats and rams came out from the bushes, and after them came several dozen natives. Behind them rose the voices of still others. They, probably, were withdrawing deep into the country, getting away from the Abyssinians who were going along the river.

Our position was rather difficult now. The natives, seeing how few of us there were and how weak we were, would most probably attack us. We, extremely exhausted, could not withstand a protracted fight, all the more so since our arms were very insignificant—just one rifle with 30 cartridges and one revolver with 10 cartridges. It seemed to me that it would be much better for us to attack them unexpectedly, rather than wait to be attacked. Not losing a second, I galloped at the natives and they, startled by my sudden appearance, scattered in all directions and hastened to run away. Carried away by my example and forgetting their weariness, Aulale and Ababa ran headlong in pursuit. I attacked the second group of natives, who were more persistent than their first comrades, and I even got into a fight with one of them... The natives abandoned their herd, and our path was now free. I stopped and began to call my *ashkers*.. But they did not respond. I fired a shot, but no answer followed. I waited for them for about 20 minutes, calling and firing shots, but they didn't raise their voice in reply. It was useless to look for them now. To wait longer was pointless and dangerous. If they were alive, then they, probably, worn out with thirst, were now hurrying straight to the river. With the burdensome feeling of not knowing what had become of my companions, I left this place behind. I began to come upon many signs of livestock, heading to the south. It must be that the natives went this way, driving their herd in the opposite direction from the Abyssinians. To my amazement I still didn't see traces of our detachment, which by my calculations I should have found already.

The sun had already set and it was becoming dark when I got to the forest by the river. To my horror, I came upon the following scene: on the edge of the forest lay an Abyssinian killed with a spear and beside him lay his horse. He was probably one of the scouts who had separated from the detachment. A bit farther, in a hidden clearing in the forest, there lay about in the grass regularly arranged rope nets, stretched on wooden frames for loading donkeys. This must have been the bivouac of those whom the Abyssinians frightened off. In a thicket of the forest, I stumbled upon a hunters' lair, arranged under a large branchy tree and surrounded by dense bushes. In the middle of a circular area, a sagene and a half in diameter [3 meters], was the hearth, and beside it was a unique basket, an arshin and a half [42 inches] in height. Twigs were stuck in the ground and connected with hoops. The bottom of it was located at half an arshin [14 inches] from the ground, and in the basket were placed pieces of dry wood and coal.

The dense forest was not quite so uninhabited as it had seemed at first glance...

Forcing my way with difficulty through the thicket, I continued to go toward the water and finally reached the steep bank of the Nyanya. It was impossible to water the mule at this place, and having fastened its lead to my saber, which I drove deep into the ground, I, grabbing hold of a liana, let myself down from a height of several sagenes [a sagene is a little more than two meters] to the river and greedily began to drink its warm water. Using the same liana, I climbed back up. To my great happiness, I found my mule—now my only companion—in the same spot where I had left it, and my fears that some Idenich would kill it from ambush or that it would break away, frightened accidentally by a wild animal, were not justified.

I left the forest and again began to look for traces of the detachment. My recently quenched thirst flared up again now to a much greater degree; and my body, which before this, had been dry, was completely covered with perspiration.

Along the way, I frequently came upon gullies. It was impossible to go farther in such conditions. I had to wait for the moon.

The moonless black tropical night was now in the full strength of its mysterious beauty. It was terrifying to feel yourself completely alone, lost in the middle of an unknown, hostile land. There were no signs that the detachment was near, and I tried in vain among the night sounds to make out the neighing of a donkey. It was to no purpose... Only an elephant was forcing its way into the forest through the thicket, and from the river sounded a hippopotamus and the piercing cry of a night bird... Getting down on the ground and tightly tying the mule's lead to my hand, I leaned against a high hill built by termites and dozed off. Exhausted, and not having had anything to drink all day, the mule stood hanging its head. Sometimes, having sensed a wild animal in the vicinity, it snorted in fear and pricked up its ears.

I was in a state of both sleep and drowsy consciousness. I held the mule tightly, listened hard to each rustle, and was ready for the most desperate self-defense; but, at the same time, fantastic pictures went through my imagination one after the other. This was really a waking dream... In thought I was carried away to my family, to my comrades in the regiment. I remembered petty incidents of my life and, facts were interwoven with fantasy in a continuous chain of images.

Finally, at about 12 o'clock at night, the moon came out and I set out farther in search of the detachment. The whole time I followed along the steep edge of the steppe to the north, and after an hour I began to come across frequent tracks of mules and horses. Still a bit farther, I came upon a wide trail trampled down by people on foot and by horses. The tracks led to the north: there was no doubt that they belonged to our detachment. I rode at a trot along the trail, time and again stumbling upon the bodies of men and animals who died during the march, and my mule threw itself to the side in fear. In low places near the bodies, hyenas already reigned; and in the quiet of the night there resounded either the growling or the groaning of a lion— long-drawn out, heard from afar, but not seeming loud.

At about three o'clock in the morning, I reached the place where our bivouac had been located on March 25. The detachment had left it, and the trail went far in the middle of dense grass and bushes. I rode quickly in the high grass. Suddenly, at several paces in front of me, in the light of the moon, there shone the blades of spears, and I saw three natives. I quickly shot at the middle one with my revolver and galloped at them. The middle one fell, and the others rushed into the bushes. The meeting with natives indicated that our bivouac was near: they were probably roaming close to it. Actually, in a little while, I heard nearby the loud neighing of a donkey, which at this memorable moment in my life joyfully resounded in my heart, like the voice of the herald of my salvation.

My servants, having waited for me with alarm, came to meet me with burning logs. My meeting with Zelepukin was the most joyous. He, poor fellow, was already beginning to grieve and getting ready to go on a search. It was already four o'clock in the morning. I quickly had a bite of a stale flatcake.

Ababa and Aulale arrived almost at the same time I did. Pursuing the natives, they had stumbled upon the road by which the detachment had gone; and, tormented by thirst, they had set out straight for water, leaving me alone.

This day's march did not come easily to the detachment either. The *Ras* ordered his troops to go straight through the waterless steppe, in order to avoid the bends of the river and the bushes on its banks. Several dozen captive women and children died because of this, since they were unaccustomed to protracted walking and endured thirst badly.

Of our soldiers, five died from sun stroke.

MARCH 31

We avoided the bivouac of March 24 and came close to the bivouac of March 23.

Our marching column had increased now almost to double what it had been before, from the quantity of livestock that had been taken, and captive women and children. The *Ras* did not have the spirit to force his soldiers to give up their booty.

Our soldiers were in a state of bliss: donkeys carried reserve provisions, relieving their masters of this heavy burden which they otherwise would have had to carry on their heads. Captive boys carried guns and shields or drove cattle which had been taken. And captive women, quickly submitting to their fate, already went for water, tore up grass for mules and ground meal. My boys also got several donkeys for themselves and grieved that they had not succeeded in capturing a Negro woman who would relieve them of the necessity of grinding meal themselves.

Vaska gradually got better. They carried him in their arms during the march. He is a remarkably intelligent boy and already knew my name and Zelepukin's, and could already ask for food and drink, etc., in Russian.

We hunted for elephants and wounded several of them, but the elephants got away.

April 1

We set up camp half an hour's distance ahead of our stopping place of March 22. The commander-in-chief decided to go from here straight to the Kibish River, in order to avoid the dense and thorny thickets which we had found ourselves in on March 21.

April 2

At two o'clock in the afternoon we set out, taking with us as much a supply of water as possible, and went until complete darkness. We set up camp at eight o'clock in the evening.

April 3

At two o'clock in the morning we got up and, orienting ourselves by compass, moved farther on. Having avoided the thickets, the arrived at the grassy steppe before sunrise.

At six o'clock in the morning we stumbled upon a lion and killed it. The vanguard saw it when it was quietly going away from the approaching detachment. They notified the *Ras* of this, and we began to rush so as to cross its path. The *Ras* shot at the lion first. Then others. The lion fell, turning its head toward us. It was still alive. Several Abyssinians came galloping up to it and killed it with sabers.

The sun soon rose and lit up the mountains which rise along the Kibish River. We set out to the familiar summit, near which we had set up camp on March 20. The way there still seemed very long. It became hot. The water we had taken with us was all drunk up by nightfall. Our column spread out, and the weaker began to fall behind. First the captive women and children began to fall and die. There was no one to pick them up, and they were thrown on the deserted steppe, since whoever could rushed with all his strength to water.

At about ten o'clock in the morning, we saw a herd of giraffe at about a verst [two thirds of a mile] from the detachment, and the *Ras* still had the endurance to hunt them. Accompanied by several officers, he galloped after them. But the hunt was unsuccessful: horses, stepping in cracks in the soil, fell. My friend Ato-Bayu broke his collar-bone this way, and I made him a bandage, using for this his long belt.[106]

At about twelve noon the vanguard horsemen reached the river and having drunk and gotten as much water as they could, galloped back to help their comrades on foot. Only at four o'clock in the afternoon did the detachment assemble. We had lost from sun stroke four Abyssinians and two Galla. About a hundred captives had been left behind. Zelepukin, who went with the transport in the middle of the column, had seen all kinds of horrors during the march and arrived very downcast.

"How awfully pitiful it is to look at the captive Shankala (Shankala is "Negro" in Abyssinian), your Honor," he said. "They walk, then stagger, then fall and lie. The master lifts her, beats her, but already, evidently, she has no strength left. He can't pick her up, so he throws her aside and leaves."

The temperature at noon was 32° Reaumur [104° F] in the shade.

APRIL 4

It is Holy Saturday. The detachment sets up camp at the Kibish River, and a select command of ten men from each regiment with an officer is sent to the fort at Kolu to lead the detachment which had been left there. Muruta Babus went with the select command. He was infinitely happy when he found out that they would let him go free. He danced in front of the tent of the *Ras* and sang, improvising in his language, laudatory songs in honor of the *Ras*. The commander-in-chief generously gave presents to Muruta. I also gave him a shirt, and we movingly said good-bye to one another. This is an amazing man, patient, hardy, never showing fatigue and, in spite of his age, remarkably cheerful. He was a favorite of the detachment, and the soldiers called him "Komoru" ("king" in the Shuro langauge). During marches they always joked with him, making him, like a parrot, pronounce all kinds of swear-words. And Muruta, to the general satisfaction, willingly did all that. One time he fell ill. This happened suddenly when he was more than ever necessary, serving as our guide (March 14-15). They made him a stretcher, and he almost constantly stayed with the commander-in-chief, who rode behind him, and the whole marching column. Long and thin, Muruta got even worse, and for three days could eat nothing. But, in spite of that, he never complained; and to all our questions, he answered only "bushi, bushi" which means "well."

With his intelligence and understanding, Muruta stood out from the other interpreters. In him appeared the undoubted superiority of the mountain-dweller race to which he belonged, over all the other tribes who dwelt in this area.

Muruta was very friendly with me, and called me none other than Benti-Babus, which means "great wizard."

In Holy Week, the Abyssinians adhere to the most strict fast. On Good Friday and Holy Saturday they eat and drink nothing. On the march, they refuse food and drink only on Saturday. I did not want to lag behind the Abyssinians in this and also today ate and drank nothing.

Since we had to stay at this bivouac for several days to give time for the detachment setting out from Kolu to reach us, I built myself a small lean-to and moved into it from my low torn-up tent. Not moving, I lay there the whole day, bathed in sweat and with impatience awaiting the cool of the evening.

The army was given an order in which it was added that soldiers observe cleanliness in camp and bury all garbage deep in the ground.

The *Ras* sent me a large bull as a present on the occasion of the breaking of the fast. At sunset, my *ashkers* slaughtered it beside my lean-to and swarmed there, sharing the carcass, looking forward to the delight of breaking the fast.

That night our detachment did not sleep. Here campfires burned, and whoever could got ready to meet the coming holiday. Already several times a chorus of donkeys neighed—they were the cocks of our detachment. But midnight still didn't come and, in anticipation of it, soldiers sat around the fire and quietly chatted. The officers by the light of candles made from the epiploon of rams, in an undertone read the Psalter or the Gospels. This night was unusually solemn and, as always, full of expectations. Finally, from the tent of the *Ras*, a shot resounded—Christ is risen! And through our whole bivouac, gunfire began to crack in a thunder peal, and piercing joyous cries spread out: "I-li-li-li-li." Zelepukin and I exchanged a triple kiss [Easter greeting] and began to break the fast with milk and meat, dreaming of salt, which we hadn't had for a long time. After several minutes, a messenger came from the *Ras* with an invitation for me to dinner.

April 5

Easter Sunday. The *Ras* arranged a large feast for all our detachment. The food, however, was very simple, consisting of unleavened bread flat-cakes and fresh meat, which the Abyssinians, after a protracted fast, ate in incredible quantities. My *ashkers*, for example (there were eleven of them in all with me), succeeded in annihilating an entire bull in two days. Vaska's stomach swelled and became hard, like wood, but apparently that didn't harm him. He was happy, recovered, and his wound healed. Zelepukin followed him around like a nanny and lay down to sleep beside him, not being squeamish about the fact that Vaska behaved badly at night and only swore about this each morning.

April 7

I went hunting. On the damp sand of the riverbed of the Kibish River, there were fresh tracks of lion paws and of rhinoceroses; but in spite of searching hard, I didn't shoot any wild animals. The day before, lions had roamed near our bivouac and had slaughtered several donkeys and one woman. At night I set out on the hunt.[107] With one of my *ashkers*—Aregau—I climbed a tree, fastening myself to the branches with a long strap, and tied a little goat to a bush. As soon as it became dark, from the direction of the river, there was heard, similar to deep breathing, the growling of several lions. The goat was on the point of beginning to rush about, but it did not bleat. We waited in vain all night long. The lions did not come to us. In the morning, limping on both legs which had become numb during the night, I returned to the bivouac and snatched a hasty bite to eat.

In the north, approximately 15 versts [10 miles] from the place where we had set up our bivouac, a high mountain was seen, on which I found it necessary to climb to survey the vicinity. It seem to me that it would be possible from there to at the same time see both northern and southern summits which were already known to me and to "connect them among their azimuths." I decided to do this quickly. This time I couldn't go without letting the *Ras* know. He ordered a convoy of 26 men under the command of an officer to accompany me. In addition to them, I also took three of my *ashkers*: Tekla Giyorgis, Ababu, and Abto Selassie.

Crossing the Kibish River, we, along the low-lying steppe which stretches along the River Omo, set out straight to the mountain, which turned out to be much farther away than I had assumed. Only at ten o'clock in the morning, after going for four and a half hours, did we reach the foot of the mountain. Here a high steep stone ridge rises 1000 meters straight up from the valley of the River Omo. Dense settlements of natives huddle together along ledges. Apparently, the summit of the mountain is completely populated. We found a trail which led up and started to climb. My soldiers followed me very unwillingly.

As soon as the natives noticed us, they filled the mountains with alarm cries; and their warriors, armed with spears and shields, began to come running together in groups, and the women and children escaped, driving the livestock. On a ledge of the cliff, a hundred paces in front of us stood an old man. He threw handsful of dust in our direction, probably as an incantation. When we approached, the old man hid behind a tree. I ordered Abto Selassie to catch him, and my ashker swiftly went after the old man and, in a moment, disarmed him and took him prisoner. The decrepit old man was not at all confused by this and coolly continued to smoke his long pipe. We led the prisoner forward and went farther. A group of about a hundred warriors, having occupied a narrow passage, blocked the road to us. I told my men not to fire, and we calmly went closer. When we were only 50 paces from the warriors, from their group I heard the cry "Halio" (peace). I also answered them "Halio", and having stopped the detachment, tore out a bunch of grass as a sign of my peaceful intentions, and in earnest approached the three natives in front. They pointed to the old man, apparently asking that we let him go; and I did so. Then I, with signs, expressed to them that I demanded them to put down their weapons, threatening that otherwise I would kill them with a puff of my gun. They understood and began to carry out my request, and in the group of natives, the old ones who were more prudent and who wanted peace, forced the young ardent ones to obey. The road was now clear and we went farther. However, my soldiers turned out to be too frightened to go ahead. They unanimously began to refuse and asked me, in the name of the God of Menelik and of Wolda Giyorgis to go back. I couldn't agree to their demands. Having come so close to the goal I had set myself, for me it would have been too painful to renounce it now. Moreover, the natives were not acting especially hostilely toward us, and retreat seemed disgraceful to me. With harsh expressions, I began to reproach the soldiers, called them "mice" (the most insultng expression for an Abyssinian warrior) and, having called my three *ashkers*, I went forward decisively, having told the soldiers that whoever of them wanted to could go back to the *Ras*. My decisiveness had an effect on them; and the soldiers, this one grumbling, that one justifying himself, reluctantly followed me. We had not succeeded in going several hundred paces when the natives, who had seemed conciliated, began again to get ready for hostile action. It must be that the party of the young, brave warrians got the upper hand; and they, quickly hiding behind rocks and trees, began to overtake the tail of my detachment. In front of all of them ran a mountain dweller of enormous size with decorations made of ostrich fathers on his head and three spears in his hands. He was already just 50 paces from our rear and, jumping high, he performed his war dance and aimed his javelin at one of my soldiers. To tarry longer was unthinkable.

A shot burst out. Its rumble and the sight of the dead man turned the attackers into retreat. We went farther; and when we had gone off a significant distance, a crowd of natives gathered around the dead man. I saw through binoculars how they examined his wound and finally, digging a grave, buried him. Others, having watched this scene from the mountain, were also frightened by it and didn't dare attack us. As we passed by, they hid beind houses or, sitting on rocks at several hundred paces from our route, they showed us the road with their spears whenever we began to doubt which of the trails to choose to climb to the summit. The higher we climbed, the more densely populated it became. Near one group of houses we took a break and drank some marvellous milk and thick kvass, which my askhers had procured.

At 12:30 we reached the crest of the mountain. I was disappointed in my expectations. From here you could see well to the south; but to the north, the horizon was blocked by the high Mount Say, which was about 15 versts [10 miles] from the place where I found myself. Nevertheless, I stopped and began to plot on my plane-table the territory which opened up from here and with surveying compass took azimuths on the salient points. For more than an hour, I conducted this painstaking work. My soldiers kept pestering me, to hasten our return. There was not a single native visible on the crest of the mountain, and our bivouac was six hours away. I just had to take several more azimuths to the northeast, and I told the soldiers that they should calmly go back down the cliff, and I would catch up with them very soon. There stayed with me only Ababa, who held my mule and carried my three-eighths-inch caliber rifle, Tekla Giyorgis, Abto Selassie, and the senior man of the convoy. The others had already gone a hundred paces from us, and I was taking the last azimuth, when suddenly I was surprised by a startling change which took place in the surrounding terrain. The apparently uninhabited bushes and bare rocks came to life. Everywhere were seen the black shapes of armed natives. The foremost of them was now some hundred paces from me.

Our position was critical. There were only five of us, with four guns, only 30 cartridges each for three of the guns and a hundred for mine, and 50 for my revolver. I myself at this moment was unarmed, since I had taken off my saber and revolver, which got in the way of my observations. They lay several paces from me. At this minute, we were completely in the power of the natives. The soldiers who were leaving could not return to us in time. To leave now would mean condemning ourselves sooner to certain death. It was necessary to quickly undertake something which could delay the natives even a little and give time for the rest of my men to come back to help.

"Halio!" I called out to the native who was closest to me, who, hiding behind a tree, was approaching me. I went to meet him as I was, with only my plane-table and my compass in my hands. He stopped and, having hidden, answered "Halio." His comrades, amazed by such a turn of events, began to watch what more would happen.

Having approached to about five paces from the tree behind which the native was, I stopped and began to beckon him to me. My opponent indecisively came out of hiding and went toward me, saying "komoru", which means "king." I reached out my hand to him, and he, in the air, kissed it. Then I said "Dir" and, squatting, made the native squat. We began peaceful negotiations, and time was gained. I took the warrior's spears and, having indicated that I demanded that he lay them on the ground, made him do that. Then I began to call the other natives near him, who were, with curiosity, watching this scene, making them lay down their spears, beforehand, and then kiss my hand. Soon twenty men had gathered around. They squatted beside me. I showed them my compass, let them listen to my watch, and finally, having called the senior man of the convoy and having ordered him to take my place in the ceremony of kissing hands with newly arrived natives, I myself rushed to my gun and put it on. Now on our hillock there were already 15 Abyssinian men, and the time had come for us to go. Having called out several times "halio" and "dir," we, satisfed that all had turned out so successfully, began to go back down the mountain.

But we hadn't succeeded in going a hundred paces when suddenly behind us there sounded loud trumpet sounds and the place resounded with howling and war cries of the natives. They surrounded us and, wildly jumping and "playing"[108] with their javelins, swiftly attacked us. The site of the battle was closed and very awkward for us. On the north and west grew dense bushes, and to the east the mountain steeply came to an abrupt end. Our trail twisted along ledges of the precipice. We took hold of our guns and quickly began to shoot, aiming the fire on the foremost, who fell about 20 paces in front of us. I fired five cartridges from my three-eighths-inch caliber rifle, and while Ababa reloaded it, let loose ten cartridges from my rapid-firing Mauser revolver. It was difficult to miss at such a close distance, and almost every shot hit its target.

The accuracy of our shooting had a stunning effect on the natives and stopped their charge. We were particularly helped by the circumstance that the natives couldn't steal up on us and that they dragged their dead and wounded comrades far back; because although our fire was effective, there were too few of us and we had too small a reserve of cartridges to be able to hold out for long. The natives only had 20 paces to go to reach us, and we would find ourselves in their arms.

After several minutes of heated fighting, the distance between us and our enemies had increased to a hundred paces. Somehow the natives' spirits had fallen, and they only sprinkled our side with stones from slings. We already didn't have much ammunition left. Stopping fire and dividing my soldiers into two units, which should provide cover for one another consecutively, I began to descend, little by little.

Our enemy was stunned. As soon as we moved down, they took heart again, and, not daring to attack us, resorted to another means of action. Our trail lay along ledges, and groups of dare-devils, having separated from the main mass of the enemy, began to occupy salient points above the road and to push off falling rocks onto us from there. It is impossible to say that rocks flying down with a crash, rebounding on all sides from the stone ledges they encountered produced a particularly nice impression. It seemed to each of us at that moment that the rock was falling directly on him, and each rushed to hide behind the cliff face or to bend down low to the ground. Howling and wild cries of the natives accompanied each rock fall. Although, luckily, they had not yet caused real damage, they caused some panic among my soldiers. In order to counteract the intentions of the enemy, we in turn began to occupy areas from which we could fire on the ledges where the natives were preparing rock slides, and in this way, to some degree, stopped them.

Only at five o'clock did we get down the cliff. We passed the boundaries of the settlements completely safely, if you do not count one soldier wounded in the arm by a stone from a sling and one dead mule. Late at night I returned to camp.

The *Ras*, who was worried about my long absence, waited for me impatiently, and as soon as he learned of my return sent to ask me to go to him. They had already reported to him all the details of the fight. Congratulating me for the victory, he at the same time began to reproach me.

"Why didn't you say that you were going to fight? I would have given you more soldiers. I do not understand how you stayed safe and how your soldiers did not run away. Death must have seemed inevitable to them. You are Saytan (the Devil). But you should know that your present bravery is not yet true courage, but rather the ardor of youth and inexperience. Believe me, that only when you have experienced retreat and been wounded will you begin to understand danger, and your inexperienced ardor will change into the conscious courage of a warrior hardened in battle." He was right.

APRIL 10

We reached the Karka River. Along the way we hunted elephants, but unsuccessfully. At night, from nine o'clock to ten o'clock there was a heavy cloud-burst, and the insignificant Karka River turned into a stormy stream, which we crossed with difficulty. Before sunset, soldiers who had set out for grass saw elephants near our very bivouac. We pursued them and wounded several, but they got away from us, thanks to the swiftly approaching darkness.

April 11

We marched around the course of the Karka and set up camp at several versts to the west of the place where we had had the fight on April 8. Because of the cloud-burst the day before, the mountain climb turned out to be very difficult. Many of the donkeys which had been captured at the mouth of the Omo and were unaccustomed to mountains, stopped.

April 12

We were forced to stop and wait for the detachment coming from Kolu. The troops were allowed to disband for foraging for provisions; and, as an escort for them, several small detachemtns were sent in various directions. I and Zelepukin climbed the crest of a hill from which I made several observations. Our foragers returned to the bivouac at this time loaded with booty, and on their heels, behind them followed natives. From above it was perfectly clear to me that the natives were returning to their dwellings with their wives and children to gather the thrown away and broken crockery and to rake together the grain which had been spilled.

The whole day, the commander-in-chief kept looking through his telescope at the mountains opposite, from which the troops from Kolu should come.

April 13

At noon, on the summit of the opposite ridge, Abyssinian tents shone.

April 14

The detachment which had come from the fort at Kolu united with ours. All my bagage arrived, and I luxuriated now, surrounded comfort which for a long time had been unprecedented. I laid out my large tent, set up my bed. Instead of the coarse flat-cakes, cooked over again with difficulty from home-made meal, in front of me lay marvellous wheat. I even found a piece of soap in one of the packs; and with delight, I washed myself with it. But there still wasn't any salt...

During our absences, those troops who had stayed in the fort suffered from chicken pox and dysentery. The animals also suffered much since the grass turned out to be insufficient and of poor quality. The natives carried on a little war, constantly annoying the fort and attacking foraging parties. Only one of my *ashkers* had died—Wolda Maryam. He was one of those whom

Zelepukin called "recruits." He distinguished himself with excessive foolishness and glutonny, thanks to which he died. Several days ago, when the detachment was going through the land of Kira, Wolda Maryam ran into the bushes. Having seen there a ram, he slaughtered it and, in spite of the calls of his comrades, stayed there to eat it well.

April 15

The detachment broke camp and headed north. We crossed one of the spurs of Mount Say and went down on its eastern side. It was a short march, but very difficult. The transport stretched out far, and the rear guard only reached camp at evening. The natives treated us hostilely and kept attacking our flanks. Many were sick. Several days ago some new illness appeared, and yesterday one of the servants of the *Ras* suddenly died from it. Before he died, the sick man was unconscious; and when he died, he nose turned out to be full of pus.

April 16

The holiday of the Mother of God. There was a day of rest and a dinner with the *Ras*. My universal instrument had broken several days before (the web in it broke), and I was busying myself today with fixing it. In the absence of a web, I attached to the eye-piece two of my own hairs, plucked from my arm. In the tube, they appeared like strings. In order that their thickness not affect the accuracy of the observations, I used the following system: I observed the upper edge of the sun with the lower edge of the hair, and the lower edge of the sun with the upper edge of the hair (on average, the thickness of the hair subsequently amounted to 2-1/2).

April 17

We went ten versts [seven miles] north, following along the foot of the mountain spur. Ten versts to the east stretched out a dense forest, which extended as far as the River Omo. Through a telescope, from above, we saw a herd of elephants in one of its clearings. But there was already little time left before sunset, so a hunt didn't take place. A large snake attacked one soldier during the march. He was riding in dense grass, somewhat separated from the rest of the detachment. We suddenly saw the head of the snake rise over the grass. The soldier cut off its head with his saber. The snake was five arshins long [twelve feet].

April 18

A day of rest. The whole day we fought with the natives. Time and again, gun shots resounded from the mountains. I conducted solar obsrvations, determined the declination of the magnetic meridian and was startled by the magnetic anomaly I detected in this place. I took magnetic azimuths on very distant mountains from two spots a hundred paces from one another, and obtained a difference in azimuths of 5° in whole numbers.

April 19

The holiday of George the Victorous. This is the name-day of the commander-in-chief, and therefore is the occasion for a feast and day of rest. In the bivouac, all night long gunshots were fired. It turned out that one of the colonels had died of this new unknown illness, and soldiers and friends of the deceased gave him military honors, shooting around his tent. The illness is spreading wider and wider in the detachment and carries away several victims a day. Among my people also things are not going so well: yesterday evening Zelepukin fell ill. At two o'clock in the afternoon, he went to the river to wash his underwear, and, probably from the strong sunlight reflected off the river, his left eye began to itch and some pus appeared. By evening he eyelids had swollen so much that I could hardly open them with my fingers to instill eyedrops. Zelepukin suffered badly, but tried not to moan. I had never seen such a severe form of inflammation of the eyes and already despaired of saving them.

April 20

The detachment marched to the foot of Mount Jasha. The *ashkers* carried Zelepukin, having wrapped his eyes in a kerchief. One ashker led his mule and two others supported the sick man from the sides and deflected upcoming branches from him. On arrival at the bivouac, I climbed to the crest of the mountain ridge. I was accompanied by three gun bearers with instruments and my gun. The crest rose 400-500 meters above the bivouac. The climb was very difficult. I hurried in order not to let noon-time pass, and when I had climbed to the summit, I was completely worn out. But I was rewarded with the fact that from there I could see Mount Kuras in the south and the bottom of Mount Bokan in the north both at the same time. Having set up the universal instrument, I began to carry out observations. I posted my gun bearers around as guards, since the territory was apparently very restless and fresh traces of natives and their livestock were seen around, and nearby from time to time gunshots of the Abyssinians resounded.

April 21

The detachment climbed the mountain ridge and set up camp not far from the summit of Say and several versts north from the place of my observations the day before. Part of the detachments scattered through the vicinity searching for provisions. Several reserves were sent to support those who were foraging. They were posted on hills five versts [three miles] from the bivouac. The commander-in-chief went up one of the nearest summits and almost until evening observed through his telescope the individual fights which were breaking out all the time between Abyssinians and natives.

They called this place Deche. Its inhabitants were of the same nationality as the Beru, Kassi, Kira, Say and other mountain-dweller tribes. They are very warlike. Guns did not stun them, as they had their neighbors. And they bitterly defended their property.

My *ashkers* also went after booty and had a hot time of it. They with difficulty defended themselves against natives who attacked them in one of the ravines. They had already used up nearly all their cartridges when, fortunately, help arrived in time. They brought back to camp a ten-day supply of grain and several captive women and children.

April 22

A detachment, consisting of healthy and free men from the regiments of *Fitaurari* Chabude, Gebra Maryam and Kanyazmatch Dubye—all together about 1000 men—was sent to reconnoitre the space between Mount Say and Mount Beru. I went along with this detachment. Zelepukin was doing better, and I wasn't afraid to leave him alone for several days. The main strength of the army would wait in place for the return of the reconnaissance detachment or for its report on where to unite again. We climbed to the crest of the mountain ridge which stretches to the west from Mount Say. The population is dense here. On the summit of the ridge, a crowd of warriors blocked our path. They, wildly jumping, threatened us with spears and retreated in front of us. At about 11 o'clock in the morning, we climbed up one of the summits. There had been rain during the night. Thanks to the especially transparent air, the distant Kaffa Mountains were distinctly visible. I stopped here, set up my instrument and began to conduct solar observations, and then took azimuths on the summits that could be seen. The soldiers during this time in part dispersed to get themselves sour milk or turcha. The sun was already almost at the meridian, and I was tensely waiting for the moment when its upper edge would stop rising and once again begin to separate from the lower edge of the hair, when suddenly, almost beside me the natives' horn blared, and there resounded the piercing scream and howl of their war cries, and they attacked us. Not far away whistled several rocks thrown from slings. One fell on the leg of the tripod and almost toppled over the instrument. The Abyssinians began to fire back. Rather than tear myself away from the instrument at the most important moment of observation, I continued what I was doing under rather unusual circumstances for astronomical work. The natives suffered significant loses and then retreated. We went farther, and they followed us at a respectful distance.

To the right and to the left from the narrow trail stretched a continuous series of farmsteads, with intervals of dense plantings of kocho banana trees. Time and again, skirmishes broke out between us and the natives. At four o'clock in the afternoon, we climbed one of the summits, on which was found a farmstead which was outstanding in its dimensions. Beside it was a holy grove. Probably this was the house of the local princeling. We stopped in its wide courtyard. In the courtyard, there were four large houses, with thatched roofs which extended to the very ground. Opposite stood two barns, of which one stood on the chopped down trunk of a tree five arshins [12 feet] above the ground. In the middle of the courtyard there rose a pyramidal burial mound, about a sagene high [2 meters], surrounded by a circle of stones. At its apex, there lay several pieces of coal, a ram's bone which had been picked bare, and a piece of elephant dung. The doors of the houses were tightly propped shut with strong thick boards. On order from *Fitaurari* Gebra Maryam, the soldiers broke them down with the butts of their guns and went into the dwellings. But after several seconds, from one house they carried out an Abyssinian already killed with a spear. Several muffled shots resounded from there, and from under the doors a stream of blood appeared... There wasn't anyone in the other houses. I also entered these dwellings in order to see them. Bending low, I climbed through the little door. After the bright afternoon sun, at first I couldn't see anything inside. Only after some time did my eyes begin to distinguish the surrounding articles. I was struck by what I saw. It seemed as if I were in an ancient temple or some dungeon. Thick molded columns supported the ceiling. On one of the walls among the columns hung two large drums of the same shape as those in Abyssinian churches. Here stood a large harp and lay several iron bells and trumpets made of whole elephant tusks. In the middle of the house, around the hearth stood three clay urns. To their base was attached a thick stone slab. To the right of the entrance lay a large oxhide which probably served as a bed for the masters of the house. The left of the house communicated with a cow stall where a black cow was tied up. Everything was black, blackened with smoke. The columns were made of thick logs, braided with brushwood. They were coated with clay and decorated with characteristic moulded designs, just the same as the natives' tatoos. Inside baskets, with which the columns were braided, were found stores of all kinds of goods, and in the urns lay some articles probably having special significance for the natives. Here were coffee beans, wrapped in small pieces of skin, and pieces of some kind of tar, and smooth little stones, gathered from the bed of a river...

The inhabitants of this place belong to the same nationality as the Beru, Kassi, Kolu, Dami, Kira, Deche, and other mountain-dweller tribes which inhabit the ridge of the southern part of the main mountain range. This people had already struck me by its contrast with the other inhabitations of the surrounding areas. The mountain-dwellers by appearance do not resemble either the Shuro or the Gimiro; and by culture, although clothing is unknown to them, they stand incomparably higher than the Shuro and almost on the same level as the Gimiro. Judging by what I had seen of their sacrifices, holy groves, and tombs, and finally judging by the hearths surrounded by urns which I found in almost all the houses, their religious cult should be comparatively high. They call God "Dadu." This name, by the way, is similar to Dedu ("thunder" in the Gimiro langugage) and Deda ("heaven" in the Sidamo language), which seems significant to me. These tribes are completely isolated by Negro settlements from other Ethiopian tribes: the Sidamo, Gimiro, Kaffa, and finally the Abyssinians. These mountain-dwellers never even heard of the existence of the Abyssinians nor of their seemingly not too distant neighbors the Kaffa; but, nonetheless, in character, way of life and culture, I found among them many analogous features, which led me to think that all these tribes are related to one another. I encountered among these savage tribes the same musical instrument as among the Abyssinians— the large harp; and found even a board for playing gebeta. Among them, as among the Sidamo and Gimiro and Kaffa, there is sacrifice and divination with the innards of sacrificed animals. The houses are built with the same thoroughness, and their fields are cultivated with the same industry as among the Gimiro and Sidamo. This all the more confirmed me in my supposition that all these represent a series of tribes who are related to one another, beginning with the Abyssinians in the north and ending with the mountain-dwellers in the south. Perhaps in ancient times, all the Ethiopian highlands were populated by one and the same people, but then from the northeast came Semites and, mixing with the aboriginees of the country, produced the present diversity. The Semitic invasion spread from the northeast to the south and west; and in this regard, it is startling the gradualness with which the quantity of Semitic blood tells in the various tribes. The Tigreans seem to be the purest Semite, then come the Shoans, and finally the Kaffa and Sidamo. In the Gimiro, Semitic blood is not at all noticeable; on the contrary, they seem to have mixed with Negroes; and the mountain-dwellers stand out among all these tribes. The inaccessibility of their mountains, the distance from the sea, and their isolation have preserved the purity of blood of this people; from which, it seems to me, that one should consider them the original inhabitants of the Ethiopian highlands.

The sun had already set when we set up camp on the banks of a stream. The natives surrounded us and bothered us incessantly. The exchange of fire quieted down only at night. Expecting a night attack, we took measures...

April 23

The night passed comparatively peacefully. The alarm was raised twice, but it turned out that the natives were simply coming to take away their dead. At dawn, we set out and began to climb Mount Kastit. At nine o'clock in the morning, we were at its summit, which rises 2600 meters above sea level. A strong wind blew. The temperature was only 7° Reaumur [48° F]. It drizzled a fine rain, and the half-naked Abyssinians shivered from the cold. Even I, who was now no longer used to the cold, became numb in my hands. The weather, by far, did not favor observations. Only in the south I could make out the mountain I called the Tsar's Cylinder, and in the east Mount Dime, and in the west Mount Jasha. At nine o'clock in the morning, we went back down Mount Kastit and went west along the ridge of the mountain range which stretches in this direction.

As soon as the sun warmed up, the natives again surrounded our detachment and gave us no peace with constant attacks.

At twelve noon we reached Mount Meru. From there Kanyazmatch Dubye and *Fitaurari* Gebra Maryam went north with the whole reconnaissance detachment. I was worried about the health of Zelepukin, and there was no special need for me to continue the reconnaissance since the geographical position of the Emperor Nicholas II Mountain Range was now already well-known to me. Therefore, I separated myself from the detachment and went straight to the bivouac of the main forces. With me went my *ashkers* and several dozen Abyssinians. We walked until sunset, the whole time surrounded by natives, and set up lodging for the night at the foot of the mountain range, to the north of the place where I had taken solar observations the day before. It grew dark. I hastened to orient myself and to see if the bivouac of the main forces wasn't visible from the mountain. Having called my gun bearer Abto Selassie, I set out to a nearby hill. One of the officers, having noticed that I went only accompanied by one gun bearer, followed me. Behind him his twelve-year-old son carried his shield.

I had spent 12 hours in the saddle that day and hadn't eaten anything for a full 24-hours. I do not know if it was for this reason or for some other, but I was in some kind of a dreamy-philosophical mood: how many victims had the conquest of this land cost? It seemed to me brim-full of violence and injustice. Of course, a new phase in the history of peoples is always paid for with sacrifices. But world justice and individual justice are quite different from one another. Murder always remains murder for us, whatever goal it may accomplish, and it is especially immoral in relation to these peaceful, industrious people who never did harm to us, whose land we now take away by force, using the superiority of our weapons...

A narrow trail rose steeply to the mountain. I went along it, when suddenly ahead, at several paces from me, there appeared the shape of a native carrying something on his head and a long spear on his shoulder. He was also climbing this ridge, but from the opposite side. Unexpectedly seeing one another, we both stopped. Under the influence of my mood, I didn't even think to undertake any aggressive measures against him. It seemed unthinkable to me that he himself would begin to attack me, even though behind me walked two men with guns... I had a saber on me, but I didn't intend to take it out of its scabbard. My Mauser revolver, which I always wore on my waist on the march, this time I had left in the holster of my saddle, since the belt on which I carried it was broken. How great was my amazement when, instead of running away, my opponent in a moment threw the burden from his head and rushed at me with his spear. I took out my saber and cried to my people who were still below and didn't see what was happening: "Belau!" (Go ahead! Shoot!) The native stopped ten paces from me, having aimed the spear at me, he made the end of it shake quickly and chose the moment for the blow. I waited for there to ring out a shot and for my crazy enemy to topple over dead, but there was no shot... Seeing that I was waiting with my saber for his blow, the native, apparently, could not decide whether to stab me with his spear or throw it at me... Suddenly, he quickly bent down, took hold of a large rock, and threw it at me with force. I managed to duck, and the rock flew over my head. After the first stone followed a second and a third!... "Belau! Belau!" I cried out to the soldiers, but they were busying themselves with something or other a few paces behind me and did not fire. To turn around myself and take my gun would have meant to expose myself to certain death. Finally, a shot rang out—the officer had fired. In haste, he missed. Abto Selassie also took out his saber and we rushed at the native... At the same time there resounded a second shot of the officer, point-blank, and our opponent toppled to the ground... He spasmed for a long time, having bared his teeth, with a repulsive smile on his face. During the last skirmish he struck at one of us with such force with his spear that it pierced through a leather shield, at that time held up under the blow by the gun bearer of the officer.

It was a strange coincidence of circumstances. My revolver, which I always wear with me, turned out to be today in the holster of my saddle. Abto Selassie for the first time carried my three-inch-caliber rifle behind me. It was loaded and the bolt was at safety, but Abto Selassie didn't know how to cock it. The other gun of my ashker had a thick cartridge caught in it. It loaded halfway in the cartridge-chamber and then wouldn't move either forward or backward. But the strangest of all was the fact that several days before this occurrence I had a dream in which the general picture of today's fight was repeated and that I had told it to Zelepukin at the time.

We returned to the bivouac. We took along the spear of the native. It was evident that this wasn't its first time in battle: there were recent traces of blood on the end—probably Abyssinian. My dreamy-philosophical mood had completely gone away. War is war, and not a tournament; and the more the one with superior strength can defeat his enemy, the better.

April 24

Night passed rather peacefully. At noon, we joined up with the main forces, and our dear boys had stocked up several days worth of grain. Zelepukin had recovered. My little Vaska joyfully ran to meet me and from afar called out to me in Russian, "Greetings, your Honor!"

April 26

Gunfire kept up all night long—the last honors which were given by friends and comrades to warriors who had died that night. A new illness was spreading widely among the soldiers.

April 27

I was very sick. I had come down with the new illness and in the evening took to my bed. I had a high fever, and my head ached.

My eyes were watering and hurt. My throat glands were somewhat swollen. Learning of my illness, *Ras* Wolda Giyorgis quickly sent to me one of his *ashkers*, Lyj Ababa, who, it turned out, treated the strange unknown illness by a method he had learned from Arabs in the northwest low-lying regions of Abyssinia near Kassala. Lyj Ababa took a look at my throat and having felt the throat glands with his little finger, pressed them hard. Due to this, some pus came out, mixed with blood. Then he had me rinse my mouth and eat a piece of stale bread, strewn with red pepper. With this, the treatment ended; but it is amazing that after this I immediately felt better and my head began to ache much less. Lyj Ababa is now the savior of our detachment. Daily, a mass of sick men turn to him, and a huge percent of those get better, thanks to him. It happens that this illness affects not only the throat glands, as in my case, but also those of the nose; and he somehow can break through those as well.

Yesterday a report came from Kanyazmatch Dubye. He was waiting for us with his detachment, several dozen versts to the north. This morning we set out for there. There was a downpour at night, and the rivulet which flowed near our bivouac turned into a stormy stream which it was quite impossible to ford across. The detachment crowded on the bank of the rivulet. The commander-in-chief had his chair placed right at the water, and we waited for it to go down. After the an hour and a half, the level began to go down quickly; and after two hours, individual dare-devils crossed; and, finally, the whole detachment went. Women loaded down with all kinds of household goods were sometimes taken by the water, but a chain of soldiers was posted along the course of the stream to save them. The detachment set up camp at the settlement of Holki.

April 28

We cross the land of Okol and united with the detachment of Kanyazmatch Dubye. The inhabitants came to express their submission to the *Ras*, and the commander-in-chief gave the troops strict orders not to go off to the side of the road; and to make sure of this, he posted guards all along the way.

Although I hadn't fully recovered, I felt much better.

April 29

A day of rest. I felt worse again. In the morning there was a long meeting of the commander-in-chief and his leaders. The whole territory we had passed through was divided into five bands which extended from the boundaries of Kaffa to the south.

In them he stationed those regiments which had had land to the east of the River Omo before:

1) *Fitaurari* Atyrsye received Shuro and all the lands to the west of it, going up to the boundardies of the the domains of *Dajazmatch* Tesemma. 2) *Fitaurari* Ubye received Jiri, Jasha, Mera, Masha, Beru, Kassi, Kolu and the course of the Kori River. 3) *Fitaurari* Damti received Kastit, Maja-Tirma, Menu and the lands to the soutwest of it. 4) The regiment of the late *Dajazmatch* Andarge received Say, Deche and the course of the River Omo. 5) *Fitaurari* Imam received Golda. The first four regiments had to set up camp not far from Mount Wyta and wait here for the arrival from Kaffa of the rest of their transport and supplies of cartridges. Then they were ordered to go to their territories and set about the complete conquest of them. *Fitaurari* Imam would follow us for another few days' march and then independently go to wage war on the militant land of Golda.

This division of the land was announced to the troops in an order. Soldiers of the units who were staying were forbidden, under pain of having their hands cut off, from sending to the homeland for their wives or their baggage, which was the usual reliable indicator that a soldier intended to desert.

My friends came to me to say good-bye, and my tent was full of people.

April 30

Our detachment went north, and those who were staying accompanied us for a long time. *Fitaurari* Atyrsye was sick and went with us. The severely ill likewise went with us, and at the tail of our column there stretched out a long file of stretchers.

May 3

I felt very bad on May 1 and 2. On May 1, when I crossed the Sebelimu River, I was so weak that my *ashkers* had to hold me up along the way. Lyj Ababa again came to press the glands, but there was no more pus, and probably, my old fever had simply returned. Today I felt better. I used the opportunity to write letters home, their first news of me after a five-month silence.

We continued to fight with the natives all the time. They had become so impudent that at night they started to break into our bivouac, causing alarm at the tethering posts. At night, firing on them was mixed with salutes for the dead.

May 4

We crossed the Kilu River. At night there was again a violent storm and thunder. My tent was blown away. After the rain the climb up the mountain became so slippery that the pack mules were in no condition to make it up, and the soldiers carried the packs up the mountain in their arms. Many animals were stuck in the road.

My *ashkers* got sick. Zelepukin also came down with a fever.

May 5

We marched to the very borders of Gimiro. The soldiers said farewell to war, and those who for the whole march had not succeeded in killing anyone, resorted to all kinds of truths and untruths in order to fill this deficiency. Among them is even established a special sport. When the detachment abandons a bivouac, they hide in lean-to cabins and wait for when natives come to the abandoned position, and then shoot at the natives from ambush. But this amusement sometimes costs the hunters very dearly, and many have paid with their lives.

May 6

We went through the border forest by the same trail by which we had crossed this frontier at the start of the campaign. The trail which we had cleared was in places obstructed by enormous trees which had been ripped up by a violent storm, and we had to clear it again. We entered Gimiro; and cheerful sounds of flutes let the inhabitants who about the arrival of the army. The Gimiro came out to greet us; and on meeting the *Ras*, they fell down on their knees and kissed the ground and beat their chests with their hands to express their joy on the occasion of our safe return. The governor of the area, Ato Kassem, came to the bivouac. The old man wept with joy. We greedily tried to get news from him; but here on the outskirts, there was little that he knew.

Interesting speculation had circulated about us among the Gimiro when we had set out the first time. They said that we would go down from the mountains into a low-lying desert covered with fog. Guides would refuse to lead us, but the *Ras* would go ahead anyway and would die with his army. Others claimed that we would all be carried away by water.

May 9

We entered Chana. I again climbed Mount Bokan. It rained at night, and in the morning the air was exceptionally clear. I took advantage of this to take azimuths on distant mountains.

From the bivouac at Chana, I set out with several *ashkers* and twenty soldiers of Ato Kassem to hunt for elephants. Zelepukin also went with me. We walked up until it was completely dark, going down from the western slopes of the main mountain range. The trail lay among very dense forest. When it had become quite dark, we stopped at the solitary farmstead of a Kaffa. The owner of the property lived in a small cabin with his wife and two children. His house had been burnt down during the conquest of Kaffa. Now he was finishing building a new dwelling, which was already almost ready. There remained only to cover the roof. A heavy rain was falling. We had no tent with us, so we cut banana leaves with our sabers, covered the roof with them, and spent the night in the house which was being built.

May 10

We set out at dawn. It was very fresh and damp, and the thermometer indicated 7o Reaumur [48o F]. We turned north and went along the western slopes of the mountain range. We crossed the River Menu, which at this place is still an insignificant mountain stream, and crossed other tributaries of the Sobat. At twelve noon, we entered the region of Bita and stopped at the house of its leader, Bita-*Ra*shi, at the natural boundary of Kushore. The farmstead of Bita-*Ra*shi was surrounded by banana plantations; and inside a tidy courtyard, enclosed by intricate wattle fencing, stand several small houses. Bita-*Ra*sha is a tall, elderly, typical Kaffa grandee. He came out to meet us himself, surrounded by his servants, and received me very hospitably.

He is a Christian, one of the number converted by the missionary Massaey. In his house he keeps a small crucifix given to him by Massaey. Bita-rasha is from the Amaro tribe which always gravitated toward Christianity and was one of the first that responded to the appeal of Massaey.

May 11

We passed a sleepless night. Bugs and fleas bit us so much that even the Abyssinians who were used to them could not sleep; and the whole time, we tossed and turned. In the morning, we set out and went to the forests where elephants kept themselves. At ten o'clock in the morning, from the summit of a ridge, we saw below, in a clearing of the dense forest, a herd of elephants. We left our mules and horses here; and by ourselves, going around the elephants, we began to approach them in such a way that the wind blew from them to us. The forest is so dense here that you can only force your way along elephant trails. Bita-rasha led us; and, stepping carefully, he walked ahead, holding his spear at the ready in case of an unexpected encounter. I followed him, with Zelepukin behind me, and, finally, stretched out in a file, walked the rest of the *ashkers*. When we came to the place where we had seen the elephants, they were no longer there; and we ran along their fresh tracks. Jumping across deep holes, pressed by the elephants' feet, we then forced our way across a boggy swamp, crossed a small mountain ridge and went into another, even denser forest. Complete quiet reigned there, and the elephants must be not far away. We held our breath and moved without making noise... Suddenly a Kaffa stopped and pointed out to me with his finger some dark-brown mass, which, like a wall, obstructed the trail, just a few paces ahead. This was the belly, chest, or hind quarters of an elephant. I was in no condition to figure out which. I was afraid that my impatient *ashkers* would not restrain themselves and would begin to fire; so I shot at the bulk I saw. Shots from Zelepukin and my *ashkers* rang out behind my back. The forest began to rumble, trees began to crack, and the whole herd, in panicky fear, broke into a run. The elephant I had wounded also ran, and having separated himself from the rest of the herd, bellowed piercingly in a thicket. We rushed in pursuit. My *ashkers* flew like whirlwinds, jumped across toppled down trees and hummocks, and shot on the run. Zelepukin and I also began to pursue the elephants, but soon had to fall behind. On one of the trails, on the leaves of bushes, on the right side, blood was found; and I went to look for the wounded elephant. But there were so many elephant trails in the forest, that I soon lost its tracks. Soon I stumbled upon another elephant and wounded it, but it also went off into a thicket. From afar, I heard the shots of my *ashkers*, But they soon fell silent. Evidently, the elephants had gotten away. I lost all hope for a successful hunt and began to return to the place where I had left my mule. That was seven versts [four miles] away. With me went Zelepukin, two Kaffas and the gun bearer Aulale, who this time carried only binoculars. Having climbed to the crest of one mountain ridge, we suddenly saw below, on the opposte side of a rivulet, in the arch between two forests, the whole herd of elephants. It must have turned back and now was going from one forest to the other. We were 800 paces from them. I quickly got down on one knee and opened fire on the herd with frequent fire from my three-eighths-inch caliber rifle. The puzzled elephants stopped for a moment, then circled around one large tree, and went back into the forest. Under the tree, one elephant lagged behind and lay down, and in the thicket several wounded ones bellowed. At a run, I rushed down the mountain to the elephant which had fallen. But when I got close, as it turned out, the elephant had gone away. Zelepukin and I rushed along various trails to look for the wounded animal. I also made the Kaffa look, but they had made up their minds not to and stayed at the edge of the forest. Suddenly, in front of me, the bushes started to break... The cracking quickly got closer. I stood behind a turn in the trail, but after a few moments everything grew quiet. The elephant stopped somewhere quite nearby, having hidden itself now—it must be behind some tree—and waiting for me. Severely wounded elephants continually do this, and then they are very dangerous. I strained my sight to see it in the dense thicket, and cautiously moved in the direction of the place where the cracking had resounded just before. Aulale also went with me and suddenly cried out in a voice which wasn't his own, "There it is!" Hidden behind a large tree, twenty paces from me, with a bellow, the elephant was now rushing headlong in attack. I shot, and it went toppling over, weightily, just five paces from me. The bullet had hit it in the head. To be sure, I shot it again. Then with my saber, I cut off the customary Abyssinian trophies —the ends of the trunk, tail, and ears.

The dead elephant turned out to be a female; and it probably had calves, since milk flowed from its udders. I wanted to take a photograph and sent Aulale for the equipment. The mule was three versts [two miles] from us, the road went through forest, and Aulale asked that I give him my rifle. I gave him the three-eighths-inch caliber rifle and was left with a saber near the dead elephant.

The Kaffa ran to me and, after a quarter hour, the other *ashkers* arrived. Following the tracks of the herd, they had come to this same place. Zelepukin was looking for another wounded elephant; so I sent all the *ashkers* to help him. Just two Kaffa stayed with me. After several minutes, frequent shots resounded not far off. Then resounded the cries of my *ashkers* that I should run because the whole herd of elephants was coming at me. Actually, I could hear them bursting through the thicket not far away. Both of the Kaffa who were with me hid in a moment. Beside the dead elephant stood a large tree. Its roots were shaped like a niche. The elephant trail went to the left of me, and from that side I was hidden by bushes. To the right of the tree, the bushes were sparser. I sat tight in that little cavern-like niche. Closer and closer, the forest cracked; and the tramp of several hundred elephant feet became deafening. Doubtless, they were coming straight toward me. But where would they pass through: to the right or the left of the tree?

Suddenly, to the right, just beside me, appeared an enormous head, wide swinging ears and weighty trunk... I sat, holding my breath. Did the elephant notice me or not? It had already gone past me when suddenly it turned back sharply and, as if rooted to the ground, stopped in front of me. It looked at me with its little glistening eyes, moved forward, gathered up its trunk, lifted the end of it high as if getting ready to make an attack with it, moved back a bit, and, finally, quickly turned and went away. The first danger had passed, but the wounded, and therefore the most dangerous elephants might be running behind. Besides, the corpse of an elephant which had just been killed lay nearby me, and everyone knows that elephants in this case are vengeful.[109] One after the other, elephants ran past me. When what seemed to be the last one ran ran past, and I thought that the danger was over; suddenly I heard trampling, and one more elephant heavily ran by me. It was wounded, and blood flowed from its side. Having run past a few steps, it, like the first elephant, turned sharply and came at me. It stopped just five paces in front of me. Its eyes looked terribly evil. It stamped in place, sucked in its trunk, as if intending to cruelly take revenge on the man who had finally fallen into his power. Like two of the worst sworn enemies, we stared each other in the eye. At that moment I didn't not think that God would bring it about that I could ever describe this episode. Its outcome seemed so certain that I now remember how I, from second to second, expected my death...

But suddenly, it is incomprehensible why, the elephant cried out, twirled its tail and, having turned sharply, ran off.

I came out of my shelter. In front was heard the cracking noise, going farther away. I am alive, and for my salvation I see only God's Providence.

On the mountain they sang the victory song *Adoy Shebae*, with which the *ashkers* celebrated the victory of Zelepukin, who had also killed an elephant. The first to run to me were the Kaffa who had made off. They knew that the elephants had gone through here. They had heard the scream of one of them, and had expected to see my remains. They were greatly overjoyed when they found me unharmed. Soon the triumphant Zelepukin came with the *ashkers*. We measured the distance. From the place where I sat to the trail by which the elephants ran turned out to be seven paces; and from the outermost tracks of the forelegs of an elephant it was just four paces.

It was already four o'clok in the afternoon. Having entrusted Bita-rasha to extract the tusks the next day, I hurried to rejoin the detachment; and in the evening, we arrived at the main bivouac.

May 12

The detachment crossed into Dimbiro. It kept rainging the whole way. The *Ras* received sad news—the death of his favorite grandson, and the whole detachment put on mourning. The commander-in-chief grieved greatly.

May 13

We crossed to the foot of Mount Bonga-Beke. I outdistanced the detachment. On the road to Bonga, I met the *Nagada-Ras*, He was riding to meet the commander-in-chief and was bringing him honey, beer, and bread as a gift. He treated me to several cups of tej and invited me to spend the night at his house. He sent one of his *ashkers* to tell his wife to set aside a place for me to stay.

The wife of the *Nagada-Ras*, the pretty Alamitu, received me very hospitably and treated me to an excellent dinner, which was attended by her friend, the beauty Tsadike, and two monks. The monks had just arrived from Addis Ababa. They had seen Russians there and talked about the amazing jigitovka [acrobatic, trick riding] of our Cossacks. It's hard to express the degree to which it was pleasant to hear this first news of my own people.

May 14

We entered the town of Andrachi. The troops we had left there came out to meet us. The wife of *Ras* Wolda Giyorgis, *Woyzaro* Eshimabet, sent one of her *elfin-ashkers* to congratulate the *Ras* and me on our safe return. In front of the entrance to the town stood a crowd of inhabitants and all the clergy with crosses and censers. Relatives and friends kissed three times on meeting. Women and children cried out with joy "I-li-li-li-li-li!" Side by side with this, wailing and gun salutes for the dead resounded.

We went straight to the church, where a prayer of thanksgiving was offered. Then the detachment dispersed to their homes, and the *Ras* went to the tomb of his grandson.

May 16

I rode out to Mount Adaudi, which is about 40 versts [27 miles] from Andrachi. Here I made observations, and at night I returned home.

May 18

I sent my baggage to Addis Ababa.

May 20

I got ready to go to Addis Ababa. Before leaving I went to take my leave and bid farewell to *Ras* Wolda Giyorgis. He overloaded me with gifts, which represent each of his military distinctions. He gave me his marvellous mule, taken from the prince of Gofa; a horse with silver dress; the silver spear of the captive king of Kaffa, which he had thrown at the Abyssinians who took him prisoner; complete battle dress; and a shield decorated with silver. But most precious to me was a gold saber, which the *Ras* received after a battle for distinguished service from the Emperor himself. The *Ras* asked me to take this weapon in remembrance of my fight of April 9 on Mount Say; and in a letter to the Emperor, he asked Menelik to confirm this reward for me.

As a remembrance, I presented the *Ras* with my true comrades—my three-eighths-inch caliber rifle and my Mauser revolver.

Our parting was in the highest degree touching. Over the four months which we had spent together, we had come to knew one another well, and I sincerely liked and had grown to respect the *Ras*. I rarely met such an honorable, energetic, and noble person, who at the same time is a prominent leader, deeply devoted to his sovereign. I saw in him an ideal man, who passionately loves his homeland, always ready to sacrifice his own interests for it...

June 5

I arrived in Addis Ababa and found here our whole mission in assembly (to the great joy of both me and Zelepukin). Up until the very last day, we had not had reliable news about where our countrymen were.

June 14

I set out for Russia as a messenger. At the same time as I, my comrades—Lieutenants Davydov, Kokhovskiy and Arnoldi—also had to leave, along with a command of Cossacks who had finished their term of service. The Emperor Menelik received me in a farewell audience and told me, in Russian, "Good-bye!" The Empress Taitu could not receive me because of illness and sent her marshall of the court to give me her best wishes. On the day of my departure, the Emperor awarded me a gold shield—an outstanding military distinction, given only on rare occasions.

We were cordially accompanied by the chief of the mission, Acting State Councillor Vlasov, and his whole staff, as well as Madame Vlasov. At noon we left Addis Ababa.

Summing up my stay with the army of Emperor Menelik II, I consider it necessary to say the following:

By order of the emperor, a fifteen-thousand-man corps, in spite of the immense region over which it was quartered, concentrated incredibly quickly and set out on a campaign to annex to the realm of Ethiopia vast lands which lie to the south of it, which no one before this had explored, and which were completely unknown. In the course of just four months, this corps annexed to Abyssinia an area of just over 40,000 square versts [about 18,000 square miles]. Garrisons are posted in the newly conquered lands, and these regions should now be considered definitely lost for any other power which might have had pretensions on them.

An expedition which would have cost any European power millions, was carried out by the Abyssinians almost for free, if you don't count several hundred men killed and several thousand cartridges shot. I suppose that with these words all has been said. However, concerning Abyssinia, you should not fail to recognize here the enormous strength of a powerful state, which at any moment can easily bring together a two-hundred-thousand-man army.

Many consider the Abyssinian army to be undisciplined. They think that it is not in condition to withstand a serious fight with a well-organized European army, claiming that the recent war with Italy doesn't prove anything.

I will not begin to guess the future, and will say only this. Over the course of four months, I watched this army closely. It is unique in the world. And I can bear witness to the fact that it is not quite so chaotic as it seems at first glance, and that on the contrary, it is profoundly disciplined, though in its own unique way. For every Abyssinian, war is the most usual business, and military skills and rules of army life in the field enter in the flesh and blood of each of them, just as do the main principles of tactics. On the march, each soldier knows how to arrange necessary comforts for himself and to spare his strength; but on the other hand, when necessary, he shows such endurance and is capable of action in conditions which are difficult even to imagine.

You see remarkable expediency in all the actions and skills of this army; and each soldier has an amazingly intelligent attitude toward managing the mission of the battle.

Despite such qualities, because of its impetuousness, it is much more difficult to control this army than a well-drilled European army, and I can only marvel at and admire the skill of its leaders and chiefs, of whom there is no shortage.

In recent centuries, the Abyssinian people have endured many conflicts. Now, perhaps, better times are coming for them. They have united and are setting out on the big road to peaceful prosperity.

God help them!...

On July 1, I left on the deck of the French steamship "Irauadi," which sailed that day from Jibuti; and on July 19, I arrived in Petersburg.[110]

Appendix

("Mountain" signifies the language of the mountain-dwellers of Beru, Kassi, etc.)

English	Abyssinia	Kaffa	Sidamo	Gimiro	Shuro	Mountain	Idenich
God	*Egziabeer*	Ier, *Iero*tone	Tosa	Ka, Kiy	Tuma	Dadu	Tumu[111]
devil	saytan	seytano	talakh	shembato			
king	atye, *Negus*	tato	k'ati	tend			
human being	sou	asho	asa	ats	men		
man	wand	anam	atu	ych	meniti	yablya-kus	
woman	set	mache	mach	mych	makanja	yabko-git	
father	abat t'anikho	t'abo	abo	ba	bie	kule	machu
mother	ynnat	t'ande	ayo	tyn	aya	kibo	yachi
wife	myst	t'amyche	macho	mych	munin		
child	lyj	t'abusho	—	tana, t'anans			
son	wanlyj	anambu-sha	atumana	ychtana			
daughter	setlyj	macheb-ushe	machana	mychtana	honiti		
brother	wandym	t'amano	ita	ych	gotene		
sister	ykhet	mane	mycho	tymych	wono		
sky	samay	gumo	deda	char			
sun	tsakhay	abo	aua	ober	godya	chaja	sus
moon	charaka	agano	agyna	erb	mulmul	atsum	tagis
star	kokab	tajo	deda	char	darsa	muninya	
thunder	nagedguad	teo,	gicho—	dadu			
land	medyr	shovo	gade	dod	ba	elu	ba

English	Abyssinian	Kaffa	Sidamo	Gimiro	Shuro	Mountain	Idenich
country	ager	shovo	entesaa	shedod	ba	elu	ba
mountain	korebta	gepo	zoze	gag	tunto	dum	kumul
water	wakha	acho	assa	so	ma	ay	ma
river	wanz	ago	shafa	—	ma	ay	ma
rock	dengay	t'ato	tutcha	—	bet	lyalu	be
tree	enchet	mito	missa	ynch	tunoto	inchi	chamo-chi
grass	sar	mocho	masha	—	habay	wogi	lanjoy
fire	esat	kako	tamo	tam	go	alu	kacho
city	katama	keto	gedo	—			
house	bet	keto	kesa	ket	tuo	i	goru
clothing	lybs	kordo	afyla	simar	afila		
trousers	suri	shenafilo	adiya	shaul			
sash	makanat	buro	—	—			
spear	tor	gino	tora	mayt	ber	bekyn	ber
shield	gasha	gacho	gondaloye	ges	kulto	gyasu	gasha
bow, arrow	kast	—	—	—	berkondo		
dagger	chubye	shiko	masha	shef			
war	tor	iro	alaba	chanengasa			
horse	faras	macho	fara	fara			
donkey	akhiya	—	—	—	sigra	ara	sigra
cow	lam	mimi	niza	kash	bi	oti	bi
bull	bare	gato	bora	—			
ram	beg	bacho	dorsa	dor	zunku	mederu	zynka
goat	fyel	emito	desha	kets	tonga	esku	noncha
food	mygyb	mao	meo	mem, mm	amido	itsa	tila
bread (flat cakes)	*injera*	kosho	ukussa	budu, gonjo			
cooked dough	gunfo	buto	—	koys			
soup	marek	mecho	yto	ach			
mashella, durra (grains)	*mashella*	yncho	mallo	zanga	liba	libessa	liba
corn	bakhr-*mashella*	—	badela	—	—		
barley	gebs	sheko	bencha	—	—	gobsu	
banana tree ("musa enset")	muz	kocho	meka	—	—		

English	Abyssinian	Kaffa	Sidamo	Gimiro	Shuro	Mountain	Idenich
poa (grain)	t'ef	gasho	gashe	gach	—	sima	
elevzina (grain)	dagussa	dagocho	—	—	bara		
pea	ater	ato	—	wadya			
wheat	sindye	teto	sarga	temb	—		
head	*Ras*	kelo	—	tynd	—	saru	saba
arm	yj	kisho	—	kuch	—	kuchu	sio
foot/leg	ygyr	bato	—	to	—	asu	dari
stomach	hod	tifo	—	shul	—	chon	kyango
mouth	af	koko	—	no	—		
tongue	melas	echio	—	gash	—		
nose	afencha	mudo	—	sit	—		
ear	joro	wamo	—	way	—		
beard	tim	isano	—	—	—		
eye	ayn	—	—	an			
I	enye	ta	tena	tan	dian		
you (singular)	ante	nena	nena	nen	denu		
he, she	ersu, ersua	bina	asa	int	dua		
we	enya	tana	inena	nona	diana, diane		
you (plural)	enant	itosh	intena	inenta			
they	yrsachou	bonosh		inena			
1	end	inko	etu	mat	kona	koy	done
2	hulat	guto	laa	nam	rama	dagyn	ramyn
3	sost	kemo	eza	kaz	sizi	kadu	sizi
4	arat	audo	oda	od	uch	kukum	buy
5	amyst	ugo	siesha	uksh	achana	uchu	haena
6	sydyst	harto	usupona	sanyn	shuch	yaku	ile
7	sabat	sanuato	lapu	nanyn	hach	tusu	iasabe
8	symynt	shimito	ospu	nyatyn	lud	zet	isi
9	zoten	itio	odupuna	chystyn	sal	sakal	sakal
10	asyr	ashiro	tama	tam	tamokita	tomu	tomun
11	aeraend	ashiroito	tamanetu	tamomata	tomokikona		
20	haya	hio	latama	hatam	—		
30	salasa	shasho	etama	kastam			
40	arba	abe	odama	otam			
50	amsa	ago	meshama	uchutam			
100	mato	balo	cheta	bach			
1000	shi	humu	sha'a				
good	malkam	gatso	tafa	soytekush	bushi	chonkus	jash

English	Abyssinian	Kaffa	Sidamo	Gimiro	Shuro	Mountain	Idenich
bad	kefu	gondo	pta	itnes	gessa	chala	gersa
big	talak	ogo	loa	ee	buyda	babue	buy
little	tynysh	gisho	tika	ushkese	tino	*eras*	chino
many	beu	mito	—	tik	—	muchachiz	buy
few	tekit	gisho	—	ushkesse	—	mera	yashish
strong	bertu	manjo	loasa	band	messo	babugondi	konidum
weak	dekapa	gidaka-acho	labanesa	gamas wyknes	lyut	bersasay	konidala
rich	kaptam	ganecho	odiasa dureasa	ketnes	—	—	—
near	kyrb	kate	—	ugis	aja	danta	ajay
far	ruk	nibe	—	ekma	ranga	okukizo	rena
yes	auy	ekha	e	io	e-e	y-y	e-e
no	aydolem	kontone	i! i!	ushesigis	iong	i! i!	i! i!
there is	alle	bete	—	itituk	—		
there is not	elem	alo	—	kaygush	—		
right	kan	kano	—	—	gurg	kuba	seti
left	gra	iocho	—	—	gurza	kanga	nangiten
hello	endyet walkh	digone	saro	dantet	ilayban	karaay	
what?	mynou	amone	—	—	korilo		
in front	wadafit	afoche	—	—	tunoko		
behind	wadakhuala	gubek-ache	—	—			
today	zarye	hanoga	—	—	mita		
yesterday	telant	icha	—	—	—		
tomorrow	naga	yacha	—	—	mirache		
day after tomorrow	tanagodiya	sharta	—				
truth	unat	iberone	—				
thank you	*Egziabeer istelyn*	Ier to simbo	loasa	kayu tsmek			
this	ikh	hine	kana	—	dia		
went	heda	amabete	beda	—	koydo		
found	alkhedam	amache	—	—	koydoiong		
saw	ayokh	beke	—	bekeyti			
did not see	alayokhym	bekeache					
ate	banakh	maate	meda	munayti	tyl		
did not eat	albalokhiym	matache	—				
heard?	samakh	—	—	—	shigida		
killed	gaddelkh	utete	aykeda	—	nissa		
said	nagerkh	getete	io*teda*	gayti			

English	Abyssinian	Kaffa	Sidamo	Gimiro	Shuro	Mountain	Idenich
born	daiedkh	shiete	ieleda	—	denu		
give!	syt	imbe	—	uts nanu	acho	itsta-tan	inje
go!	hid	ambe	—	ham	iodo	enti	kaush-ausha?
stand!	koy	—	—	—	tesso		
eat!	bela	mamot	—	mnayk	muga	baeno	mato
drink!	tata	—	—	ushunt			
well (interjection)	bel	—	—	ga			

Notes

B: = Bulatovich, author
K: = Katsnelson, editor of Russian reprint
S: = Seltzer, translator

1S: In his reprint of the Bulatovich book, Katsnelson made some very minor abridgements. I've compared his text with the original and restored the original material for completeness.
2K: This trip is described in From Entotto to the River Baro.
3S: P.N. Krasnov later led the Don Cossacks against the Bolsheviks during the Civil War. After that unsuccessful venture, he went into exile in Western Europe and became a novelist. Then, under Hitler, he led a detachment of anti-communist Russian exiles against Russia as part of the German Army in World War II.
4S: Artamonov figures prominently in Solzhenitsyn's August 1914 as an incompetent general responsible for the Russian defeat at the Battle of Tannenburg. He also wrote about his experiences in Ethiopia, but his observations were buried, in the Russian archives until 1979, when they were published for the first time by "Nauka" [Science] Press in Moscow, as Cherez Efiopiyu k Beregam Belogo Nila [Through Ethiopia to the Banks of the White Nile].
5B: The MacDonald expedition did not take place because of a mutiny of his soldiers. The unfortunate result of the Fashoda incident is well known. The actions of Bonchamps and Clochette ended in complete disaster and the death of Clochette.
6K: King Lebna Dangel (David II) reigned from 1508 to 1540.
7B: According to a legend I heard from Abyssinians, 48 nations were subject to David II. The army that they paraded was huge: when David once gathered it for review, it pitched a camp which extended from Gondar to Gojjam. At the sight of his power and in sorrow that he had no one with whom to measure his strength, David ordered that the earth be beaten with whips; and turning to God with a prayer to send him an enemy, he set fire to a pile of incense (according to some, to a pile of carts), the smoke of which raised its column up to heaven itself.
8B: Gran was a native of the Harar region, which at that time belonged to Gallas who had adopted Mohammedanism. In 1539, having raised the flag of the Prophet among the Moslem population of the coastlands and having declared holy war, he invaded Abyssinia, burning and destroying monasteries and churches. Inspired by the ideas of Islam, Gran directed

9B: his attack particularly toward northern and central Abyssinia, the most cultured area and the religious center of the empire, and destroyed the city of Aksum. In 1545, in Damby at Lake Tana, Gran was killed.

9B: An Abyssinian monastery is located next to the Russian Inn in Jerusalem. Abyssinian pilgrims often visit our churches. Met by other Europeans with contempt and arrogance, only among Russians do they find sympathy and help.

10S: Father of the future emperor, Haile Selassie.

11B: The detachment of *Ras* Makonnen consisted of 7,000 of his own troops; 6,000 of Menelik's from Gondar, infantrymen under the leadership of *Dajazmatch* Demissew, governor-general of the western Galla lands; 4,000 irregular Galla of *Dajazmatch* Gebra Egziabeer, the ruler of the Galla kingdom of Leka; 4,000 irregular Galla of *Dajazmatch* Joti, the ruler of the Galla kingdom of Wollaga; 3,000 of Menelik's *tabanja-yaji*, infantrymen under the leadership of *Dajazmatch* Waldi (who was sent in the summer of 1898 as ambassador to the President of the French Republic); and 1,500 men of *Dajazmatch* Haile Maryam. *Ras* Makonnen conquered Beni Shangul and reached the sandy steppe which stretches along the right bank of the Nile. At the beginning of April 1898, his detachment returned safely to Addis Ababa.

12B: *Dajazmatch* Tessema reached the mouth of the Sobat River and hoisted the Abyssinian flag on the right bank of the Nile.

13S: Now Lake Turkana.

14B: The Abyssinian military hierarchy is very involved. It is difficult to express it as a table of ranks. The sequence of grades is as follows:
Negus negast—Emperor, commanding all armies
Negus—king, commanding the army of his kingdom
Ras—field marshal, commanding his province or one of the armies of the Emperor or of a *Negus*
Dajazmatch—roughly, our field general or lieutenant general; he can independently command a separate army or a detachment in the army of a *Ras*; in the latter case, he corresponds to our corps commander.
Fitaurari—major general; he can also command a separate army; when he commands a regiment, he corresponds to our colonel
kenyazmatch—colonel
grazmatch—lieutenant colonel
balamberas and yamato-alaka—a grade equivalent to the
Russian captain
likamakos—adjutant general
azzaj—marshal of the court
elfin ashker—page (literally, servant of the bedroom);
elfin ashkers are recruited from boys raised in the courts both of the emperor and of the *Ras*es and other commanders; although they perform the duties of ordinary servants, they can attain the very highest posts. Promotion in the grades does not take place successively as in the Russian army, but in accordance with the personal choice of the commander. As a result, any captain or lieutenant can be promoted directly to *Ras*. The main difference between the Abyssinian military hierarchy and the Russian lies in the fact that the general principle of service is personal, and each com-

mander has the right to promote his subordinates to the grade just below his own. Therefore, for instance, there is no such thing as a colonel as such, but rather there is a colonel of such and such a general or *Ras*, or of the Emperor himself. Thus, in order to judge the official position of a person, it is necessary to know for whom he serves. For instance, a colonel of the Emperor counts as higher than a general serving in the army of a *Ras*.

15B: At noon in the shade, 15° Reaumur [66° Fahrenheit]; at night before dawn -2° Reaumur [28° Fahrenheit].

16B: I took more men than was absolutely necessary because of possible losses and also so that the men, feeling that there was a surplus of them, would more prize their posts. This measure protected me, to some degree, against the possibility of strikes and mutinies among the servants, which are very frequent among the Abyssinians.

17B: Large white cloaks of cotton material, like a Roman toga.

18B: From the fruit of the *kusso* a medicine for tapeworm is prepared.

19B: By the way, I consider it appropriate to mention the different action of the three-eighths-inch-caliber rifle when shooting with a bullet with a filed end and an ordinary, whole bullet. The first goat I hit at a distance of 150 paces with an ordinary whole bullet, which pierced both lungs of the animal and went through a rib, taking out a square centimeter, the splinters of which appeared in the wound. Despite such a serious wound, the goat galloped two hundred paces and only then dropped dead. I shot another goat with a filed bullet at a somewhat greater distance. This one also had both lungs pierced in the upper part, and its bones and heart remained unaffected. But this goat didn't take another step. It fell on the spot.

20K: Gurage is one of the peoples of Ethiopia who live in its central and southwest regions. There are Christians and Moslems among them. The Gurage engage in basic agriculture in combination with cattle-raising; they also have artisans. There are various theories regarding their origin. Some consider them descendants of Tigreans; others descendants of Sidamo, who took the Tigrean language and subjected it to some significant changes. In any case, the Gurage language belongs to the Semitic family. (M.V. Rayt, Peoples of Ethiopia, Moscow, 1965, p. 16).

21S: An "express" is a rifle "possessing high velocity, flat trajectory and long fixed-sight range." Encyclopedia Britannica, 11th edition, 1911, vol. 23, p. 335.

22B: A shamma is a white mantle with a red stripe. It is similar to a Roman toga. By custom, it is worn only by free Gallas.

23B: Aba Dula and Aba Jefar are not the personal names of these individuals but the names of their war horses—Dula, Jefar; the word "aba" means "owner" or "rider".

24K: Apparently, Aba Jefar acknowledged himself to be a subject of Menelik II in 1881. (G. Sellassie, Chronique du regne de Menelik II, roi des rois d'Ethiopie, vol. I, Paris, 1930, p. 175, footnote 3.)

25B: The tribute paid by the king consists of an annual payment in money of 7,000 talers and payment in kind of 5,000 to 7,000 skins full of honey, 300 to 400 ukets (an uket is one pood 28 pounds [64 pounds total]) of elephant tusk and, at the request of Menilek, civette (musk), iron artifacts, cloth, meal etc. Besides the income from his own lands, which is spent on the upkeep of the court and the army, Aba Jefar himself has some customs duties and income of about 100,000 rubles a year from marketplaces, and besides gets a significant sum from his subjects in the form of taxes—at the rate of 1 piece of salt (20 kopecks) a year from each household and 4 kuna (a basket of fixed measure) with a portion of each kind of grain.

26B: They usually load 6-8 poods [216-288 lbs.] on a mule.
27B: On the bank of the Gibye River, I killed a bird the like of which I had never before come across in Abyssinia. It was particularly large, with black feathers, and in general resembled a stork. The males had a unique crest on the head.
28B: Kogo, a banana-like tree.
29B: Both Christian and Mohammedan Abyssinians consider the meat of an animal slaughtered by a person of another faith to be a profanation.
30B: This mountain ridge, unknown up until now, was discovered by me. See more lower.
31B: See lower.
32K: Originally a region in the southwest of Ethiopia where the Sidamo people, including the Kaffa, settled. This was taken by Negroids, who, up until the present, remain in part on the Ethiopian-Sudanese border and are known under the general name of "Shangalla" (from the Amharic word for Negro). The Negroids were gradually forced out or absorbed by Cushitic tribes, which consequently received the name "Sidamo," speaking Semito-Hamitic languages. (They have no written language.) Apparently, they settled the whole region between the Blue Nile and Gojeb, but in the fourteenth century were driven away by Galla to the mountains of the southwest. For classification of Sidamo languages see: M.M. Moreno, Manuale di Sidamo, Milano, 1940. Kaffa or Gonga is in the Gonga language group, to which also belong the languages Shinasha, Bosha or Garo, Mao, and Sheka or Mocha.
33K: This legend is not in keeping with the oral tradition established by F. Bieber. The population of the country of the Minjo tribe, from which the king's clan derives, is imputed to be Kaffa. In agreement with this tradition, up until 1890, there were 19 kings who had succeeded one another from the first—Minjo (1390). The version about the descent of the dynasty of the kings of Kaffa from Zara Yakob, cited by A. K. Bulatovich is unconfirmed. (See, F. Bieber. Kaffa. Ein altkuschitisches Volkstum in Inner-Afrika, vol. II, Modling bei Wien, 1923, pages 494-533). About the time of government of separate kings, also see: C.F. Beckingham and G.W.B. Huntingford, Some Records of Ethiopia, 1593-1646. London, 1954, Pages LVII-LVIII.
34B: The double name of the country indicates the origin of this tribe. The more ancient name—Enareya (which means "slaves")—was given to it by the Abyssinians who conquered it. The more recent name—Limu—it obtained from the name of the Galla tribe which took possession of it afterwards.
35K: The name "Sidam" first occurs in Ethiopian literature in the sixteenth century. It is possible that it originated from the western Semitic root "sid," "sad" meaning "to travel" and the suffix -ata, where of course a was trans-

formed into o. See, E. Cerulli, Peoples of South-West Ethiopia and its Borderland, London, 1956.

36K: In actuality, in Kaffa right up to its conquest by Ethiopia, the people preserved many of their distinctive peculiarities, in particular in the political and social structure of the country. (See, F. Bieber, Kaffa..., and also G.W. Huntingford, The Galla of Ethiopia, The Kingdom of Kaffa and Janjero, London, 1955, p. 103).

37K: Members of this council were called "Mikirecho." The clans A. K. Bulatovich writes about were called Hiyo, Amaro, Ako (Ukko), Mechcho, and Minjo. The king belongs to the last of those. In the opinion of F. Bieber, the general number of clans attained 37. (F. Bieber, Kaffa, Ein altkuschitisches Volkstum in Inner-Africa, Volume II, Modling bei Wien, 1923, pages 53-55). E. Cerulli counts only 25 (E. Cerulli, Etiopia Occidentale, volume 1, Rome, 1932, chapter 20). Apart from those indicated, the following clans were considered privileged: Girgo, Argeppo, Dingerato, Yachino, Kalichcho, Kullo, and Matto.

38B: One of the regimental commanders of the *Ras*.

39K: A.K. Bulatovich's guess about the origin of the name *Iero* is not confirmed. *Iero* or Yaro was originally the god of the sky, the representation of which after the spread of Christianity in Kaffa in the sixteenth century was combined with representations of the Christian God.

40K: The last king of Kaffa, Gaki Sherocho (nicknamed Chenito), ascended the throne on April 6, 1890 after the death of his father Gali Sherocho (nicknamed Galito), who had reigned since 1870.

41B: One of the *Ras*'s regimental commanders.

42B: This work involved great difficulties. Each time, as soon as I got ready to take observations, I was surrounded by a crowd of curious people, whom my *ashkers* only managed to chase away with difficulty. In addition, the weather did not favor this work. I don't know if it was chance or if it is a common phenomenon at this time of year, but every day the sky, which had been clear after the morning fog dissipated, was covered with clouds at noon.

43K: Konta is one of the tribes of western Sidamo (Ometo) who live in the region of the middle course of the River Omo.

44K: Kulo is one of the tribes of the western Sidamo.

45K: Kusho, more exactly Kucha, is one of the tribes of the western Sidamo. The region where they settled is the right bank of the middle course of the River Omo.

46K: Gofa is one of the tribes of the western Sidamo, who live in the region of Konta, to the south of the River Omo, in the area of its confluence with the Irakhino River.

47B: I do not know how correct it is to have given them the name "Sidamo", since that name is completely unknown to the people themselves. By type, the Sidamo resemble Kaffa and Abyssinians, but in them there is an inconspicuous presence of Semitic blood, as in the Kaffa. Moreover, the difference between the Sidamo and the Abyssinians in the shape of their eyes and their expression is striking. Both the Kulo and the Konta consider themselves as having come originally from the region of Dembea in Gojjam, which is populated by the Agau tribe, who likewise differ from the other

Abyssinian tribes and also, apparently, from strangers of Semitic blood. The Sidamo are a very intelligent, capable and hardworking people, who worship war. They are very brave, but cruel and bloodthirsty. Killing in war among them has been elevated to a cult, and he who returns from a raid without tangible evidence of his victory is subjected to general scorn like a coward. The women are also very warlike; they accompany their husbands to war and during battle encourage the fighters, carrying to them jugs with intoxicating beer. The Sidamo culture stands at a relatively high level of development. Agriculture, cattle-raising and bee-keeping thrive here. They mine iron, from which they fashion steel and iron spears, daggers, ploughs, etc. They also get a lot of cotton, from which they make cloth which is well known in Ethiopia for its durability and good quality. The clothing of the Sidamo does not differ from the clothing of the other non-Abyssinian tribes. Their armament consists of metal spears of the most diverse shape, a dagger at the waist and a large round shield.

They believe in God who abides in heaven and whom they call Tos (a word from the same root as *Deontos* in the Kaffa language). They also worship many other secret spirits on whom their well-being depends. They know the names of Christ ("Krystos"), Mary ("Mayram"), George the Victor ("Giyorgis"), and together with this the Devil ("Satana"), etc. They don't ponder over the nature of God, and don't try to express to themselves the relationsihp of Him to those beings in which they incidentally believe. From their point of view, those are superfluous details, the knowlege of which is necessary only for magi who have remarkable significance. The priest-magi knows medicine for illness, and also knows those who have caused calamities and the means to propitiate them. They also know how to arrange to avoid misfortune. You just have to bring the priest enough gifts and a sacrificial animal, which, having thrown it down on its right side, he slaughters in a sacred grove... They collect the blood of the sacrificial animal in a cup and drink it, having mixed it with ashes beforehand. By examining the internal organs, the priest tells fortunes or gives advice or demands another sacrifice if the first seemed insufficient for the god.

Among the Sidamo, the conception of life after death is very vague. They say that a man who had good qualities during life will be good also after death, and that one with wicked qualities will be bad. When someone dies, the accepted practice is to celebrate a funeral feast, at which, as a sign of mourning, the relatives smear their heads with mud, dress in their oldest clothes, tear out their hair, and scratch their faces with their fingernails until they bleed. The dead, wrapped in cloth and palm branches, are buried in deep graves, at the bottom of which, under one of the sides, they dig out caves where they place ivory and various ornaments which belonged to the deceased. The death of a prominent person is usually accompanied with bloodshed. Often the favorite wife of the deceased kills herself; and the relatives, assuming that the cause of death was the "evil eye" of some evil-wisher, set out to find the enemy. Sometimes the priest points this person out or, if he does not know him, they determine who it is by the following rather original method. They set an ambush on a major road. The first man who falls into this ambush is proven to be the sought for evil-wisher of the deceased and is killed. The relatives of the murdered man take revenge in turn, and bloody clan fighting arises.

The family life of the Sidamo is very similar to that of the Gallas and the Kaffa: they have polygamy; wives are bought and are slaves to their husbands. Boys are circumcized.

The form of government is monarchy. The throne is inherited by the eldest son. They have a council of elders—representatives of clans who reside in the state. This council helps the king in government affairs and in administering justice. The king receives special respect. On meeting him, his subjects throw themselves on the ground with the words "Mokua ganda," which means "For you, I will bury myself alive," to which he replies, "Mokua pyata," which means, "Don't bury youself."

48B: For the Eucharist they do not use wine, but rather ground, dried grapes mixed with water. It is brought from Gojjam or Harrar. Several churches, however, grow vineyards themselves.

49B: At each church there live many clergy: several priests, deacons, and monks, and finally, *debtera*, i.e., student-scribes. These are people who are preparing themselves for an ecclesiastical vocation, but, for various reasons, have not taken holy orders. *Debtera* lead a worldly life, but belong to the clergy. They teach children in church schools, busy themselves with copying books, and sing during the holy service. Among them are found people who are in the highest degree well-read and, from the Abyssinian point of view, educated. One of the *debtera*, who enjoys great respect among his comrades and parishoners, is designated by a *Ras* to manage the church in which he lives, and the church property.

50B: These rattles consist of a handle to which are attached two parallel copper plates, joined above at a pivot. On the pivot are put copper rings, which, striking the plates of the instrument when it is shaken, produce a very pleasant sound.

51B: Afilye is prepared in the following manner. The back leg of a ram is freed from the tibial and shin bone; the meat is cut in long thin strips which hanging on the end of the bone form a kind of flower cluster. Then the meat is dipped for several minutes in a boiling sauce, made from butter, pea meal, red pepper and other spices—and the dish is ready.

52B: This instrument is called masanko. Made in the shape of a rhombus, it is trimmed with leather; and one of its corners is furnished with a thin long end. There is only one string on the masanko, on which they play with a bow. Singers, as far as I was convinced, have mastered this instrument to perfection. The musical taste of the Abyssinians is quite different from ours. European music produces no effect on them, and they do not like it. They prefer their own songs, with a tune which, for the most part, is elusive to our ears, with endless trills, and changing from note to note. For the expression of great feeling, the singer must sing, unnaturally, through the nose, and add hoarse guttural sounds.

53S: Bulatovich is quoting the concluding lines from the poem "Song of Prophetic Oleg" by Alexander Pushkin (1822)—"The company feasts on the shore; The warriors recall by-gone days And battles where side-by-side they fought with sabers."

54S: According to legend, Saint Vladimir (c.956-1016), the prince of Kiev, received ambassadors from all the major religions before deciding that his nation should convert en masse to Orthodox Christianity. Moslems forbade drinking alcoholic beverages; so Vladimir replied to their ambassadors that it would be counter to the Russian spirit to refrain from drinking.

55B: Lemd, amfara, saber with silver decoration, silver shield, kalecha—are the same as our orders with swords. A saber decorated with gold is a rather rare distinction, given only to senior officers and generals and corresponding to our gold weapon.

56B: The regular units taking part in the expedition (in my further account, I will refer to them by regiments), and the places where they were stationed before the campaign are as follows:

1. Regiment	Atyrsye	1000 men	land of Kuchya
2. " "	Faris	800 men	" " Koshya
3. " "	Gabro Mariam	800 men	" " Konta
4. " "	Chabude	800 men	" " " "
5. " "	Ubye	600 men	" " Gofa
6. " "	Imam	2000 men	" " Melo and Dime
7. " "	Damti	1000 men	" " Banko, Ara, & Shangama
8. " "	Dubye	500 men	" " Kulo
9. " "	Alemnekha	500 men	" " " "
10. " "	Andarge	300 men	" " " "
11. " "	Zamadyanekha	600 men	" " " "
12. Wolda	Tensaye	600 men	" " Limu
13. Zavanog (personal guard of *Ras*)		500 men	

The strength of the regiments is approximate. The number of guns was 10,449.

57B: The way they conduct lawsuits is interesting. The litigants warrant the rightness of their claim with property, and, in more important matters, even with their life. The formula of this guarantee is as follows: "I accuse so-and-so of such-and-such! Now, say what you will stake on the fact that this is not so? I give one measure of honey! (two measures or three, and so forth)." The cost of one measure of honey equals about a taler. The value of a guarantee depends on the importance of the matter. If the judge finds that it is too little, then he himself indicates a larger size. Then the law-suit proper begins. They bring in the evidence, call witnesses, etc. The losing side, in addition to a fine for the use of the person who won the suit, still pays to the court the monetary warrant, which goes for the use of the court.

58B: In Abyssinian, this is known as *fokyr*. Victors in battle cry out in almost the same expression when an enemy falls at their hands and also when they notify their leaders of their victory.

59B: These white men could not be any other than Bottego and his comrades. And since the Gimiro knew so little about them—knowing only of their trip—I could conclude that the Gimiro inhabit a small area somewhere to the side of the movement of the Italian expeidition; otherwise they would have had more accurate information about it. On the other hand, I concluded that in the neighborhood of the Gimiro there should be either a tribe quite alien to them—both by customs and by language—or a wide uninhabited zone. This assumption was later confirmed: to the southwest of the Gimiro there is an uninhabited, low-lying valley of the Joba River, and to the southeast live the Negro tribes of Shuro, etc.

60B: *Nagada-Ras* is the head of the merchants. In Abyssinia, all merchants are subject to several *Nagada-Ras*es, and Vadym Aganokh is one of them. All the merchants who live in the lands of *Ras* Wolda Giyorgis are under his leadership.

61B: *Woyzaro* Eshimabet is a sister of Empress Taitu. Wolda Giyorgis is her third husband. She married him several years ago in a church ceremony. She is a very intelligent woman, educated in the Abyssinian manner. The *Ras* worships her. Like all noble Abyssinian women, she is very pampered.

62B: The eldest daughter of the *Ras* and two daughters of his wife had gone off with their husbands. The second daughter of the *Ras* was widowed. Her husband, *Dajazmatch* Andarge, was killed in the Aussi campaign in 1896.

63B: The 30 *ashkers* were distributed as follows: the most senior—Wolda Tadik; his assistant and chief of the transport—Aboye; two of *elfin ashkers* (household servants) of mine—Tekla Giyorgis and Ambyrbyr; two cooks Adera and Inasu; the chief stable-man—Ordofa and his assistant—Ababa; 14 ashker-bearers; two herdsmen who during the march carried sticks from the tents—*tarads*; and six weapon bearers—Faisa, Aulale, Haile, Ambyrbyr, Abto Selassie and Wolda Maryam. There were four horses and 19 mules. One of the stable-men led my personal horse in front of me and in case of need I sat on it; and the three senior servants—Wolda Tadik, Aboye, and Abto Maryam—rode the other three horses. Three mules were saddled for me, and I rode on them in order. One mule was Zelepukin's. And on the remaining 15 mules was found our load of transport, with a weight in general at the beginning of the march of about 70-80 poods [2520-2880 pounds]. This consists of 50 poods [1800 pounds] of meal, cartidges, one large and three small tents, medicine chests, supplies of clothing, underclothing, cooking and dining equipment, salt, wax for candles, some bottles of liqueur, several boxes of dry broth (Magi) and wineskins with oil.

64B: Express rifle, 500 mm caliber rifle, two 3/8" caliber rifles, Winchester and shot-gun.

65B: Dake-rasha in translation means "chief of the Dake region." He comes from the Uka clan and up until the subjugation of Kaffa was a member of the "council of seven."

66B: The right of such a ceremonial passage belongs only to Rashes within the limits of their rgions.

67K: Kusho, or more accurately Kucha, is one of the tribes of western Sidamo. The region which they inhabit is the right bank of the middle course of the River Omo.

68B: The residents of the harem led a life which was quite closed, never seeing anyone except the guard eunuchs. The king never visited their lodging. On his command, they were brought to the palace. Tato Chenito was generous. He surrounded his wives with luxury, gave them gold and silver ornaments, and dressed them in long silk shirts trimmed with gold chains.

69B: The astronomical position of both of these mountains was subsequently accurately calculated by me. Mount Dime was determined to be several minutes further south than Donaldson determined it, not to speak of the difference in longitude, which amounted to about six minutes both for this mountain and for the mouth of the River Omo.

70B: The Menu River flows into the Sobat.

71B: Up until recently, this greeting, used by the Kulo tribe, was completely unknown to the Gimiro, who copied it from their conqueror Abyssinians who came from the land of Kulo. Not knowing one another's languages, the Abyssinians used for conversation with the Gimiro a third language which was the least well-known for they themselves, thinking that it must probably be better known to the Gimiro. I noticed this kind of behavior more than once in other circumstances: this tendency to express oneself with foreigners in any language which is the least understandable for the speaker. For instance, our solider-medical orderlies who were with the Red Cross in Abyssinia, in converstaion with the natives used French words such as "march," "mange," etc. Likewise, when Abyssinians enountered a European who was unkown to them, they talked to him in Galla.

72B: For this they use a damp twig of a special, very flexible tree. Before use, they lightly chew the end of the stick, which does not have a core inside. When it splinters from the chewing, they clean their teeth with it, as a toothbrush. The sap of this tree stimulates much saliva.

73B: In general, I noticed how much all the customs of war, which are learned by long experience, were in the flesh and blood of each Abyssinian, including the procedures for safeguarding reconaissance parties, and the way of life on the march. Already for several marches before this, near the eastern Gimiro border, they had established among themselves procedures for night watches—in which the guards stood along the edge of the tethering posts—and they themselves determined the punishment for insufficient vigilance, which included taking a gun away from the guilty party and giving it to someone else who didn't have one.

74B: Now Beni-Shangul has been conquered by the Abyssinians.

75B: Here they clear the forest in the following manner: at the root they make a campfire and when it begins to smolder, they fan the fire until the trunk at the base has burned through sufficiently. Then they topple it down.

76B: Their teeth stick out in front, and the lower incisors are usually knocked out.

77B: One of the regiments, in order, was designated as the rearguard. Its responsibilities included: protecting the detachment from the rear; picking up the wounded, sick, and those who lagged behind (who they seated on mules of soldiers in the rear guard); rendering help to those who were left behind with pack animals, and, without fail, conveying their loads to camp, even in case of the death of the animals.

78B: Custody of coffee and its brewing is always the responsibilty of the treasurer.

79B: A similar method of obtaining salt is also known in the land of Gof.

80B: Lent lasts for seven weeks; or eight weeks, counting Shrovetide. For the week before Lent there is also a three-day fast—Noy-Ney.

81B: Besides, I didn't want to confirm the firmly established opinion among Abyssinian soldiers that Europeans on the march stuff all their holsters with all kinds of supplies and eat constantly on the march.
82B: However, it was not the Abyssinians who did this, but rather the irregular soldiers of the *Ras*, savage Kulo.
83B: The Aussi campaign was in 1896.
84B: It turned out later that I was not mistaken.
85B: It seems that Donaldson Smith met such disfigured women on the left bank of the Omo River.
86B: The Abyssinians developed this ability to innoculate against small pox themselves. They innoculate a child with human small pox from someone else who is sick, introducing it into a cut on the skin by the mother. For the most part, those who undergo this operation recover; and since the illness is in childhood, it leaves almost no traces.
S: According to Dr. Pascal Imperato, "The practice of variolation is a very old one in Africa, and the Ethiopians had it centuries ago. I studied it closely in West Africa. The practice actually spread smallpox and didn't give the results Bulatovich and many other early observers were led to believe." Dr. Pascal cites two of his articles on this subject: "The Practice of Variolation Among the Songhai of Mali, Transactions of the Royal Society of Tropical Medicine and Hygiene. Vol. 62, No. 6, pp. 868-873, 1968. "Observations on Variolation Practices in Mali," Tropical and Geographical Medicine. Vol. 26. pp. 429-440, 1974.
87B: Gebeta is a very widespread game in Abyssinia. Each player is given a little hole which is either carved in a board of simply dug in the ground. (There are 12 holes in all). At first four little round balls or stones are placed in each hole. The first player takes all the balls from his holes and distributes them one at a time, in order, to the right and to the left, to the following holes. From the hole in which the last ball was placed, he takes out all the balls lying there and continues in the same manner until the last sphere arrives either at an empty hole or at one where there are three balls. In the latter case, in other words when the ball is added to three already found in the hole, all four balls are taken out of the game and become the property of the player who took them away. When all the spheres have been taken away, they begin the game again. This time each player fills only as many holes as he has enough balls to fill with four balls per hole. The game keeps going until someone no longer has a single ball. I was very surprised that people in Kassa had the board which is necessary for this game.
88B: The Battle at Embabo took place in 1886 during the war of Menelik against the Gojjam *Negus*.
89B: Do not look skeptically at this number, my compatriots, asserting that people in Kharkov, Kiev, and other provinces easily endure such heat. If their thermometer shows this temperature in the shade, let them try tying the thermometer to the end of a rope and twirling it around for five minutes. Only then will they find out the actual temperature of the air. In the sun, my Reaumur thermometer indicated 50°, and sometimes even more. But besides, by the general assertion of the majority of those with whom I happened to be in Africa, it was noticed that there is a striking lack of

correspondence between the indications of a thermometer and the sensation of heat. I do not know what to attribute this to: the closeness to the Equator, the brightness of the sun, or properties of the air and soil.

90B: In number 195 of "The Russian Invalid" for 1899 the following is published: "Staff-Rotmister of the Life-Guard Hussar Regiment Bulatovich, who travelled in Africa, thanks to his participation at the beginning of 1898 in one of the Abyssinian expeditions to the southern regions of Central Africa, managed to cross through lands which had previously been completely unknown to Europeans and to discover a large mountain range which rises along the western bank of the River Omo and extends for several hundred versts from north to south.

"Up to this time, the existence of this mountain range was unknown to science. It was assumed that there was a mountain height to the west of the River Omo, but this was still unconfirmed. Previous explorers (Chiarini, Cheki, and Monseigneur Massaya) only passed through and investigated the northern spurs of this mountain range. Travellers who discovered Lake Rudolf (Count Teleki, Hohnel, Donaldson Smith, the 1896 expedition of Bottego, and the 1897 expedition of Cavendish) shed much light on a part of Central Africa the geography of which was still unknown. Nonetheless, a significant space found between 7° north latitude and Lake Rudolf and between the Omo and Nile Rivers remained still completely unexplored. The first European who passed through part of these regions and who discovered here an enormous mountain range was Staff-Rotmister Bulatovich. First, he crossed the northern spurs of the montain range in 1896. The detailed investigation of the whole mountain range, in all its extent, was carried out in the period of time from January 24 to April 23, 1898. For the whole time of his journey, Staff-Rotmister Bulatovich used every opportunity to conduct accurate astronomical observations, and along with these made a detailed map of the route. In all, he calculated the astronomical position of 13 points and composed a detailed map of the journey...

"The Emperor Nicholas II Mountain Range is located between 8° 30' north latitude and 36° 30' east longitude, and 6° north latitude and 36° 30' east longitude. In the north, it separates into several mountain ridges, which constitute the watersheds of the Rivers Gibye, Giye Enarza, Gibya Kake, Didessa, Dobana, Gaba, and Baro. "The main mountain range, which stretches along the River Omo, constitutes the watershed of two enormous basins: the Omo and Lake Rudolf on the one side, and the Juba and Sobat Rivers, consequently the White Nile and the Mediterranean Sea on the other. In the middle part, the mountain range rises above the River Omo 1,000 to 1,500 meters at a distance of only 30-40 versts from its course. And the waters of its western slopes, being so close to what would seem to be its natural basin, are driven off by it for 10,000 versts [6,700 miles] to the distant Mediterranean Sea.

"The average height of the mountain range above sea level is 2000 meters. Its northern part is the highest, where separate summits—Tulu Jiren, Jimayangech, Bacha-aki-Kela, and Gida—attain altitudes of higher than 3,000 meters. The summits of Gonga-Beka, Boka, Yta, Shashi, Say, Kastit and Jasha attain heights of 2,500 meters above sea level.

"Unlike most ot the mountains of the Ethiopian highlands, the mountain range of Emperor Nicholas II shows no signs of volcanic origin. It is a system of uniform, even bulges with rare hill-like summits.

"The rocks found there include sandstone, granite, and gneiss. The only metals the natives mine are iron and copper. The veins of quartz often found give reason to think that thorough geological exploration might uncover other metals.

"The water which flows down from this mountain range forms the following rivers: from the eastern slopes the water goes down into the Gibye River which arises in the Guderu Mountains, as well as the rivers Gibye Enarza and Gibye Kake. At the confluence of these rivers, it is called the 'Omo.' Farther to the south, the Gojeb and Gumi flow into it, and at the confluence with the Gumi it is called 'Shorum.' Still farther, the Kibish River flows into it, and from here the river is called 'War.' The mouth of this many-named river at the point where it flow into Lake Rudolf is called 'Nyanya.'

"From the western slopes of the mountain range flow the rivers Baro, Menu, Bako, Kilu, Shebelimu, Chomu, and Kori, which unite to form the Sobat and flow into the Nile.

"The structure of this mountain range is different in the eastern than in the western part. The eastern slopes are very steep and precipitous, and the rivulets which flow down them are for the most part fast mountain streams. The western slopes are gently sloping and go down down very gradually, and the rivers on these slopes flow much more slowly.

"This mountain range has great climatic significance. Located close to the Equator, in the region of two trade winds, significantly high above the rest of the territory, it attracts a great quantity of rain clouds, and hence the greatest part of the rain falls on its eastern slopes. With regard to climate, the mountain range is divided into three zones. The middle section of the mountain range in which Kaffa is located is extremely humid; and, at the same time, it has the highest elevation. Thanks to the abundance of water and the regularity of the temperature, the soil of Kaffa is distinguished by its fertility. A large part of the area of Kaffa is covered with dense forests in which the trees attain gigantic dimensions. Coffee trees, which grow wild in this part of Abyssinia, are found in great abundance. There are two rainy seasons: one in February to March and the other in June, July and August.

"Although the northern part of the mountain range is also distinguished by a humid climate, it has only one rainy period in June, July, and August; it doesn't have the spring period as in Kaffa.

"The southern part of the mountain range is distinguished by a drier climate. Here rain falls both in the spring and in the summer periods, but in much smaller quantities.

"The climate on the plateau to the south of the mountain range is very dry. Rain falls very rarely here, and the rivers are dry stony channels in which water is held only in rare holes.

"The vegetation here is very meager. The soil is rocky and strewn with fragments of mountain rocks.

"The tribes who inhabit this mountain range belong to seven separate ethnographic groups and speak different languages.

"The northern end is inhabited by Galla (Oromo). They are divided into several independent states: Guma, Gomo, Gera, and Jimma, which at the present time have been conquered by the Abyssinians. Only Jimma preserved its conditional independence.

"Kaffa, which occupies the middle part of the mountain range, is populated by a tribe of Semitic extraction. In the distant past, Kaffa was a strong, rich, and vast southern Ethiopian empire. In 1897 it was subdued and annexed to Abyssinia.

"The eastern slopes of the mountain range which border on Kaffa are populated by Sidamo tribes and constitute the states of Kulo and Kontu, which at the present time have been subdued by the Abyssinians. To the south of Kaffa live Gimiro tribes, divided into small states which are dependent on Kaffa: Sharo, Shevo, Benesho, Yayna, Duka, and Kaba. This tribe is probably a mix of Sidamo and Kaffa with Negroes.

"To the south of the Gimiro are found the Negro Shuro tribes, which probably are related to Nilotic Shilluks. The southwestern end of the mountain range is populated
by a tribe which by type, language, and way of life differs completely from Negroes and resembles the Sidamo tribes. There are some grounds for supposing that these tribes are a remnant of the original inhabitants of the Ethiopian plateau which remained intact and which, mixed with Semites, formed the tribes which now inhabit Ethiopia. The plateau to the south of the mountain range is inhabited by Idenich nomads, who are probably related to Shuro Negroes but are in a more savage state.

These tribes are at extremely different stages of cultural development. The most developed are the Kaffa. They constitute a separate state, have already experienced centuries of political life, and are divided into classes. The least developed are the Idenich tribes. In translation the name "Idenich" means "sons of non-humans," and this name is given to them by their colleagues, by savages.

"The different names which they use for God testify to the diversity of these ethnographic groups. The Galla (Oromo) call God 'Wak'; the Kaffa 'Ier'; the Sidamo 'Tosa'; the Gimiro 'Kiy'; the Shuro and Idenich 'Tuma'; and the original inhabitants of the Ethiopian plateau call God 'Dadu.'

"The mountain range, being inhabited in its whole extent by diverse tribes, divided into many small independent states, does not have a special name which belongs to it. Each of these states carries the name of the territory they inhabit, but there is no name for the whole mountain range.

"From now on it's name will be the Emperor Nicholas II Mountain Range."

91B: I calculated the latitude by the least of the observed zenith distances, correcting it to a half diameter of the sun, taken from the ephemerides. The longitude was determined graphically at the intersection of the latitude with the azimuth, taken at one of the earlier determined mountains in the north or northeast.

92B: The supply of salt which I had with me had run out the day we crossed the border. Abyssinians do not carry pure salt with them on the march. Rather, they make due with crushed red pepper with only a small addition of salt. This mixture is called dylykh.

93B: However, the Europeans' fear is completely understandable after the unworthy and distorted descriptions of Donaldson Smith.

Donaldson Smith spent some time at the residence of General Wolda Gabriel, waiting there for permission from the Emperor Menelik for a trip across Abyssinia to Lake Walamo or Abasi. Menelik had to refuse him in view of the fact that the Walamo tribe had still not submitted to him, and he himself was just getting ready to go against them. The Abyssinian general gave Donaldson Smith the most cordial welcome and assigned him a place to stay in his very own house. Wolda Gabriel provided him and his whole caravan with provisions and, on parting, gave Donaldson Smith what was extremely necessary for him—several excellent camels and, in general, conducted himself as a true gentleman and perhaps even with excessive generosity toward this white man who obviously had a hostile attitude toward the Abyssinian nation. The American took all the gifts of the Abyssinian, gave him nothing in return, and in his books even reproached Wolda Gabriel for begging, only because one of the general's retainers told Donalson Smith that his master very much liked his gun. Moreover, Donalson Smith described in ridiculous form both General Wolda, who had shown him such kindness, and his family as well.

94S: There is no simple English equivalent of the Russian word "sal'nik." Found in the abdomen of a sheep, "white fat" is a paraffin-like substance which is basically like fat, but with a higher melting point. It looks like rounded agregates of white spheres. (Thanks to Alexander Chaihorsky for this information. He became familiar with "sal'nik" as an explorer in Northern Mongolia.)

95B: When it is 30° Reaumur [99° F] in the shade, in the sun the temperature is greater than 60° Reaumur [167° F].

96B: I collected rocks as best I could; but to my deep distress, a large part of the collection, including all the granite, was lost. They were usually carried in a sack placed in a pack. The ashker to whom the collection was entrusted, figuring that it only aggravated the mule, which was worn out anyway, and that the stones had no value in and of themselves (he says, "you can find as many rocks as you want everywhere") threw them away.

97S: The vernier or "nonius" is a small ruler on some measurement devices which helps to measure fractions and make fine adjustments.

98K: Murle is a nationality which lives in the east of the Republic of Sudan and in Ethiopia on its southwest borders. The Murle-Pibor (from the Pibor River) are distinguished from the Murle-Buma (from the Buma Plateau) by their place of settlement. A.K. Bulatovich is talking about the Murle who live in the lower reaches of the River Omo, of whom there are considerably fewer. The Murle language is related to the group of the languages of Central and Eastern Sudan.)

99K: Murdu or Murzu is a nationality which is close to the Murle and which lives in the lower reaches of the River Omo, farther north than its bend. The Murdu language belongs to the group of languages of Central and Eastern Sudan.

100B: Here, for example, is one of these dialogues:
—*Et Tekhedalekh?* (Where are you going?)
—*Bandera tekela.* (To set up flags.)
—*Myn tybelalekh.* (What do you eat?)
—*Komora.* (Sour fruit.)
—*Myn tytelalekh?* (What do you drink?)
—*Aguara.* (Heat).
—*Myn tyshekamalekh?* (What do you carry?)
—*Fujigra.* (Gun.)
—*Yamanny ashker?* (Whose servant are you?)
—*Eras makara.* (Servant of "*Ras* of troubles," a nickname of *Ras* Wolda Giyorgis).

Or here, for example is another saying: "Be *frenj*o hid no auajyu. ("With the foreigner there is only one order—go forward!") "Be Bayu emmaymmechyn gud ayu." ("With Bayu [Ato Bayu] we saw impossible things.") "*Be Melke etafan ba kork.*" ("With Melke [secretary of the *Ras*] we defiled ourselves during Lent with meat of antelope"). "*Te shiambel gadel ishalal.*" ("Better the masses than the colonels.") And so on, including the most unflattering image of the majority of the leaders.

101K: The Masai is a nationality which lives in Kenya and Tanganyika. In the nineteenth century, the region of their settlement extended as far as Lake Rudolf. Their language belongs to the southeastern group of Nilotic languages.

102B: The Kulo are one of the brutal Sidamo tribes (see above). They are so blood-thirsty that they showed no mercy even to captured livestock, and if they couldn't take the livestock with them, they slit the animal's throat and threw it on the roadside. They were not members of our regular army and had a position in the detachment like Turkish bashi-bazouks.

103B: See the appendix.

104B: The Mountains of Nakua are noted approximately correctly on the map of Donaldson Smith. The Mountains of Moru do not appear on his map. The western bay of Lake Rudolf was discovered by Bottego in 1896 and confirmed by Cavendish in 1897. Neither Bottego nor Cavendish found its native name. Captives from the Murugu tribe called it "Labur." That is exactly what my captive Turgana called it for me. This name (Labur) is found in Cavendish, but he uses that name for the mountains which are found to the west of the Cape of Vaska.

105B: This river is noted on the map of the Italian expedition of Bottego and is there named Moritsio-Seki.

106B: The belt which Abyssinians wear around their waist is a long (about 14 arshins [32 feet]) band (half an arshin wide [7 inches]) of light cotton material (which weighs about one and a half to two pounds). It is very useful on the march. It serves as an abdominal band or girdle, uniformly pulling in the stomach. In case of wounds, it is useful as a bandage. It is also very convenient to carry a bandolier in this belt.

107B: In this territory there are so many lions that the Abyssinians call it Yaambasa-Myeda—the Lion Field. Incidentally, they called the fort at Kolu Yadagusca-Myeda—Field of Dagusa (a type of bread grain), and the mouth of the River Omo—Yaakhya-Myeda, i.e., Donkey Field.

108B: They raise the spear high and aiming it at the opponent, they make it vibrate by fast action of the hand.
109B: As hunters assert, elephants often destroy all the trees in the place where any one of their herd has been killed. The danger from wounded elephants is corroborated by all the travellers of Central Africa: Prince Ruspoli fell victim to an elephant wounded by him. Count Teleki, Cavendish, and I saved ourselves from them only by some miracle.
110B: I spent from September 9, 1897, to July 19, 1898, on my journey. In all, not counting trips by train and steamboat, in that time I covered about eight thousand versts [five thousand miles], during which there were only four extended stops: 1) from October 15 to November 16-42 days; 2) from January 9 to January 21-12 days; 3) from February 26 to March 4-6 days; and 4) from May 5 to May 14-9 days. There were 33 days of short stops. There were 211 days of marching.
111B: In the language of the inhabitants of the mouth of the River Omo, God is called not Tumu (which the other Idenich tribes call him), but rather Niyaguch.

Selections from the introduction to Katsnelson's edition

A.X. BULATOVICH—HUSSAR, EXPLORER, MONK

Isidor Saavich Katsnelson

Africa has hidden and still hides much that is unknown, unexplored, enigmatic. Even today there are regions of Africa where the foot of an explorer has never trod. Kaffa (now one of the provinces of Ethiopia) remained a legendary country up until the very end of the last century—"African Tibet"—having fenced itself off from the outside world. Foreigners were strictly forbidden access to this country. Even now, we know less about it, its history, morals, customs, and the language of the inhabitants and the neighboring tribes to the south and west than about any other region of Ethiopia. The first traveller and explorer who crossed Kaffa from end to end and compiled a detailed description of it was the Russian officer Alexander Xavieryevich Bulatovich.

The life path of A.X. Bulatovich was truly unusual. Having begun in one of the most exclusive educational institutions of tsarist Russia and in the fashionable salons of Petersburg, in the circle of brilliant guard officers, he dashes across deserts, mountains, and plains of the least known regions of Ethiopia; across the fields of battle and hills of Manchuria; a solitary monastic cell and monasteries of Mount Athos embroiled in fanatic scholastic arguments; across First World War trenches soaked with blood, saturated with stench; and tragically, senselessly comes to an abrupt end in a little hamlet in the Ukraine.

The posthumous fate of A.X. Bulatovich was no less amazing. At the very end of the last centry and before the First World War, he repeatedly found himself at the center of attention of the Russian, and, at times, also of the foreign press. But then he was completely forgotten.

To a considerable extent, the cause of this was the October Revolution and events of succeeding years. But, however it came about, up until recent times almost nothing was known about A.X. Bulatovich. Even the year of his death given in the second edition of the Big Soviet Encyclopedia—"around 1910"—was incorrect.[1] His discoveries and observations did not receive full appreciation. In any case, no one who wrote about him indicated that he was in fact the first man to cross Kaffa.[2] Only now, when searches have been begun in the archives and some people who knew A.X. Bulatovich or were related to him have responded,[3] his image has become more distinct and the great significance of his journeys and of his scientific work is becoming clearer.

However, this research is still far from complete. Much apparently needs to be amplified, and also, possibly to be made more accurate. For instance, we now know almost nothing about the last three to four years of his life, and the circumstances of his death are known only in the most general way. We will try here to sum up briefly all that we have learned about him in recent years.

A.X. Bulatovich was born September 26, 1870 in the city of Orel[4]. At that time, the 143rd Dorogobuzhskiy Regiment, which was stationed there, was commanded by his father, Major-General Xavier Vikentyevich Bulatovich, who was descended from hereditary nobles of Grodno Province. X.V. Bulatovich died around 1873, leaving a young widow, Evgeniya Andreyevna, with three children.

The childhood years of Alexander Xavieryevich and his two sisters were spent at their wealthy estate known as "Lutsikovka" in Markovskaya Volost, Lebedinskiy District, Kharkov Province.[5] Already at that time some traits of his character and world view took shape: courage, persistence, passionate love for his native land, and deep religious piety.

In 1884, Evgeniya Andreyevna moved with the children to Petersburg. It had come time to send them to school. The girls entered the Smolny Institute. The elder daughter soon died of typhus. A.X. Bulatovich, who was then 14, began to attend the preparatory classes of the Alexandrovskiy Lyceum—one of the most exclusive educational institutions.

Having passed the entrance examinations, A.X. Bulatovich was admitted to the Lyceum. His only difficulty on the exam, strange as it may seem, was in geography, which he just barely passed. Subsequently—right up to graduation—he studied excellently, advancing with prizes from class to class.[7] Future diplomats and high government officials received their preparation at this Lyceum. Therefore, the pupils mainly studied foreign languages —French, English, and German—and jurisprudence. In other words, A.X. Bulatovich received an education in the humanities, but that didn't prevent him from becoming a capable mathematician, as indicated by the geodesic and cartographic surveys he conducted.

In 1891 A.X. Bulatovich finished the Alexandrovskiy Lyceum as one of the best students and went to work in May of that same year in "His Majesty's Personal Office in the Department of Institutions of the Empress Mary," which directed educational and beneficial institutions. He was awarded the rank of the ninth class, which is "titular councillor." However, a civil career did not entice him; and following the family tradition, he submitted an application and enlisted on May 28, 1891 as a "private with the rights of having volunteered" in the Life-Guard Hussar Regiment of the Second Cavalry Division, which was one of the most aristocratic regiments. Only a select few could become officers of such a regiment.

After a year and three months, August 16, 1892, A.X. Bulatovich received his first officer's rank—cornet. After another year, he made his way onto the fencing team, formed under the command of the Horse Grenadier Guard Regiment, with the task of becoming a fencing instructor. He stayed here for a half-year, then on April 10, 1894, was sent back to his regiment, where he was first appointed assistant to the head, and then, on December 24, 1895, head of the regimental training detachment.

Although A.X. Bulatovich was taught in a civil educational institution, he acquired riding skills in childhood and youth; and through persistent training at riding school and at race courses, he became an excellent horseman—possibly one of the best of that time. That was not an easy accomplishment: Russian cavalry and Cossack regiments always had a reputation as first-class horsemen. According to trainer I.S. Gatash, who served in the stable of A.X. Bulatovich, (quoted by V.A. Borisov who found the old man), "For Alexander Xavieryevich, the horse he couldn't tame didn't exist."

Thus, interrupted only by races and other horse competitions, the years of service in the regiment passed rather quietly, until events which at first glance did not have any relation to A.X. Bulatovich suddenly broke the settled tenor of life of the capable, prospering officer.

At the end of the nineteenth century the colonial division of Africa among England, France, Germany, Spain, and Portugal was completed. Only Ethiopia had preserved its independence, together with the almost unexplored regions adjacent to it on the south and southwest, plus some difficult-to-reach regions of the central part of the continent. Italy, which had joined in the division of Africa later than the other European imperialistic powers, felt that it had been done out of its fair share. Only at the end of the 1880s did it settle in Somalia and Eritrea.

Now, according to the plan of its leading circles, should come the turn of neighboring Ethiopia.

[Katsnelson describes the events leading up to the Battle of Adowa]...

In Russia, a collection of goods was organized to help the sick and wounded Ethiopian soldiers [from the Battle of Adowa], and a detachment of the Red Cross was sent. The decision to do this was made in March 1896, and 100,000 rubles was allocated for expenses. Aside from the leader—Major General N.K. Shvedov—61 men joined.

It is hard to say what directly prompted A.X. Bulatovich to apply for inclusion in this detachment to which he was assigned March 26, 1896. One of his fellow travellers, F.E. Krindach, in a book that was published in two editions but which is now very rare, Russian Cavalryman in Abyssinia (second edition, St. Petersburg 1898), "dedicated to the description of the 350-verst trek, outstanding in difficulty and brilliant in accomplishment, which was carried out under the most extraordinary circumstances by Lieutenant A.X. Bulatovich in April 1896," considered it necessary in the introduction "first of all to establish the fact tha A.X. Bulatovich was assigned to the detachment at his own request, as a private person."

A.X. Bulatovich strove to prepare himself as thoroughly as possible for the jouney. We know about this not only from his first book, but also from other sources. For instance, Professor V.V. Bolotov, historian of the early church, a man with great and deep knowledge in this area, having mastered many new and ancient eastern lanuages, including Geez and Amharic, on March 27, 1986 wrote "... there appeared an Abyssinian Hierodeacon Gebra Hrystos [Servant of Christ] and told me that he wanted me to see Hussar Guard Bulatovich who is going to Abyssinia. It turned out that Bulatovich wanted to know which grammar and dictionary of the Amharic language to get..." Apprently, his progress was considerable, because a year later when A.X. Bulatovich had extended his theoretical preparation and supplemented it with practice, this same V.V. Bolotov reported to another addressee "... in March there was no one in Petersburg who knew Amharic better than I did. Now Life-Guard Kornet A.X. Bulatovich, who has returned from Abyssinia, speaks and even writes some in this language."

The trip to Ethiopia turned out to be longer than anticipated, due to obstacles put in their way by Italians who hadn't given up hope of consolidating their position in Ethiopia. Naturally, any help to Ethiopia, even medical, was undesirable to them.

In any case, the detachment was not only denied entrance to the port at Massawa, despite previously obtained permission, but a cruiser was even dispatched to keep watch on the steamer with the Russian doctors. Therefore, N.K. Shvedov and his companions sailed from Alexandria to Jibuti, where they arrived on April 18, 1896, as indicated in the book written by F.E. Krindach, who we now let tell the story, since Bulatovich himself doesn't mention anywhere the events of the first days of his stay in Africa.

> While the caravan was being formed, the state of affairs[38] made it necessary to send ahead to Harar an energetic, reliable person, in view of the fact that the rainy season was rapidly approaching. One of the prerequisites for successfully completing this mission was to travel as fast as possible. To carry out this difficult and dangerous mission, they asked for a volunteer. Kornet (now Lieutenant) A.X. Bulatovich accepted the offer. The small Jibuti settlement buzzed with the most diverse rumors and speculation relating to the possible outcome of undertaking such a journey, which would be immense for a European. Not knowing the language and the local conditions, being totally unprepared from this method of travel—on camelback—and the change of climate—all this justified the skepticism of the local residents, the majority of whom did not admit the possibility of a successful outcome. It is 350-370 versts [233-247 miles] from Jibuti to Harar. Almost the whole extent of the route runs along very mountainous and, in part, arid desert, and permits only travel with a pack animal.[39]

The decision to dispatch A.X. Bulatovich as a courier was finally made on April 21. Taking a minimal quantity of the simplest provisions and only one waterskin of water, A.X. Bulatovich set out on the route, in spite of the fact that on the way he could count on only two springs, of which one was hot and mineral.

On that very day, April 21, at 10 in the evening, A.X. Bulatovich, accompanied by two guides, left Jibuti. Even though he had only had a few hours to practice riding on "the ship of the desert," on the first leg of the journey he went for 20 hours without stopping. By the end of the following day, they had covered 100 kilometers. It is impossible here to describe all the troubles of this fatiguing and monotonous journey. The distance of greater than 350 versts [233 miles] A.X. Bulatovich managed in three days and 18 hours, in other words about 6-18 hours faster than professional native couriers. In the course of 90 hours spent on the road, the travellers rested no more than 14. No European up until A.X. Bulatovich ever achieved such brilliant results. This trek "made an enormous impression on the inhabitants of Ethiopia. Bulatovich became a legendary figure.

The author [that is F.E. Krindach] had occasion to hear enthusiastic accounts of this trek."

However, Alexander Xavierevich couldn't stay long in Harar. The detachment, having arrived after him, intended to continue on the way farther to Entotto when orders came from the Negus to wait. Since the rainy season was approaching, which threatened many complications to making further progress, N.K. Shvedov decided once again to send A.X. Bulatovich ahead, so he could in person explain the situation and have Menelik change his order.

> The immense crossing from Harar to Entotto, about 700 versts [466 miles], despite the difficulty of the route, Bulatovich accomplished in eight days. It turned out that Abyissinians, accustomed to Europeans who came to Abyssinia for the most part chasing after personal profit, couldn't understand the unselfish purpose of this detachment. Therefore, several rases were opposed to the arrival of our detachment in Entotto. Bulatovich's explanation not only convinced Menelik to expedite the permission, but even inspired him with impatience for the rapid arrival of the detachment.
> ... On July 12 the detachment reached the residence of the Negus and was met by Bulatovich...[42]

The completion of this mission nearly cost Bulatovich his life. The road from Harrar to Entotto went through the Danakil Desert. The small caravan (Bulatovich was accompanied by seven or eight men) was set upon by a band of Danakil bandits who took all their supplies and mules. By chance, on June 2, 1896, they were met by N.S. Leontiev, who was going from Entotto to Harrar. This was the first meeting of two Russian travellers in Africa. Judging by the words of N.S. Leontiev's apologist Yu. L. Yelts, Leontiev furnished A.X. Bulatovich with all necessities and gave him letters of recommendation to Frenchmen who were living in Entotto in the service of Menelik.

A description of the work of the Red Cross Detachment is a separate subject which has been sufficently covered in works and publications which were sited above, and in the stories of individuals who were members of it.

Even several Englishmen, who were forced to accept the presence of Russians in Ethiopia, couldn't help but note that the mission sent to them rendered "unselfishly and with good will" help to the wounded. At the end of October 1896, the detachment curtailed its work and in the first days of January of the following year, they returend to Petersburg.

As for A.X. Bulatovich, through N.K. Shvedov, he submitted an application for an excursion "for a better understanding of the circumstances in Abyssinia at the time the Red Cross Detachment left the country" and permission to carry out a journey to little known and unknown regions of western Ethoipia. He also wanted to go into Kaffa, which was living out its last days of independent existence. This request was supported by the Chief of the Asiatic Bureau Chief of Staff Lieutenant General A. P. Protseko, who noted the energy of A.X. Bulatovich in striving to as much as possible become better acquainted with the country, and his knowledge of their language and also that the information collected would be very helpful for the further development of relations with Ethiopia.

Menelik categorically forebade crossing the borders of his realm, since this would mean unavoidable death for the traveller. On Oct. 28, 1986 A.X. Bulatovich was received by the Negus. Having obtained all necessary permissions, on the following day he left the capital and with his fellow travellers set out for the River Baro. This expedition lasted three months. He returned on Feb. 1, 1987 and then just two weeks later on Feb. 13 again set out on a trip, this time to Lekemti, and then to Handek —a region in the middle course of the River Angar and its left tribuaries and of the valley of the River Didessa. Here A.X. Bulatovich took part in an elephant hunt and occupied himself with learning about the country, its people and the natural conditions. On his return on March 27, 1897, there was prepared for him a ceremonial reception at the residence of the Negus, who on the folowing day gave him a private audience. Leaving the capital on March 25, A.X. Bulatovich arrived at Harar on April 4, in Jibuti on April 16, from where on April 21 he sailed to Europe.

On December 6, 1896, A.X. Bulatovich was promoted to lieutenant with seniority dating back to August 4, and for help of the Red Cross Detachment; and for his successful expendition he was awarded the Order of Anna in the third degree.

The material he had gathered in the time of his trip, he put into the form of a book, entitled From Entotto to the River Baro. An account of a journey in north-western regions of the Ethiopian Empire and published it on orders of the General Staff. It appeared in September of that same year 1897. Thus A.X. Bulatovich wrote it in a very short time.

[Katsnelson discusses reactions to that book and then goes over details of the second expedition and a third expedition in 1899.]

Returning to Russia [after the third expedition], A.X. Bulatovich intended to pass through the Sudan and Egypt. But the English Resident in Egypt, Lord Cromer, at first absolutely refused to grant permission for passage, claiming this was because of "disorder in of the region." However, the true reason was different: Harrington, the representative of England in Addis Ababa, "had already for a long time considered

Staff-Rotmister Bulatovich as a very energetic and knowledgeable man whom the English should beware of." Naturally, they didn't want to let into the Sudan this wise, experienced, and observant traveller, who could bring back for the use of Ethiopia any information he gathered. Only under pressure of the Russian general consul in Cairo, T.S. Koyander, was Lord Cromer forced to give permission for the passage of A.X. Bulatovich through the Sudan. But it was already too late. He set out for his native land by the route he had taken previously, intending to visit Jerusalem and then Iran and Kurdistan.[115] However, he was forbidden to travel to both of these countries by the Minister of War, A.N. Kuropatkin.[116]

Stopping by at his mother's residence in Lutsikovka, A.X. Bulatovich returned to Petersburg at the beginning of May 1900. But this time, too, his stay in his native land turned out to be brief—even shorter than before. On June 23, 1900, in accord with personal instructions of the Tsar to the Chief of Staff, he was sent to Port Arthur to the command of the Commander-in-Chief of Kwantung Province, for attachment to one of the cavalry or Cossack units operating in China.[117] What gave rise to this assignment is not known. Probably, the hurried departure prevented A.X. Bulatovich from reworking and publishing his notes from his third journey that he had brought back with him from Ethiopia. Subsequently, he never returned to those notes, and one must suppose that a significant part of them perished together with the rest of his papers.

At the completion of military activities, on July 8, 1901, A.X. Bulatovich returned to his regiment. After a month, he was assigned, at first temporarily, and then permanently,[118] to command the Fifth Squadron. On April 14, 1902, he was promoted to the rank of "rotmister" [Captain of cavalry]. He was also awarded the Order of Anna of the Second Degree with Swords and the Order of Saint Valdimir of the Fourth Degree with Swords and a Bow.[119] On August 21, 1902, there followed permission to accept and wear the Order of the Legion of Honor[120] that had been conferred on him by the French government. At that time, too, he finished, with first-class grades, an accelerated course at the First Pavloskiy War College.

A brilliant military career awaited the intelligent, talented, courageous guard officer. But after returning from Manchuria, the life of A.X. Bulatovich suddenly changed. The events of the last decade of his life are still far from clear. A few separate episodes and dates show through more or less distinctly, but even those were established only recently. It remains to hope that subsequent research will be crowned with success, and we will be able to get a fuller and clearer idea of this unusual man.

December 18, 1902, A.X. Bulatovich was released from command of the squadron; and, as of January 27, 1903, he was discharged into the reserves "for family reasons."[121] Apparently, it was at this time that he made the decision to take monastic vows.

What led to this act that amazed not only all of fashionable Petersburg, but even his closest friends? We can only guess. A deeply religious man, perfectly honest, kind, inquisitive, he fell under the influence of a preacher and mystic who was well-known at that time—Father Ioann of the Kronstadt Cathedral. By other accounts, he was oppressed by unreciprocated feelings for the daughter of the commander of the the regiment, Prince Vassilchikov. Undoubtedly, his experiences in the field of battle, the bloody brutalities of war played a large role. Apparently, it is more correct to speak of the sum of all these causes, but, for the present, it is impossible to give a precise answer.

After taking monastic vows (probably in 1906, because on March 30, 1906, he retired from the army), "Father Anthony," as A.X. Bulatovich now called himself, set out for the "Holy Mountain" of Athos. According to his own account, up until 1911 his life was "secluded, silent, solitary." He was entirely occupied with his own religious activities, and never went beyond the walls of the monastery. "I kept myself away from all business and did not know what happened in the outside world, for I read absolutely no journals nor newspapers." In 1910 he was made a hieromonk, and at the very beginning of 1911, Father Anthony set out for the fourth and last time to Ethiopia.

In 1898 by Lake Rudolph, Alexander Xavieryevich had found a badly wounded boy named "Vaska," had nursed him back to health, and then had taken him back to Russia, baptized him, taught him Russian, and looked after his education. According to M.X. Orbeliani, Vaska was a "kind, gentle, and unfortunate boy," who had suffered much from his mutilation. Entering the monastery, A.X. Bulatovich took Vaska with him as a lay brother, but Vaska suffered from constant mockeries. Finally, when an opportunity arose, Bulatovich sent him back to his native land. Missing his ward, after a three year separation, Father Anthony, in his own words, "wanted to see him and give him the Holy Eucharist." So Father Anthony went for a year to Ethiopia.[122] What he did there, aside from "giving the Holy Eucharist," was determined quite recently from the report of the charge d'affaires in Ethiopia B. Chemerzin to the Ministry of Foreign Affairs in December 15, 1911.[123] It appears that it was not just anxieties about saving the soul of Vaska that attracted Father Anthony to Ethiopia.

On his arrival in Ethiopia, Father Anthony was sick for the first two months.

At this time, the Emperor Menelik had been severely ill for a long while. He didn't appear at official ceremonies and received no one, which had led to the spread of rumors that he had really died and that his death was being concealed by those in court circles.

Using his old connections and his relationship with the Emperor, Father Anthony not only obtained an audience but even got permission to "treat" the royal patient. Praying, Anthony sprinkled and massaged the body of the Emperor with holy water and oil, and applied wonder-working icons. But, of course, he did not succeed in bringing about any improvement in Menilek's health. As a result, B. Chemerzin notes with irony, it was established that the Emperor was alive and that all the rumors that someone who resembled him had been substituted for him were absolutely false.

Next, A.X. Bulatovich tried to found in Ethiopia a Russian Orthodox ecclesiastical mission and an Athonite monastery. On an island of Lake "Khorshale" [Lake Shala?] he wanted to found a monastery with a school, where the children of local inhabitants could get an elementary education. He assumed that the money to do this could be collected by voluntary contributions, of which he himself would collect the greater part. However, the impracticality of such projects and the lack of sympathy both in Ethiopia and also at Mount Athos for the proposed undertaking prevented its accomplishment. On Dec. 8, 1911, A.X. Bulatovich left Addis Ababa forever, "taking with him only hopes and not a single firm pledge from the wealthy," as B. Chemerzin expressed it.

Unfortunately, our knowledge of this fourth and last visit by the Russian traveller to the country he so loved is limited to this general description. Almost all documents of the period of Menilek's reign were destroyed at the time of the war with Italy in 1936. As for the papers of the Russian Embassy, in 1919 tsarist diplomats gave them to the French Embassy "for safekeeping"; and in 1936, they were taken to Paris, where they were burned along with other archives in June 1940.[124]

In 1912-13, A.X. Bulatovich got caught up in a conflict between two groups of Athonite monks, known as the "Name Fighters" and the "Name Praisers."[125] (Father Anthony sided with the latter.) This affair took such a scandalous turn that Father Anthony was forced to leave Mount Athos. The scandal at Mount Athos received wide publicity, and from January 1913 stories about the mutinous monks and their leader appeared from time to time in newspapers. Over the course of 1913-14, the name of A.X. Bulatovich didn't leave the pages of the press, giving occasion for all kinds of wild tales, often based on gossip and the desire of petty reporters to snatch fees.[126]

SELECTIONS FROM THE INTRODUCTION TO KATSNELSON'S EDITION

Having taken on the role of defender of the "Name Praisers," A.X. Bulatovich was caught up in a storm of activity: he wrote and published polemical articles and brochures, sent letters to his followers, recommended that they stand fast and not give in to their opponents. The Synod assigned him to residence in the Pokrovskiy Monastery in Moscow. But, instead, he lived first with his sister, M.X. Orbeliani, in Petersburg, until he attracted the attention of the police to her and her husband; then at his mother's house in Sumy, and next at Lutsikovka.

As soon as the war began, A.S. Bulatovich left Lutsikovka. On August 21, 1914, he went to Sumy and from there to Moscow and Petrograd and obtained an appointment in the active army. "Holy wars are defensive. They are God's work. In them miracles of bravery appear. In offensive wars, there are few such miracles," he wrote a year before that. From 1914 to 1917, Father Anthony was a priest in the 16th Advanced Detachment of the Red Cross. Judging by the stories of people who met him, he here once again exhibited "miracles of bravery," in spite of his age, his eye disease, and the cassock of an ecclesiastical pastor.

After the end of the war and the disbandment of his detachment, in Feb. 1918, A.X. Bulatovich sent requests from Moscow to Patriarch Tikhon and the Synod for permission to retire to the quiet of the Pokrovskiy Monastery, to which he had been assigned before, because his situation was "quite disastrous." The request was granted, but without the right of religious service, apparently because of the "heretical" beliefs in which the applicant continued to persist.

In the summer of 1918, A.X. Bulatovich applied to the "Holy Council" with a new petition, for removal of this restriction and for transfer to the Athonite St. Andrew Monastery in Petrograd. The answer to this request is still unknown, but could scarecely have been positive, because at the end of November 1918 Tikhon and the Synod looked into the application of "the excommuncated Hieromonk Anthony (Bulatovich)," who "professing 'God-making' reverence for the Name of the Lord, rather than agreeing to revere the Name of the Lord relatively, as today's church authority requires, has separated himself from all spirital contact, henceforth until the Holy Synod has held a trial on the substance of the matter." The issue was passed along to the authority of the Moscow Diocese for "further consideration."

Apparently, not waiting for a decision, A.X. Bulatovich preferred to go to Lutsikovka, where he spent the last year of his life, about which almost nothing is known. Only very recently was it established that he was murdered by bandits on the night of December 5-6, 1919.

The great and terrible years of revolution obliterated the memory of A.S. Bulatovich. And even more, the fanatical Father

Anthony almost completely overshadowed the courageous traveller of unknown African lands.[127]

Indeed, this affair that absorbed all the thoughts and motivated all the deeds of A.X. Bulatovich at the end of his life seems to us unwarranted and even bad. But it was also a manifestation of discontent with existing reality, of inner discord. Raised and educated in certain surroundings, he could not surmount the errors and prejudices of his time and his circle. However, even amid these errors, let it be said that honor, straigthforwardness, stoicism, sincerity, and courage were in the highest degree inherent in A.X. Bulatovich. Namely these characteristics, in combination with ardent patriotism and sense of duty, impelled the young hussar officer to accomplish in four years the deeds that glorified his name and placed him in the ranks of the most outstanding Russian travellers.

Notes

[Ts.G.V.I.A. and G.I.A.L.O. are references to Soviet Archives.]

1. Bolshaya Sovietskaya Entsiklopediya, second edition, volume 6, p. 258.
2. For example: M.P. Zbrodskaya, Russian Travellers in Africa, Moscow, 1955, pp. 62-66; M.V. Rayt, "Russian Expeditions to Ethiopia in the Middle of the 19th and the 20th Centuries and their Ethnographic Materials" in African Ethnographic Collection, volume 1, Moscow, 1956, pp. 254-263.
3. V.A. Borisov worked strenuously on such searches, and graciously shared the results with me. The sister of A.X. Bulatovich, Mary Xavieryevna Orbeliani, who now lives in Canada, answered and sent her recollections of childhood and youth, which contain information which, naturally, no other source could provide. S. A. Tsvetkov, who from 1913-14 was secretary of A.X. Bulatovich, and who died several years ago in Moscow, turned over some interesting material. G. F. Pugach, president of the Belopolsky Regional Office of the Society for the Preservation of Natural and Cultural Monuments, let me know the exact date of death of A.X. Bulatovich.
4. Service Records of Staff- and Ober- Officers of the Life Guard Hussar Regiment on January 1, 1900 (Ts.G.V.I.A., P. S. 330-463, line 149). In any case, he was christened in Orel in the church of the 143rd Dorogobuzhskiy Regiment. See: GIALO, f. 11, op. 1, d. 1223, line 76. In the reference sent from there (No. 499 from Dec. 9, 1962), apparently, the year of birth—1871—was erroneously indicated. Compare, in the same source, d. 1185, lines 12-13; Ts.G.I.A. U.S.S.R., f. 1343, op. 17, d. 6777, line 12.
5. Now the Lutsykovsky Village Soviet of the Belopolsky Region of the Sumskiy Area ("Sumsky Area, Administrative-Territorial Divisions," Sumy, 1966, p. 15).
6. G.I.A.L.O., f. 11, op. 1, d. 1166, line 258—petition of E. A. Bulatovich.
7. G.I.A.L.O., f. 11, op. 1, d. 441, lines 10, 188-189, 264, 351, 415, 441.

SELECTIONS FROM THE INTRODUCTION TO KATSNELSON'S EDITION

8. G.I.A.L.O., f. 11, op. 1, d. 1223, lines 77, 80.
9. Ts.G.V.I.A., P.S. 330-463. Service Records of Staff- and Ober- Officers of the Life Guard Hussar Regiment on January 1, 1900, lines 149-155. A copy of the service record of A.X. Bulatovich is likewise in the files of the commander of the armies of the Kwantung Region (Ts.G.V.I.A., P.S. 308-178). Data about his military service were determined from these records, which go as far as 1900. Dates are given in the "old style."
10. "Government Herald" from August 19, 1892.

[Note that this is only a selected portion of Katsnelson's introductory article. The original footnote numbers are retained here.]

38. This "state of affairs" consisted of obstacles created by the English, who were likewise striving to prevent the establishment of direct contacts between Russia and Ehtiopia. For example, they in every way made it difficult to obtain camels for the caravan. The railroad from Jibuti to Addis Ababa was then only beginning to be built.
39. F.E. Krindach, Russian Cavalryman in Abyssinia. From Jibuti to Harar, St. Petersburg, 1898, pp. 12-13.
42. Note of the president of the Russian Society of the Red Cross M.P. Kaufman (AVPR, Political Archives, document 2015, lines 2-9).
115. Letter of A.X. Bulatovich from February 8, 1900 (Ts.G.V.I.A., f. 400, op. 261/911, d. 92/1897, chapter 4, lines 8-10).
116. Telegram of A.N. Kuropatkina to the Russian Consul in Jerusalem from April 4 1900 (Ibid., line 11).
117. In accord with the reply of the General Staff from June 23, 1900 for Number 33673 (Ts.G.V.I.A., P. S. 308-178).
118. Ts.G.V.I.A., f. 3591, op. 1, d. 157. Order of the Life Guard Hussar Regiment from December 8, 1901.
119. "Record of Rotmisters of the Guard Cavalry by Seniority on May 1, 1902," Saint Petersburg, 1902, p. 23.
120. Reference of the State Regional Kharkov Archive, No. 15 (187), from June 16, 1962.
121. Ts.G.V.I.A., f. 3591, op. 1, d. 160, line 57.
122. Hieromonk Anthony (Bulatovich), My Conflict with the 'Name-Fighters' on the Holy Mountain, Petrograd, 1917, pp. 10-11.
123. A.V.P.R., "Greek Department," d. 678.
124. Czeslaw Jesman, The Russians in Ethiopia, London, 1958, p. 150.
125. The Synod in a decision from August 27, 1913 for Number 7644 conferred on the adherents of this "heresy" the designation "Name Idolators" (Ts.G.I.A. U.S.S.R., f. 797, op. 86, d. 59, line 80.)
126. Namely in the supplement to Russian Word—the weekly of Spark (Number 9 for 1914) there appeared photographs of Alexander Ksaveryevich with captions, which were used by I. Ilf and E. Petrov in Twelve Chairs as the source for the story of "Hussar-Heretic" Count Aleksey Bulanov.

127. Thus, for example, A.X. Bulatovich isn't even mentioned in an essay on the history of geographical discoveries in Ethiopia by N.M. Karatayev. See: Abyssinia (Ethiopia). Collection of Articles, Leningrad, 1936, pp. 1-83.